Minetown, Milltown, Railtown

MINETOWN, MILLTOWN, RAILTOWN

Life in Canadian communities of single industry

REX A. LUCAS

UNIVERSITY OF TORONTO PRESS

Toronto and Buffalo
Printed in Canada by
University of Toronto Press
ISBN 0-8020-1812-2 (cloth)
ISBN 0-8020-6123-0 (paper)
Microfiche ISBN 0-8020-0137-8
LC 70-166934

To the memory of Carl Addington Dawson, 1887-1964

pioneer Canadian sociologist, and the teacher

who introduced me to Canadian communities

Introduction

There are two distinctive, legitimate, approaches to the study of human activity. One establishes patterns and trends of behaviour through the use of census data, without ever talking to the people under study.[1] The other approach, the one taken in this book, begins with an individual, his hopes, fears, problems, solutions, and the habitual associations of his daily round of life. After informal chats or formal interviews with many individuals, the sociologist begins to see persistent patterns, some shared by all, others shared by certain respondents. During the course of the interviews it becomes clear that some respondents think that their problems are personal, unshared, and not understood by others, but other perceptive respondents are aware that many share the same difficulties because they see them as arising from a common source in their place of work, their community, or their nation. The sociologist has the advantage of listening to more people in more communities than any one respondent; this enables him to locate patterns about which many individuals are unaware. The accumulated advantages are even greater if, as in this study, the sociologist is able to undertake all of the interviewing, rather than relegating the work to others. This approach is time-consuming but rewarding because of its enlightening results.[2] Further, after many formal and informal interviews it becomes possible to prepare questionnaires that are meaningful to the respondents. Questionnaires are useful because they can tap a larger and more diverse sample than any researcher can interview in person.

1 A good example of this emphasis is John Porter, *The Vertical Mosaic* (Toronto, 1965).

2 Both approaches have their advantages and perils. Without taking up this issue in detail, I should mention that the census approach forces the investigator to produce an ideal model of society, against which existing practices are evaluated. This tends to produce a reification of the model; behaviour is judged as though the reification were real life. This is legitimate as long as one goes along with the model and does not ask about possible alternatives. By this method, it is easy to create "non-problems" in the view of the citizens. In defence, it has long been recognized that sociological problems are not necessarily recognized social problems.

With the individual interview approach, however, the respondent sets the criteria against which he evaluates his life. His model may be as unrealistic as that set by the sociologist, but at least it is not imposed. This approach is true to life but is restricted to life experiences and does not introduce broader and more theoretical alternatives. The individual describes his life, taking into account his ideal model and the social restrictions within which he lives.

The two approaches ask different questions of different materials and so raise different issues. Each throws light on the state of man.

The first patterns for this book were found after interviewing many people in Railtown, Ontario. In a quite different community, Milltown, Quebec, one could trace the rather distinctive round of life that characterized that town. After a study of Minetown in the Maritimes, it was found that similar underlying traits characterized life in all of these distinctive communities. These patterns were confirmed in interviews and in questionnaire replies from a much wider range of communities of single industry throughout Canada.[3] It is these common patterns, intrinsic as they are in communities of single industry and with a population of under 30,000, that I have chosen to report here. These common traits are found, regardless of the type of industry, and they persist over time. Data collected over almost two decades have not become dated despite the illusion that changes in mass communication and urbanization have revolutionized the life of man. There are important changes, of course, but basic patterns and relationships persist.

Sociologists such as S. D. Clark[4] and C. A. Dawson[5] have described community development on the frontier, and early Canadian community life. Books like *Canadian Frontiers of Settlement*[6] provide important documentation of an era now past. These publications suggest an obligation to keep the record up to date, pursuing continuity by carrying research findings from the past into the future. This book is concerned with a type of contemporary Canadian community based on twentieth-century technology, on which there are few published data.

Important studies are being carried out by undergraduate and graduate students in Canadian universities. Useful data are accumulated in these unpublished documents, and I have placed considerable relevance on these resources. It is very gratifying to find that other observers have noted similar phenomena and have shared many of my conclusions.

The nature of this book is influenced by the approach to the study of human behaviour. If it had been based upon the census, the illustrative material would have been statistical in nature. As it is pri-

3 Notes on data and sources are found at the end of the book.

4 S. D. Clark, *The Developing Canadian Community* (Toronto, 1942).

5 Carl Dawson and Eva Younge, *Pioneering in the Prairie Provinces: The Social Side of the Settlement Process* (Toronto, 1940).

6 W. A. Mackintosh and W. L. G. Joerg, *Canadian Frontiers of Settlement*, 9 vols. (Toronto, 1934-40).

marily based on many observations, interviews, and informal chats, the basic building blocks are the informed opinions, persistent behaviour, and perceived problems of the citizens of communities of single industry. Some would argue that this approach provides many subtleties but little rigour; quantitative data are defended in the name of rigour, but can be criticized as lacking in concern with meaning in human terms. Fortunately, the two approaches are not mutually exclusive. When it seemed practical and illuminating, I have used statistical data, as exemplified in the chapters on the Healing Arts and on Marriage and Migration of Youth; these data, however, are interpreted in the light of the qualitative material from the interviews.

The five hundred or so informants, of course, remain anonymous. Because of this guarantee, they were able to talk freely and candidly; their confidence in my professional ethics is appreciated. To reinforce this guarantee, the communities remain nameless as well. Naming communities arbitrarily would be unethical, particularly when community identification is immaterial, for the patterns are similar; differences are local variations on the major themes. Other sociologists, newspaper reporters, and commentators working under different auspices and different and legitimate ground rules were able to name their communities and respondents. When utilizing their material, in the interest of consistency I have taken the liberty of substituting "[the community]" for the name. The information is in the public domain, so anyone interested in the identity of these communities may look up the references. The communities in which the detailed studies were carried out have been named Railtown, Minetown, and Milltown.

My indebtedness to many people is illustrated on every page of the book. I wish to express my great thanks to each respondent, not only for the information so freely shared, but also for the warmth and friendliness with which my requests were received. These warm friendships, brief though many of them were, have enriched my association with this great sprawling land, Canada. When a community name is mentioned on a newscast or in casual conversation, it is rewarding to a Canadian to be able to visualize the town and to remember with warmth the shared encounters with its citizens.

Some studies involved colleagues, students, and research assistants. Some part of their work and interest is reflected in this book. Jean Burnet, Catherine D. MacLean, S. D. Clark, and G. Grant Clarke made many helpful suggestions. The writing of this book was aided by a grant from the Canada Council which provided for a summer research assistant and the typing of the manuscript. As research assistant, Alexander Himelfarb made major contributions to the book as well as looking after many of the essential details.

Minetown, Milltown, Railtown

1

The community of single industry

Canada, like most nations, maintains a number of myths. One is that Canada is a young country, another is that Canada is classless if not egalitarian.[1] These, like all myths, contain some elements of truth. Compared with ancient China, Canada is young indeed; but seen beside the emergent countries of Africa, the stance of Canada as a youth of over one hundred seems somewhat forced. In comparison to a caste system, Canada seems to be a model of classlessness, but financial inequalities among Canadians, if nothing else, cast doubt on egalitarianism.

THE URBAN DEFINITION

A myth-in-the-making that appears with increasing regularity in newspapers, periodicals, and political speeches is that Canada is an urban nation. It has been adopted by many social scientists. Martin, for instance, states: "We need not insist on the importance of the urbanization process as a basic factor in the transformation of our society. This is quite obvious. At least three-quarters of the population of the province [Quebec] live in urban communities and very few areas indeed remain free from the dominating influence of such centres."[2] In the same vein, Porter notes "In a country where, in 1956, 40 per cent of the population lived in fifteen metropolitan areas, the following observation written a few years earlier by Leslie Roberts seems a little strange: 'The people of Trois Pistoles and the loggers of the Charlottes are too busy working and building to have time for self-analysis – and these and others like them comprise the great majority of Canadians.'"[3] A further indication that the definition has been accepted is that urban sociology and institutes of urban study are in vogue in the land.

To the traveller, however, this definition seems contrary to sensory evidence. As one person put it after driving from Ottawa to Toronto, "I had never realized before how many people in Canada live nowhere." Indeed, the data for this book were collected from a wide range of individuals, living in small communities of single industry

1 See J. Porter's elaborate rebuttal of this myth: J. Porter, *The Vertical Mosaic* (Toronto, 1965).

2 Y. Martin, "Urban Studies in French Canada," in M. Rioux and Y. Martin, eds., *French Canadian Society* (Toronto, 1964), p. 251.

3 Porter, *Vertical Mosaic*, p. 134.

under a variety of circumstances. Some interviews, for instance, were held in a construction shack with the never-ending sound of bulldozers in the background; outside stood rows of temporary prefabricated bunk houses; beyond, the few very new houses were dwarfed by the large construction project which represented the future industry upon which this embryo town would depend. Other interviews were conducted with teachers, administrators, and workers in a community of new houses neatly laid out along curving boulevards; the streets were filled with children and young adults; there was not an old person in sight. Still other interviews were conducted in dusty communities of unpainted frame buildings which have nestled helter-skelter around the pit head of the mine for more than eighty years. All of these communities had two common characteristics: they were built around a single industry, and, in part because of this, the population was small.

We need to look a little more carefully at the urban character of Canada. What is meant by urban? How many Canadians live in cities, towns and villages? What is a community of single industry? How many are there?

First, the sources of the urban definition will be considered. The Dominion Bureau of Statistics has made a major contribution to this definition. The Bureau reports, for instance, that the farm labour force declined from a peak of 1,293,000 in 1939 to 725,000 in 1958,[4] and that according to the 1961 census 69 per cent of the population lives in urban areas.[5]

Most people picture 69 per cent of the Canadian population hurrying up and down escalators, or driving cars back and forth to work on crowded city streets. They see the great majority of Canadians criss-crossing urban areas in subways and city buses, eating in smart restaurants, shopping in downtown department stores or suburban plazas, and enjoying first-run movies and the ballet. They visualize them as availing themselves of the services of large specialized medical complexes, famous law firms, great universities, and noble cathedrals. They also see the crowding, the lack of planning, the pollution, the smog, and the impersonality of it all. They see all this, that is, until they know that the Bureau's definition of urban includes villages of 1000 population.

4 Dominion Bureau of Statistics, *Canadian Statistical Review, 1959 Supplement* (Ottawa, 1959), p. 35.

5 Dominion Bureau of Statistics, *Census of Canada 1961*, vol. 1, part 2, bulletin 2 (Ottawa, 1962), table 21.

Traditionally, the notion of urbanism suggested the distinct social qualities of human community: a special mode of existence, a way of life found only in a city. Wirth includes in these distinct qualities a complex division of labour with a diversified occupational structure which forms a major basis of a system of social stratification, high territorial and social mobility, marked functional dependence of the population, substantial personal anonymity in interpersonal contacts and segmentation of social roles and role interactions, reliance on indirect moves of social control, and normative deviance.[6]

The term urban, then, seems to involve at least three major dimensions – demographic, economic and social-cultural. The census definition, however, involves only the demographic element.

> In the 1961 census the Dominion Bureau of Statistics treated as urban areas the locality falling into one of the following categories: 1. incorporated cities and towns and villages of at least 1000 population, 2. unincorporated agglomerations (generally considered as towns or villages) of at least 1000 population, and 3. built-up fringes of incorporated cities, towns or villages (of at least 5000 population) with a population density of at least 1000 persons per square mile.[7]

This definition may be useful for some purposes, but a community of 1000 people certainly does not have the social characteristics or urban life that were described by Wirth or Burgess.[8]

Communities with a population of 1000 or, for that matter, 30,000, do not have urban qualities.[9] Nor do they incorporate what Park thought to be a crucial urban characteristic, "the freedom of the city" to be able to choose, whether it be a particular church, doctor, or way of life.[10] This freedom of choice, as we shall see, is one of the crucial social characteristics that distinguishes the urban area from

6 L. Wirth, "Urbanization as a Way of Life," *American Journal of Sociology*, XLIV, no. 1 (1938-9), pp. 1-24.

7 Leroy O. Stone, *Urban Development in Canada* (Ottawa, 1967), p. 5.

8 Ernest W. Burgess, "The Growth of a City: An Introduction to a Research Project," in George A. Theodorsen, ed. *Studies in Human Ecology* (New York, 1961), p. 37, reprinted from Robert E. Park, Ernest W. Burgess, and R. D. McKenzie, eds., *The City* (Chicago, 1927), pp. 47-62.

9 Harvey W. Zorbaugh, "The Natural Areas of the City," in Theodorsen, ed., *Studies in Human Ecology*, p. 45.

10 Robert E. Park, *The Human Communities* (Glencoe, 1952), p. 86.

the small community. The ranges of choice are severely limited in a community of 1000.

Springdale, the *Small Town in Mass Society*[11] studied by Vidich and Bensman, is an urban area by the demographic definition, yet it is perhaps an exemplary small town with its lack of anonymity and its world of myth. This suggests then that the census definition does not have a meaningful social reality. The major problem is that the demographic category is often reified and confused with observable social phenomena. Many transform the statistical definition of urban – communities of at least 1000 – into a social reality of flesh and blood, bricks and mortar, and complex institutional city life. It is then that people talk about a reality that does not exist.[12]

If urban connotes size, excitement, and variety, then metropolitan suggests super and complex urbanism. It is difficult to envisage Waters (population 2064) near Sudbury, Ontario as urban, and the citizens of the community probably do not realize that they are classified as metropolitan in a demographic sense.

Although the percentage of Canada's population living in communities of 100,000 and more is steadily increasing, over the years the population distribution has been remarkably stable. In 1891, for instance, 25.4 per cent lived in incorporated communities of 5000 to 30,000 compared with 24.7 in 1951. Over the sixty-year period the percentage distribution changed less than one per cent.[13] The per-

11 A. J. Vidich and J. Bensman, *Small Town in Mass Society* (Garden City, NY, 1960).

12 This problem is discussed by D. R. Whyte, "Rural Canada in Transition," in M. A. Tremblay and W. J. Anderson, eds., *Rural Canada in Transition* (Ottawa, 1966), pp. 1-8. For a variation on the theme using 10,000 population see Pierre Camu, E. P. Weeks, and Z. W. Sametz, "The People," in B. R. Blishen, *et al., Canadian Society,* 3rd ed. (Toronto, 1968), p. 43 (from their *Economic Geography of Canada* (Toronto, 1964), chap. 3); Yoshiko Kasahara, "A profile of Canada's Metropolitan Centres," in Blishen, *et al., Canadian Society,* p. 68; Nathen Keyfitz, "The Changing Canadian Population," in S. D. Clark, ed., *Urbanism and the Changing Canadian Society* (Toronto, 1961), p. 5.

13 Leroy Stone in his monograph on *Urban Development in Canada* cautions us about several other problems which are associated with the more technical aspects of census taking. He suggests that the figures might be somewhat misleading because of (i) "mistakes in the identification and mapping of the boundaries of densely settled built-up areas on the fringes of incorporated cities," and (ii) "mistakes in the classification and 'bounding' of unincorporated towns and villages." As Stone points out, only further work will deter-

centage distribution of the population living in incorporated areas of 30,000 and under was 44.4 in 1951 compared with 59.5 in 1891.[14]

The incorporation of areas involves a further series of definitions often unrelated to social reality. The difficulties arise because most provinces have four types of local units: rural municipalities, villages, towns, and cities. As Rowat points out:

> In two provinces ... the rural areas are not municipally organized ... Newfoundland, Nova Scotia have no incorporated villages, while PEI had none until after passing a new village act in 1951. British Columbia is unique in having no towns.
>
> It should also be noted that in all provinces except Nova Scotia and New Brunswick, the northern sparsely settled areas are not municipally organized. These areas, for the most part divided into Local Improvement Districts, are usually administered directly by the Provincial Departments of Municipal Affairs. In British Columbia as much as 25 per cent of the population lives outside organized municipalities, but elsewhere the proportion of the population thus excluded is very small.
>
> The rural municipalities across Canada have been variously named: "districts" in British Columbia and Alberta, "rural municipalities" in Saskatchewan and Manitoba, "townships" in Ontario, "townships" and "parishes" in Quebec, "counties" in New Brunswick and "municipalities" in Nova Scotia.[15]

Rowat notes other incongruities:

> Only five provinces for instance have established minimum population for cities, these range all the way from 100 in British Columbia to 15,000 in Ontario (or 10,000 by special legislation). Ontario and Quebec require a minimum of 2000 for towns, while Saskatchewan requires only 500. Moreover the provinces have no requirement for villages and towns to change their status with population growth. So even within a single province, as a result of an uneven growth in population, it is quite possible to find villages that are larger than towns, and towns larger than cities. Indeed, some of

mine the extent and direction of such possible errors. (Leroy O. Stone, *Urban Development in Canada* (Ottawa, 1967), p. 6.)

14 These figures were taken from Dominion Bureau of Statistics, *Ninth Census of Canada, 1951,* vol. 10 (Ottawa, 1956), Table IV, p. 37.

15 Donald C. Rowat, *Your Local Government: A Sketch of the Municipal System in Canada* (Toronto, 1962), pp. 17-8.

> British Columbia's villages are actually larger than many of her cities![16]

According to the Dominion Bureau of Statistics there are 4196 municipalities in Canada. Hefferton states that there are approximately 1300 communities in Newfoundland alone but that 1034 had a population of less than 500.[17]

Rowat points out that Ontario and Quebec account for two-thirds of all municipalities in Canada and "rather surprisingly the number of rural units in Canada (over 2200) still exceeds that of urban units (about 1800)."[18]

Although not particularly meaningful, statistics show that the average population of communities in Canada is only about 3200. This average includes the large cities.[19]

POPULATION IN COMMUNITIES OF 30,000 AND LESS

A large portion of the Canadian population, then, lives in very small communities, and the majority of communities in Canada are small. The communities with which the present research is concerned need discussion. Before making refinements, we need to know what proportion of the Canadian people live in communities of 30,000 or less. This is easier said than done.

A step-by-step procedure is necessary in order to estimate the number of people who live in communities of 30,000 or less in Canada. First, the populations of communities of under 30,000 can be accepted as they appear in the census although, as we have seen above, the census defines these people as urban.[20]

16 *Ibid.*, p. 20. The difficulties that these arbitrary and inconsistent definitions can lead to are well outlined by Richard Laskin in "Nonagricultural, Semiagricultural and Agricultural Service Centers," in Tremblay and Anderson, eds., *Rural Canada in Transition*, pp. 114-77.

17 S. J. Hefferton, "Planning for Small Towns in Newfoundland," *Community Planning Review*, 8, no. 1 (March, 1958), p. 11.

18 Rowat, *Your Local Government*, p. 21.

19 *Ibid.*, p. 133.

20 The 1961 definition specifies that all cities, towns and villages of 1000 and over, whether incorporated or not, were classed as urban, as well as the urbanized fringes of (*a*) cities classed as metropolitan areas, (*b*) those classed as major urban areas, and (*c*) certain smaller cities, if the city together with its urbanized fringe had 10,000 population or over. The remainder of the population

We find that 1,372,666 Canadians live in communities of 1000 to 4999; 932,936 live in communities of 5000 to 9999; communities between 10,000 and 29,000 account for 1,965,592 people. We have, therefore, a total population of 4,271,194 who live in communities of 1000 to 30,000 by census definition.[21]

These figures, however, do not account for communities whether incorporated or unincorporated with a population of less than 1000. The rural population by census definition totals 5,537,857. However, this "rural" population includes a scattered farm population which does not form communities in a demographic or social sense.[22] The farm population for the 1961 census was 2,072,785.[23] We subtract the farm population from the total rural population to give the non-farm population living in communities of less than 1000: this figure is 3,465,072. If we add this to the population of 4,271,194, already established, we now have a total of 7,736,266.

A number of communities between 1000 and 30,000, however, although incorporated and politically separate, are an integral part of metropolitan areas; Metropolitan Toronto, for instance, has within its boundaries a number of such communities including Leaside, 18,579; Weston, 9715; Mimico, 18,212; and so on. Bloomenfield de-

was classed as rural. The main differences from 1956 (*Census*) resulted from the exclusion of any non-urbanized fringes within metropolitan areas and the inclusion of urbanized fringes adjoining those smaller cities covered in (*c*) above. (Dominion Bureau of Statistics, *Census of Canada, 1961,* bulletin 1.1-7, inside front cover.)

21 Dominion Bureau of Statistics, *Census of Canada,* vol. 7, part I, series 7.1, Table 2, pp. 2-26, 2-27.

22 The census definition of a farm and non-farm population has developed over a number of years "from the 1931 census for the first time, the rural population could be separated into the farm and non-farm components." "The accuracy of the estimate depends upon the validity of one basic assumption. It was assumed that on average the number of people per household on each occupied farm was the same as the number of people per rural household." "In each census the rural farm population was identified by farm residence and farms were defined in terms of size, value and volume of production or sales, and location. The rural non-farm population was the difference between the rural population and rural farm population." In 1951 a farm, for census purposes, was "a holding on which agricultural operations are carried out and which comprises (1) three acres or more in size, or (2) from one to three acres in size with agricultural production in 1950 amounting to $250 or more." (DBS, *Census of Canada, 1951,* vol. II, page xi; Isobell B. Anderson, *Internal Migration in Canada 1921-1961* (Ottawa, 1966), pp. 80-1.)

23 *Census of Canada,* vol. 7, part 1, series 7.1, Table 2, pp. 2-4.

fines the metropolitan area as "primarily a complex of closely related centres of population located within daily commuting distance to the central city and thus has two main parts – the central city or metropolis and the nearby centres whose economies are closely linked to that of the central city."[24] Although many of these communities are socially distinct from the metropolitan area and may even sustain industry apart from the rest of metro, as in Oakville, Ontario, all the political communities of 30,000 and less that come within the census definition of metropolitan must be removed. This is a population of 1,731,883; this, when subtracted from our accumulated total, gives a final population of 6,004,383 who live in communities of 30,000 or less.

Many community characteristics, deeply affected by size, will shape the lives of the additional 2,072,785 people who have been designated as farm population. Those patterns that arise intrinsically out of the size of community, then, affect the lives of 8,077,168 people. When we discuss levels of medical practice, recreation, and various institutional and professional services, that are affected by the size of the community, we will be describing the lives of almost half the population of the nation who live in communities of 30,000 and less.

Size of community, however, is only one focus of the analysis. Detailed consideration will be given to communities of single industry with a population of 30,000 or less. This is a much more restricted proportion of the population. We now turn to a consideration of this rather special category of community.

TYPES OF SMALL COMMUNITY

Communities with a population of 30,000 or less clearly need further specification. We know something of the size of the community, but not much about the social patterns within it. Communities with a population of 30,000 or less include market towns, fishing villages,

24 "In 1961, the census metropolitan area was comprised of an incorporated city of at least 50,000 persons and a surrounding area large enough for the whole metropolitan area to contain nearly 1,000,000 or more persons. The part of the metropolitan area surrounding the central city (incorporated) should have (1) at least 70 per cent of its labour force engaged in non-agricultural activities, and (2) a minimum of population density of 1000 persons per square mile in its built up segments." (Stone, *Urban Development in Canada*, pp. 5-6.)

pulp and paper towns, railway towns, mining communities, manufacturing towns, county seats, agricultural villages, tourist resorts, small communities with several industries, and so on. This variety incorporates different types of social patterns. Agricultural communities for example, are made up of independent capitalists, and the concerns and patterns of life are quite different from those in a mining community, where miners work as employees of a large bureaucratic organization.

Firm in the belief that the age and economic base of the community affect the ongoing life of the citizens, sociologists have worked on typologies within which like communities could be grouped. S. D. Clark, for instance, distinguished between the fishing and agricultural community of the Maritimes, the gold rush community of the Yukon, the prairie community, and the frontier community. Clark,[25] like Dawson,[26] Innis[27] and Lower,[28] was interested in the new frontier community.

In 1936, E. C. Hughes proposed a five-class typology of French-Canadian communities. These were: (i) the old, settled agricultural parishes; (ii) the new agricultural and fishing communities; (iii) the old small French towns which, of late, had been invaded by industry; (iv) the new frontier towns where industry came first; (v) the former English towns where French farmers had moved in as labour. Montreal and Quebec were seen as special cases.[29]

Still maintaining the distinction of the economic base, Falardeau notes that

> a new, meaningful typology ... should be established with regard to the degree of industrialization. Two leading questions should guide

25 S. D. Clark, *The Developing Canadian Community* (Toronto, 1962).

26 C. A. Dawson, *Group Settlement: Ethnic Communities in Western Canada,* vol. 7 of W. A. Mackintosh and W. L. G. Joerg, eds., *Canadian Frontiers of Settlement,* 9 vols. (Toronto, 1934-40); C. A. Dawson and Eva R. Younge, *Pioneering in the Prairie Provinces: The Special Side of the Settlement Provinces,* vol. 8 of Mackintosh and Joerg, eds., *Canadian Frontiers of Settlement;* C. A. Dawson and R. W. Murchie, *The Settlement of the Peace River Country: A Study of a Pioneer Area,* vol. 6 of Mackintosh and Joerg, eds., *Canadian Frontiers;* C. A. Dawson, ed., *The New Northwest* (Toronto, 1947).

27 H. A. Innis, *Industrialism and Settlement in Western Canada* (Cambridge, 1928).

28 A. R. M. Lower and H. A. Innis, *Settlement and the Forest and Mining Frontiers* (Toronto, 1936).

29 E. C. Hughes, *Bulletin of the Society for Social Research* (University of Chicago, 1936), pp. 1, 2, and 8.

> the choice of the criteria of classification: which was there first, industry or the community? And at what period in the history of the province has industry given rise to or transformed the community.[30]

Following in this tradition, Garigue states:

> More recent research enables us to submit the following scheme which envisages all the Quebec communities as located somewhere along a continuum, one extreme being the single-industry, company-town type of community, like Arvida, the other extreme being the non-industrial, administrative or educational centre, such as perhaps, Nicolet de L'Assumption. The classification is as follows. (1) single-industry, company owned communities. (2) Single, dominant industry centres, which are subdivided into (*a*) pulp and paper centres; (*b*) textile communities; (*c*) mining towns; (*d*) hydro-electric and chemical centres. (3) The mixed, industrial-commercial towns. (4) The predominantly trading centres. (5) The non-industrial towns, which may themselves be subdivided into many sub-categories.[31]

Montreal and Quebec are also considered as special cases.

> This typology is only tentative, but in our opinion, points in the right direction by assuming that the most telling feature of contemporary communities is the extent to which their existence and social organization depend on industry. It is in the light of this basic factor that comparisons between the population volume, the economical structure, the occupational and ethnic distribution and the complement of institutions of different categories of communities assume their full meaning.[32]

Garigue suggests that the structure of these types of communities affects the structure and size of the families who live within them.

A simpler typology was used by HRH The Duke of Edinburgh's Second Commonwealth Study Conference on the Human Consequences of the Changing Industrial Environment in the Commonwealth and

30 Jean-Charles Falardeau, "The Changing Social Structures of Contemporary French-Canadian Society," in Rioux and Martin, eds., *French Canadian Society*, pp. 108-9.

31 Philippe Garigue, "The French Canadian Family," in Mason Wade, ed., *Canadian Dualism* (Toronto, 1960), pp. 181-200.

32 *Ibid.*

Empire held in Canada in 1962; communities were divided into (I) Communities with a single industry; (II) Communities with a dominant industry; and (III) Communities with diversified industries.[33]

John Dales also draws attention to the nature of the economic base. He calls pulp and paper, saw- and planing mills, non-ferrous metal, smelting and refining, and asbestos products "resource-located" industries,

> whose location is likely to be largely determined by geographical factors and especially by the location of natural resources ... they are all "early stage" industries closely tied to the natural resources they process ... the products of resource-oriented industries are usually quite mobile and ... therefore the industries which use these products as raw materials are normally quite foot-loose.[34]

COMMUNITIES OF SINGLE INDUSTRY

As communities of single industry are the second major focus of this book, the working definition excludes communities characterized as agricultural, fishing, hunting or trapping, market towns, county seats, tourist resorts and the like. In these types of communities the working population is basically made up of small capitalists, entrepreneurs and government officers who carry on a particular and distinctive way of life that differentiates them from the population of a community with a single industrial base.

There have been several recent studies related to this subject matter, but each has arrived at a slightly different set of delimiting criteria. One study, for instance, identified 155 communities of single enterprise with a total population of approximately 189,623 (more than twice the population of Prince Edward Island). This study excluded "permanent married men's quarters associated with armed forces camps;" ghost towns of the past that have been abandoned; "communities with one major, but not the sole, industrial employer," and communities "in which there is no company owned housing or in which company housing is a small proportion of the total local

33 HRH The Duke of Edinburgh's Second Commonwealth Study Conference, *Conference across a Continent* (Toronto, 1963), pp. 160-281.

34 John H. Dales, "A Comparison of Manufacturing Industry in Quebec and Ontario, 1952," in Wade, ed., *Canadian Dualism*, p. 212.

housing"; and the many "projected new towns which are in the drafting board or in the conception stage of creation" at the time of the survey.[35] In the present study, data were not collected from communities without population, whether abandoned or projected, but the criterion of housing ownership was not used. The owner of the housing is an important issue, as we shall see, but not an adequate criterion upon which to select communities of single industry.

A later study by Ira M. Robinson was concerned with resource-based industries. His working count of single industry communities was 161.[36] But, by restricting consideration to resource-based industries, he excluded the many isolated one-industry railway towns across the nation. This definition also excludes the smelter town that is removed from the mine and the textile mill town. These types of community of single industry are included in the present study.

Richard Laskin tackled quite a different problem; he worked to locate "nonagricultural, semiagricultural and agricultural service centres located in predominantly agricultural areas in Canada."[37] Some of his nonagricultural centres are communities of single industry and others are not.

Leonard Marsh's source book covers all types of communities in Canada, from frontier towns and prairie towns, to the suburbs and inner cities of the metropolis. His book contains a valuable list of 160 Canadian resource-based communities.[38] By his definition, he excludes railway communities. Many of the smaller saw mill towns were not appropriate for his purposes.

The Center for Settlement Studies, University of Manitoba uses the term "single-enterprise community." They present a map indicating

35 Institute of Local Government, Queen's University, *Single-Enterprise Communities in Canada* (Ottawa, 1953), pp. 6-7.

36 Ira M. Robinson, *New Industrial Towns on Canada's Resource Frontier,* Programme of Education and Planning Research, Paper no. 4; Department of Geography, Research Paper no. 73 (Chicago, 1962).

37 Laskin, "Nonagricultural, Semiagricultural and Agricultural Service Centers," pp. 114-74.

38 Leonard Marsh, *Communities in Canada; Selected Sources* (Toronto, 1970). The list of communities is to be found on pp. 183-8. This is a very valuable book because it brings under one cover a wide range of obscure and hard-to-find material. A number of authors whose work is cited here is well represented. Although not relevant to the subject matter of this book, it was rewarding to see material from Carl A. Dawson and Eva Younge, *Pioneering in the Prairie Provinces: The Social Side of the Settlement Process* included in this valuable source book on Canadian communities.

about 200 single-enterprise communities.[39]

When is a town a one-industry town? Clearly, the single industry and its employees require the service of shop keepers, doctors, and other personnel. So our interest is concentrated upon those communities characterized by a single industry and its supporting institutional services. The single industry eliminates communities with one resource base which supports two competing companies: on this basis, E. C. Hughes' Cantonville of *French Canada in Transition*[40] is excluded. This criterion also eliminates Jean Burnet's Hanna in *Next Year Country,*[41] because of the mixed economic base. Donald Willmott's study of Esterhazy[42] does not come within the criteria because the town was affected by both the potash mine and agriculture. Miner's *St. Denis*[43] of course, has an agricultural base, and Janek's *Isolated Communities*[44] is a study of Labrador fishing villages.

There are few communities of single industry that do not have a tourist lodge, or a printing shop or sawmill or other small "industry." In order to simplify the problem of selection, the working rule of thumb was that at least 75 per cent of the population had to work for the single industry and its supporting institutional services. This means that we would not eliminate an isolated northern railway town

39 Center of Community Studies, University of Manitoba, *Nature and Purposes of Single-Enterprise Communities, First Annual Report* (June 1968), p. 49.

40 E. C. Hughes, *French Canada in Transition* (Chicago, 1943).

41 Jean Burnet, *Next Year Country* (Toronto, 1951).

42 D. E. Willmott, *Industry Comes to a Prairie Town* (Saskatoon, 1962). Other Studies from the Centre for Community Studies, University of Saskatchewan are concerned with agriculture or the non-industrialized northern part of Saskatchewan.

43 H. Miner. *St. Denis: A French-Canadian Parish* (Chicago, 1943).

44 O. W. Janek, *Isolated Communities: A Study of a Labrador Fishing Village* (New York, 1937). Similar objections rule out four studies published by the Institute of Social and Economic Research, Memorial University of Newfoundland, St John's, Newfoundland: Noel Iverson and D. Ralph Matthews, *Communities in Decline: An Examination of Household Resettlement in Newfoundland,* Newfoundland Social and Economic Studies, no. 6 (1968); Cato Wadel, *Marginal Adaptation and Modernization in Newfoundland,* Newfoundland Social and Economic Studies no. 7 (1969); Robert L. Dewitt, *Public Policy and Community Protest: The Fogo Case,* Newfoundland Social and Economic Studies no. 8 (1969); Ottar Brox, *Maintenance of Economic Dualism in Newfoundland,* Newfoundland Social and Economic Studies, no. 9 (1969). For an evaluation of these four studies see Jim Lotz, "Resettlement and Social Change in Newfoundland," *Canadian Review of Sociology and Anthropology,* 8, no. 1 (Feb. 1971), pp. 48-59.

if it had a small sawmill employing a handful of people. But we would eliminate a railway town on the prairies, because it has quite different bases – the railroaders, the farmers, and the market town entrepreneurs serving a considerable hinterland.

Combining all the criteria, then, we have the following working definition. Our concern is with communities of single industry with a population of less than 30,000 in which at least 75 per cent of the working population serves the single industry and its supporting institutional services. One almost ideal community of single industry has 3066 working in the sole industry. These employees and their families are supported by 398 employees manning the telephone, post office, hydro, hospital, civic administration, and schools. In addition these are all served by 40 professional people and 115 business establishments ranging from jewellery stores to coin laundries. Many of the communities are somewhat more complex than this one.

The communities answering this description are mainly built around resource-based industries and transportation – mining towns, smelting towns, textile towns, pulp and paper towns, sawmill towns and railway towns. We noted above that eight million Canadians were deeply affected by those community characteristics which depend on the size of the community. There are fewer who are directly influenced by the characteristics that arise out of the single industry.

The counting and location of these communities was not easy. Neither the census nor the many business and industrial directories are of direct assistance. The list was accumulated through a variety of procedures. The easiest, but not the most practical procedure was to visit the community. The second was long, complicated and not very scientific: it consisted of consulting directories, lists, government brochures, articles, pamphlets and the like, to assess available information.[45] The task was not made any easier by the differences in municipal definitions and boundaries from directory to atlas, nor by inflated claims of industry by local groups.

As was suspected, the communities of single industry tended to be small. Only a handful had a population exceeding 8000. The single-industry aspect of the study, then, is basically concerned with a total of 636 communities with a total population of 903,401. Almost a million people in Canada are directly affected by the qualities intrin-

45 See Laskin, "Nonagricultural, Semiagricultural and Agricultural Service Centers."

sic in a community of single industry, as well as those intrinsic in community size.

The significance to the nation of these patterns of community life is much greater than might at first appear because of the traditional migration of young adults, from small communities in general and communities of single industry in particular, to urban communities. This segment of the population has been brought up in communities of single industry, and its basic ways of life, patterns of interaction, attitudes, and expectations have been formed within the context of the community of single industry.

INDUSTRY, TECHNOLOGY AND CONTROL

Canadian communities of single industry are distinctly and fundamentally different from the long list of famous communities studied in the United States of America. All of these community studies have a common theme which suggests explicitly or implicitly that in the past each autonomous community maintained itself through the work of independent hoers of rows who hoed in rustic simplicity while independent craftsmen made beautiful but useful objects. Some version of this Jeffersonian ideal seems to lie at the origin of each community studied. A recurrent theme is town-meeting democracy; often these idealized norms and myths are accepted as though people had acted that way.[46] The scenario suggests that simple honest folk carried out their allotted work, governed themselves with honest, homespun democracy, and that all was utopian. Then tragedy struck in the form of a highway, a railroad, a mass production industry, a war, a government, a bureaucracy, or a depression; whatever it was that struck, it was an impersonal force from outside the safe and happy community. From that point on, there were problems; people were no longer in control of their own work, lives, recreation, or community.

46 It is generally assumed that because there were town-meetings, people attended and liked to attend. That this was not so is illustrated in the early records of the Plymouth Colony. See D. Pulsifer, ed., *Records of the Colony of New Plymouth in New England* (Boston, 1861), XI, pp. 10, 54, 92, 155, 156, 170. Fines for non-appearance were persistent during the colony's history. See also Samuel Deane, *History of Scituate Massachusetts from its First Settlement to 1831* (Boston, 1831), p. 100. In Plymouth in 1636, a fine of three shillings was ordered for absence from the polls in the annual election.

It is not surprising that the early beginnings of these communities were based upon agriculture and simple crafts – the arch-typical Jeffersonian ideal. So we find that West's Plainville,[47] Martindale's Benson,[48] Warner's Jonesville,[49] Lyford's Vandalia,[50] Vidich and Benson's Springdale,[51] Iverson's New Ulm[52] and Homans' Hilltown[53] are all agricultural market towns suddenly confronted by new outside social conditions, procedures and influences. Warner's Yankee City Series[54] traced the transition from craftsmen to mass production workers in a bureaucratic structure imposed and directed from outside the community; the Lynds[55] show the effects of industrialization and depression on what had previously been a county seat of 6000 people. Even Lantz' Coal Town[56] began as an orderly agricultural community in 1804, before the first coal shaft was lowered in 1904. In Blumenthal's Mineville,[57] miners are tempered by farmers and stock-raisers. Hollingshead's *Elmtown's Youth,*[58] Steiner's Tipton,[59] Williams' *An American Town,*[60] Wilson's *Quaker Hill,*[61] and

47 James West, *Plainville, USA* (New York, 1945).

48 Don Martindale and R. Galen Hanson, *Small Town and The Nation* (Westport, Conn., 1969). In the first chapter the authors discuss the place of the small town in a mass world. They discuss and illustrate the local and translocal forces in much the same way as has been done above.

49 W. Lloyd Warner, *Democracy in Jonesville* (New York, 1940).

50 Joseph P. Lyford, *The Talk in Vandalia* (Charlotte, NC, 1962).

51 Vidich and Bensman, *Small Town in Mass Society* (New York, 1960).

52 Noel Iverson, *Germania, USA: Social Change in New Ulm, Minnesota* (Minneapolis, 1966).

53 George C. Homans, *The Human Group* (New York, 1950), chap. 13. Homans notes that his account is based on D. L. Hatch, "Changes in the Structure and Function of a New England Community since 1900," PhD thesis (Harvard University, 1948), and C. C. Zimmerman, *The Changing Community* (New York, 1938), pp. 249-70.

54 W. Lloyd Warner and Paul S. Lunt, *The Social Life of a Modern Community* (New Haven, 1941); W. Lloyd Warner and Leo Srole, *The Social System of American Ethnic Groups* (New Haven, 1947); W. Lloyd Warner and J. O. Low, *The Social System of the Modern Factory* (New Haven, 1947).

55 Robert Lynd and Helen Lynd, *Middletown* (New York, 1929); Robert Lynd and Helen Lynd, *Middletown in Transition* (New York, 1937).

56 Herman R. Lantz, *People of Coal Town* (New York, 1958).

57 Albert Blumenthal, *Small Town Stuff* (Chicago, 1932).

58 A. B. Hollingshead, *Elmtown's Youth* (New York, 1949).

59 J. F. Steiner, *The American Community in Action* (New York, 1928).

60 J. M. Williams, *An American Town* (New York, 1906).

61 W. H. Wilson, *Quaker Hill* (New York, 1907).

Sims' *Hoosier Village*[62] are in the same tradition. Even Dollard's *Caste and Class in a Southern Town*[63] and *Deep South*[64] by Allison Davis, Burleigh Gardner and Mary Gardner, maintain this theme, although their major foci are on other problems. All of these studies set up an idealized or mythical past by which the present is evaluated. It is in this context that we can understand the titles of several recent books – *Small Town in Mass Society,*[65] *Small Town and the Nation,*[66] or *Eclipse of Community.*[67]

In direct contrast, Canadian communities of single industry are twentieth-century products of an age of industry and technology. They are communities of today, relevant, with few past memories. They are new communities, and their very existence depends upon an advanced technology, a complex division of labour, and a sophisticated system of exchange. With few exceptions they have a short past, because they were born of technology; the oldest of the communities are products of the coal and rail ages; the newest have been created to supply industrial metals. Their inhabitants have no lingering myths of days gone by; they know that their community, jobs, and lives depend upon twentieth-century science and technology.[68] They know that their situation is bounded by bureaucracy and a precise division of labour which in turn depends on a complex national and international division of labour. They know that their future depends upon impersonal forces outside their community such as head office decisions, government policies, and international trading agreements. They do not presume to be their own gods. Their interest in local government is as casual as such interest always has been. These are empirical assumptions, implicit when families moved to communities of single industry, and part of the accepted fabric of life for those who are born there. Their behaviour cannot be interpreted on the basis of a nostalgic past. These are men, women, and children of the twentieth century!

62 N. L. Sims, *Hoosier Village* (New York, 1912).

63 John Dollard, *Caste and Class in a Southern Town* (Garden City, NY, 1957).

64 Allison Davis, Burleigh Gardner, and Mary Gardner, *Deep South* (Chicago, 1941).

65 Vidich and Bensman, *Small Town in Mass Society.*

66 Martindale and Hanson, *Small Town and The Nation.*

67 Maurice R. Stein, *The Eclipse of Community* (New York, 1960).

68 This is precisely the point made by E. C. Hughes when he talks of "the new frontier towns where industry came first" (*Bulletin,* pp. 1, 2 and 8), and Falardeau, by "which was there first, industry or the community?" ("The Changing Social Structures," p. 108).

2

Stage I Construction of the community

Although certain patterns of behaviour are characteristic of communities of single industry they are influenced by the stage of community development. Clearly patterns are different when bulldozers are still clearing the town site from when the community has been established for as few as twelve or as many as a hundred years. In this chapter the initial stage of construction will be considered.

COMPANY PLANS AND RESPONSIBILITIES

Geographical position often forces sponsoring companies to provide a fully serviced community in addition to an industrial plant. Other corporations have the choice of building a new community or adding housing to an existing one. One company, for instance, added a town site to an existing town; it became responsible for most of the expenditures connected with this plan:

> We built 45 houses on the town site in the existing town. Schools, churches, police and fire services were all established there already and we felt it was better economics to move into an established community where improvement could be made rather than to try to set up completely new services on a raw site. So the schools were increased and a water and sewage system was put in; this was the town's idea. It amounted to a large capital assistance grant from us to help them with this new development.[1]

Other firms have located close to established communities. This simplified the setting up of an elaborate town site because the new population could draw upon many services from the established communities: "We are located between two towns and these towns have provided neighbours, some living accommodation and certain services. So here it was necessary to build everything for some people, but it was not necessary to build everything for all people. Our neighbouring town is a natural commercial centre."

One town began with a town site "for the senior members of the company and those with specialized skills and specialized experience who had to be brought here from outside." The remainder of the workers were to be housed in neighbouring communities. It was ex-

1 For a study of the social implications of such a move, see Donald E. Willmott, *Industry Comes to a Prairie Town*, Centre for Community Studies, University of Saskatchewan (Saskatoon, 1962).

pected that the workers would also use the institutions of the settled communities. As time went on, however, the new town site grew beyond original expectations; despite this, the company still maintains the largest privately operated bus company in Canada to transport those workers who do not drive their own cars to work from the neighbouring communities.

But many, if not most, of the communities of single industry are located in inaccessible areas with no houses or institutional services. The company is obliged to build the industrial plant and houses for the employees. Additional provision has to be made for the streets, waterworks, sewers, power, telephone, landscaping, stores, schools, churches, offices, theatre and hotel; in short, the physical complement of a complete community.

In the old days, the single-industry community consisted of nothing much more than a number of simple frame houses with very few services other than electric lights and perhaps running water. Even in the early days, there were some attempts to construct model communities. These were often altruistic attempts to translate Utopian ideals into reality, to bring culture to the working classes, or the luxuries of London to the wilds of Canada. Many communities of single enterprise have been built according to plans drawn up by leading town planners, architects, and engineers.[2]

In contrast some towns of single industry arose through short term expediency. One mining executive reported:

> In the very beginning you could probably call this a company town. We started from scratch, we built our own town site, we built the stores and operated them and so on; but we got out of that very, very early, and now, other than owning some houses, we don't really have any formal connection with the town other than being a major tax payer.

On the other hand, in a community under construction, the manager explained

> ... here the company is building the houses. They are renting them for a nominal sum. They rent the whole thing for fifty dollars. This gives you a three-bedroom house with full basement, living-room,

2 Ira M. Robinson, *New Industrial Towns on Canada's Resource Frontier*, University of Chicago, Department of Geography, Research Paper no. 73 (Chicago, 1962).

dining-room, kitchen, all very modern, new, and beautifully finished. This doesn't begin to pay for the cost, maintenance or anything else.

The excessive cost is borne in order to attract people to the new community, and keep them. Another respondent explained the complications that arise when services are provided for a small maintenance staff at an isolated power dam:

We have thirty-five employees to maintain the dam and we had to build them facilities because of the isolation of the area. In doing so, we had to look after numerous other people. Eventually, by the time we look after thirty-five people, we have seventy-five to eighty families, including the school teachers, the shopkeepers and the men who maintain the houses, and so on down the list.

Sometimes the company itself does the building, but many industries use sub-contractors and sub-developers. If not directly involved, however, the company often offers indirect subsidies to attract and keep shops which offer goods of reasonable quality. One executive outlined the plans that the company had for the community:

The general plan is as follows: two years ago we built 16 housing units, last year we built 96 housing units which brings us up to 112, and this year we are planning on 87 units; there are to be 455 units in three more years. We have bunk houses with two men or one man to a room, and here we can house up to 750 people, at two to a room. This allows us for 1200 working men – 750 in the bunk houses and 455 in the housing units. We are leaving allowances for other services – the shopping area, theatre, hotel and so on. Next year we probably will have to do something more about recreation, but we would like to leave most of the recreation to clubs, and most of these other services to private individuals. We have made arrangements with a corporation that will look after the first phase of the shopping area. It will build a shopping area that will involve banks, stores, and so on. It will probably be given the title, and will either sell or rent to some of the major stores and banks.

In isolated regions, the company finds itself involved in assembling and maintaining programmes as well as buildings. When, for instance, the individual enterprise risks are high, the company provides for the entertainment of its employees: "An isolated town must make employees comfortable. In my opinion, the company could have gone much further in their contributions to the town but I also think that few townspeople appreciate fully the company's contribution."

Some companies built recreation centres as one of their first community projects, to provide a short-term and, hopefully, a long-term substitute for the elaborate facilities available in urban areas. "This is one of the few towns where the company went into recreation and then followed through; they started here with no community at all and much has been done by the company regarding recreation. They built this building which is pretty concrete evidence; and they also built the golf course and tennis courts, and all of these are actively supported." In another community, the recreation director explained that, "Originally the company had to maintain a recreation programme to keep people amused, to make the place attractive when it was very isolated and there was little diversion."

It is clear, then, that each company became involved in activities far removed from its expert knowledge in industry. This may involve only the building, painting, and the maintenance of a few company houses or the planning, development, and maintenance of a complete community.

Years later, some companies find themselves with strange tasks still left over from the early days. One mining company official noted ruefully, "we still own the sewer and water supply." An official of a manufacturing company noted, "the mothers insist that the evening curfew be blown on our whistle. We do it. Very few children go home, but apparently the mothers like it. We blow it and that's it – we don't try to enforce it!" Another company executive said, "we had to make a graveyard here." Or, in another community, "we did all landscaping and grass mowing," or "the company still owns the hospital." Or again, "the tenant has his storm windows put on and his grass cut." The company is forced like all landlords to maintain the property: "As far as maintenance is concerned, we decorate the interior every four years and the exterior when needed. We repair the normal wear and tear and the tenants look after the stove, refrigerator, taxes and water and all the rest of it." One other respondent noted that in the old days the company delivered coal and ice to every household.

Regardless of the particular plans and responsibilities assumed at the beginning of the development, each community began with construction; the original people in each community of single industry were construction workers. The work habits pattern of these men and the nature of construction work affect the behaviour characteristic of this initial stage of community development.

CONSTRUCTION WORKERS

Work moves from conference rooms and architects' and town planners' drawing-boards to the chosen location near the resource to be exploited. Contracts are awarded and construction begins. The recruitment of labour is not an easy task. Nor, as Bradwin pointed out before World War I, may the recruitment and the availability of labour be taken for granted:

> Migratory labour of the camps is not aimless in its flow. There is on frontier works a fixed rotation, it proceeds from lumber camps outward to the railway work and thence to the mines and mills of industrial centres. And seldom is this order reversed; the prospector is not going to revert to navvying until compelled by circumstances, while the navvy looks back on the routine hours of the bush camp as a memory of days to be forgotten; henceforth his gaze is outward. When the English-speaking navvy does occasionally return, it is because of a stripe [promotion] of some kind, or when a slackening of industry throughout the country causes him to fall back on the winter camps which do not fluctuate so readily as other frontier works.[3]

The building of a mill, a dam, railway yards, a town site, requires particular specialized knowledge but all construction requires a variety of skills; the site becomes the focal point for many men with differing career and work patterns. The construction workers converge upon the area for diverse reasons; they bring with them a variety of skills.

1. Mobile Construction Workers

These men work exclusively on construction. They have periods of work, characterized by long hours and high pay, and periods of un-

3 E. W. Bradwin, *The Bunkhouse Man: A Study of Work and Pay in the Camps of Canada 1903-1914* (New York, 1928), p. 184.

employment, because their work follows the construction season as well as the vagaries of the industry. These erratic work patterns are anticipated, and the gaps are filled in with unemployment benefits during long periods of vacation.

There are a number of sub-types within this general category of worker. One is the man who moves from job to job and lives with his wife and family in a trailer.[4] Then there are the workers, crucially important for the large construction firms, who contract to build the dams, town sites and major installations in various parts of the country. These mobile construction workers live a more precarious life; they move from job to job and have at least a tenuous contact with one or more construction firms. However, they are unencumbered by trailers and spend long periods in isolation on construction jobs far from road or rail transportation.

Most mobile construction workers, in whatever sub-group, have, beyond the initial construction period, only a fleeting contact with the community of single industry, as explained by a respondent:

> Construction workers are now here and these men will move on as the construction is finished. Almost invariably in this part of the world, new workers come in and take over the houses that construction workers have put up. Construction workers almost never stay in the community or carry on in the industry which they have constructed. Instead, they move on to start construction somewhere else.

2. The Get-rich-quick Worker

This is a different type from the mobile construction worker in that he has not worked in construction in the past and in all probability will not do so in the future. He works in construction for a brief period in order to accumulate enough capital to invest in some other type of occupation. Construction makes this possible because it needs a wide range of skills, and while work is at its peak long hours are worked at relatively high pay. The nest-egg seeker may spend several years of his work-life in construction before returning to a quite different occupation. "At first we have unlimited working days and a

4 Peter M. Butler, "Migrants and Settlers: The Influence of Geographical Mobility on the Retention of Extended Kinship Ties," unpublished MA thesis (University of New Brunswick, 1967).

minimum of a ten-hour day. Some people came in and would collect $13,000 over a couple of years. Many people worked sixteen hours a day, most of that overtime. Now (at the present stage of construction) you work from eight to four, with no chance to make big money."

There are a number of hazards to the get-rich-quick approach. One is to be able to withstand the primitive and unfamiliar conditions on the construction site and stay on the job; the individual must resist temptation of playing poker or taking periodic binge-holidays. Tales circulate about men who have moved out of a construction site with anywhere from $10,000 to $50,000. It is difficult to establish whether this is myth or reality.

3. Tradesmen and Skilled Workers

Construction, also, is characterized by the presence of a number of skilled men such as tin-smiths, plumbers, electricians and welders. These differ from the first two categories in both their level of skill and their work patterns. They work entirely within their skill range and have their trades papers. Basically they are urban workers, and are brought to the construction site by a contractor or sub-contractor for a specified period of time with a specified contract. The attraction of this periodic foray from the city is the high hourly pay, longer hours, and the bonus received from the sub-contractor. This type of work is attractive to them at a time of high unemployment or when there are few urban construction jobs. One contemporary respondent stated: "All our skilled men come from Montreal. Actually, we have to sub-contract, so the plumbing, heating, and the roofing is all done by Montreal sub-contractors who bring in their own Montreal personnel." Some of these skilled tradesmen take on this sort of work infrequently but some work on construction jobs exclusively for a few years, still within the employ of a city-based contractor.

4. Immigrant New-comers

Many construction jobs have knots of immigrants carrying out their first work in Canada. "About 25 per cent of our work force is Italian – straight off the plane" or "there are a number of men who have stayed all year; many of these lingerers among the labourers are Portuguese." At least one of the immigrant group must be able to speak English or in some way communicate with his superiors.

The construction job provides room, board, high wages, as well as the opportunity to accumulate money, but it is a matter of chance if construction work permits the immigrant to integrate into the larger society and labour market. The nature of the work and the way of life trap some immigrants into a life's work at construction in isolated places. Although it is exceptional, there are a number who spend the summer working on construction in isolated places in Canada, and the winter in Italy. Apparently international commuting provides these workers with a congenial way of life.

5. University Students

North American university students have provided seasonal manpower for a number of occupations for many years, including jobs at tourist resorts, on survey parties, and in many types of construction. Not all students are willing to live in isolation or work long hours during their "vacation." Nevertheless, a number from all faculties, whose past and future work patterns are quite different from those of the other workers, take construction jobs during the summer. Often they move from labouring jobs to white collar positions in the office or stores at the construction site.

6. Unemployed Tradesmen

Construction sites also attract tradesmen, carpenters, electricians and so on, who move in and out of the construction work force. During periods of unemployment in their own trades, these men appear on construction sites near their home city. They are attracted to construction on a temporary basis; their stay is usually short. These men differ from the mobile construction workers because as tradesmen they have skills, but they also differ from the tradesmen on the subcontract team because construction site work is an exception to their general work pattern rather than an integral part of it. In periods of high employment very few of these part-time construction tradesmen are available, so no construction firm depends upon them.

7. Marginal Farmers

The bulk of workers at many construction sites have an entirely different kind of life work pattern. These men consider themselves farmers and are land based. They come from marginal rural areas characterized by unemployment or under-employment. Traditionally, their way of life has consisted of subsistence farming, with forays into the work world to augment their cash incomes. This type of farmer characteristically cuts pulp wood in the winter, and works on county roads or carries out unskilled work during certain seasons of the year. These men are useful to the construction industry for two reasons: first, their work needs are seasonal – they do not seek a full-time job – and their season coincides with the peak requirements of construction. Secondly, these men are semi-skilled; although they cannot read blueprints or work at jobs demanding sophisticated skill, they provide "common sense," "good solid rough carpentry," and they are "good with their hands." Each province has a large reservoir of workers of this type.

In eastern Canada, construction supervisors discussed these men in broad stereotypes, for example, "French Canadians, Newfoundlanders, and Maritimers live in a different type of atmosphere and tend to want to work on the seasonal level and then return home for one reason or another." Or, as another contractor explained:

> To many this is their way of life. Newfoundlanders, for instance, are used to working six months of the year and they don't want to work any longer. They keep one eye on their bank account and one eye on their unemployment insurance book. This goes not only for the people from Newfoundland but also New Brunswick, the north shore, the south shore (of the St Lawrence) and parts of Nova Scotia. They don't want to work twelve months. They keep a little house and family at home and they can eat regularly; their food is good basic stuff – it isn't high cost – and many can live quite happily on what they earn in a season, the baby bonus, and unemployment insurance. This pattern, as long as it lasts, fits *our* needs.

The limitations of the rural marginal worker are indicated by another contractor:

> We have no particular trouble. They make good labourers, good carpenters – rough carpenters – but the trouble is, we can't get any trades for finishing [buildings] ... We build a beautiful house – and they are the people who leave hammer marks. So there is no finishing from them. We can't even use them for painters. They slop great gobs of paint on and it all runs down the wall and a perfectly good

> house is ruined – so we have a real problem to get people who can paint and finish a house. This is the sort of thing; when it is done badly, you can't repair it, and it is all very difficult.

The construction requirements fit the work needs of these men; in many instances the work relationships are almost formalized:

> All our construction must be done in four months of the summer. We must pour the foundations, put up the house, close it in and then we can get it finished inside. The sub-contractors work eighty hours a week and they push the contractors who push us to have things completed so they can work. By May the first, we start our excavations and if we are lucky we do our basements in June. This year we are having difficulties because instead of the usual six feet of frost we have twelve to fifteen feet. We are working seventy men at the moment, that is, all winter; this will go up to three hundred men in the summer. They don't have to be terribly highly skilled in the trades. We get them to come from rural areas for six months; 5 per cent of them go home early, but most of them stay for the whole summer. As soon as there is snow, they want to go back and at the beginning of December, they are all home. At the beginning of April they begin to move in here again.
>
> I like them, they are good men. When they work, they do something. They work nicely and they work very hard. And they are clean. They come back year after year. We keep a record of these men and this record is forwarded to our agent and when we order men, he gives them priority. He notifies men who have been here before and who have been successful. We have troubles getting the number of men because of transportation. We can't bring in five men because a DC4 holds more than that; on the other hand, if we have to have a group of carpenters, they bring their tools, and these are heavier than the men quite often; so one of the problems is, if you need five truckdrivers how do you bring them in?
>
> We pay for their transportation in and then take it off their pay so that they pay it indirectly. If they are sick, they go back, but if they are in hospital and we know them, we pay their hospital bill and their fare and they pay us back. We usually try to fly them direct by a chartered flight but it is extraordinarily hard to get them there with transportation. Fifty per cent of our workers here are single and fifty per cent are married and they are surprisingly middle-aged, both the single and married ones.

8. Unemployed, Unskilled Speculators

One respondent noted that "a big construction job is a bit like a honey-pot, and does it attract flies." He is referring to the unemployed, unskilled workers who apply at the site for a job. They hear rumours of work through their own peculiar underground communication network which is part of their sub-culture. This is a subculture of unemployable youth who hitch-hike across the country, or occasionally ride the rods in the traditional manner, "looking for work," the unemployed and unskilled who ask "is there any work in Toronto?" or declare "there is no work in Edmonton." They can be convinced that there is "no work" in a city by a fellow traveller in a bus terminal who says that he has been around for a week and hasn't found any work. On the basis of similar hearsay, these chronically unemployed arrive at a construction site or as close to it as they can get. As Oswald Hall suggests: "As in most cases of migration, those who move are rarely the most enlightened or the best equipped to make such a venture. Rather, it is those on the fringe of employment and near the margin of subsistence."[5]

The more isolated construction sites are protected from the constant application of this type of labour. However, they are faced with the problem of the unwanted, the unskilled and the unemployable, who somehow reach the site and must then be taken out. These people have been called "migrant headaches." The experiences faced by authorities in one quite isolated area serve to illustrate the problem:

> One of the major problems that we had to face was the influx of hordes who hoped to get jobs and if there was no work they were stranded with no way to get out and no money to get out. It was really pretty bad last summer; we were inundated by people who came to the community looking for work, but came uninvited. There was no work for them and they were on our hands. The problem was how to get them out of town [because of isolation]. We had many who were literally on our hands, starving; we produced meal tickets for them and this was not very satisfactory and we will not do it again. It is estimated that at the peak of this influx there were twelve hundred unemployed people here who had to be cared for. This is a little ironical because we do not have a serious unemployment situation locally.

5 O. Hall, "The Social Consequences of Uranium Mining," *University of Toronto Quarterly*, XXVI, no. 2 (Jan. 1957), p. 235.

Another informant in the same project enlarged upon these problems:

> In mid-March we even had 300 immigrants who arrived in a group by air, unannounced. These people were new immigrants to Canada and there was no work for them. We are quite often stuck with a great number of people; they sleep on the beach, they sleep on the boats, they are sleeping everywhere, and they become a problem. Actually, the police handle the problem and it is purely seasonal.

If there is a period of high employment this large reservoir of bodies is tapped, but they are seen as poor, unskilled and unreliable workers who pose more problems than answers for the construction industry.

9. The Local Labour Force

A new construction site creates a boom in the immediate area. Most of the sites are isolated so the population is sparse and lives marginally.

Many of the local inhabitants have the temporary opportunity of working on a regular basis for the first time in their lives. The very marginality of the bush-workers, farmers, Indians, and others who live on the fringes of habitation leads to great difficulties in integrating them into even the work force of the seasonal construction industry.[6] This point is made by a respondent:

> Here the way of life is thoroughly primitive. These people are used to being their own bosses and doing their work at their own time in their own way – as a result, in most instances they are not on time [punctual] . The notion of punctuality is quite foreign and the question is just what to do about this? They are pretty good workers although they are not very dependable. If they are hired on, they work the week and they go home for the weekend, and their weekends are pretty flexible, and they return here on Wednesday.

The availability of these men and the desirability of good relations with the local population lead to the inevitability of their employment. Their life work patterns are not related to construction work or any other work that requires industrial discipline; these men have

6 *Ibid.*, pp. 231-3.

not sought work but become employed because of the intrusion of industry into their locality and their way of life.

10. Bunk House Based Workers

This tenth group differs from all others because, although the men maintain a low level of skills, their work-lives are linked forever with the frontier. Such men spend their lives in jobs as helpers in the cook-house or labourers in saw mills. They are "loners" who talk little of their past; it is impossible to tell how many of them are single, divorced, or separated. Their lives are spent in the bunk house with the simple pleasures of cribbage and tobacco. They work to save a bankroll and talk about what they are going to do when they get "outside." They convince their work-mates that they will never return again. Within a week of departure they are back, penniless and somewhat sheepish. They tell a story of liquor, women, and robbery. They claim that the "city is no good." Somewhat cowed, they begin another stint of work in isolation. Many of these men are illiterate, some are periodic alcoholics, all have a low level of skill and make the bunk house on the fringe of civilization their only home. They carry out tasks that few others are willing to do, such as pot-washer, dishwasher, general kitchen help, and the dirtiest labouring jobs. Little is known about the origins of these career lines or how they end. It can be argued that Canada owes the development of its resources to the work of these perpetually marginal bunk house men who are able to live forever in social privation on isolated construction sites.[7]

THE CONSTRUCTION JOB

It can be seen, then, that construction workers represent a wide range of backgrounds, socio-economic levels, skills and work patterns. Despite the diversity, they all hold two things in common: they are all male, and they share (along with their employers) a desire to work long hours and earn overtime pay. They all share the construction job, which involves long hours of work, distinctive types of behaviour, and the insecurity of seasonal work.

7 For a vivid description of the "bo" and the "floater" at the beginning of the century see Bradwin, *The Bunkhouse Man*, pp. 52, 109-10.

1. Hours of Work

If the workers are to leave the amenities of the city then they want it to be financially worthwhile.[8] On the other hand, the contractor wants to get the maximum work accomplished with great speed in as little time with as few men as possible:

> This year, our work force is working a ten-hour day. Last year, they were working a twelve-hour day and they got time and a half for overtime. Now actually it is much better for people in this situation to work a twelve-hour day than a ten-hour one. Last year the total work week was seventy-two hours; now it is sixty hours. No good man wants to work less than ten hours a day because he comes up here to make money and there is nothing else to do. Our problem is that he may cause trouble when he sits and talks: he is inside, he gambles, he does a lot of things; he is not tired enough. So there are problems there. On the other hand we miss 72,000 hours in four months, and these are four crucial months because our building season is very short here. So the four months you have 280 men, a difference of two hours a day adds up to twelve hours a week, twelve times two hundred and eighty is 72,000 hours.

It would be anticipated that the long work hours, the isolation, and the fact that the work force is all or predominately male would affect behaviour.

2. Behaviour

With the variety of career lines that come together in a construction job many problems are raised that are not so important in an ordinary work situation. Conflicts regarding the rate of work, the ethnic backgrounds, religion, working conditions, and pay arise. The variety of work expectations, the type of work itself and its location in a sprawling construction site lead to careful supervision of work. One contractor suggested that:

> You can't supervise a large construction job like this too carefully. The foremen go around, but we have cost sheets and we know who is working and who isn't and we just simply tell them, if they are

8 For an account of men taken to the construction site in handcuffs and manacles see *ibid.*, p. 57.

> not working, that they are supposed to accomplish this or that and they have only accomplished a small amount and they had better get a move on. The big secret is if you are working in a house, six men in a house, unsupervised, or only periodically supervised – no two men in a room, otherwise they start talking.

Despite attempts to co-ordinate and integrate the work, the size of most construction sites means that it is possible to have men laid off for lack of work in one section, whereas in another section work is at a standstill for lack of workers with the same skills. Changes in the weather, unexpectedly rapid progress on one section of the construction, or a sudden exodus of workers, all produce instability in working arrangements. Field supervisors are able to improvise; they work with instability, and in what supervisors, in the more orthodox bureaucratic structures, would call chaos.

Many workers attempt to take advantage of this situation by claiming that they have skills which they do not, or by attempting to be re-employed in another section at a higher rate of pay, or to move from the construction to the nucleus work force of the sponsoring company. These are old tricks and most of the seasoned supervisors are aware of them. One supervisor described the situation in the following way:

> We have an arrangement with the company here that they won't take our employees and we won't take theirs. If the employee wants to change the arrangement, he must go out for three months and then come back. This is a very good idea. For instance, not too long ago I had a bricklayer who didn't have any tools. Well, we rustled up some tools for him and he started working and I could see by the lean on the wall that he wasn't a bricklayer. I asked him to tell the truth, and it turned out that he lived nearby and had a large family. He did work when he could find something, and he had inquired and knew that we needed bricklayers up here, so he came up to work as a bricklayer. As a reward for telling the truth, I kept him on and put him in as a labourer where he belonged. In no time flat he was sneaking around, looking around again, and disappeared; I found that he was in the cafeteria working as a cookee.

This is a male work world and, by and large, a work world frequented by young to middleaged men. A few construction jobs are located near a highway where it is possible to have a trailer and wife and carry on an uninterrupted family life, or have access to a community with amenities for leisure hours. Otherwise, it is an isolated male social world which takes over many of the characteristics of life in the armed forces. Recreation and leisure time is filled with talk – mainly of sex and past adventures – poker and beer. Construction firms attempt to control the use of beer and liquor on the site. When beer is available outside the construction site, liquor is forbidden within; this forces the men to leave the camp to do their drinking. On the other hand, the construction firm often maintains a canteen or a club on isolated sites. The hours of these outlets are restricted.

Behaviour in this male world is different from that of the same men in mixed company; the men themselves make this distinction. It would be surprising, then, if there was not criticism of their leisure time activities. Opinions differ about the extent of the deviance. Hall, for instance, reports that on one construction site, "in an average week, seventy or eighty prisoners are shipped out by bus."[9] In contrast, Butler suggests little more than noisy weekend parties among married construction workers in a trailer camp.[10] On one mining construction job, one man evaluated behaviour: "It is quite a law-abiding community and even during the worst of construction we did not have many criminal problems. I would say that arrests averaged about three per day and many of these are 'protective arrests' – usually people who are drunk and if not taken into protective custody would be robbed or beaten up or something." The men's behaviour and the amount of conflict depends on a number of complex factors including the ethnic make-up of the camp, the local customs, the control of liquor, the hours worked, the quality of the food, the accommodation, and the recreation. There are probably more arrests and more conflict when the workers come into periodic close contact with the settled community; their behaviour is different from that of the local inhabitants and a great deal depends on whether the behaviour of the construction workers is defined as a free-wheeling boom town atmosphere,[11] or deplorable and threatening drunkenness.

In days gone by, working conditions for the men in the camps were not always the best. These conditions, of course, have changed for

9 Hall, "Uranium Mining," p. 235.

10 Butler, "Migrants and Settlers."

11 Robinson, *New Industrial Towns,* p. 86. See also A. Phillips, "Our Wild Atomic City," *Maclean's* (May 25, 1957).

the most part.[12] But it still remains that life, for the isolated bunk house group, is very restricted. The social isolation has changed little since the early twentieth century:

> The social life in a bunk house community is self-contained. The very work of any distant camp is performed in comparative obscurity. The men themselves, dwelling in a camp often miles remote from the nearest hamlet, are thrown largely on their own resources during their spare hours. This continues often through varying weeks and months at a time.
>
> ... Even with healthy men, this manner of life exacts tribute of the innate powers of mind and body. Workers under these environments are allowed to give but not to take. A restlessness pervades their days which ultimately infects not only their thinking, but their habits of life. As the months drag on there is a weariness of heart, a blank feeling that gets the better of the whole man. Take any set of men, however carefully selected, and let them be thrown as intimately together as are the men in a bunk house, hearing the same voices, seeing the same faces day after day, and they soon become weary of one another's society and impatient of one another's faults. And these be men who under ordinary circumstances would be able to dwell at peace with their fellows.
>
> The natural reaction is shown in the current unstableness of labour so common in camps. There is the frequent desire to shift work, "jumping" it is called, even though the move lead to little betterment for the individual. It is the fact of a change that is desired. Restless, "taking his time" on the slightest pretext, the casual labourer in camps is in some respects the legitimate offspring of the bunk house.[13]

Bradwin sums up the situation well when he states:

> Despite appearances sometimes, sobriety is also a characteristic of the bunk house man. He should not be judged entirely by his conduct when, between jobs, he visits a frontier town or some city at the front. The test of his industry is the long months of patient service in some camp on construction. He is dependable through many

12 See Trevor Jones, "Great Slave Lake Railway: They couldn't have picked a better name," *The Last Post*, 1, no. 1 (Dec. 1968), pp. 32-8. Alan Edmonds' description of life on Canada's contemporary construction project "Power," appears in *Maclean's*, 82, no. 9 (Sept. 1969), pp. 42-54.

13 Bradwin, *The Bunkhouse Man*, pp. 83-4.

weeks; he works contentedly in isolation foregoing the recreation, the sports, and the amusements of a more orderly life.[14]

He graphically evokes the spirit of the frontier community in that era when the men looked for relaxation and diversion:

What are the social out-croppings? Time spent around any of the frontier towns reveals this in all its crudeness. The situation is simple. Men, both English-speaking and foreign-born are deprived during months at a stretch of the companionship of women, of home ties, and all that elevates life in a man; they are starved by isolation and monotony. When they again reach the outskirts of civilization, the frontier town with its "aurer" its music and noisy hilarity entices them from their deepest resolves. Vice too frequently pervades such places and, in divers haunts, drugged potions aid in "rolling" the victim.

The all-night orgies, the drunken sprees lasting for days in some top room of a hotel or lodging house; the busy rigs with their pimpish outriders who ply their ghoulish trade, the snake-room with half a dozen forms crouched upon the cot or dirty floor, spuming and snoring off the poisons of a protracted drunk; and then the group, silent, sore, sick and seamed with debauch, rounded by a "pilot," who gather in the zero weather late of a December night to catch the train en route for months more of life at camp, such is the vicious circle in which these men are held helpless – the obverse of life conditions in camps and shacks through previous months of work. It is a characteristic of Canadian life which produces a shudder: the curse of hardness overspreads it, and the price of hardness is hideousness.[15]

3. Seasonal Work and Mobility

The construction firms themselves have many problems other than their employees. The variety of problems are illustrated by three separate instances. One, for example, is the question of supply:

You learn by your mistakes and this year we will have some advantages. We have all our materials in the yard and they are all here

14 *Ibid.*, p. 215.

15 *Ibid.*, p. 163. See also S. D. Clark, *The Developing Canadian Community* (Toronto, 1942).

now so that we can really go when the ground is ready. We have the material on the job. This wasn't possible before because the transport wasn't ready to bring too much along. Anything we order is three weeks away and there are always additional delays. We once had something coming that took two and a half months.

In addition the construction firm is alert to weather, flies, and fire. "There is no sickness, this is a very healthy place in which to live. The air is different. There are mosquitoes, but if we can spray DDT at the right time, it can be quite effective. We do have clouds of black flies and mosquitoes here in wet weather and in dry weather we fear fire."

In this quickly changing, highly mobile, unstable world where all are strangers to each other, the problem of theft is grave. There is always the threat that men will steal from each other and from their employer. A standard gift of a rural family to a boy who is about to make his first venture to a construction job is a money belt. A construction supervisor notes:

They all have their own tools. This raises another thing – we do have the odd problem with theft. Things get lost. There are several thousand yards of PX wire which disappeared; now we can't go to see if it is hidden under someone's bed; they carry their tool chest to and from work and I understand that even a labourer goes to work with a tool chest! However, we have worked out a new system so that next year we can bring all the locked tool boxes together in a central location; if they need an extra tool they go with the supervisor and unlock their tool box and take it out. Once there is something hidden in the tool box, there is nothing we can do about it.

The workers themselves do not consider removing things to be theft; it is scrounging. These workers, like most employees, feel that removing items from the company is fair game. This is well illustrated by the account given by a magistrate about behaviour of workers on a construction job for which no town was supplied:

When construction is around and when the installations are being built, there is an awful lot of excess material rolling around – stuff that was being burned, stuff that was being wasted – so people began to take this scrap material off the site and the authorities had no objection. But of course, along with this scrap, you also got a

> lot of new material, and everyone is busy on the site scrounging. There is a nice story of a man who every night went out past the gatehouse with a wheelbarrow, and the wheelbarrow was filled with chaff, and each night the guard would burrow down in the chaff to try and find out what was in the wheelbarrow and it was always empty, apart from the chaff. This happened night after night, week after week, until the man retired. It was his last day on the site. On his last night, sure enough he came up with his wheelbarrow and it was filled with chaff. The guards looked through it and they said "what have you been stealing all these years, what have you had hidden in that chaff?" "Hidden in the chaff, nothing," said the man, "hell! I've been stealing wheelbarrows."

Construction work is temporary. The work patterns of the men, their career lines, and perhaps even their motivations all suggest that this is a highly mobile population. All except perhaps the bunk house group give up many non-monetary rewards for money and isolation – enforced savings. The turnover of population is extremely high, although the contractor attempts to keep it as low as possible. The actual rate is influenced by many factors, most of them beyond the control of the contractor. For instance, the availability of out-going transportation affects the impulsive departure. If the man can get into his car and drive away at any time he wishes, he is in a different situation from the man who must depend on a weekly plane. The quality of food, accommodation, recreation, weather and friendships affect the mobility of the men.

Rates of mobility, as such, have little meaning. Both Hall and Robinson suggest fifteen to fifty per cent a month. In one location "One construction boss ... reported a turnover of four to one; this means that he had to hire four men to keep one on the job."[16]

The most interesting figure given by a construction supervisor was the turnover of two hundred and five per cent. It is not clear what this figure means except that it must be a lot!

In many respects, the construction firm is powerless to do anything about the mobility rate. This account suggests an intangible set of circumstances over which the contractor has no control.

> At the period of very high turnover, we noticed that the workers are like birds on a wire. One decides early one morning – he gets

16 Robinson, *New Industrial Towns,* p. 85; Hall, "Uranium Mining," p. 23.

out of bed and says he is going home – and you will find five or six before the plane leaves, all going home, and you will find that they are all from the same village. If they are going home to the village, they have two reasons for going – one of them is very sensible and one of them is very silly. On the silly level, if Joe is going and he gets there first, then he will be the hero of the community and he will have the way with all the women; he will have stories to tell. On the other hand, they all go because they can share a cab from the airport to whatever distant community they live in.

Unstable as they are these construction workers are the first inhabitants of the community of single industry. They are essential to the establishment of the community. They affect the future of the embryo community for two reasons. First, some construction workers still live in the community when the future citizens arrive. This period of overlap in which two rather different populations come together lasts for a few months up to several years. Second, although not the rule, some of the original construction workers stay on as citizens of the town.

We now turn from stage I, the brief or prolonged period of construction, to consider the recruitment of the population of the emerging community.

3

Stage II The recruitment of citizens

While construction progresses, the corporation is active in other areas. Key professional and other expert personnel have to be attracted to the new plant and community. Semi-skilled and unskilled workers must be recruited. Some recruits are eager to move, but most are reluctant, even though arriving as original members of the work force and first citizens has many advantages.

The incoming employees and future citizens of the community begin to arrive long before the roads, street lights, and homes are completed, and often before the industrial plant is finished.[1]

RECRUITMENT

The townspeople eventually outnumber the construction workers. Longer-term construction workers are fewer and more stable than the earlier ones, and the two rather distinct groups may live in close proximity for as many as ten years. Also, some construction workers break their habitual career lines and shift from construction to permanent work in the new plant - from construction stores to company stores, for instance. Others have jobs that keep them in the community until the final days of construction; they lose contact with other construction workers and have friends and acquaintances among the permanent townsfolk. Still others stay because of the attractiveness of the area, they "like this part of the country." Whatever the motivation and social influences, few towns of single industry cannot boast of at least a handful of "old-timers," there before settlement began.

These "left over" construction workers are a minority. Most employees are recruited by the company. The initial selecting and sorting of employees provides the original citizens of the community. From the point of view of work patterns, four types of recruit within two broad categories are involved.

1. Transferred Employees

Two types of recruited employees combine to form one broad category - employees at present in the service of the company in one or

1 This recruitment and settling process seems to be much more protracted and complex than Robinson suggests. Ira Robinson, *New Industrial Towns on Canada's Resource Frontier,* Department of Geography, University of Chicago, Research Paper no. 73 (Chicago, 1962), p. 86.

another branches. Traditionally, a company selects key experienced men from its employees elsewhere to administer and supervise the technical and scientific activities of the new plant. These men are transferred and promoted, and are usually recruited with the least difficulty because mobility is generally accepted by management and professional people. The company assumes that management, professional, and scientific personnel accept mobility as a way of life; mobility is seen as a mutual advantage to company and employee. These expectations, generally reinforced by past practices, make mobility a condition of employment although it is seldom specified contractually.

Reimbursement of expenses usually covers out-of-pocket costs only. It is generally accepted that in urban areas the short-term financial losses caused by real estate fluctuations have to be borne by the employees; but mobility, when viewed on a career basis, is indicative of salary and status improvement; any losses are balanced by the higher positions with higher salaries achieved through the knowledge and experience gained by geographical mobility.

This does not mean that change of residence does not affect the employee or his family. Often the decision to move is ultimately in the hands of the employee's wife and family. A change means severing friendships and a web of relationships in the community in which they are living, to move to a frontier community among strangers. The wife is particularly interested in the schooling available for children, shopping facilities, recreation, and the type of house she can expect. Many wives feel that they have married their husbands for better or for worse and the husbands' careers may require considerable sacrifice on their part. As we shall see later, some wives are not able to adjust and this has implications for family and community life in small towns of single industry. Despite the exceptions, most of the supervisory personnel and their families accept the transfer without question.

Other employees who are transferred have non-professional skills which are needed in the new location. These personnel, unused to moving, present a more serious difficulty. The intellectual, emotional, and social unacceptability of mobility may be so severe that moving may be a disservice to the employee, his family, and the company. Further, the chance of a tradesman being able, on a career basis, to recover possible losses arising out of relocation by salary improvement is questionable. The move is put on a voluntary basis; rejection of the offer is without prejudice. The family of a man at this level experiences difficulties in re-establishing itself that are not met by personnel to whom mobility is a way of life. As one respondent explained:

> First, people at this level often have substantial investment in their homes. Mortgage payments are quite low and as a result of not being able to retrieve their equities immediately, their budgets at the new location are upset. Secondly, the people at this level appear to rely more heavily on primary relationships within the community. Their limited social experiences are of little help for their re-establishment in the new community ... Although most of these employees experience difficulties, there are some exceptions to the general rule. The employees of oil and gas industries, for instance, resemble more closely the construction workers; even those at lower position levels appear to be more flexible.

Another informant said: "Family ties were extremely difficult to break. They must be given at least a promotion and the assurance that they could return if they didn't like the place out there, with the further assurance that they would get their job back with at least the rate they had when they left."

2. *New Employees*

The other types of personnel that must be recruited roughly parallel the two just discussed, but fall into the second major category of new personnel. New administrative, scientific, engineering, and like personnel are required to fill out the management complement of the new plant. Young engineers, scientists, and potential administrators, usually from the graduating classes of universities, are attracted. They are often lured with promises of adventure on the frontier and the rapid advancement often associated with "getting in on the ground floor."

The fourth type is made up of new semi-skilled personnel who carry on the bulk of the work in the new industry. These men come under the supervision of the experienced administrative staff and take on-the-job training given by the skilled personnel transferred from other branches of the company. Whether mine, paper mill, manufacturing concern, smelter, or railway, the educational requirements are minimal.

The sifting of these personnel and their families is responsible for the peculiar social characteristics of the community of single industry in the second stage. The new personnel for a new plant in an isolated area have many resemblances to construction workers. People from various ethnic and religious backgrounds, with differing educational attainments and social statuses, are brought together in an isolated community. At the beginning all are strangers to each other.

The transferred personnel have a career line already invested in the company, but the new recruits do not have these vested interests. It is not surprising that there is a high turnover among the new personnel. One respondent said: "The turnover is tremendous, probably for every three men that have come up here, you have one who stays. As a result, this whole place is characterized by insecurity. Anyone you talk to about the future says 'I hope to get out of here soon, I am fed up.'"

In another community, a union official said, "They had to hire 1800 men each year to maintain their work force of 800. I should know, because I had to make out the union forms for all these men." In a mining community, one man said, "At the beginning there was the influx of high paid drifters but now it has settled down and people who are here are people who want to stay." Another observer said "The one basic problem is greater than all others as far as this community is concerned. All of the people consider themselves to be living here temporarily. According to the people, there are no full-time residents. This makes it extraordinarily hard to interest citizens in the future of the town, a future which, in their words, they will not share."

EARNINGS AND ISOLATION

Many citizens have easy answers to account for this period of change and unrest. Basically, they attribute the mobility of the population to a quest for quick money, "The majority came in to make a good deal of money; it turns out that they do not save, and they always have the feeling of temporariness; you cannot build a town if everyone thinks they are temporary. The people feel that they are not going to be here permanently. The people don't work hard civically and put in roots." Some may have taken the job for quick money, but such a goal is difficult to achieve at this stage of community development. This is indicated by a member of the clergy who states:

> Anybody who wants to come up here and work furiously for a few years, make a pot of money, and pull out, finds it now impossible. Five years ago, you could come up here for a number of years, make $35,000 and save it, if you had that in mind. I know someone who did - saved $35,000 - because he wanted to buy a farm, a big farm, a well-equipped one with certified cattle. Now with the abbreviated hours, the forty-eight hour week, this type of person doesn't come up any longer.

Another person suggests, "Almost everyone universally 'hates' the place. They admit that they are here for the money - they don't like the place and they spend most of their money on consumer goods."

One characteristic of the community referred to over and over again in interviews is the isolation. A great many of the social difficulties are attributed to this community characteristic. Isolation and earnings are often linked, as in the following quotations:

> The interesting thing is that they are caught here earning very high money but with very high expenditure in order to live like human beings; but they are taxed at the same level of ordinary citizens. I have been campaigning for lowering taxation for isolated workers for some time. When you take into consideration the position they are in, they should have some deductions. For instance, in a normal year each individual must spend at least $500 in getting out.

Or,

> Travelling is a must and they have the money to do it and I would say they are some of the best travelled people in the world. Many of the people here are Europeans and they go back [to Europe], but other people get out from the isolation and go to Florida and various other places.

More exotically,

> Everything is far away from us, the distance and the isolation and the money produces a very peculiar situation - you have a father, a mother, and a child, and together their income is $600; this seems like a lot but if they go on vacation for a month, this will cost them at least $2000 and it takes quite a while to accumulate a backlog like that. As soon as the vacation is over, they come

back, they have little purpose in life really, beyond saving for the next vacation. They are looking for thirty-three days of Florida or Acapulco and they want exotic holidays like this.

Some people suggest solutions or potential solutions to these problems. A union member feels that many people get fed up with isolation, they get "bushed" and wish to live in civilization for a short period. He feels that they should not have to leave their job in order to do this:

> The problem is that when a man wants to get out, he really wants to get out. From the very beginning, when we first came in here unorganized [the union] we tried to convince the company that instead of holding a man here and having him quit and leave, they could institute a system of leave of absence after so many months. After this time you have the right to take so many weeks leave of absence with pay. If they did, I think they [the company] would save much in the long run. A man who is up here for a long time gets "bushed" - this means he gets cranky, he is grouchy and hard to work with; the grievances are high because the men are irritable, and just from a purely safety viewpoint I think this would be worthwhile. Along with this, of course, is the cost of leaving. This is very high and you get people trapped, and again you get the sort of attitude or frame of mind which doesn't do the union, the company, or the employee any good.

Alternatively, a member of the clergy suggests that the people in the initial stages of this sort of community should have isolation pay similar to the armed forces, or income tax benefits:

> I think there should be some deductions [from income tax] for people here, or they should pay people isolation pay as they do in the armed forces. Actually, the workers here pay $1500 a year in taxes and we get no services; we get no services at all from the federal government except the post office, and that is a money-making proposition. We either need a northern allowance, or better, an allowance to account for the cost of living, or else a deduction from income tax.

Many claim that people come to these new communities to make money; the fact that they do not make money traps them as permanent residents, as the following comments suggest:

> A funny thing though; people who have been here any length of time, although they are determined to get out, cannot, because they can't accumulate enough money to leave. For instance, if they try to sell their furniture, they only get half price for it; if they try to crate it up then it's going to cost them hundreds of dollars to get it out. It is hard for these people to save money, because when you are in a situation like this, you like to get out and you like to see civilization again and there is no place you can go that doesn't cost an awful lot of money. People can't save.

All residents share isolation and its influence on net earnings, but the impact of this shared situation on particular individuals varies considerably. The different effects on new and transferred personnel has been suggested. In addition, respondents indicate that other social characteristics such as marital status, social and ethnic background, career expectations and personal qualities, such as friendliness, all deeply influence the contentment of the individual and the length of his stay.

SINGLE EMPLOYEES

One informant said with an air of explaining everything: "The single men, several thousand, live in company dorms under rather poor conditions. The single women – and there are about fifty – also live in company dorms although these are much more elaborate than the men's dorms." Another informant was more detailed in his comments:

> In the bunk houses, things are not too bad if we can have one per room which is what we have now; generally we have a man who sweeps and washes the bunk house – the tenants look after their own beds, except for the males who have their beds made for them. If you have one per room we have accommodation for 100 trades, labourers, as well as our specialized people. So each janitor looks after about 20 rooms in each bunk house. Any damage anyone does, he is charged for it, if it can be found out by whom it was done. The charges run from three dollars to ten dollars. We don't charge for the material, just for the labour.

Dormitory accommodation, whether shared or on a one person per room basis, may be appropriate for some levels of employees but other employees, particularly university educated men, object to this type of accommodation. This was made explicit in an interview that began as an off-work evening chat with a young geologist in the "male staff bunk house" of a northern community of single industry. The geologist said,

> Then the company wonders why people leave. Do you realize that in our section of forty-one professional people, twelve have left this year and more are going? The result is that it is a very demoralized department. As soon as three or four people make up their minds to leave, the whole department becomes demoralized and it becomes a plague. Most of them are going out because of the isolation and the facilities. You make reasonable money here – you spend it too – and one may as well live with more amenities. There is not much point in having a college education if you are going to live under these conditions.

During the interview, as the evening wore into morning, other unmarried professional engineers and geologists joined the speaker. One had returned from a cribbage tournament at the recreation centre, one had been drinking with a blind date (he was the lucky one), one had just returned from playing poker and lost $125 in his last hand so that his night's take was only $350, another had been in his room reading philosophy. Most of the discussion centred around women and plans for a big party on Saturday night and the problem of finding enough women to half go round the guests at the party. As the hours wore on, they discussed leaves and what they did on their leaves; isolation, leaves, women, and housing conditions were the major topics and the subject of major complaints. It was also clear from the group conversation that the promotions and political deals within the work structure had great impact upon the group. (This group of young professional men, who lived in one bunk house unit had beaten the liquor availability problem by sacrificing two of their rooms which they had converted into a common room, with a well-stocked, pay-as-you-drink bar. This was their social centre. During the extended interview it became apparent why the bar bills were high.)

The conversation draws attention to the sex ratio of the communities at this particular stage of their development. This ratio is crucial to young graduates who are in the marriage market. One study showed that the number of males to 100 females ranged from 143 to 1119.[2] It should be remembered that this ratio does not reflect the number of females eligible for marriage because the rates include married females. "It is impossible to hold an engineer here who is engaged to a girl down south."

In one emerging community a respondent estimated the number of females: "As far as female staff is concerned, we probably have a staff of 60 plus 20 waitresses; of these probably 25 per cent are married. There are very few daughters; none of them old enough [to work for the company, or, for that matter, marry]."

At this stage when the predominant population is made up of child-bearing adults and their offspring, there are few baby-sitters. One executive suggested some of the implications:

> There doesn't seem to be much double working although husband and wife, when they do work, run into difficulties and we have to cut it out. During the early days, we had a husband and wife both working and the children were running wild in the streets and we had the police moving in – so we had to lay down new rules by which married women were not permitted to work.

The atypical sex-ratio might seem an open invitation to prostitutes. A clergyman volunteered:

> As for prostitution, there is the odd [occasional] prostitute, but she is watched pretty carefully. You have far more bootlegging than you have prostitution and the bootleggers really make money. For a 48-ounce bottle you pay from $30 to $40 with a $2 tip to get it out to you by cab. But the Mounties keep this pretty well under control. Somebody was caught recently with liquor in his car and was fined $1500.

At this stage the unbalanced sex ratio has further implication because the single, unattached, but yearning males are in close association with married couples as well as the few single females. This poses problems when males on the make, liquor, and dancing are combined. One informant explained carefully,

> We have a lot of dances and they are all open. We allow stag lines, but we can cut them down by raising the price. Usually one of our dances is five dollars, or three dollars a couple. If we want to restrict the stag line, then we raise the price for stags. We do that for our main annual dance; we will have the price for stags at ten dollars.

2 *Ibid.*, p. 82.

This problem of holding the young unattached professional was considered in some detail by an older professional person in a well-established community who, reminiscing, said:

> If you are going to have to keep your young engineers you are going to have to give them a lot more than was given to us here. Now I am a great believer in one furnishing his own entertainment, but the young fellows today expect more and you will have to give them more. Our first winter here, we were very isolated. In the middle of the first winter the company opened the first movie house. A bunch of us used to call ourselves the first-nighters. We hit every movie on Monday, Wednesday, and Friday. That was the bulk of our activity.
>
> There was a lot of drinking, a lot of guys getting drunk; a lot of running around with women, you know the type I mean. But this is not what I wanted out of life. I wanted something more so I left. Got married and came back eighteen months later. I've been here ever since and I love it. It [the community situation] was pretty hard at first. We didn't know anybody, but we formed our own groups and clubs. We formed, for example, the Thursday evening club. We met every Thursday evening and it was pretty intellectual – somebody would give a paper. The evening would start around eight o'clock and finish around ten-thirty. Then, we would have a party once a month. We met in the basement of the church here.

MARRIED EMPLOYEES

Although many are quick to attribute the rapid turnover to footloose single men with no family responsibilities, and to those in quest of quick money, this is hardly a sufficient explanation of the phenomenon. The exodus of married employees is very high, as one company executive explained: "We own at the moment 585 dwellings. Actually, 175 people have moved from one house to another, and 285 tenants have moved from town. In other words, 85 per cent of the occupants of these houses have been here only two years [of a potential 7 years]. This will give you some idea of the turnover in the houses." In another community, a respondent explained,

> Among the householders there is a tremendous turnover of population, you have a 50 per cent turnover over a three-year period. This means it will be a long time before they are property owners,

> and before town offices can be elected, as people will not accept nominations when they are simply waiting to go. When you have a whole town that is waiting to go, you are in difficulties. The company had a survey not too long ago, and there are no people in the town who wish to own their own property. There have been no applications received, although theoretically, they could send them in; I expect that after ten or fifteen years, things will still be temporary. This feeling of temporariness is the natural outcome of being isolated; isolation without a road – even if you had a road it would still be isolation because the road would go nowhere.

In still another community, a citizen said,

> Theoretically people will purchase their houses – but not in the near future. There would have to be all sorts of differences in the situation. When people don't feel that they own the house and can't make internal changes without company permission they are unhappy; but I don't think they can risk purchasing because if they are laid off – if anyone is laid off – they would have this large investment which they couldn't pay off and there are no job alternatives in the community.

Nevertheless, it is a vicious circle because if a family comes to settle, it requires a house. "It is hard to get a house and this discourages married families from settling down. This is one of the reasons why two or three years ago the turnover was 105 per cent." In fact, families settling into this type of community have a number of problems to face. These were outlined by several respondents, for instance:

> At the moment of course, the town site belongs to the management and it still controls the houses; there are tremendous [large] families and the recreation of children is a problem. The handling of the children situation raises all sorts of difficulties, not only in school but in off hours. At the moment we seem to be running at the average of 3.7 children per family and currently there are 400 children here. This is a much higher birth rate than the national average. As for accounting for children in the housing, basically they are planning on three-bedroom houses. They have a few four-bedroom houses which are for the supervisory workers [sic], but they are not planning on more than three-bedroom houses for the average worker.

The fact that the high mobility rate is not expected to be a temporary phenomenon is suggested by the following comment,

> Most students go along to grades 9, 10, or 11. Of course, we have very few older children along here at this point. I don't think we have many scholars, but when children reach the beginning of maturity, this is another reason why parents begin to pull out: they go south where their child can get education. This produces another realm of instability. We are hoping to get a university in this area!

The situation is complicated in the case of the married employee because the life he leads depends not upon himself and fellow workers alone, but upon his wife and family. At this stage, the views of the wives are of crucial importance. These views depend to considerable extent upon the background and expectations of the women:

> If the married men can bring their wives and children, if there is education, then they're all set. But we lost two or three last year who were engaged. They worked a year, were thinking about getting married, but mothers-in-laws are problems. If the mother-in-law doesn't think that the daughter should go to the north, then, in many cases, he has had it. Occasionally you find a man who finds the kind of wife who will follow her husband wherever his work takes him. In this situation everything is fine.

Many wives immediately adapt to life in an incomplete isolated one-industry town. As one respondent suggests:

> As far as wives are concerned, most of them have a wonderful time. They find all sorts of outlets – if they mix, and if they are energetic. They have a tremendous number of problems to solve – they have to set up a school organization, they have to look after a library, they have to be active in church work. Once the problems of the community are settled, and as the children grow older, they become more sociable, and life dissolves into bridge parties and coffee parties and the usual routine. Wives generally go out [of the community] twice a year, once for a holiday with their husbands and once home to see the parents or some other item [sic].

Preliminary findings of a study conducted for the Center for Settlement Studies, University of Manitoba, suggest that the most satisfied wives and homemakers in communities of single industry were women who

> had been brought up in small towns or on farms; those who had been raised on the Prairies or in another northern or mining town had particular advantages; had lived away from their home town environment at least once before going to [the community of single industry] ; in addition to living away from home after marriage, had lived away from their families for a few years before marriage.[3]

SOCIAL BACKGROUND AND EXPECTATIONS

In cases of high mobility it may not be the marital status but the professional and career expectations of the employee that are crucial:

> Among the engineers you will find the mining engineers and geologists are pretty well OK. They have chosen their career and intend to carry on in it - they know that a great deal of their work will be in isolation in the north. Electrical engineers and mechanical engineers, however, have trouble; they are usually geared to production. We can certainly use them, but the rest of their engineering friends are not here. This job is one of many alternatives for them and quite often they get restless and decide to go out to the bright lights.

This same informant noted that "Most professional men are free till they reach their forties, and then they find that it is sort of hard for them to displace themselves or dislodge themselves. It is hard for them to get a job after forty and they tend to stay." One astute administrator noted, "The major problem, I think, of a place like this is isolation. This isolation takes over a different significance for single people and married and it varies according to the level of education." He then went on to enumerate the number of variables such as marital status, ethnic affiliation, career line, motivation, friends,

3 Center for Settlement Studies, University of Manitoba, *Third Annual Report* (Winnipeg, 1970), p. 176. *The Proceedings - Symposium on Resource Frontier Communities, December 16, 1968* published by the Center are of relevance to this chapter. One resident from each of four communities of single industry presented prepared answers to a set of questions concerning factors affecting living, permanence, educational facilities, and income in their home communities. The communities involved were all in stage II. See also, John S. Matthiasson, *Residents' Perception of Quality of Life in Resource Frontier Communities,* which appears in this series.

family, and the community structure from which the person came, making quite fine distinctions between the various types of motivation, expectations and patterns of life.

He first separated those from metropolitan areas and those from small towns and farms. "All I can say is that few from metropolitan areas tend to stay; most of the people who stay here are from small towns or from farms." This respondent refers to differences in way of life; obviously neither a raw unfinished community nor a community of single industry can offer the services of a metropolitan community. Urban citizens have different expectations than small town citizens. This will be explored more fully as we proceed.

Ethnic and cultural differences can be crucial. For instance, a French-speaking professional speaking of a community in Quebec stated:

> Oddly enough, I think that English-speaking people fit much better in this community than French-speaking. Certainly, when recruiting from universities, the English-speaking will ask about the pay, the hours, the kind of job, and the challenge. French-speaking students will ask about these but they seem to be mostly preoccupied with social life; what do they do in the evenings? Is there a library? Are there dances? What sort of recreation is supplied? This could probably be accounted for in several ways. But in my opinion, the English form clubs wherever they are; they also have a notion of going through sacrifices now for future benefits. The French-speaking people tend to be tied up with a large family circle and to make their social life within this circle, so have difficulty adjusting to an anonymous group.

The ability to fit into this emerging community is affected by yet another variable which one informant located precisely:

> One problem that has never been solved, is the person who comes from a very close and tight family – this is a real problem and I don't see any technique of getting around it. For instance, people come from a little village where there are twenty families who are all inter-related and who are all inter-connected. These people tend to form a social life all their own; it goes on within the family, with an untold number of brothers and sisters, and many cousins, living hard by. These people are quite lost when they get out in a strange land, and if a wife comes from this type of area and family, she just

> simply can't cope with the North. We have had several women whose husbands had very good professions and liked their work very much, but the women were going quietly batty – they had to go.

Respondents living in communities at this stage of development note obvious and important variables; the ability to make friends, for instance: "None of these people will stay unless they find compatible friends. But some people don't get along anywhere, and they just don't make friends here.

Clearly, kinship expectations, ability to make friends, ethnicity, and the like are not unique to communities of single industry, but the social implications of these variables take on added significance in this type of setting.

The limited leisure diversions available often seem more appropriate to the labourer than to the professional. For instance, in one community, an informant stated,

> On Saturday or their day off, the boys go in and drink a lot of beer; the place closes at 10:30, and then what can they do? Well, for somewhere to go, they go over to the cafeteria for a cup of coffee and something to eat, and if somebody looks at them twice, then a fight starts and this raises problems. But it is amazing how few problems there are considering the isolation and the lack of outlets that the single people have in the area. Everyone has a card which admits him to meals, and on this card he can have five meals a day, or six meals if he wants to, or even more. He's supposed to have three. Legitimately, he can have four if he works an extra shift or some overtime. These people eat prodigious quantities and for the first few months the diet of most of them is pretty bad – filling up on pastries, pies, and sweet things – later it settles down, but they still eat very large quantities. It is known by all that the T-bone steak is served every second Sunday – each steak weighs about a pound – people will consume as many as four of these at a sitting.

PHYSICAL FACILITIES

The problems of isolation and earnings, however intensely felt, focus the residents' attention on facilities for recreation. They want a place to get together "to have fun" – but the limitations of space force them to discover that the tastes of the top scientists and the labourers are not necessarily compatible, what is suitable for adults is not necessarily useful for toddlers.

One respondent takes up the general question of physical facilities and its relationship to keeping personnel in the community:

> I realize now that one of the dire problems is a place for young people to meet. There is no place for these young people to congregate either accidentally or on purpose. I understand that there is a large turnover of nurses at the hospital and from speaking to the department heads here, I understand there is a pretty high turnover in young engineers, also. Engineers today don't grow on trees. It is impossible to get trained men, so that we've got to hold on to these fellows and train them, and fix it so that after their [on-the-job] training they'll stay with us. I see a problem in helping them to get oriented here. Actually, I don't think much has been done about it. I will admit that now you have a problem of a place to meet; if you are going to throw young nurses and young engineers together, you've got to give them a place to dance. That is the normal way of passing time. The next question is where you are going to dance.

Another respondent in another community shows concern about a similar problem:

> The problem here is what to do after work. In the old days [stage I] when you worked long hours it was very good ... The position of the men in the bunkhouses is rather bad. You have 1000 men, and I think they are lonesome. Whether they are married or single doesn't make any difference, they are just lonely people and as a result there are far too many parties and far too much fighting. Part of this is aggravated by long hours of leisure ...
>
> I don't think many of the bunkhouse people use the recreation centre. A great deal of what they do there is organized in teams, for the few and not for the many; for instance, curling – a great deal of space and time is spent on curling and there are very few who have had any experience or any interest in curling as compared with, for instance, ice hockey, which should have been the first investment. As it is now in ice hockey, they play some, but when you have done a day's work and it is 25 below zero there is a limit

> to how long you want to play [out-door] hockey. As far as the children are concerned at that temperature they are forbidden to play fast hockey. Breathing deeply in the very cold air can harm lungs. An arena is very much needed here.

COMPANY AND TRADE UNION POLICY

The company is not a passive bystander in this process. Attempts to cut down the extreme mobility are made through hiring, interviews, and selection procedures: "We try to select employees on the basis of their willingness to work for a length of time. We usually tell them, 'If you are only interested in coming up for two or three months we are not particularly interested in having you. But if you are interested in coming up for a few years, then we are.'"

This, however, is complicated by their need for certain skills. For many of these skills, the company has to compete directly with urban employers:

> As far as the project is concerned we find that we have more difficulties in some areas because of lack of skills, especially all mechanical skills. As far as good mechanics are concerned they can earn as much in Montreal as they can here, so there is not much point in coming here, although they can get more hours. They don't get much more pay, but they get more take-home pay by working more hours.

Throughout this period, it is not only the company that has the problem; unions are affected directly. The shared problem of an unstable and mobile work force tends to make the union and the company allies and confederates. This is made even more apparent because both are starting with clean slates, with no background of traditional disputes and revengeful counter moves:

> The major problem here is to have a stable population, a stable work force who feels that it is worthwhile living here, who can live for the moment in a company house, but eventually in their own houses, who will develop their own recreation, who will stay and not want to go out to the bright lights. Now in this place, where you have around 1300 people, 700 quit over a winter, that is, in the nine months. Three-quarters of all the problems that we have

arise out of this; both the company and the union have the same problems.

The instability of the work force makes it almost impossible to carry on union activities. Local union responsibilities, like community concern and dedication to daily work, are not of major importance to someone who is leaving next week:

> Attendance is poor to good, depending on the agenda. The routine meetings, treasurer's report and that sort of thing, are very poorly attended. Of course, one of our main problems here is that with the rapid turnover of personnel we have a rapid turnover of leadership, and so you might call the executive and find that two have left. You might talk to someone, make some plans, and find that he is gone the next day. I think the only way that you can get the union to work, is to really assign enough staff. Most unions are understaffed because you can't really count on your executive types remaining too long.

INDUSTRIAL DISCIPLINE

Social control in the form of industrial discipline and penalties is part of all industry. A mine supervisor said:

> There is a system of penalties involved; sometimes it is one day, three days, four days, up to ten days. Usually for major sins the guilty have a day off, four days off, ten days off, and then they are fired. If they muck things up so that production stops for several hours, you might as well go home and not come back. Anybody who sleeps on the job has committed a very serious offence because there is a great deal of moving machinery. Quite often a person will work in his house during the evening and the night, go to work tired the next day, fall asleep. This has a penalty of ten days off work the first time, and you are fired the second time.

Nevertheless, infractions do occur, and penalties are imposed:

> As far as infractions that require discipline are concerned, we have had 591 cases issued by the company in the last year. Most or a good proportion of these come up for grievances. The biggest problem is the missing of a shift. This to us is a major sin, because it is

> very expensive. Particularly in the winter when it is 40 degrees below zero and the man is employed high on a windy hill, it is a great temptation not to come in. We can't allow things to become too lax or too loose and we have rules of when you should phone in and that you can't get off the shift. This type of thing probably accounts for 30 per cent of the infractions.

Discipline and control do not stop with work penalties. As the work situation tends to stabilize, for instance, the company tries to reduce the amount of costly overtime. "At the moment there is very little overtime. What overtime there is is checked on very closely."

COMMUNITY DISCIPLINE

Company control moves far from the work situation into the community, firstly to control the buildings erected.

> Within the town itself we control the sorts of buildings that go up rather stringently. First of all we have city by-laws which are based on the National Building Code; there are provincial laws, and on top of that we own all the property and sell all the lots; before we sell any lot we introduce restrictions as to what may be built upon it. The conditions are written into a contract, and before land is sold these must be adhered to according to the stipulations. Up until ten years ago outsiders would apply for a lot and permission to build, whether it be a garage or what have you, and if the company felt that they were reliable and that there was room for their services they would give permission; if not, they wouldn't.

Control also moves to outer boundaries of the new town-site to try to control fringe development. "We try to control squatters." Hall notes the ribbon developments that arise outside the town boundaries of the mining community, and states "The latter community is planned to prohibit these on the grounds that they soon become unsightly slum-like areas, and that it is too costly to provide utilities and other services for them."[4] The planting of trees and gardens are of concern to the company:

4 O. Hall, "The Social Consequences of Uranium Mining," *University of Toronto Quarterly*, XXVI, no. 2 (Jan. 1957), p. 234.

> Then again we have had trouble. Usually some young couple would want to make their place look lovely, so they would want to put in a few trees, and a hedge. But what they put in, did not particularly mean anything to them – they would just put in whatever they had their hands on. But we are against willow. It wrecks the sewers, the water mains, the sidewalks – everything. We have had so much trouble in the sections of town with these trees that we will do anything to discourage their use. Townspeople do not understand this and feel that we are interfering. But the story you heard – that we will not allow these people to plant gardens – is definitely untrue, and, in fact, against our policy in every way.

Of course, the company keeps control of those who are to be tenants in the company owned houses. The allocations vary from community to community. In all communities, the key personnel are given first choice. Often each department is assigned a number of houses, and the department head makes the allocations within his department. Others work on a centralized system of allocation.[5] In the early days, specific allocation is based upon fecundity, rather than status: the employee with the largest family rather than the person with the highest status is given the largest house. One company felt forced to go further than this, and laid down rules on who could keep boarders in their houses "so that housing conditions aren't too crowded." But this was difficult to enforce and police.

While the sorting process is going on, the officers of the company are appraising their new employees. They do not necessarily like what they see, as explained by one executive:

> You can categorize people as the go-getters, the people who go ahead, the person who barely gets there, the person who is pretty solid, or perhaps, better still the go-getter who goes ahead, and the person who barely gets through. And then there are all the people in between. Now the go-getter is fine; he can go ahead, he gets promotions, everything is excellent; the one who barely gets through – well, we are stuck with him – we probably shouldn't have him here, but, we carry on with him. Usually he can do a fairly adequate job; he also realizes that he is doing much better here than he can

5 For a more elaborate discussion of housing and housing policy, see Institute of Local Government, Queen's University, *Single-Enterprise Communities in Canada* (Ottawa, 1953), chaps. 4 and 9.

> do elsewhere and so he stays. Now it is the in-between people who are bright – not top, not bottom – the very solid people who we need, but who stay two or three years; they usually leave because they don't see any promotion coming up. They should be persuaded to stay. Anyway, most of the people in this category come to the North either for money or to get ahead faster. And for that reason there is a great turnover.

Social control, however, is a two-way process. The new residents do not hesitate to remind the company (landlord) when it has been remiss. "People certainly don't hesitate to tell you when there is anything wrong. There was a broken water line yesterday and we must have received twenty-five calls about it."

> And again in the old days we used to maintain about 85 per cent of the houses – in other words we used to paint the outside every four years and inside – oh, about the same. The maintenance used to amount to 60 per cent of the rent, and as the rent was very low indeed it meant that very little maintenance was done. We used to have great difficulties with accusations of favouritism, and all sorts of pressures were brought to bear. If we moved in to service a house or to paint a house on a street we would be sure to get calls from all the women on that street who also wanted their place done. We permitted them to do their own interior decoration. This they had really to do if the house was to be kept in good shape, because the rent was $13 a month in the depression.

THE EMERGING CONTROLLED VERSUS UNCONTROLLED COMMUNITY

The types of controls discussed above introduce a number of problems very early in the life of the community. Usually the company was accused of being authoritarian, paternalistic, high-handed, or acting as a "big brother." Certainly, interpersonal relationships, among those affected by decisions and those whose job it is to implement these decisions, were bound to be affected. When, however, no provision was made for a planned and controlled community beside a new development, problems also arose, but they were problems of a different order. The lack of stringent controls also affected interpersonal relationships, as this disillusioned respondent stated:

> Everyone here is temporary and asks what sense it is to organize a town, to pay taxes, to build a better house, and so on. Everyone is always ready to move. There is no goal. Holidays are considered to be merely a day of pay lost. One thing that is free is big ideas but no one goes ahead on any of these – so if you have a street cleaning campaign, which everyone agrees is a good idea – people say: "If you want it go ahead and do it." It is very difficult to get community spirit – community enterprise – operating on this level.

The quality of the housing is also affected:

> At the outset there was no mortgage money available in the town. The population was felt to be too unstable by firms and banks that normally deal in mortgages. So, not having mortgage money available, people started building with what they had. This meant that they had very little capital to invest and they put together bits and pieces of scrap lumber and so on, to build a house. This meant that the best they could do to house their wives and families, was to put up shacks. This in turn meant that the zoning laws of construction could not be rigid; families had to be sheltered and 2000 houses were built. Many of them were shabby but nevertheless the families were rather decent people.

McCutcheon and Young, in evaluating such a community, state that because of high transportation and labour costs in the area most dwellings are of a "very low standard."[6]

> Money was needed for services, garbage collection, and so on, and a poll tax was put on people at $10.00 a year. There are also a lot of legal permits, usually around $5.00; there is a business tax and a dog tax and a propane gas tax, and the revenue is used for garbage removal and so on. All help is scrounged but the people generally are against community efforts to produce cleanliness and order. Actually we are bursting at the seams – we now have 1600 acres and 12 miles of roads and we double in size every 18 months and need guidance and help.

On a different level, the problems of hitching a new town site onto an older community are illustrated in this quotation.

6 M. K. McCutcheon and R. C. Young, *Canadian Geographer*, no. 4 (1954), p. 62.

> Whether the number of miners came from Northern Quebec and Northern Ontario, these were the right kind of types. At the peak, about 550 miners entered the area. The area has more than doubled its population. There has been friction between the old-timers and the miners, but this was not practically evident on the surface. The miners have a tendency to get drunk and uproarious; the police force has had to be increased, but I don't know of any serious social disturbances.

On the other hand, an irate citizen accused the invading industry of "polluting the water, killing off the fish, destroying a lot of wood property, ruining the tourist business, and bringing in a lot of people who have different kinds of standards than the local inhabitants, and who created a great expansion of the schools which, now that the company is laying off men, will leave the local people with debt." He further accused the company of raising the ideals of the people in the area to a higher standard of living; subsequently there was no basis to support this standard. Another respondent noted that:

> Each person is special and wants special privileges; everyone is against everything as far as rules and regulations on a technical level are concerned. The authorities wantonly gave away strips or blocks of land, and all they [the citizens] had to have was permission. The tenants thought this land was being given to them and many picked up two or three places. They then scrounged for materials both legally and illegally and built several shacks which they rented from "our land."

During this first hectic period of adjustment, when potential employees come and go, when some stay to take employment with the company, settle into a house, make it a home, and begin to interact in ways conducive to community life, several important processes operate which affect the community throughout its existence. Along with the sorting out of individuals there is a concomitant sorting of age categories and ethnic groupings.

THE BEGINNING OF THE AGE CYCLE

Almost all of the migrants are young, including the professional and supervisory transfers. The population that settles in the community is young, and those who are married begin to raise a family. People in new communities are eager to tell you that they have the highest birthrate in the country, or the highest proportion of children under such-and-such age. For example, these are statements given by informants in very different communities:

> We have a population of 16,000. The average age of the population is 34, and we have 5000 children of school age or below.
>
> There are very few old people in this town. I can think of only one person who is over fifty.
>
> There is relatively little done for teenagers in terms of recreation, basically because there are so few of that age-level in the community. There are probably no more than 60 teenagers in all [population 12,000].
>
> At the moment we have 1230 at the plant for whom the average age is 29.

Or

> We have been actually operating the high school for ten years, and as yet the bulk of our population hasn't moved into high school. We are talking about a young community here and old people are relatively new. It's only about five years that we've seen grey-haired people on the streets.

Once started in this way, the populations in isolated communities of single industry begin a demographic age cycle that continues in perpetuity unless broken by an influx of new population at some later period, or by a sudden expansion in the industry. This characteristic population-age cycle has important social ramifications that will be discussed in more detail in a later chapter.

THE BEGINNING OF THE ETHNIC DISTRIBUTION

The second process that takes place during the population sorting period is the emergence of a particular ethnic and religious mix that characterizes the community from that time on, barring drastic changes. This bringing together of certain groups from the population is described by Hall:

> It remains to be seen just which segments of the mining population will be mobilized to come to the new area. Italians have pre-

> dominated in the group that has migrated from Europe to the mining areas in recent years. It may be that the most recent group will also be the one most ready to move again, but there are few guides on which to make guesses. The initial group may be exceedingly, even distressingly, mobile from the point of view of the employer who is looking for stable workers.

He continues,

> In so far as the population of the nearby areas is predominantly made up of French-speaking Canadians, associated with the forest industries, the mines and mill will inadvertently acquire a work force largely French-Canadian in background and orientation.[7]

The skills and education of the incoming individuals fix the limitations on the types of jobs open to them. Stereotypes arise; for instance, "Indians tend to have no vocation – they are just labourers; their basic background and training has been that of a nomadic life, and they can't get away from this. Out of every ten Indians hired, probably five are very good workers." Eventually, certain jobs are seen as appropriate for particular ethnic groups, all arising out of the inadvertent initial population sorting. Carlton notes this: "Once granted seniority many of these first English-speaking workers were able to rise quickly upon the swelling body of French and immigrant labour, to positions of virtual tenure in the lower levels of management."[8]

Although the ethnic distribution, conflict and interaction are quite different in each community, the processes remain the same. These are of importance, and will be considered in some detail at a later point. The importance of ethnic selection at this particular juncture is based upon the origin of these distributions, and the impersonal processes through which this selection takes place. At a later point in the life of the community when ethnic lines have hardened and consolidated, many forget the accidental factors that started the pattern. The data presented here confirm Hall's analysis:

> However, it has never been possible to plan *all* aspects of the life of any community; moreover the difficulties of adhering to a plan

7 Hall, "Uranium Mining," pp. 231-2.

8 Richard A. Carlton, "Differential Educational Achievement in a Bilingual Community," unpublished thesis (University of Toronto, 1967), p. 49.

> usually deepen as time goes on ... it will not be possible to prescribe what sorts of migrants will or will not be admitted. Yet in the course of time, it is precisely the characteristics of the population that give the main pattern and coloration to a community. In the sense that [this] is a one-industry community, the population is, of course, highly selected; it will represent a very narrow group of occupations. However, in terms of the *cultural* and *social* backgrounds of the migrants to the area the community is at the mercy of forces beyond its control.[9]

This does not mean that the company or community is powerless to control all aspects of community life. It seems to be much easier, for instance, to control, to some extent at least, the institutional migration. Early in the development of the community, decisions are made about which grocery and departmental chain stores will be given the opportunity to establish themselves in the town. This, of course, includes the policy of exclusion: "The company would never let Jew stores in the town, so they [Jews] built their stores outside the town limits, and we all do our shopping there."

We have seen, in this chapter, that personnel are recruited from present company employees on both professional and lower levels in various centres. In addition, personnel are recruited from outside the company; this recruitment is usually accomplished by locating professional employees among the graduating classes of the universities and attracting sub-professionals from the general labour market.

For a number of years employees come and go. The reasons for the high mobility level are obvious – the isolation of the community, the facilities offered, the expectations of the single personnel and the wives of the married men. Gradually, both industrial and community discipline take effect. In this confused and fluid period of uncertainty, the future of the community is established; two general characteristics of the population emerge from this flux. One is that the great majority of the population are young. This fact, barring subsequent expansion, establishes the age cycle which has many ramifications for the future of the community. The second characteristic, largely unpredictable, is the ethnic affiliation of the immigrants. These ethnic characteristics, although important to the future of the community, are not the major focus of the present discussion.

9 Hall, "Uranium Mining," p. 231.

We now turn to chapter 4, and the third stage of the development of the single-industry community – the transitional period. This involves the shift of responsibility from the company to the citizens.

4

Stage III Transition

As we have seen, most companies feel that in order to develop a resource, it is necessary to build a basic community as well as a plant. Once the plant is in operation and a fairly stable population established, the company is usually anxious to leave the vexing problems of real estate, social planning, community activities and local financing. It prefers that the conflicting social aims be decided by citizens, councillors, and mayor within a community budget according to provincial requirements for municipal affairs. This inclination on the part of the company is supported by the provincial legislators who have made local self-government mandatory.

Like many protestors, the local citizens are reluctant to exchange their status, about which they had bitterly complained, for one involving the responsibility, cost and work of taking over the decisions of their community. Once the shift has been announced, the complaints of the local citizens are long and varied; perhaps one of the reasons for this is that when "forced" (as a number put it) to own a house, they no longer have the luxury of being in the community but not of it; no longer can they say, "we could be out of here tomorrow." This reluctance on the part of citizens to take over their own affairs ("it will cost us twice as much") is a good indicator of the conservative local government that they institute, conserving, among other things, their tax dollars.

The transition from company-employer-landlord-planner-legislator to a company concerned only with the business of running an efficient industry, is difficult and complex. Traditionally local office holding, voting rights, and taxes have been based on ownership or rental of property. The shift of the ownership of the physical community seems to embody a shift in citizen commitment.

Sooner or later, the majority of companies transfer ownership of houses,[1] non-industrial facilities, and major community responsibility to the citizens of the community. It is sooner, on the part of the railways; traditionally they have built their physical plant, and a handful of company houses for senior personnel, and let the employ-

1 For a discussion of this see: Institute of Local Government, Queen's University, *Single-Enterprise Communities in Canada* (Ottawa, 1953); also, Center for Settlement Studies, University of Manitoba, *Proceedings – Symposium on Resource Frontier Communities, December 16, 1968* (Winnipeg, 1968); J. S. Mathiasson, *Resident Perceptions of Quality of Life in Resource Frontier Communities,* Center for Settlement Studies, University of Manitoba (Winnipeg, 1970).

ees get on with the job of building and organizing some sort of community. It is later for those communities dependent on an industry whose management attempted to maintain utopia in the backwoods. For instance, after fifty years of complete company control, one official talked of the transition:

> The local arrangements consisted of house rent, but practically all services were almost free for nothing, the employees being almost wards of the company. But this policy was changed and we worked out an arrangement that if a person rented a house for ten years we more or less just gave them the house.
>
> This sort of paternalism did have its points because at the time the wages were extremely low – when the unions pushed the wage up, it was no longer necessary to supply all the basic services originally developed. Service had to be supplied by the company or else nothing could be done at all, because when this place was started it was cut out of the forest itself – there was nothing here.

Another company executive summed up the process which had taken place in a community after twenty years of company control:

> The company owned everything and it has sold the houses; it has handed over to the citizens, the new owners, the school, the shopping centre, and the parks. There is actually little land that now belongs to the company, and what there is will probably remain undeveloped. The rest of the land has been handed over for subdivision.

Another company was planning the transition after five years of responsibility in a yet uncompleted community:

> There is a fairly active community spirit, this is nurtured because the company itself does not believe in paternalism and part of its policy is very specifically that we should not remain in any business but industry. This has been stressed on a number of occasions. It would be much easier to run the community according to the paternalistic system in the short run, but in the long run this policy would probably be disastrous. We hope to incorporate the town soon. It would be managed by a mayor and a council. Probably at the beginning the council would be company-appointed with a town manager, and there would be some sort of a tax rate. This is to get back a little bit of money on our investment, and it is much

better if it can be made into an almost normal community. At the moment we are paying 98 per cent of the taxes, but we would like to get some back from the storekeepers and others. This also would permit other people to build homes – that is [the personnel of] whatever oil company is in here, the Department of Transport, the storekeepers, the bank managers, and so on. These people would build homes, and then the oil companies and so on would pay taxes on them.

THE TRANSFER OF HOUSING AND ASSETS

The general pattern is to dispose of the houses at a nominal price, usually paid for in terms of monthly rent: for instance, in a coal mining town, a company informant said:

> There were some company houses, but these have all since been sold – actually we are using the word "sold" rather loosely – we gave them away. They went to employees who paid a small rent. The rent accumulated, and at the end of so many years it meant that they owned their house.

Two others reported their arrangements. In one community:

> By and large our house sales have been made so attractive that people could not afford to refuse. First of all they were all assessed by CMHC, and then they were asked to pay 10 per cent down and mortgage over 30 years with land free. This really means that they can buy a house for the rent that they would pay in ten years, and very few have turned this down. After that they can do anything they want. We give a guarantee, by the way, that we will buy the house back within a ten-year period, but this isn't necessary because it is found that they can sell privately, or if they move, they can rent and make a very large profit.

In the other community:

> The sale of the houses now is at such an attractive rate that employees actually would not dare refuse – they are selling the wartime housing for $3000 complete. Granted, this isn't the best housing in the world, but the houses can and have been remodelled to make very attractive homes; whereas out in the new area a serviced lot alone is worth $3000.

Other assets were transferred to the new authorities in various ways. One company, for instance, sold the community's physical services piece by piece:

> The city has bought many of its assets from the company. We started when we bought the sewer; we also bought the water system – now we didn't pay the full price for it by any means, in fact we bought it for $450,000 on a loan over a 25-year period. We have acquired the sidewalks, the sewers, and the water lines – in other words all the fixed services.

Another company wrote the entire physical services off their books, but stipulated the type of financing the community should use in the future:

> When the company turned over the entire physical assets of the town including the water works, the sewage, the roads, and everything else for the sum of $1.00, it also stipulated that no money should go into reserves, that the town should be operated on a pay-as-you-go basis. There is some debt because of the tremendous number of schools that are being constructed and the new need for increase in classroom space. We also need a new water tank and water main and sewer and that kind of thing.

Community administrative systems and councils were set up, and had to face the problem of maintaining the town and the assets they now controlled:

> Our mayor and Council meet on the first and third Wednesday of every month, and there are a tremendous number of committee meetings in between which are open to the public. Within one of the subdivisions of the municipal government is the recreation agency, which is a community association within which are 70 affiliated clubs. These are indirectly sponsored by the company, which provides all the root facilities; they are all left over from the company régime. Now all of this is in a period of transition. The company used to maintain the playgrounds, the schools and so on. The company is gradually getting out of this.

Conflict of interests and difficulties often arise when the elected representative is also a company employee. The cross-pressures are particularly difficult because of the vulnerability of the company as major tax-payer. One major fear of many companies is that when direct control of the community is lost, they will become victim of irresponsible activities because it is ultimately the company who pays:

> The conflict of being an employee and playing the role of mayor is usually not incompatible at all. From time to time a question comes up where something does come into conflict. For instance, the treasurer of the town was saying to the mayor that they would have to increase the assessment of the company for more income to the community. The mayor may not welcome increased assessment of the company for which he works.

Some companies have introduced some protection for themselves; one such plan is explained by the town manager:

> As you probably know, any loan that is made by the city isn't voted on by a majority of voters by number, but by a majority of voters by the evaluation of their property; so therefore, the company can block any legislation on the percentage of assessment. In fact, the company blocked the first project the town started on. They have, of course, legitimate right to do this because they are responsible for over 70 per cent of the budget.

The shift is never total. Every company maintains a few "company" houses, and many have an arrangement to buy houses back if requested to. There are at least two commonly expressed reasons for this. First, and probably more important, the company often transfers management, scientific, and professional personnel from one branch to another. It is clear that in a community of single enterprise the real estate market does not operate in the same way as in a more complex, larger, and more diversified community. Housing is kept available for a small group of employees who shift from branch to branch and community to community. Secondly, the company has to make some provision so that it can discharge an inefficient worker:

> We might be able to make some general arrangement with sales similar to a Central Mortgage agreement, but we would have to have some sort of a clause stating that we would be willing to buy back the property. Otherwise you couldn't fire someone, because he wouldn't be able to leave this house and would have to stay here with no means of support.

Another company maintains houses tenanted by widows of former employees and pensioners: "We certainly would not put these people out; we maintain the house till they die and then sell the house."

A more eccentric reason, found only once in the sample, was the retention of a large housing development to maintain an informal rent control. In this community rents of company houses were still less than thirty dollars for a substandard seven room house in the 1960s. As a citizen said, "What happens if the company suddenly dumps all their houses on the town?" The answer, obviously, is that without this basic alternative, rents are apt to rise considerably.

TESTING OF COMMUNITY-HELD DEFINITIONS

This period of transition clarifies many issues, confirms many widely-held values, shows that other widely-held norms are not valid, and stimulates wide-reaching social changes. Some of these changes, such as the unemployment of the large group who worked permanently at maintaining the company houses, seem to have been unanticipated. Much of their work is now taken on by the individual family on a do-it-yourself basis.

Before the change, the citizens complained about the undue authority held by the company over the small details of life, including such things as the colour scheme of the house, the planting of a hedge, the cleanliness of the house, and the paternalism that invaded all aspects of living. Once the changes of status were announced, however, there were many objections. As one informant put it, "It is a good thing that the change-over did not have to be put to a vote, or we would never have had the changes made." One government official who presided over the transitional period of a number of communities commented:

> The people at the moment are getting all municipal services free of any responsibility and do not want to make any change. Although there will be no change in the cost at this point, or in the next few years, they fear, and rightly so, that it will cost them much more in the future. At present, although the company and the town are kept separate, the company performs many of the administrative services free of charge; for example, many professional men work for the company and are used in the town; their company secretary

is a lawyer and he acts for the town and no fee is charged; the engineering and planning problems are looked after. The company hired a consultant, who submitted a report and this was accepted in most details by the board of the company. The company was partly interested in cost, but mostly in the problems of responsibility; first the houses, which had all been company-owned and rented, were sold. Then, the company rid themselves of telephone, light, and heating in order to set up the Municipal Act.

As a result of the reluctance of the citizens to take over all power, authority and responsibility, the company finds itself with residual problems long after it has divested itself of original duties. After many years, sets of patterned expectations, responsibilities and obligations are not easily forsaken. The populace is reminded that rights and privileges also involve duties and obligations. Feuds about the distribution of responsibilities are often prolonged:

> The town's growth and expansion are somewhat limited and controlled by the fact that the company reluctantly owns the sewage and water system. It refused to expand it. Community taxpayers refuse to take it over. We find that we give the city its water supply, not that we want to particularly, but we started by bringing in a water supply and we have continued that all along.

On the other hand, the company may find itself paying for services that it is not given. This is illustrated in the following account:

> We get absolutely no service from the community. We get no water, no garbage collection, no fire protection. The last water main stops about a mile down from the plant; we look after our own water. However, we are citizens of the community, and we don't mind paying our taxes, but as we have always pointed out, we will pay taxes on the same basis as everyone else and for services that we use. Well, now they need some money and the mayor told me quite informally that they have decided that they are going to charge us a water rate, for the water we would have used had we been using the city's water (if you can follow that). They were going to charge us for the amount of water we would have used; I said, "Well, we aren't going to pay for something we are not getting." However, we discovered that this is absolutely legal, and they could charge us for what we weren't going to use. So, my next tack was to say, "All right, if we are going to pay for something we are not going

to use, you put the water in; we will pay a water tax, but we will use the water." "Oh, well," said the mayor, "In that case, we have to put in the mains to get it to you. It is a mile away and this will cost us $40,000 and we will have to charge you for that." To make a long story short, after many meetings with our head-office people the final compromise was that we would pay the town $2000 a year as a special grant in lieu of water tax, and this will be fine until they decide they need more money. It is a $2000 gift.

Reluctance or not, it has been found that the transition has meant that many of the citizens of the community look upon the town with new eyes. In the first place, many as property owners see it as a viable community:

The community itself has always been considered to be very temporary, so you have a preoccupation with impermanence here. It has discouraged buying for some time. The present working out of purchases and building is certainly giving the whole community a greater feeling of permanence and the people have invested in property in the town.

Once the company relinquished control, and sold houses to the employees, the interest in and the care of the property was enhanced, despite grave forebodings to the contrary. "Interestingly enough many predicted that the houses would go to wrack and ruin, others predicted that they would improve – actually the houses have had much better care. It is possible to care for your house when you own it and you can do the looking after of it."

In addition, there was no interference with the strict community zoning maintained by some companies after the transition. An executive stated:

The time and effort that is put into housing, the great care taken in the community to maintain the zoning laws, these are no longer the responsibility of the company but of the city fathers. The city fathers could change the zoning laws at any time. This has been the experience in other communities where pressure is brought to bear; people or the city fathers will make an exception or change the law to suit a property owner ... We must admit, however, that this sort of thing hasn't occurred. We don't have gas stations in residential areas, and by and large the town is much better now that it is in private hands. The properties are kept up much better

> than before – people take a pride in their property – other than the odd exception which you will find anywhere.

EMERGENCE OF NEW ORGANIZATION

In some communities, it was found that when the employer-landlord-social arbitrator sequence was broken, there was far more freedom.

> The present municipal system is much better than the old one. In the early years problems did arise and there was no formal way that grievances could be given to the company. People would complain, or a delegation would work out a petition and come and meet members of the company to voice their objection. This meant that the only contact that people made with the corporation was invariably in terms of complaints and this wasn't particularly good; there was no adequate representation so they only met over problems.

In a short time, commercial builders move into a lucrative market:

> One of the facts of life here is that we are very short of housing. Up until a few years ago we were definitely a company town in the traditional sense. We have moved, over the last few years, to a municipality, and the company is determined to stay out of the housing business. There is a growth in demand and we have not been able to keep up with this demand. The company built all the houses in the first place. These are now being sold to citizens, usually the tenant, and now we are developing subdivisions where the contractors build houses for speculation and for sale. The influence of Central Mortgage and Housing has been very great because you are having private enterprise and contractors building, but within specification of the CMH.

Private building was encouraged, as this young engineer explains, by problems within the local situation.

> The main reason that I built my own house is rather long and involved. We used to live in a block [row] house, and with two children and one child expected the space was very inadequate, and we needed more bedrooms. It was impossible to carry on with only two. We actually had no intentions of building, but put our

name in for an end block house position because the end house was larger than the centre ones and boasted three bedrooms. However, although my name was on the top of the list and I had all the priorities necessary, it just didn't come up and other people got preference. After waiting for some little time I got impatient. The reason why my priority was disregarded was that there were some families in block houses who had as many as five children, and they obviously had top priority. I didn't object when two families of this sort moved in, but then the company policy on housing changed and the company decided to sell all the houses that it maintained. The residents of the houses, or the people who were then tenants, had first choice and after that other people could apply for buying the house. A number of families who did not want to buy the house in which they lived were then shifted by the company to other accommodation, and some of these went into the end block house that we were hoping to get ourselves.

Originally the company assigned houses to employees and the houses assigned depended on a number of factors, the major one being size of family. When it was decided to sell the houses, some people were in very desirable homes. They got an extremely good deal because the sale was based upon the rent that had been paid rather than upon the price of the house.

EVALUATIONS

Evaluations of the era of company control vary. One mining executive in a town of recent origin explained why the company was pleased to relinquish responsibility:

A company town is a headache – both for the company and for the people, even if it is run by a municipal board. The problems are still blamed upon the company. After things have settled down people begin to have a sense of martyrdom, they want a better salary, they want a better home, they want the cake and the frostings too. They have a secure job and they have amenities, they won't leave for more amenities, things that they can't have here, without taking a lower salary, which they don't want, so they tend to blame the company.

A political leader suggested that the company sponsorship in the community was a great advantage to the residents, at least in a monetary way, but that it did not benefit the company:

> You can't give away too much. Look what happened. Our company provided a grand recreation centre and yet we had the worst strikes.
>
> Nearly all the companies are getting out of housing except one. They have a good thing there; good for the people. Good housing, well maintained by the company. The company doesn't interfere. These people have an improvement district which is wonderful for them. Now they want to form a municipality. They are crazy. This way they get all kinds of services, without all the problems of municipalities. They now want their own hospital and school. I still say they are crazy. The company town isn't necessarily evil. People get low rents and cheap services.

On the other hand, a labour leader in a community of single industry suggested that there were compensations other and perhaps more important than monetary ones:

> The company town was all right as a start – but there was always the same group in control. With a new set-up a lot will depend upon who is on the council. In the old days 90 per cent of the people in the town worked for the mill. This is not so now, because there are many people who provide services who have no direct relation to the company. There should be no resentment toward the forthcoming council, but at the moment there is a difference between the plant and the outsiders and the kinds of businesses that they have (and they are now all permitted to build houses). On the whole, people are complacent. They have their houses permanently and think a council is all right. It should be the people who run a town, not one man. The one man is a one-man dictator. The fire protection, the water and the telephone – since the company has got out of all of that, we think there is quicker service, but you pay more – eventually you will pay more. But you feel captive when you pay your rent to the company. It is much better if you own your own house; then you know that if you are fired from the company you can at least keep your house.

THE COMPANY AS CITIZEN

The single industry also takes the role of institutional citizen. Because of the large number of employees and its wealth, the policy of the company in relation to the town has wide-reaching effects. Whether it plays the role of leader, follower, or non-participant in community affairs, it has great influence upon the attitudes and relationships in the community. Such simple decisions and policies as the size, frequency and extent of donations to worthy causes affect the relationships among the people in the community.

Officers of the companies are usually aware of the influence that their decisions have, and most realize that they are deeply involved, whether they want to be or not:

> As far as the town is concerned, we are very much embroiled, even if we don't necessarily want to be. By embroiled, I mean indirectly so; we attempt not to interfere in the town at all, but when such a large proportion of the tax dollar comes directly from us, we do find that we are involved in every project ... We are indirectly involved in the community whether we want to be or not, simply through our own employees.

Previously a few examples of the community political safeguards were noted; these included a general directive on how community projects were to be financed, or an ultimate veto as major taxpayer. Most industries, however, attempt to keep aloof from local politics:

> I would like to point out that these employees are involved in civic affairs as individuals, not as representatives or as part of the company as such. But we do pull our weight. For many years we have had employees at the management level as members of the city council – again as individuals and not as representatives of the company.

In another community much the same idea was expressed:

> On town council there are several councillors who are employees of ours, but this is only accidental. They happened to be employees because we supply most of the employment. They don't represent the company in any way.

Although company executives claim this to be so, and in many cases it may, in fact, be so, most citizens are convinced that the company does wield an undue influence. Here is one illustration of this sentiment: "Most of the men on the council work for the company so that pretty well what the company says goes. It's unfortunate, but a practical reality."

It should be noted that people refer to "the company," "the community," or "the people" in much the same way as they refer to "the government," as though there were consensus about what the corporate group thinks, says, wants, and does. Although this is rarely, if ever, the case, people speak as though it were so, and presumably conduct many of their relationships on this assumption.

As we have seen previously, policy regarding the company's role in the community has varied from supplying and maintaining recreational services and encouraging the growth of social and recreational groups, to non-participation. Clearly, the types of interaction and attitudes emerging from these different approaches will themselves be quite different. The following comments were made by a citizen of a community in which the company took a leadership role, provided recreation centres, subsidized activities and, in general, took the role of fairy godfather:

> As far as the town goes, there are many things wrong with it. But I believe that it all stems from one thing. Too much paternalism on the part of the company. They have taken the initiative, inadvertently I believe, from the townspeople. They have led them every step of the way. So what happens? A tremendous void where there usually exists a community spirit.
>
> There is no leadership outside the company. In fact it's reached the point where the company *must* take the lead or else it is criticized. They unfortunately have substituted company spirit for community spirit, but you can't be associated with the company twenty-four hours a day. The lack of community spirit means the lack of co-operation among townspeople in almost all civic projects. "Don't bother with the thing," is the attitude, "the company will handle it."
>
> There is no feeling of MY town here. Rather it is the COMPANY's town. What to do? For one thing, make the townspeople pay for some of the privileges. The only place that I associate with belonging in this town is the golf club, because there I pay for the privileges that I get. I go out there and feel that it is MY club and I can use its conveniences because I'm paying for it. That is the only way ...

My God, it's a basic psychological premise that the recipient of charity ultimately hates the giver. Give these people back their independence, if it isn't too late.

Perhaps it has reached the point where there are people too listless to care ... Let them work out their own problems. They can and will if not allowed to become soft and weak by that doting mother, the company.

In contrast, during a campaign in preparation for a vote on local option for a beverage room, one citizen wrote in the local paper:

Local railway officials are gentlemen; but the railway policy that they are requested to support is entirely a negative one. THOU SHALT NOT. What has the railway done to help the employee to profitably or pleasantly occupy his leisure time? What provision is made here or in other towns ... Libraries? Reading rooms? Gymnasiums? Billiards? Pool tables? Table tennis? Bowling alleys? Shower baths? No, none of these! Keep sober or else ... nothing to help the men keep sober ... nothing to make him forget a hard day's work. Wake up, you top policy-makers, and give your hard-worked, hard-driven officials something to fill in the employees' time pleasantly and profitably. WHAT AN INSULT TO THE INTELLIGENT PEOPLE OF THIS TOWN!

On the other hand, one official of a welfare service when commenting on the role of the company in the community, said that it was not enough to give money, but that the time and talents of the company officials were necessary contributions:

The people in industry certainly have a lot to give. Many of them are very generous with their money, although I'm not so sure that they are quite as generous with their time. Of course we get a lot of support from industry, in pledges and so on, for our campaign which we just completed, of $200,000. There aren't any real top notch executive types on our board, they are industrial types and we have representatives from the industries but we don't really get a lot of service out of them. They can't afford the time or don't seem to be able to. They're very nice people, mind you, and gave quite large gifts to our campaign but we very seldom have mine managers on our board.

Most companies have a rule of thumb, if not a policy, which they attempt to maintain: One executive said: "We have no set position –

we donate – we help out – but we will not administer it. There are no members of staff on any committee. We make this a policy; there are no overseers on it and these are not company representatives – they are simply good citizens." The following explanation is perhaps typical of most companies:

> At the moment we have one member of the company or one employee of the company who happens to be a council person, but he is a councillor in his own right and not as an employee of the company. If I happen to meet him, that is fine; we chat, but it has no significance. I would chat with the mayor or to anyone else, but not as a company representative. We do discuss things informally but we don't attempt to wield any particular influence in the community. As far as donations to projects are concerned, well as far as churches are concerned – that is simple; we just don't give to any denominational interests. Hospital is a more complicated problem – here we feel we have some obligation and there are a number of other things where it is quite difficult to know what one does.

Often the influence of the company is indirect, such as "the feeling" that the company does not approve of some facility or policy. Perhaps this could be illustrated by reference to the perennial Canadian controversy on prohibition (through local option). In one quite large community, one informant noted:

> I want you to understand that we do not like to drink all the time. In fact I don't like scotch or rye; I am used to drinking cognac, an aperitif, or a small glass of something in a social way. In Italy we have a great deal of pleasure in the place where we drink, rather than in the drink. This is lacking here. Here, if people want to drink, they buy a bottle. The bottle is consumed at home. When I ask them why, they say that the town has no liquor license because the company does not want it. There is a great lack of a place for congenial people to meet together. It also points to the fact that you can never get away from the company. It is bad enough to live in a company house, but even in the community, if you want to do this – no, you can't – the company doesn't like it, etc. You always feel that you cannot really live and breathe freely without offending the company. This may not be true but it is the impression received.

In a heated wet/dry controversy carried out in the local newspaper of a railway town some years ago, one advertisement noted the informal arrangements in a "dry" town:

> TO THE WOMEN OF THE COMMUNITY
> I think most of us will agree that over the past thirty years an enormous quantity of alcoholic beverages have been illegally consumed by honest, reputable men of our town. Like the little boy, when told that they cannot, they immediately set out to show that they can. By virtue of their occupation, the majority of men in this town know their very livelihood is in jeopardy if they are found by the authorities in one of these unsavoury places. And do not think that some of these men are not "found in" from time to time. Many families have only the leniency of the authorities to thank for the fact that the husband and father is still gainfully employed ... The very atmosphere of bootleggers' places is degrading morally as well as mentally. Not a very pleasant picture, is it?

To which, in the next issue, a "dry" replied:

> The writer (who hasn't the intestinal fortitude to sign his own name) further states that for railroad men the beverage rooms are OK because they won't have to sneak out of them the way they do from the bootlegger's. Well, when I read up my rules, though I never did pass them, Rule G said that "to even be known as a frequenter of a place where liquor was known to be sold was sufficient cause for dismissal." That sounds very plain to me as if it also included the beverage room. While we are on this subject, should a railroader and the head of a family be so unfortunate as to get caught coming out of these proposed beverage rooms, do these new sponsors promise to see that his family, who will suffer by his dismissal, will be taken care of by the profits they hope for? They seem to have overlooked that point too, ladies.
>
> Today I was told by a hotel man [from a neighbouring community] that there were five licensed places in the town and FORTY BOOTLEGGERS. He told me that some were doing a flourishing business too, and it prospered after the beverage rooms closed. How does that sound, Mr Ghost Writer, for your law and order, for your better enforcement under the Beverage Room Act and your lessening of the amount consumed? Kid yourself, if you like, but such facts are hard to overcome. This information may come as a shock to the small group of women who had decided to vote

> "wet" because they wanted to take the profits away from our local bootleggers. From what I heard today you just play right into their hands. You will just have more beer consumed until closing time in the beverage rooms, and then still more at the larger number of bootleggers.

Many suggest that the company in a community of single industry becomes the scapegoat, regardless of its policy. Any inadequacies in the community, its services or social life can conveniently be blamed on company policy, if for no other reason than that if the company was not there, the citizens and their institutions would not be there either. Inadequacies within the urban area may be blamed on a "they" – but the "they" is diffuse or impersonal or perhaps both. Reference is made to "city hall" or "the government" or "industries," "the planners" or, more conveniently, just "they." The use of the scapegoat influences the interaction within the company and the kinds of attitudes, values, initiatives, and interaction found among the citizens of the community.

As one company manager pointed out, "You are damned if you do and damned if you don't":

> If you are asked to serve on something or if you are asked to help out on something, if you say "yes" then you are told that you are running the community – that it is a company town, that the company is pushing the people around. If you say "no" – well, it is typical company, they are not interested.

In this chapter, then, we have noted that authority and responsibility are transferred, sooner or later, from the company to the population. Sometimes this shift is gradual, and sometimes it is very rapid, but it is always accompanied by great ambivalence. Like all arrangements that concentrate and centralize authority, the control of the community by the company focuses discontent and criticism. Once this authority is discontinued, however, there is a realization on the part of the people that the new arrangements will require more work and more money from them. The new situation also lacks the convenient, and often important, scapegoat. Although the dominance of the company remains (as major tax-payer and employer), blame for the niggling details of community and home housekeeping becomes more diffuse.

We now turn our attention to the fourth stage – maturity, to explore the community patterns that persist over time.

5

Stage IV Maturity

After a number of years, quite different characteristics emerge in the community of single industry, the community faces different types of problems and is characterized by different types of interpersonal relationships. At this stage few adults leave the community, older people retire and live out the remainder of their lives in the town, but youth is forced to emigrate. The mature phase of the community of single industry, as its name suggests, can only come about through time. Perhaps one of the surest indications that maturity has been reached is a number of men, retired from work, and choosing to remain in the community.

THE PENSIONERS

With the retirement of the original recruits, the community for the first time takes on something like a usual community age distribution. For the first time since its inception, the community of single industry has the very young, the middle-aged and the very old. But because the entire work force, and so the great majority of the townspeople, was in the twenty-five to thirty-five age bracket when recruited, although all ages are represented in the community for the first time, the aged are now over-represented. The age cycle referred to in Chapter 3 is perpetuated.

Older people perform baby-sitting chores, provide role enrichment in the family, and share their knowledge and experience with their children. But a disproportionate number of pensioners influence the broader sweep of community life; some of these implications are noted in a study of a railway town:

> ... the pensioners ... are often pointed to by people as a good reason for supporting or opposing some proposed project. The standard argument of those opposing a proposed town project is that the pensioners cannot afford any raise in taxes, or are not able to give any money towards it, thought by some to be a virtuous expression of self-interest. One case in point was the proposed building of a covered skating rink "for the children." The town council holds that the undertaking of this cost would be too much for certain of its citizens, meaning of course, the pensioned people. The opponents of the council immediately press the matter as being more important for the children of the town. They claim that the

pensioners are reasonably well off, and besides, there was no need to raise taxes because of it. "The pensioners, the pensioners, that is all they talk about, the pensioners." On the other hand, there is the strong feeling about hurting the income of these older people: "The townspeople wouldn't favour any centennial project because they wanted to raise $12,000. But most people are pensioners here, and only get a low fixed income."

... The pensioners are the immobile element. Their whole life has been tied up on the community; it is here they worked and here they intend to die: "My wife is buried here, and my grave is all prepared."[1]

CHANGE IN THE MOBILITY RATE

In marked contrast to the first three stages, the mature community is characterized by lack of mobility of the major part of the adult work force. One respondent noted,

> People are very reluctant to move or transfer. They have their own home, they invested a tremendous amount in this home – in fact, it is their life saving really, and they are very reluctant to leave this. This is understandable. In most of these towns, people all own their own houses. This would be a nice study – the difference between the situation where you can have easy rental as against homes owned by the individuals. The own-home can be dysfunctional in certain ways. On the other hand, the rented houses should not belong to the company, I don't think. I don't think the town should be company owned or company built, but the houses should be owned by councils which are independent of the company so the employees can't be put out. We [the company] own a few houses, but a very, very small percentage – very few houses.

By this period, not only has a house become a home but employees have invested a great deal of their work life in the company in terms of work, seniority, skills and fringe benefits. There is little movement from work: "We have a very low turnover here at the

1 Alick Andrews, "Social Crisis and Labour Mobility, A Study of Economic and Social Change in a New Brunswick Railway Community," unpublished MA thesis (University of New Brunswick, 1967), pp. 86-7.

plant now. Very seldom does it go over one and one-half per cent of the labour force." Many of the workers continue to work late in life if permitted to, "Certainly workers continue long after they need to continue. We have one man with 71 years' service and we have another who has 68 years of service."

A number of respondents noted that the worker saw few opportunities to make a change. "As far as the workers see it, they have very little opportunity to move away and find new job opportunities and most of them stay in close to their homes." Or "There is little turnover in the work population mainly because there are no alternatives in the area. The only alternative is found in the service industries, and these, of course, are bound up with the only industry in a monetary way." The range of alternatives, seen by various members of the community, will deserve more detailed consideration later on in this study.

As time goes on, there is a tendency for a number of individuals in the same family to work for the single industry. This point might be illustrated by an extreme case:

> The population grew with the industry and all the families in the area have depended a great deal upon it, and we have many, many members of the same family working for us. This we find has advantages and disadvantages. We can have – in fact, it is actually quite common to have – twenty members of one family working for us. This is a little bit difficult sometimes in labour relations because if you affect one member of the family, you affect 25 in the firm – you have them all mad at you. On the other hand, if a relative dies, you suddenly have 25 people off to a funeral. But, generally speaking, we think it is a good idea, and, by and large, the advantages outweigh the disadvantages. You have families devoting their entire life to the company. You have a father, and all his sons and all his daughters, working their whole life here.

The number involved from one family is extremely large in this case, but it is not atypical of sawmill towns, railway towns, mines, and mills. The above quotation fits the stereotype of a paternalistic family concern. Actually, the respondent was discussing work relations in one branch of a very large, and highly unionized, mass production corporation.

OCCUPATIONAL INHERITANCE

Stability and occupational inheritance, however, raise a new set of strains, and introduce a different type of mobility. One mine manager noted: "I would say we have 100 per cent occupational inheritance. The children take over from their parents, even those who are going on to university and become part of the local work force during the summer are reluctant to leave." Part of the reluctance to leave is seen as a product of the isolation of the community as pointed out by a union leader:

> One of the basic problems of the Union is that it is a one-industry town and the dominance of the one industry in the community. Many people have grown up in this community and have lived all their lives here. The isolation is quite noticeable and many, many of the people here have never been outside. A good number of the youth are raised here and, of course, work in the plant because it is the "natural" place to work.

Parents are anxious to keep their children near by, as a group of labour leaders noted. These men were concerned about the third generation:

> All five of us union leaders had fathers in the town – we all have sons here but the sons will have to leave town; they cannot stay and it is a great disadvantage. They will have no connection with the company but they can have first choice as apprentices and that sort of thing. We think it is a good idea that the company supports education and scholarships.

A personnel manager in a large plant illustrated the same point:

> We have actually two problems here: the young men and the old men. Seventeen per cent of our work force is skilled labour. This year sixteen students graduated from the technical school here. The company was able to absorb 10 of these. That was fine – this year. But the graduating classes are going to become larger while the number that we will be able to take will become smaller. This creates dissatisfaction not only among the boys graduating from school, but also among their fathers who invariably work for the company. I can visualize the typical young man coming out of

technical school, a good education, nothing for him in the district. They won't go into labouring work. A typical example happened last week. One of our old employees came in with his son who had done two years of technical school and for some reason was stopping there. He wanted a job for the boy. I told him that there were no apprenticeships open, and I suggested that inasmuch as his son was a strapping boy, and with his education, he could go into the production line and get a job there which would probably make him a foreman in about three years. I thought he was going to hit me. He pounded the desk and cursed and told me that no son of his with an education would work in production, and that was the thanks he was getting after twenty years with the company, etc., etc. That is the type of thing that is recurring more and more frequently. These men have undoubtedly stated over and over to their sons that an education would take them out of the labouring work so they come in here, and what are they offered? A job on production. It's a problem. But I think they are wrong. My son, if he is going to go into industry is going to have to do practical work. He is going to understand what the men think of the jobs he will have to boss. The stubborn pride of these men, however, now stands in the way because production is so far below them.

FORCED EMIGRATION

A recurring theme is the assumption of workers that the company (as the single major employer) has an obligation to employ their offspring. At this stage, it is impossible for the company to absorb the sons of all its workers. Many companies inflate artificially the educational requirements for what is, basically, unskilled work, but even this does not stem the tide.

Youth is a big problem. They have big families here and we cannot absorb all the young men. As a guide, we do not accept anyone with less than grade 11 education. There is great competition for work in the mill. Many youths have to go away.

Regarding the youth of the town, until 1940 we could absorb all and most of them stayed because staying in town was the "thing to do" and you could get security. At the moment we can't absorb any – we find that two-thirds of the 51 graduates stay here

> in hope and it usually is a vain hope; three of four enter the company as apprentices and about 13 go on to higher education.

Where do these youths go? Some go on to higher education, and career lines different from those of their parents; the school dropouts must try to find work elsewhere.

> As far as we are concerned there is relatively little retirement and so there is not a ready market for youngsters to come into the company. These unemployed youths will try their luck outside. Many go to new "boom" towns, to try to get on as unskilled labour there. Most of them return without very good results, because these places have their own labour market and their own pool of labour.

The daughters have even greater difficulties, because the work force is basically male. The few clerical jobs and service occupations cannot possibly provide jobs for all the girls. The major alternatives for the girls are marrying within the community or finding work outside. "Employment level is high and future looks bright for employment. There is a shortage of marriageable females because there is no work for them to any extent. They leave town. To avoid the problem of leaving town or finding themselves in unsatisfactory jobs, girls tend to take the opportunity to marry early."

So stability in the community necessitates mobility on the part of youth. This outward mobility will be discussed later. This need for youth to leave the community is accounted for, to some extent, at least, by the age cycle discussed earlier. There are periods, every forty years or so, when youth can be absorbed. Periodic expansion can also account for more jobs for youth; extensive expansion, however, is not characteristic of resource-based industries. The period of stability, in the small town, produces among the youth some candidates for construction forces and the first stage of settlement of a new community of single industry where their skills, or lack of them, can be utilized.

As we have seen, in a period that can be as short as fifteen or twenty years, profound changes come over the mobility patterns and the values and aspirations of the population. One man who had observed these changes described them in these terms:

> In the construction days, in the early days, for each person on the job there was one new person arriving and one person going. When the company tried to sell its pension plan it involved, of course, a

> feeling of permanence and staying. Many people who had been there for six years – and that made them oldtimers – said they certainly wouldn't take out a pension plan because they didn't intend to stay. They now have sons working here – they have stayed on and those sons have married the daughters of other workers. This means that they have grandchildren here and these are the people who will not leave.

AN UNCERTAIN FUTURE

Even the adults in a community of single industry are made vulnerable because of the single industrial base. Periods of optimism, deep pessimism and an overriding ambivalence and resignation are characteristic of many citizens, as they realize that their welfare depends upon international markets, changes in technology, or depletion of the resources upon which the industry is based. These threats, common to so many career lines, represent an exaggerated threat in a community which can offer no viable alternatives. One citizen expressed some of these fears while discussing a local building boom:

> The older people of the north cannot understand this building and speculating that is going on; I don't know really why it's happening. It is happening in spite of a real depression in the area. Funny, it has been a tradition in the north for people never to be too certain of their future. People don't really believe that they will stay for sure. We had a very small home originally and my Dad would never build anything very pretentious because he was always thinking he might have to leave here; they were never for many years convinced that they would be staying. The idea was – save money, don't spend it; keep it in a sock, so to speak.

Mining is the classical example of a non-renewable resource. One mining executive said, "What we are doing as a mine is to liquidate operations, but that, essentially, is what any mining venture is at the best of times – what you are mining has absolute limits, and so therefore liquidating operations is the same as mining." Derelict communities scattered through the northern country are evidence of the short life of many sawmill communities, gold and copper mines; the declining coal-mining industry of Nova Scotia, the eclipse and revitalization of coal mines in Alberta and British Columbia document the very real threat to those whose lives depend on these types of industry. One study lists 28 "ghost towns" in British Columbia alone.[2]

One respondent tried to explain what it was like to be permanently futureless: "We have no security. The town is not settled and you tend not to save or put money into a permanent home. Ever since we have been here there has been no future. Even though most of us have been here a good number of years. It is all tied to the ore that has been found." Many respondents, however, noted that it was very difficult to know how long basic resource of the town would last. The experts do not know for sure, either, for unexpected deposits are found, and changes in technology permit the mining of low-grade ore which was uneconomical to mine in earlier days. The mining company tends to look upon the operation with pessimism, if for no other reason than the certain knowledge that it cannot go on forever, and that the local population should be forewarned. One labour leader explained:

> Of course the situation is bound to deteriorate because they are working here with a depleted resource, but I think some adjustment has to be made in an industry that is built on depleted resources to produce more pay while the resources are there. It is very hard for the population really to know what is going on. The mine managers have been singing the blues and they are still saying the same thing and we are still going on. At the same time you have your business men and your Chamber of Commerce who say – "well all this will go on for a long time, we are going upward and onward." Professionals tend to be local boosters at the same time so it is no wonder that the local people find it difficult to assess what *is* going on.

Another union member said "This place has a life expectancy of fifteen years. But when it first started forty years ago, it began with

2 E. T. Clegg, "A Regional Planning Analysis of a Single Enterprise Community of Settlements," unpublished MSc (Community and Regional Planning) thesis (University of British Columbia, 1958). See also, Bruce Ramsey, *Ghost Towns of British Columbia* (Vancouver, 1963). At the other end of the country, a discussion of mine closing is contained in K. Scott Wood and Harold Verge, *A Study of the Problems of Certain Cape Breton Communities,* Institute of Public Affairs, Dalhousie University (Halifax, 1966). See particularly pp. 68-9. For an overall view of the impermanence of communities of single industry in north western Quebec, see Robert McKenzie's article, *Toronto Daily Star* (May 1, 1971), p. 13.

a life expectancy of fifteen years." A government official characterized the industry of a single enterprise community as "always on the verge of closing, but never actually closing." Another respondent, referring to an industry that had closed, points out: "This town was built around a mill which produced liquid pulp. This has now been abandoned." By nature, then, the community of single industry seldom expands, it is vulnerable to changes in international markets, changes in technology, and in most instances it has a limited life expectancy, if for no other reason than that the sole reason for the town's existence may disappear.

THE ENVIRONMENT

The major industry creates more than a social structure, and a set of work conditions; it usually, if not always, creates the environment in which the population lives. The industry may have laid out the original town lots and selected the site and the physical plan of the community. Populations are fond of blaming the company for locating the town in a mosquito swamp, or on a plateau of drifting sand.

Although there are exceptions, industries affect the environment in which the population lives in another way. Many industrial processes pollute or artificially influence the environment in which the population lives. The odour that hangs over a pulp and paper town is apparent to all who drive through; waste and tailings from a mining activity are often obvious; the fluorine given off by many smelting processes conspicuously affects foliage. Other damage, such as the raising and lowering of lake levels in power projects and log drives, or the pollution of lakes with the accumulations of bark which falls from thousands of logs on the drive, is not so apparent.

Many industries emit black smoke or hydrogen dioxide or fluorine, some pour chemicals into streams and create other environmental changes. When the interviewer, as a stranger, asked about the stunted and dead trees or the red streams, tree destruction and foreign agents in the water, these were often denied. Smells, on the other hand, were considered to be shared sensory perception; but the reply to the enquiry was almost invariably: "The day that the air doesn't smell will be a sad one for this town." Certainly, by the time a community reaches maturity, the accumulated effects of the industrial process are there for all to see and smell. The author of "Miner's Wife" notes:

> Though boundless wilderness surrounds [the community] its houses are huddled together on fifty-foot lots covered with gravel, except for a few nurtured lawns. Rose says "I'd love to have enough topsoil brought in so we could plant grass and radishes and a flower or two, but sometimes the fumes from the company sinter plant blow down on this end of town and everything withers away.[3]

In another part of the nation, E. T. Clegg reports: "The toxic fumes from the ... operations at [the community] have destroyed vegetation for several miles up and down the ... River Valley ... New growth has been prevented for years by ... fumes. Coniferous growth has suffered particularly."[4] He continues, "The agricultural resource in the area has suffered from the toxic fumes ... The ... valley once had a number of good farms, but these had to be abandoned because the ... smoke destroyed all the crops. To-day the smoke is under better control, but most of the damage has already been done ... The region now imports almost all of its farm produce."[5]

THE VIEWS OF RESIDENTS

In one community the most widely discussed topics in unstructured interviews were the weather and the smoke (gas, dust). Well over 90 per cent of all the people talked to spontaneously mentioned the question of gas and smoke. Most felt that the company showed lack of forethought in not anticipating that in the choice of the site of the community over half of the residents would be troubled with a gas nuisance. For the majority, the gas had only nuisance value, but it caused considerable anxiety to others:

> One of the worst things I find in this town is the gas. I don't see how these people live in it. It's like being on the production line 24 hours a day. I think it is actually worse [outside] than being there. It nauseates me more and I can smell it more out there than I do inside [the plant]."

3 Edna Staebler, "Miner's Wife," *Chatelaine* (March, 1962), p. 80

4 Clegg, "Single Enterprise Community," p. 111.

5 *Ibid.*

> It's quite frustrating for husbands to go out and plant gardens and see everything die, for wives to clean out the whole house and turn around twenty minutes later and see this scum over everything again. Dust may sound like nothing, but actually it is a tremendous problem. No gardens. Disgruntled housewives who can't keep the house or the kids clean.
>
> I don't even bother planting flowers any more. The weather and the dust ruins them. Does a hell of a job on the house too, with the wife trying to keep the house clean. She worries quite a bit; she figures if it does that to trees and flowers, what is it doing to the kids? We are reassured that the gas and dust can't hurt, but a mother, especially, keeps wondering just the same.

This last quotation indicated some of the anxiety about gas. It seemed to the population that everyone in the community and in the area recognized the problem except the company. This had several results. Some damage was done to the foliage in the town, and the paint on some of the houses; to what extent the gas affected individuals, no one was sure; because the company seldom appeared to give recognition to the problem, many townspeople suspected the worst. Little was known of the research that the company was carrying out, other than the presence of obvious dust counters situated in the town and the fact that new filters had been installed in the plant. One citizen stated: "Good heavens, you will find a great number of people in the head office who will not admit that there is such a thing as gas – it is a figment of our imagination."

That the gas and dust had influence upon plants and trees was obvious for all to see. However it is very difficult to assess actual effects or to what extent the severity of the problem was a "figment of the imagination."

It was commonly held that it was impossible to grow gardens in the "gas area" in one part of the community. The exhibits at the local Horticultural Society Show were analysed. The following assumptions were maintained: (i) the majority of the entrants in the show had gardens in their yards; (ii) entries in the show indicated a high level of interest in gardening. The town was then divided into two areas, that area commonly defined as being in the path of the gas, and that area commonly considered to be out of the gas area. It was found that 26 people or 3.94 per cent of the population in the "gas area" submitted entries to the show, while only 2.11 per cent of the population from the "clear area" submitted entries. This would seem to question the commonly accepted belief of the impossibility of gardening in the gas area.

From the entries from the "clear area," 92.3 per cent won prizes. But among the people who made entries from the "gas area," only 42 per cent won prizes. This may indicate that the entries from the "gas area" were not as good as those from the other area, because of gas; on the other hand, this lower percentage of prize winners may be due to other reasons. Eleven people from the "gas area," for instance, won prizes for flowers and only ten people from the "clear area" won prizes for flowers. For some reason eight prizes from the "gas area" were won for vegetables, but twenty-two were recorded for the "clear area." The evidence shows that gardens can be grown in the "gas area," but this little "test" does not present any conclusive evidence. The important thing is that some pollution does exist, and that people define it as a nuisance and a threat.

In other towns of single industry, similar complaints are heard: "What do wives complain about? Mainly dust and the price of groceries"; "There is a very bad smog which makes houses hard to keep and affects gardens"; "The company admits to slight problems concerning air pollution. Everything is under control. Pollution and the killing of the forest is not discernible around the community itself." Some industries are accused of affecting the environment in several ways. One irate citizen accused the industry of "polluting the water, killing off the fish, and destroying a lot of forest."

THE VIEW OF THE COMPANY

The company officials are aware of the problem. One executive talked about it in these terms:

> We have dust counters all around the plant. These measure the amount of dust that falls from the atmosphere. The prevailing wind takes it away from the town fairly well. But this year we had a wind in the opposite direction for three solid weeks and that affected the town very much. Usually the wind blows that way for a day or two and then stops. This gives the plants a chance to recover and carry on again. Look at these pictures. They show the same two maples over a three-year period. The first two years the

> tops were affected, but with careful pruning, they were restored – they look a little flat but it is OK. But the three-week wind cancelled it all – the trees are dead. The problem was so great in some areas that we have had to buy the land from the farmers, so that we can eliminate the smoke problem.

The irony of "eliminating the smoke problem" by buying up farm land seemed to escape the informant.

Another informant in a different community seemed to be quite proud of the fact that it had been proved that the pollution in parts of the town was no worse than the smog of the large industrial communities.

> We don't get any actual complaints at the moment, although we have heard a great deal about it in the past, but we have had the federal government in and they set up a number of observation posts and found that there is far less dust and dirt than there is in the records of Toronto or Montreal and, interestingly enough, there is less here than in Vancouver, according to the federal authorities. This seems quite surprising and I will admit, however, that this does not apply to all areas. There are some which tend to have a heavy concentration of dirt and smoke.

One candid informant explained why his particular company could not admit that there was a pollution problem:

> We cannot admit that there is such a thing as smoke and fumes. You will find a great many people in head office who will deny it. The point is we have never been sued. We have bought out farms and bought an awful lot of land – but we have never been sued. We have had many claims, many legitimate and others not, but we have managed to move round them every time. This is a great problem. On the road there is a line of dead trees, which advertises the fact that the smoke does damage. We cut down the trees and the next line becomes affected. It is spreading more and more. There would seem to be two ways – either by killing the trees by overpowering fumes, or by small doses over a long period. Some areas which were never affected before are showing signs now. I think it is caused by the long period of slight contamination, followed by the extra fumes which reach these areas after we cut down the barriers of dead trees. We have a biologist and physiologist who

> work for us and test plants, farms, cattle, etc. So, under these conditions, we can hardly publicize the fact that we are perturbed about it.

Another said, rather philosophically: "On the other side of the town they are pretty well immune to the smoke problem. That is pretty clean. One way of checking is by snow surveys. About March it is pretty easy to tell which part of town is getting it."

EFFECTS OF ENVIRONMENTAL CHANGE

It is unusual for the industry to be sued. In one case the prevailing wind constantly blew smoke and cinders directly on to the house of a citizen, and the citizen sued the company. The following cryptic report of the case appeared in the local paper.

> RAILWAY IS SUED FOR DAMAGE TO PROPERTY BY SMOKE
> On Saturday afternoon last, before His Honour Judge --------------, the case of -------------- v. *the Railway* was heard. This was a case brought against the company for damage to her property by smoke. After a lengthy hearing, the case was dismissed with costs against the company.

The industry, then, creates the environment in which the population lives. However, the citizen of the community of single industry, like the citizen of an urban community, feels powerless to control his own environment, even if he feels it is harmful. But although both urban and small town dwellers are powerless to control their environment, in the community of single industry the blame can be placed squarely upon the local industry. Causes of urban pollution are much more diffuse with many more culprits involved; the farmer, who cannot control his environment, can blame impersonal forces. The blame that can be and is attached to the dominant company affects the relationships between the company, its officers, and its employees, both on the job and in the community. But, despite this, as we have seen, interaction cannot be curtailed. Often the outcome of all of this is a feeling of resignation and fatalism. Ultimately the managers are right – it would be a sad day for the town if the pollution stopped, because it would signify the closing of the industry. And so, year after year, housewives hang out their laundry in the air filled with black, greasy smuts; mature trees wilt in fluorine fumes; dinners are eaten in the stench of mercaptans[6] and children swim in polluted waters.

THE OLD-FASHIONED COMPANY TOWN

The company of single industry as it grows passes through the four stages. At each stage, the individuals involved in their various capacities find themselves in a situation which patterns their interaction and values. The time involved in passing from construction to maturity is probably not less than twenty years, but there does not seem to be any maximum time. In the past, particularly, it was possible for a town to reach maturity without ever going through the period of transition. This was, of course, a company town, with all the control and responsibility and cost vested permanently in the hands of the company.

Observers and even townspeople often use the term "company town" indiscriminantly, when referring to any one-industry community or even a much larger community with one dominant industry. The term "company town" is properly reserved for those closed company communities owned and administered by the industrial employer. In the strict sense of the term, the closed company town no longer exists, if for no other reason than that it runs contrary to legal requirements of most provinces.[7]

A number of years ago, permission was granted to enter one of the few surviving company towns in Canada. Before visiting the town, it was described in the following way by a government authority:

6 Fluorides and mercaptans are incredibly foul smelling, even in quantities too miniscule to be removed from the atmosphere by chemical processes. Air pollution by these waste products may therefore be much less than one's olfactory sense would lead one to believe.

7 See Harry W. Walker's discussion of company towns in Institute of Local Government, Queen's University, *Single-Enterprise Communities in Canada* (Ottawa, 1953), chap. 1. James B. Allen devotes a chapter to the end of the company town in the western part of the USA in *The Company Town in the American West* (Norman, Oklahoma, 1966), chap. 11. This book includes a thumbnail sketch of 191 lumber, copper, coal and industrial company towns that existed in eleven western states of the USA.

> The community is still all controlled and all facilities are supplied by the company. The company built the houses – row houses. The company owns the railway – that is the only way you can enter the town. The company owns all the land, so there is no problem of squatters on the edge of the community. There is one store from which all is bought. The industry has remained on an even keel, requiring no fluctuations in population. The number of houses exactly matches the number of employees. When an employee retires, the family has to leave the town; when an employee dies, the family has to leave to make room for a replacement.

During the visit, it was possible to carry out a number of interviews. The following are extracts from the interview with the general manager of the industry (and town):

> In this community there are 900 children between the ages of 7 and 17. Each year we have 100 babies born in the community so that there are probably 400 children between the ages of 1 and 6, which means that 50 per cent of the population is under 18. We now have a second generation that knows nothing of the outside, and this forms the hard core of our working force.
>
> This is a privately owned town and the grounds are held on a lease and have been held since before 1900. Our holdings are large enough that there had been no slum development on the outside of the town.
>
> We are responsible for everything in town including the Land-Rover, which is used as a hearse and an ambulance. We own and control all of the stores and all the mechanics (e.g. telephone) of the town. Some of our employees are unmarried and they are maintained in the mess hall, which feeds about 400. We used to have far more temporary help but now many of the older unused bunk house buildings have been removed. At the moment we have about 110 men who work on a seasonal or temporary basis. The temporary help usually work long enough for unemployment status under the unemployment insurance arrangement. This work is seasonal; some work in the summer and go home in the winter; some work in the winter and go home in the summer.
>
> We employ 800 men, one-half of them work directly in the industry, the rest of the personnel work with the railway, stores, and these are mostly permanent employees. The industry is in constant operation. We have a lot of construction work; summer road main-

tenance and so on. In the winter we have about 40 seasonal, temporary employees but in the summer about 120. Most of the construction is done in the summer. When we hire temporary employees we seek out the old and faithful ones although when they leave they lose seniority rights.

You ask about the older worker: at 55 his physical condition is not as good as it is when he is younger and he is less alert. When a man is burned out and cannot keep up, we usually put him on a less difficult job. Many jobs are created for these people – they are jobs we could do without, but the company has a feeling of responsibility toward a worker who spent 25 years with it. And we are bound by our labour agreements to pay even a sweeper a pretty fair salary. These men tend to be light tenders, workers in the shop, or they may sweep.

The problem of the older person who is in a non-competitive job is accentuated by his accommodation predicament. As this is a company town we have to plan the tenancy of our houses very carefully. We have some houses set aside for the mine, some for the mill and others for the shops. You can understand that the houses have to be evenly distributed between these. After a man has had 25 years underground and is suddenly stricken under 50 he has no right to a house, and this is written into the lease, but you simply cannot throw him out. We house probably twenty pensioners in homes at the moment (some live with their children), but at 65 the lease for the house is automatically cancelled. This is expected by the employees and does not seem to raise any acute problems – the 55 to 65-year-olds are the problem.

To be efficient I have to know all problems and approve of their solutions. If the industry and town are to run efficiently all of the problems must go over my desk.

Young people are a tremendous problem because we are limited as to the number we can hire. They prefer to stay in town rather than go outside, so there are just too many. This means that we are now doing no hiring from outside, except for a little temporary help. Sons of miners working in the mine raise internal problems of family relationships and interfamily jealousy. Quite a few of our kids go on to university or vocational training. They do not all succeed. We do not have any teenage problem. A lot of this is due to the home. The old man realizes he has no opportunity and if his children are to make any money they must look after their academic work. So children become a joint concern of the family, the school and the company. The company will guarantee a summer job for any student who goes to university.

Girls don't do so well. We employ nine altogether. Most of them work in the local stores or go out to take a business course or become a nurse. A few help out at home. There are no maids in the town.

Generally, the education level has improved tremendously. Ten or fifteen years ago many of our employees were illiterate; now I would say we have an average education of at least grade 6. Twenty-five years ago we could not write instructions, and almost no one could write a report. We have had an adult school, and in the past it has done very well. Originally, we built a building for adult school, paid the teacher who taught such things as drafting and elementary subjects. It was very good, for the people were taught to read and write and they took to it very well. The seasonal worker who was in here was so excited when he wrote his first letter back to his wife.

Originally, the company built the school for the kids – it was open to all the kids in the community and the company hired the teachers and supplied the necessary equipment. The school is heated from our steam plant; it is administered by a board and we provide a hostel for teachers at a very modest rent.

The Roman Catholics have their own school in a badly overcrowded parish hall. They want a new school building, and the company is eager that they should have it so that they can pull down the hall. The new school cost under $50,000, which was borrowed for five years. The balance is a debt on the Roman Catholic parish; the money is extracted through the company check off.

We do have a town supervisor, because I cannot deal with all the women. When I do, I am exposed to all sorts of vindictiveness – whose house I will paint, what house is being repaired, and what house is not being repaired, and so on. This poor devil looks after all of the houses; it is all administered from his office. I approve what goes into the house. There is no public relations officer here; the town is not big enough. The best guide is experience. We consider each request and situation as an individual problem.

The town is very quiet – occasionally a bit of a problem with people making beer. You can get liquor by ordering it from outside. There is sometimes some difficulty when people order a case of liquor. But most of the relaxation goes on in the woods – people like to hunt and fish.

There are a few clubs and associations in the town; only this week there was an attempt to start a service club. The Legion is strong here and has a liquor licence. There are the usual church organizations and typical church activities go on in the various halls, including dances. There is an IOOF and a K of C.

We built the entire hospital ourselves and it is quite elaborately equipped. Water, sewage and electricity are all supplied by the company at a most nominal cost. We now have two privately owned stores in town. But the company store is maintained to police the price of necessary foods. We sell a variety of goods and operate it so that we do not make a profit. All the bread for the community is baked in the company mess hall. We do all the cooking and catering, but we have great difficulties in getting good cooks and we are losing a quarter of a million annually because of inefficient [cooking] methods. The men are unhappy and gripe about the food – the food is alright, it is the cooks who ruin it. We used to give them table service in the woods-camp style, but now that has been done away with. Just the other day a workman came into my office and threw a herring on my desk. To begin with I am not very fond of herring and this one apparently had not been cured very well, and the man demanded to know if I would eat this. It gave me a bit of turn, but things like this do not happen too often these days. Thank goodness!

THE SOCIAL SETTING OF THE COMPANY TOWN

In setting down this set of administrative arrangements, three or four additional pieces of information seem to be appropriate. The speaker, an engineer by training, complained that he could never get at his real job, which was running an efficient industry. He felt he could only have an efficient industry if he had happy people working for him, and provision for this took up most of his time. He was very surprised when he was asked how he felt about the responsibilities he had in presiding over the lives of so many people. He had never thought of it that way – these were administrative decisions that had to be made and only he had the authority to make them.

The second point is that this was no family concern, but a branch of a large sprawling corporation. The respondent was fairly sure that the board of directors had no knowledge that their distant general manager made decisions on whose house would be repainted, whether Mrs Brown could have a new cupboard, who was responsible for burning the bread for the town, and whose child was doing badly at school and needed to be spoken to. The respondent attended the annual meetings of the board, and it was apparent from the conversation and questions that they did not know of these responsibilities, and from their point of view, he felt, they were irrelevant. When asked why he did not tell them of the range of his important responsibilities, he replied that it was bad enough to carry on his work as it was: "Can you imagine trying to administer a town following edicts from head office?"

The third point is that although this interview was recorded a number of years ago, the employees were represented by two international unions. Separate and private interviews were conducted with union leaders and citizens. When asked about the advantages and disadvantages of living in the community, the general consensus seemed to be that the factor of isolation was the most important and from this stemmed many minor irritations. The most pressing current issue was a letter received by the townspeople stating that in two weeks' time the local store would add 5 per cent to the bill for COD, 5 per cent for telephone orders, and a 25 cent charge for delivery. (Urban dwellers used to cash and carry chain stores might well wonder what level of service these householders expected.) Several pointed out with some bitterness that there really was no alternative to paying these charges. Another said that the store was justified in charging for delivery. If there was no direct charge, the result would be that the prices of groceries would go up for everyone. But someone else said, "But the people are perturbed. They don't like it; they would like to have an alternative."

Union members wanted to invite other stores to come into the community, but said the company would not allow it. The company wanted to have control over the stores and prices. They stated that the company gave a heavy subsidy to the store, the rents and the fuel (coal):

> We have recreation problems. We have no stadium, but recently we do have swimming. Our isolation does affect sports that involve

teams; we do have all sports in one form or another, although we lack some facilities.

Most of the houses are pretty good; most of them have three bedrooms and rent for about $25 or $30 per month. Lights are $1.50 a month extra. The company picks up your garbage and puts coal into your shed. They paint three rooms every year, so the whole house is painted every three years.

According to union leaders,

Sons are the problem - some 17- and 18-year-olds are working with the company as common labourers, and a few are on some seasonal employment. About 95 per cent of the children complete their senior matriculation.

Some people make home-brew, but if one person is going out to the liquor store, they get bottles for their friends. The last time I went out, I came back with forty bottles, but only one was for me. There is not much of a liquor problem in town - we can always get a drink at the Legion.

One big beef is that there is no restaurant in town. If you came in here, even today, and are not a guest of the company, you would starve. We have had people come to our door who were in town on business, and ask if they could have a meal with us because there is nowhere in town to eat. In fact, there are no travel facilities for people from out-of-town. The company did maintain a hotel, but now it is closed and nobody would want to live in the bunk house. That is the only facility that is maintained by the company.

The daughters mainly work in the stores. A few work for the company, some go into school-teaching and nursing [outside], some help out at home, but unless a girl gets married young, she has to get out of town. The stores here pay a girl $30 a month if she lives at home and $60 if she comes from outside - even though there is a minimum wage, even for females. As a union man, this burns me up, and when my girl came back with her pay cheque, I sent her back with it; we had the minimum wage tacked up in every store, but I don't think it makes much difference.

The place isn't free - there are gripes "behind the iron curtain." In the old days, there was no freedom of speech, but the unions have changed all that. When the town first started, we were getting 37 cents an hour and we dared not express an opinion.

When asked about being forced to leave the home community at retirement, there were no indignant responses. Instead, the replies were as follows: "A few of the older folk stay on here and live with their sons." "Most of the people have always had a home elsewhere and those who do not own one, have bought or built one since, for their retirement." "I have my home outside, where I will retire." or "I'm only 52, and I have not got around to thinking about the problem yet."

These interviews seem to indicate that in this community things are good, compared to the "old days." The interviews also suggest that patterned social usages and expectations have a great deal to do with expectations and values that people hold. There was no indignation that a life-long set of friends and social relationships would have to be terminated at retirement. Rather the replies seemed to ask – "are there other ways?" or – "well, this is the way life is, and we expect it, and make provisions for it."

THE PASSING OF AN ERA

But, although the company town seems extreme now, this type of community was essentially a prototype of many mining and sawmill communities in the farther reaches of the northland. Many sawmills, connected by private rail line to the transcontinental rail routes, were isolated fiefs boasting the sawmill, the planing mill, the drying yards, the company houses built with the products of the mill, the company general store, the community hall with barber and pool tables, the school, and the church visited every fourth Sunday by an itinerant clergyman. And this was the total life of the inhabitants, management and labour alike. And there was no way in or out of the community without the leave of the company and its railway.

As time goes on, and the structure and processes of society change, so do the structures and organization of the communities of single industry. On one hand, the sponsorship of the communities of single industry changes, with the provincial government taking an active part in the development of communities of single industry in four or more provinces.[8] The federal government or its agencies have been

8 Ira M. Robinson, *New Industrial Towns on Canada's Resource Frontier,* Department of Geography, University of Chicago, Research Paper no. 73 (Chicago, 1962), Table I. See also M. K. McCutcheon and R. C. Young, *Canadian Geographer,* no. 4 (1954), pp. 57-62.

instrumental in the initial development of several communities. Although the division of labour in Canadian society, at the moment at least, leaves the responsibility for the exploration and development and later exploitation of natural resources to the corporation (with or without subsidies), once the development is decided upon, there are now provincial and federal agencies available for the co-operative development and exploitation of the resources. So the full onus of the development of the plant and community is shared with public agencies.

The fullest responsibility, however, rests upon the corporation. The implications of these responsibilities for the lives of the individuals involved will be more precisely examined in the next chapters.

This chapter concludes our consideration of the four stages of the development of a community or single industry. Each stage - construction, recruitment, the period of transition, and finally maturity - has characteristic patterns associated with it. The periods of construction and recruitment are characterized by a high level of mobility, in and out of the community. The maturity phase incorporates a degree of stability in community population, but during this phase there is a persistent and obligatory exodus of youth.

We have also noted the genesis of two phenomena which have very important implications for the community of single industry and its inhabitants. The first is the age cycle. The fact that the majority of the original citizens are under forty results in a long series of consequences. The disproportionate number of citizens in one age bracket means that the community is subject to phases, each characterized by particular problems: in one, the schools are overcrowded, in the next, there are insufficient jobs for the youth, but more than enough school accommodation; later, there is a rash of deaths and retirements, with heavy recruitment into the work ranks.

The second phenomenon is the genesis of the ethnic distribution in the population. This ethnic distribution varies considerably from community to community, partly because of the different types of industry involved, and partly because of the geographical area in which the community is located. We would expect a very different ethnic distribution in a community in Newfoundland than in one in Quebec. The distribution of ethnic groups in the work force and the stratification system of the community will be considered in the following chapters.

In the next chapter, we direct our attention to the organization of work in the community of single industry.

6

The organization of work

The neat traditional pyramid structure of the formal organization of an industry suggests a compartmentalized and rationally organized set of responsibilities, privileges, and symbols carefully co-ordinated and articulated. The formal symmetry conceals the "dead-end" jobs, "desirable" and "undesirable" departments and types of work, and the fact that few workers in the bottom ranks ever reach the top. The formal pyramid also obscures the structural channels within the hierarchy and the informal arrangements that grow out of interaction between people. Over-simplification is particularly deceiving when the organization has many branches throughout the nation, with various skills within the organization represented by different and often competing trade unions.

DECENTRALIZED HIRING

The railway, for instance, represents one of the most complex kinds of organizations. One descriptive title subsumes a wide range of work skills and responsibilities; the individuals with these skills are based in hundreds of communities across the nation; the work day ranges from a job a few minutes from the worker's house to work-in-transit which takes the individual anywhere from a few hundred to a few thousand miles from his home; skills range from weed killing on the right-of-way, to those of a sleeping-car porter, an oxygen-welder, the first dining-car cook, diesel locomotive engineer, clerk typist, freight agent, switchman, or train conductor.

A railway organization has a central personnel department, but the recruitment and training of personnel in a Rocky Mountain railway town, or a Northern Ontario village, or even in Montreal or Toronto or Winnipeg has little to do with the formal policies of the company. In such a vast and sprawling organization, recruitment and training must be decentralized by necessity. And so, in small towns and great cities across the nation, this recruitment becomes the responsibility of local men within local social structures, who are carrying out local practices in an appropriate manner. The formal minimum requirements are taken into account, but the large areas of discretion follow local usage.

The selection of personnel, then, is not based upon the policies or directives of the national headquarters, but is the product of the informal and vital continuing relationships between particular people within a particular community; the local hierarchy reflects the ethnic groups, the status locally given to particular jobs, and to a large extent, the history of the community and its peoples.

As far as the railway is concerned, central hiring is not feasible, and to have a personnel officer at each divisional point would be impracticable. Employment is a local and often merely an incidental matter; some minor officer accepts men for vacancies. The candidate must be physically fit. Beyond that, for many jobs there are few further qualifications necessary. With rare exceptions there are few places for a university education in the larger system. The divisional superintendent, as well as other members of the staff have been, by tradition, the products of practical railroad experience.

Few laymen know what jobs on the railroad entail. So the recruits for vacancies are found among the townspeople who live in divisional point communities. There, people know what is involved in the occupation, they also know when the vacancy occurs. The skills can be learned only by experience. The skills in many departments cannot be transferred to any other industry. Most jobs are based securely on a type of apprenticeship.

The line of promotion below the higher executive positions is well defined, for promotion is inextricably tied up with seniority rights within each trade and skill. Variations of time within which promotion takes place depend upon the age of the senior men and the amount of goods and people transported by the railway. Transfers between departments and trades are seldom made. In part, this is the natural outgrowth of the seniority rules which make transfer difficult and impose upon the transferred worker a rather serious loss of status and salary in relation to others in his department. The railroader's work life is restricted to geographical divisions, and seniority is usually restricted to one division only.

A railway is not unique in this. Mines, smelters, paper mills, textile mills, sawmills, each part of a larger organizational-complex, all recruit their personnel locally. Once the employees take their places in the local hierarchy, they live out their work lives in particular departments and areas of skill. The executive of a fabricating plant in a community of single industry pointed to this phenomenon:

> Most industries face the same problem of non-transferability of employees once they have entered: we are very highly specialized here and our seniority operates on [the basis of] a seniority by

plant, by branch, by department, and by job. This complicates things a great deal in as much as it is difficult to transfer personnel from one department to another.

QUALIFICATIONS AND TRAINING

Although many railway jobs are found only in that industry, the general conditions just described are found in most industries and in single-industry communities in particular, regardless of the precise nature of the work. Some clerical jobs excepted, the educational requirements for the great majority of industrial workers are very low indeed. One manager pointed out, "We have a good work force here. The younger employees that we take on now, we don't ask any particular education although we like them to have grade 10. We get a number with their senior matriculation. There is no particular scholastic requirement for the majority of our work force provided they are reasonably intelligent." Another major employer stated: "We have extremely low educational requirements, in fact, literally none. It is preferable that the person speaks English, but this is in the general run of work." Or, in another factory "At the moment, the only requirement for an employee is that he read and write." Most of the main production jobs in the sawmill, the textile mill, the pulp and paper mill, the mine, the smelter, or indeed of any mass production unit require no other education.

RAISING EDUCATIONAL REQUIREMENTS

The instruction is usually given on the job:

> The training, of course, is informal – very little formal training traditionally. The employee would be hired, and would be given some general orientation – what the company was, how it operated – and then they would be taken to a department whose head would then assign the incoming man to an experienced employee who would, in turn, train the newcomer. This training would take, in most departments, about three weeks. They would then start with the lowest wage, with a low level of work. Supposing they were working on the spindles, they would first take over part of a job and as they got more experienced their work load would be increased, so within three months they should be assuming full work load.

This is not to say that many industries have not introduced high educational requirements for incoming employees. To the outsider, these educational requirements are admitted to be extravagantly high, and to have no relationship with the jobs to be performed. Company officials usually offered one or more of three reasons for this. The first was that during the early days (the first three stages of the development of the community), the company usually asked for few educational qualifications. However, after stability had been established for some years, when there were far more local candidates than jobs, the educational requirements were raised to grade 10 or senior matriculation. Thus one finds the incongruous situation that sons without a senior matriculation could not be hired despite the fact that their illiterate fathers were employed by the same company. One general manager said, "I have no use for personnel departments who have the kids fill out forms and pass tests and then go through all sorts of hocus pocus – why? Simply because the management has not the guts to say NO. Instead, you sit there and talk about suitability and test scores, which is absolute nonsense."

The second reason for inflating the educational requirements of employment is related to the employer's responsibility to the community population. The management well knows that if the applicant cannot find work in the community he must leave, and inflated requirements encourage the local youth to remain in school as long as possible, before having to migrate. In many communities this works, as one union man explained:

> They work hard at school and do not do much except for school work, probably because they live in isolation. The company will have nothing to do with new employees who have less than senior matriculation. The school board, the manager, and all the officials in town stress education here, and as they cannot go anywhere else without high education almost 100 per cent finish high school.

This type of plan is not without its perils, as illustrated by this account of life in a small community of single industry:

> I think education is gradually improving here – but I will have to tell you what happened just recently. We have a very amiable and very bright parish priest here who is extremely influential. He came to us, as the single employer, and he said, "Look, can't we do something about the education in the community? How about you

refusing to hire anybody under grade 9 – say this is the minimum requirement and everybody will have to go as far as grade 9." We talked this over, and we decided it was a very good idea. In the end we had several full-fledged meetings with the parish priest, the staff of the boys' school, the staff of the girls' school, and a couple of people from town; everybody thought this was a good idea – and it was agreed that the company would not hire anybody under grade 9. Actually, up until now, we have not hired anybody, of course, by law, under 16, so when an applicant comes and applies for a job, we send him to the parish priest to get his baptismal certificate; now the priest agreed that he wouldn't give the certificate to anybody who hadn't had grade 9 education. He agreed that he would advise them to go back to school and finish off their education.

Well, everything went well for about three weeks and then I began to get fathers [employees] coming in to see me; "What's wrong? I have given 40 years of my life to the company. I have eight sons working here. Our family has done nothing but work their whole lives for this company – and here my boy is refused a job, and yet you go around and you hire someone just down the street and his family has never worked here – just because he had grade 9 education. Does the job that he is going to do – working in *this* plant require a grade 9 education?" Well, I could only answer the obvious, "No, it doesn't." He said, "Well, then, isn't my boy going to get a job – or is this a type of discrimination?" So finally, I phoned the parish priest, and I said, "Look, if you want to get your people to go to school longer you are going to have to count me out, because I can't be disloyal to my local employees; one has a boy who is of age and his father and all the family want him to work here and he comes from reliable people, I can't refuse him. We are going to have to think of something else." So our little experiment in building up the education of the community didn't get very far. Actually, the education is creeping up – I would guess that most of them come in with seventh grade now. It used to be that you would have people coming in sixteen years old with grade 4 or 6, and now it is grade 7 or 8.

The third reason commonly given by business executives for requiring educational achievements beyond the occupational requirements is that they are employing individuals who may stand good chances for promotion, and so require the educational requirements for their prospective new positions.

The majority of the communities of single industry make use of their local labour pool and do not hire people from outside the community once the stability of the population has been established. One noted that company officials were sometimes deceived: "We give preference to the townspeople. Occasionally we find that we have hired someone by accident – a young fellow comes in and he gives a local address, and we find out much later that he was living with his aunt, and actually came from somewhere else."

A LOCAL RAILWAY HIERARCHY

At this point, we turn to a specific divisional point on one of the transcontinental railways, Railtown, to see how the division of labour in one particular divisional point is carried out. Railtown, with its particular history and its particular ethnic mix has, through the years, worked out a division of labour and an appropriation of prestige unique to itself, though following the general requirements of the larger system.

The railway is the sole industry of Railtown. It offers occupational opportunities each of which involves a type of work and the payment that goes with it, but it also gives the worker a status. Certain types of occupation are defined as more desirable than others; the status varies according to the job level in the hierarchy.

1. Officials

At the apex of the local hierarchy is the divisional superintendent. He is responsible for the supervision of the division. He lives in the house supplied by the company for the superintendent. Immediately below him, in the hierarchy, are the assistant superintendent and the heads of the branches which come under his jurisdiction – the master mechanic, the trainmaster, yardmaster, and roadmaster. All of these men have risen through the ranks outside of the divisional point. Each official has received promotion through transfer from one division to another, each move involving new and often greater responsibilities. The officials have the respect and sympathy of the workers under them, because they answer to the company for the employee's mistakes. Because of this, their authority, and the fact that they have risen through many jobs lower in the hierarchy, their positions embody very high status.

2. Running Trades

The men with the highest status positions below the supervisory staff are the running trades. These are often known as the big four – the locomotive engineer, fireman, conductor, and brakeman (trainman). In the past they have been referred to as the aristocracy of labour. Technological change has affected their work and their position relative to other types of workingmen.

Let us consider a youth who hears of a vacancy for student fireman occurring. The education requirement is that he must be able to read and write. He then fills out the forms, and has a medical examination. If he passes this stage satisfactorily, he buys a lunch pail, borrows a good watch and starts "firing." He is instructed on actual "runs" by a veteran foreman and learns his responsibilities and something of the locomotive he operates. Eventually he has the opportunity to work alone. He is then the most junior fireman in the system of seniority, – an "extra fireman." While on the "extra board" and while "the road is busy" he may cover much mileage and make good money. If the road becomes "slack" (few trains) he may be removed from the board completely, or be laid off, but he still retains his "rights," i.e., to return to the job when more work is available. He joins his union, which is responsible for the negotiation of his wage with the railway.

Once the fireman makes his first run, everything depends upon seniority, that is length of service in that job category. He begins on freight trains, and as men above him retire, die or move away, he may bid for the position of fireman on passenger trains. As passenger trains maintain regular schedules, the firemen on these "runs" have regular schedules and so can plan their social life. The very regularity, however, limits his income. He is not able to make extra "trips" and "make more mileage" and more money. This is an interim stage, however, for the fireman has another ladder to climb.

Depending upon the number of men ahead of him, and the rate at which the engineers above him die or retire, he will sooner or later move to the other side of the engine cab to become an engineer. This may take a few years or several decades. According to railroad commission law, before he can be considered as qualified to run a locomotive a man must be twenty-one years of age and must have been a fireman for three years.

He is then an "extra" engineer. If few trains are run, he may slip back to a fireman's job and everyone beneath him also moves down the ladder. His engineer's training again takes place on the job. As fireman, he has observed the essentials of his new job, and the finer touches can only be learned by experience.

The engineer then moves from freight to passenger engine. As he becomes older he may bid for and receive the top prestige job – a "steady run" with "good hours" on a passenger train. Occasionally men are selected to take even higher "management" jobs, but, as the railroad is so widespread an organization this selection seldom touches a divisional point.

The railroader usually works as hard as possible during his last ten years of service because his earnings affect his pension. The pension is based on the number of years of service and the earnings of his last ten years of service.

Our youngster might have found a vacancy at the other end of the train, as brakeman. In this job he learns a set of signals, how to couple and uncouple cars, the techniques of "switching" and other appropriate skills. In the same manner as the fireman, he moves to his next step, to the position of conductor. At each stage he belongs to his appropriate craft union which protects him from the "outsider."

Here, then, are the "big four" of the railway industry, "railroaders." In many respects the work is undesirable. The engineer and firemen suffer from heat and cold in the relatively unprotected engine cab. Much of their time is spent away from home driving the train to the next divisional point, handing it on to the next crew, sleeping, and driving the next train bound for their home point. But there are advantages. They were the best paid men in any industry for a long time. Petty domination by foremen is reduced to a minimum because they are completely on their own during their working hours. Their responsibility is great: their hands guide an engine which controls many lives as well as goods and costly equipment.

Much of the high status is a carryover from early railroading when resourcefulness and daring were the keynote of their jobs. Engineers, who took trains through forest fires, across burning bridges, and stopped them within inches of a "wash-out," had high status. A cloak of romance surrounded the "Knight of the Shining Rail." Now, as they operate by automatic signals, many decisions are made for them.

The statuses of these four occupations are enhanced by their direct contact with the movement of trains, by lack of immediate supervision, high pay, strong unions, monopoly and, for engineers, a romantic tradition. The skills learned by members of the running trades are not transferable to any other type of industry. Even if the skills were transferred to another railway, the worker would lose all seniority rights. These men, then, have a life career line bound up in the local community.

The fact that the differences in status, prestige, and wage are intrinsic in the job itself, and the job in relation to other jobs in the hierarchy, can be demonstrated by studies of railroading made many thousands of miles from Railtown. Andrews in his study of a railway community with a different ethnic distribution in a different province, thousands of miles distant from Railtown, states:

> The solidarity of railway employees in presenting a united front to the outside world has been a traditional stance. The policy of family members being part of the railway system, its historic role in the development of the country, supported by the "railway songs" and the ensuing pride in being called a "railroader" had produced this type of unity.
>
> As within many other organizations, a front of solidarity often hid feelings of resentment and jealousy among the different departments. Most of the critical feeling had been directed toward the firemen and engineers, who were paid the highest wages and held positions of higher prestige than those of the average railroad worker. It was charged that the firemen and engineers seemed to have their every wish granted and their desire at least taken into consideration by the company: "The engineers and firemen would lord it over the rest of us. Everything they wanted, they got. They had a union which was really a union." They were often described as asserting their authority in the extreme: "They're a bossy crowd. When they come in anywhere, it's all to do this and do that." Comments were also made on their so-called greed: "They would not give one another a mile. If one had a chance to get a few miles, he'd be quick to grab it," or "During the depression, when our department [mechanical] all got together and went on short time so that everybody got a few days of work every month, these engineers did not help one another at all."

Anti-engineer feeling was so strong that a certain rather minor incident became a well-known joke ... the engineers had to have what was known as a two-hour call, that is, the "call boy" had the duty of going to the home of the engineer at least two hours before his shift of duty began. This had to be done regardless of the fact that the shift was a regular one rather than one from the spare list for which a call would be necessary ... It was a regular shift for the engine crew and a terrible snow storm happened to be in progress at the appointed time for the call. It was 3:30 a.m. and the call boy struggled through the high drifts and cold wind to the right house, where he found the engineer dressed and ready to go to work:

Call boy: Do I have to call you every time, even when you're on regular shift?

Engineer: Oh yes, you have to call me, that's part of our union agreement with the company.

Call boy: Well, I hope the Lord calls you before the next snow storm.

This ... was considered a good joke and one which really "told off" the engineers. Some of the bitterness can be seen in this joke and it expresses the degree of resentment felt by some of the lesser paid workers.[1]

3. Operators and Dispatchers

The operators and dispatchers are directly associated with the big four, even though they work inside the station. The dispatchers are the men who plan the itinerary and the stops for the trains. They decide where the trains will meet, and what siding will be used to allow another train to pass. The operator relays his orders along the line. The great responsibility of the dispatcher gives him a high status and a certain amount of sympathy: "I wouldn't take the responsibility for anything. If anything happens, the dispatcher is usually to blame. I wouldn't like to take the blame for a dozen or so deaths in a train

1 Alick R. Andrews, "Social Crisis and Labour Mobility. A Study of Economic and Social Change in a New Brunswick Railway Community," unpublished MA thesis (University of New Brunswick, 1967), pp. 77-9. See also W. F. Cottrell, *The Railroader* (Palo Alto, 1940), and W. F. Cottrell, "Death by Dieselization: A Case Study in Reaction to Technological Change," *American Sociological Review*, XVI (1951), pp. 358-68.

wreck." (Technical advances have now reduced much of the dispatcher's personal responsibility.)

These, then, are the railroaders. Hence the big four (engineers, firemen, conductors, and brakemen), telegraph operators, dispatchers, and the transportation officials belong to the top group in the occupational stratification. All other railway employees are considered to be lesser breeds.

4. *Other Categories of Railway Workers*

(i) Shopmen

> Shopmen who handle the inspection and repair of rolling stock belong to the mechanical department and occupy the next lower rung. Their skills are in general more complex and more difficult to learn and require at least as great intelligence as those of the elite; but unfortunately from the point of view of income, they are not as easily monopolized as those of the operating department.[2]

The early career of a shopman is rigidly controlled by a long apprenticeship. For example, one apprentice's manual states that

> machinist's apprentices shall be instructed in all branches of the machinist trade. They will serve three years on machines and special jobs and they will not be required to work more than four months on any one job or machine. During the last two years of their apprenticeship they will work on the floor and will be instructed in the oxy-acetylene, thermal, or other electric welding processes.

Boilermaker's apprentices' work covers a period of sixty months. Each apprenticeship is definitely and precisely defined by the railroad.

The shopmen hold a pride in craft, but once perfection has been achieved, promotion on merit except to a minor supervisory position is impossible. Bidding systems and seniority determine shift. Although shopmen work inside, the work is difficult, tedious, dirty, and often dangerous. There is always the threat of competition from "outsiders" who have similar trades. Although skilled, shop workers have not the satisfaction of being directly identified with the more romantic aspects of railroading, the actual operation of the trains.

2 Cottrell, *The Railroader*, p. 21.

(ii) Carmen

A marked division exists between the shopmen and the carmen. Usually the carman is considered to be the lowest of the skilled railway workers. He is just as skilled as many of the shopmen; there are other reasons for his low pay and status. The low pay, which was traditionally his, attracted a less aggressive group, especially as the required skills can readily be acquired through experience without dangers of damage or accident.

(iii) Yardmen and switchmen

This group is small but important as these men look after the making-up of trains in the railway yards; they carry out the continuous switching and general duty done by the yard engine. The switchman's job is out of doors, thus it is considered undesirable. The positions of yardman and switchman are higher than that of section man, because of their special skills.

(iv) Labourers and sectionmen

Labourers do many jobs and work in various departments. There is a wealth of classified and unclassified labourer's positions, varying in wages. The jobs require little or no skill; the title of labourer has an added stigma.

The sectionmen's work on the maintenance of the way is varied. In the winter, they put shims under the rails. They handle the snow and ice – on platforms, under culverts, in sidings, ditches, etc. In spring the shims are removed, grass is burned, new ties are distributed. In summer the ties are renewed and the railway bed is resurfaced; and in the autumn they mow the right of way; remove weeds from the track ballast, repair switches and buildings, and clean out ditches and culverts.

Throughout all this work the sectionman patrols his section of track daily. Any defects are immediately repaired. The lights at the switches are refuelled and lighted. To encourage better work the railways once sponsored section competition with prizes for the best section and the best garden in front of the section houses.

The sectionman's pay was low. The majority lived in section houses, spaced at intervals along the track – an isolated life. Although some skill was required in the technique of maintaining the track, it was soon learned, and the major part of the work depended upon physical stamina on routine jobs, exposed to all weather. Technology has reduced the number of sectionmen and changed the nature of their work.

(v) The extra gang

Each summer the extra gang does the larger replacement jobs on the track, replacing rails, putting in new ballast, etc. For this type of job, seasonal workers are employed. In the opinion of the rest of the workers they do not belong to the railway at all. Their status is extremely low.

These "lower" occupations fit the category of "jobs." The skilled workers such as electricians, carpenters, or machinists, are able to adapt and transfer their skills to other industries; the unskilled labourers may also move from industry to industry. In Railtown few, if any, move from the community to transfer to another industry; nevertheless, workers with "jobs" do not have the same feeling of attachment and belonging as do those with careers directly dependent upon the railway.

(vi) White collar employees

All of the above-mentioned occupations have a direct or indirect connection with the operation of the trains and of the railroad. Within these various classifications there are various in-groups, usually built around some small skill. Nevertheless, all these employees have some feeling of identification with the physical aspects of railroading.

The clerks, messengers, and ticket-sellers are seldom considered to be connected with the railway at all, although they belong to one of the largest unions. Their functions are important, but they are remote from actual train operation.

Some clerks do become identified by their fellow employees with the classification of the railroad department in which they work. As a result a clerk or typist in one section may have a greater feeling of belonging than a clerk in another. Higher prestige is given to clerks in "important sections" by their fellows. Few railroad workers, however, consider these clerical occupations to be in the railway stratification; clerks are usually thought of as "just office workers."

In all these occupations, the duties, rights and obligations of each role are patterned. But, even more important, there are various statuses in the hierarchy built around rituals and symbols rather than along rational lines of technological activity. Association with a railway locomotive, for example, represents greater symbolic status value than actual skill.

The general outlines of the prestige hierarchy persist despite constant technological change. Over the last twenty-five years the change from coal engines to diesel probably introduced more change than any other single factor. Many traditional occupations associated with coal disappeared, and new skills were introduced. Engines needed less servicing, so that the technical economic base for many communities all but disappeared. The changing role of the fireman has had a great deal of publicity during contract negotiations over the last number of years. Shop and service skills have changed. Automatic signalling systems have shifted responsibilities. Changes in passenger traffic have introduced new work patterns. It has recently been announced that machines have been developed to do much of the work that is at present the responsibility of the section man. Extra gangs will become groups of skilled technicians instead of gangs of strong immigrant labourers.[3]

5. *Ethnic Distribution*

This hierarchical arrangement, however, involves more than the association of certain breadwinners and certain families with particular jobs. As O. Hall states, "It usually happens that the distinctive ethnic groups of a community come to be associated with a characteristic group of occupations."[4] We have noted previously that the early stages of the development of communities of single industry are characterized by little less than chaos, as a process of self-selection is carried out. However, out of that process comes the distinctive dis-

3 For a more detailed discussion of the effects of technological change on the railway see Andrews, "Social Crisis and Labour Mobility," *passim,* and Cottrell "Death by Dieselization."

4 O. Hall, "The Social Consequences of Uranium Mining," *University of Toronto Quarterly,* XXVI, no. 2 (Jan. 1957), p. 232. The same point is echoed in Ira M. Robinson, *New Industrial Towns on Canada's Resource Frontier,* Department of Geography, University of Chicago, Resource Paper no. 73 (Chicago, 1962), pp. 84-5.

tribution of jobs among the particular combination of ethnic groups attracted to the new community. Hall has stated:

> Jobs in the actual promotion of large-scale business, jobs in the organization of business and finance, and engineering jobs, involving considerable responsibility seem generally to fall to the lot of the Anglo-Saxon. By contrast, the French-Canadian has tended towards jobs of a lower level of skill and training in the industrial hierarchy. Such distributions of people among jobs are likely to be blurred and concealed in the anonymity of the metropolitan community. But in a small one-industry community the distribution of jobs among peoples becomes highly visible; moreover, the various ethnic groups in the community are likely to become acutely conscious of their place in the job distribution.[5]

Though we may agree with Hall's general statement, it might be useful to see how the ethnic distribution began in a particular community; more important, because few of the non-supervisory jobs intrinsically require high educational attainment and because skills are gained through on-the-job training, it is important to establish how the original ethnic distribution becomes perpetuated. In a railroad town, for instance, the sorting process must be based upon more than educational qualification.

It was suggested earlier that although there are infinite local variations on a theme, the people of each emerging community work out an ethnic distribution which reflects the patterned relationships and values of the community. In an all French-speaking community, one would expect a different resolution of stratification than in a community characterized by a population of English and Ukrainian background. Railtown, with its own particular ethnic mix, has developed informally its own ethnic division of labour. This tradition is directly related to the beginnings of railroading and the community.

Prior to the building of the railroad and the founding of Railtown, the land was covered with virgin forest scarred in many areas by forest fires. Small bands of Indians lived in log huts and skin tents. They lived from the forest: fish, blueberries, deer, moose and rabbits formed their main diet. The Indians shot and trapped animals for fur, and several times a year they loaded their cargo in birch-bark canoes,

5 Hall, "Uranium Mining," p. 232.

and entire families paddled across great lakes and portaged over hills to reach a trading post where skins were bartered for goods. Then the railway came, and with it, a new white population. Railway construction attracted men with many different backgrounds, languages, cultures, and skills.

From early histories and obituaries, it is possible to trace the moves of a few of the first residents of this community. One prominent citizen, for instance, white, Anglo-Saxon, Protestant, worked on the construction of the rail line, before there was a Railtown. His first work was looking after the houses used for construction work. As the rail was extended, he became the first section foreman in one area, a hundred miles east of Railtown, and as the rail was built farther west, he caught up with it and became a locomotive fireman fifty miles away. After the steel had moved through what is now Railtown, he remained at this point, and continued as a fireman, and shortly afterwards became an engineer. The first white woman arrived in town the same year and opened a boarding house. The population lived in tents for over a year, and there were two rows of box cars in which people lived. But within two years there was a hotel. The first school was held in a tent furnished by twelve rough-hewn seats, and a big stove in the middle. "The kids who sat around it fried on one side and froze on the other, but it wasn't much different at home in those days." As the railway was extended westward, men, with friends or brothers, left construction jobs to work for the railway they had helped build. As each community emerged the first citizens had to clear away trees to begin to build their houses. As railway work expanded, the population increased, and as more and more people stopped off the process of selection went on. Railtown became a divisional point, but was never a rail construction headquarters, as was a community a hundred miles east, which was described by an oldtimer:

> ... as wild as any adventure-loving youth could have wished. Men with sums of money were in danger of being killed if they so much as flashed their wealth around. There were different methods of killing them, but whichever was used, the victim was afterwards dumped into the lake. All the workmen flocked to the headquarters for construction on pay day and it did not take them long to dispose of their wages. Sometimes they went into gambling dens and were never heard of again. In those days when a man died he

was just buried and forgotten. There was no report made. Of course, scurvy was a plague that killed hundreds of workers.

For a number of years the Indians lived near Railtown and carried on their traditional way of life, coming to town only to trade skins for their ever-extending list of essential manufactured goods. Gradually, their tastes became more and more allied to those of the white population, but, at the same time, the animals within the area became scarce. Consequently, more and more Indians moved nearby and a few crossed the river and built rude shacks at the edge of the town. Their existence was marginal; trapping augmented by odd jobs. Hence, at the beginning Indians took no part in railroad work. Their main orientation was still towards trapping. Their work in the town or on the railway was temporary and seasonal labouring work. Throughout the years Railtown has grown, and more and more Indians have moved into the town. They live in their part of the community – "Lower Town" or "Indian Town." These people gradually became identified with the town and with labouring occupations in it; only a few could earn their livelihood from the bush.

The French who settled in Railtown in its first ten years came from rural Quebec. Their limited education and lack of mechanical experience as well as language difficulty, seem to have prevented the French Canadian from taking over jobs involving mechanical knowledge. Their orientation was based upon a different set of values. Their training was for the life of the community in which they had been born.[6] For instance one of the first French Canadian residents of Railtown came from a village in Quebec, followed the rail construction out west, and on his way back east, stopped, worked as a sectionman, and then opened a butcher shop.

The British, on the other hand, both from the United Kingdom and from the other parts of Canada (mainly the Ottawa Valley) had a different upbringing. Many, particularly those from Britain, had had a long apprenticeship in a mechanical vocation. Occupations such as mechanical shop trades and the operation of locomotives and trains appealed to them and fitted their background.

In this way, distribution of individuals in jobs according to ethnic affiliation and experience emerged early in Railtown's history. Poles, Ukrainians, Italians, and others were late-comers to the community

6 E. C. Hughes, *French Canada in Transition* (Chicago, 1943).

and took their place in the lower echelons, providing personnel for labouring jobs, extra gang, and sectionmen.

OCCUPATION AND ETHNIC AFFILIATION

E. W. Bradwin, in his book *The Bunkhouse Man: A Study of Work and Pay in the Camps of Canada, 1903-1914*, confirms the early allocation of work according to ethnic characteristics. Bradwin, Director of Instructors, Frontier College, had many years of first hand experience in camps. Although his phrasing and terminology is old-fashioned, his material has the ring of authenticity; although he habitually attributes the work position and capacity to "natural" factors such as "stock" and "race," he should be read in the spirit and conviction of the times.

> To the white man [born in Canada, USA, the British Isles, and Scandinavia] fall most of the positions which connote a "stripe" of some kind – officials in one capacity or another, walking-bosses, accountants, inspectors, the various camp foremen, cache-keepers, as well as clerks who perform the more routine work of checkers and time-keepers. This class also includes the cooks and helpers in the cookery, the tote-teamsters on the hauls, the drivers of scrapers and dump-wagons in the mud cuts and on the fills. The white man, too, does much of the rock work where more than ordinary skill and practice in the use of powder are essential for effective blasting.
>
> The most remunerative part of railway construction ... [occurs] at the repair camps and machine shops on construction where there are frequent calls for locomotive mechanics, boilermen, pumpmen, engine hostlers, and machinists of parts ...
>
> The different bridge crews and a preponderant part of the gangs who build the wooden trestles on the line are whites ... Many newcomers to the Dominion from Central Europe would prove useful on structural work, but have not the requisite knowledge of English so essential in the conduct of these hazardous tasks ...
>
> The French-speaking navvy is usually more accustomed to frontier conditions and is invariably an axe-man. While he engages sometimes in the routine work at machine camps and busy pits as car-knocker, a brakeman, a helper or machinist, he predominates

more usually in the trestle gangs or at the camps. Frequently, too, numbers of French-speaking navvies are found at a grade camp where a compatriot is operating on a piece of work or where the foreman in charge is of their own tongue and race ...

The French-speaking Canadian who navvies on the line is not usually literate. In this respect he lags behind the Italian, the English-speaking worker alongside him, and particularly the Scandinavian and Finn who engage in the same class of work ...

There are phases of new construction in which the French-speaking Canadian excels. Much of the earlier work beyond the steel is performed by him. He prefers to be in the van-guard. The space and freedom of the trails and water routes appeal to him, whether carrying the mail, running lines with the engineers, building corduroy roads in the low places, toting supplies up the grade, or assisting with ready axe to erect the big log company camps. He is seen to advantage at the portage where for the time the canoe and pointer must displace the heavy haul on the cache-road. With loaded back he rotates in quarter-mile trips from the "dump" to the lake, his well-greased shoepacks slopping along the muddy trail or through the muskeg, bearing his balanced loads of flour, sugar, meals, beans, tinned goods or other urgent supplies. True flies abound and mosquitoes torment, and grouch increases with every untoward delay; his *sacré*-ing is furious, and it were not well just then if some unobtrusive snag or root in path should cause a further spill ...

Most camps on railway construction have also a considerable number of newcomers from the British Isles – Scotch and English ... Their industry, their experience, often, and their natural aptitude for machinery, as well as their fondness for tools, usually assure them a permanent place. They throng the temporary machine shops and do much of the repair work.

... The Scandinavians usually work together in groups as distinct nationals, using their own language, but they readily assume their place with the best workers on the line. Their splendid physiques, their willingness and their prodigious capacity for work are big assets in performing the heavier manual tasks of the camp. Their services are eagerly sought for rock work and excavations. Many of the Swedes, also, become camp foremen and company officials on the grade ...

Before discussing the so-called foreigners found on frontier works, mention may here be made of the Indian. Strange as it may appear, men of this primal race seem exotic to camps. The bunk house itself in the Canadian hinterland signifies an intrusion upon his former domain. Camp activities of whatever kind mean ultimately a narrowing of privileges and customs that for so long have marked his mode of life.

The Indian himself draws apart from the continued labour in camps. The ordered complexity with which considerable numbers of men are handled effectively, the big machines that in their ponderous efforts awaken to new life the solitudes that he so long has called his own, may awe, or even attract for a time, but his stay in the bunk house is usually temporary. The Indian more than any other campman is rooted in his own ways, and the methods of the past ...

Foreigners ... Slavs ... display definite characteristics: slow and immobile, lacking initiative, rather careless of personal appearance, with but limited mechanical ability, not quarrelsome except when liquor is about, easily brow-beaten, for the foot of despotism has cowed their spirit; just plodders in the day's work – withal, that pliant type that provides the human material for a camp boss to drive ... In a hasty moment or as a term of reproach they are locally dubbed Russians, Bohunks, Galicians, Douks maybe, and occasionally Hunkies. The railway work with [Ukrainians] was only a way-station. Sooner or later they intended to have farms of their own in the new land. At first opportunity they gathered their earnings and located on a prairie section in the west ...

Members of the western Slavs, now comprising largely the countries of re-established Poland and Czecho-Slovakia, entered Canada during the third period of railway construction under diverse names. They were commonly listed as Slovaks, Bohemians, Poles, Austrians, Lithuanians and, in some cases, Ruthenians ... Many thousands of these people came and went on the line during the ten-year period of construction. Less purposeful in their plans and lives, they shifted frequently from work to work ... Occasionally in evidence among the Slav groups, but noticeably different, were the pure Austrians, or Hungarians, as they preferred to be called, upon an acquaintance ... The southern Slavs, including Serbs, Croatians, and other mountain races, now known as the Jugo-Slavs ...

while they are industrious plodding workers and aggressive, they suffer from a lack of English, a working knowledge of which they are not always willing to acquire ...

The Jews, while not numerous, are always in evidence during any period of railway activity when large numbers of men are employed in camps. Few Jews engage in manual work. There are exceptions, however, and persistent able workers they are even in the most strenuous tasks. But they usually prefer to do their own planning. As tailors, peddlers, jewellers, and small traders of various kinds they follow the steel, locating temporarily in the small towns which spring up in its wake.

Invariably competent, willing and possessing reliance the German-born worker was an asset to a foreman ... the newcomer from Italy displays an adeptness for work with cement – whether on excavations for concrete, erecting massive piers, or building abutments. The Italians, too, engage quite frequently at ballast pits or are found in large bodies with liftgangs on railway maintenance, particularly when they may labour under their own countrymen acting as bosses ...[7]

These, then, were the men who built Canada. It is a wonder that any survived under the conditions of work and living that Bradwin describes. That thousands left the country is not surprising.

THE PERSISTENCE OF THE ETHNIC DISTRIBUTION

Ethnic association with particular occupations has persisted. A great deal has been heard of the national patterned differences among French and English. Nathan Keyfitz, for instance, notes that:

7 E. W. Bradwin, *The Bunkhouse Man: A Study of Work and Pay in the Camps of Canada, 1903-1914* (New York, 1928), pp. 100-29. These views were characteristic of the era. See S. Woodsworth, *Strangers within Our Gates* (Toronto, 1909), pp. 132-69; W. Burton Hurd, *Racial Origins and Nativity of the Canadian People,* census monograph no. 4 (Ottawa, 1937). For an objective, nation-wide history of ethnic groups in Canada see, Royal Commission on Bilingualism and Biculturalism, *The Cultural Contribution of the Other Ethnic Groups,* Book IV (Ottawa, 1970). The excellent bibliography in Book IV is augmented by that prepared by the Department of Citizenship and Immigration, *Citizenship, Immigration and Ethnic Groups in Canada: A Bibliography of Research* (Ottawa, 1960-6).

> Logging is another activity in which the French are represented in greater numbers than they are in industry as a whole; 48 per cent of persons in all logging occupations are French. But only 40 per cent of foremen are French against 49 per cent of lumbermen, and these figures, like those for construction had not changed greatly since 1941.
>
> To turn to transport, we find that 42 per cent of the taxi drivers are French but only 20 per cent of the locomotive engineers. Since driving a locomotive is more highly regarded than driving a taxi the question arises (this writer does not have the data to answer it) why the French should have a higher proportion in the one than in the other ... Answers in general will turn on historical considerations ... There has been an improvement between 1941 and 1951, in the sense of an increase in the proportion of locomotive engineers who are French and a decline in the proportion of taxi drivers.[8]

To return from the general distribution of occupations among ethnic groups to the specific distribution as it began in Railtown, we find that the original distribution of ethnic groups in railway employment has continued. The British have retained all the top administrative jobs and desirable status-bearing occupations of the railroad. The French and the Indians have continued to work in the lower levels of the job hierarchy.

This ethnic association with occupation could hardly have been continued without some mechanism to restrict ethnic groups from certain occupations. If promotion is based strictly upon seniority there could be no system of sponsorship within the industry. Once a man is "in," the rest is automatic – no formal or informal mechanisms can stop his promotion. Instead the screening takes place before employment.

The workers in a particular department are aware when a vacancy occurs. Before the vacancy is posted, the word goes around: "They're going to be taking on firemen." On the informal level the news circulates in the running trades' work group, which is, of course, almost entirely British. Either a son of an engineer or a son of a friend of an engineer is ready to go to work at this time. He is told to drop in to see the "super," that "they will probably be taking on some men soon."

8 Nathan Keyfitz, "Some Demographic Aspects of French-English Relations in Canada," in Mason Wade, ed., *Canadian Dualism* (Toronto, 1960), p. 139.

The job is there; some "bright young lad" visits the superintendent and "would like to go on the road." Several British workers will drop over to the superintendent's office to "put in a word for Frank's son." As the superintendent finds "this lad is willing," he is given the job. This procedure, with slight variations, restricts outsiders from coming into certain occupational areas. The British group have had advance notice through the grapevine.

Often several people from various ethnic groups apply for the job. A few French have "slipped through": "They must have spoken to the roadmaster who's French."

If a man of French or "other" ethnic background applies for a job, the superintendent will tell him with perfect honesty and sincerity: "I'm sorry, but there are no openings in the crews. Too bad. If you want a job right away, they need some men in the shops and on the extra gang. Take that for now, and apply for the other job when one is open – we'll post a bulletin." When the job is posted formally, it has already been filled informally.

This is an obvious case of pre-employment ethnic sponsorship. By this informal sponsorship the train crews have been restricted to the British group almost exclusively for four decades. After sixty years of hiring by this process, the British represented 100 per cent of the managerial group, 91 per cent of the train crews, but only 15 per cent of the labourers. Management is probably aware of this mechanism; if they employ sons of reliable locomotive engineers, they have a good chance of obtaining future reliable employees.

Although the railroad recruits its employees from the town, it recruits the different ethnic groups into different levels of the occupational hierarchy. As has already been pointed out, it is difficult to transfer from one department to another. Tradition has produced mechanisms which perpetuate occupational allocation of Indians, French, and British. This process is not carried on deliberately by the company, but informally by the employees.

Nepotism seems to have been much more explicit in the railroad community studied by Andrews. In discussing the apprenticeship system (for shop work) he states:

> An applicant for apprenticeship usually had to be sixteen years of age and had to have a reading and writing knowledge of English. Each applicant was also expected to know the "first four rules of

> arithmetic." Preference was given to sons or dependent relations of [railway] employees. This was not too much of a problem in [the community], but a system of entering the son in the same work that his father had done was the general policy. The idea was that the son while growing up would be continually hearing and be aware of the type of work his father did. This, it was felt, would be a decided advantage for the boy's introduction into the system ... For example, he would know the vocabulary of his future work. Said one man, "One time a father would work all his life and then his son would be working in the same job before he retired. You could start at the bottom and work up." The company then, not only gave the official word regarding the hiring of employees' sons, but actively encouraged the placing of these younger people in the same job as the fathers had held.[9]

ETHNIC STEREOTYPES

The railroad has menial and seasonal jobs available from time to time; these provide an alternative to the unwary school drop-out. These

9 Andrews, "Social Crisis and Labour Mobility," pp. 72-3. Ethnic sponsorship and particularly nepotism is closely related to two persistent research findings – that occupation of father is the most likely occupational choice of son and that there is less upward mobility among youth from small communities. See P. M. Blau, "Occupational Bias and Mobility," *American Sociological Review* (Aug. 1957), pp. 392-9; C. F. Bolling, "Mobility Study in the Bituminous Coal Industry," unpublished MA thesis (University of Tennessee, 1960); R. Freedman and A. H. Hawley, "Migration and Occupational Mobility in the Depression," *American Journal of Sociology*, 55 (1949), pp. 171-7; E. Ginsberg, *et al.*, *Occupational Choice: An Approach to a General Theory* (New York, 1951); H. H. Hyman, "The Value System of Different Classes," in R. Bendix and S. Lipset, eds., *Class, Status and Power: A Reader in Social Stratification* (Glencoe, 1953), pp. 426-42; Mirra Komarovsky, *The Unemployed Man and His Family* (New York, 1950); G. E. Lenski, "Trends in Intergenerational Mobility in the United States," *American Sociological Review*, 23 (Oct. 1958), pp. 514-23; S. M. Lipset and R. Bendix, *Social Mobility in Industrial Society* (Berkeley, 1959); S. M. Lipset and F. T. Malm, "First Jobs and Career Patterns," *American Journal of Economics and Sociology*, 14 (1955), pp. 247-61; G. L. Palmer, *Labor Mobility in Six Cities* (New York, 1954); N. Rogoff, *Recent Trends in Occupational Mobility* (Glencoe, 1953); M. M. Tumin and A. S. Fieldman, "Theory and Measurement of Occupational Mobility," *American*

jobs do not tempt those who have an occupational orientation in a specific direction, backed up by family, school and friends; but to those whose occupational orientation is indefinite or directed toward the railroad, these jobs represent an ever-present and welcome temptation. Thus, the railroad affects various ethnic groups in differing ways and degrees; the temptation is always there, but like plans are also influenced by definitions of appropriate behaviour held by parents, peers, teachers and the youth themselves.

The ethnic stereotypes that are held in the community and among the workers on the railroad, are kept alive by railway workers. "The individual must be ethnically qualified to hold a certain job, a circumstance which has resulted in the development of a pattern of ethnic job expectations, sponsorship and rejection."[10]

Although there is ethnic association with various jobs and statuses in the hierarchy, it is not seen as such by the workers. The sponsoring of British youth for a job vacancy is usually defined as "pull." Then there is the definition of the work habits of various ethnic groups which are considered reason enough for ethnic restriction. "Indians don't know how to take care of things. Of course there are some white people who don't know, but most Indians don't know how. It happens to anyone who is lazy and shiftless and dirty." The French are not considered capable of doing mechanical work: "Have you ever seen a Frenchman who can handle a car?"

Both French and Indians are defined by the superordinate group as not capable of doing jobs which require mechanical skill. They are thought to be mentally dull and emotionally unstable, which restricts them from any job with responsibility. They are considered capable of doing the more menial, unimportant and lowly-paid jobs. These are the stereotypes maintained by the workers.

Sociological Review, 22 (June 1957), pp. 281-8; W. Wance and R. Butler, "The Effect of Industrial Changes on Occupational 'Inheritance' in Four Pennsylvania Communities," *Social Forces*, 27 (1948), pp. 158-62; W. L. Warner and J. C. Abegglen, *Occupational Mobility in American Business and Industry, 1928-52* (Minneapolis, 1955).

10 O. Collins, "Ethnic Behaviour in Industry," *American Journal of Sociology* (Jan. 1946), p. 293.

NEPOTISM

Nepotism and ethnic sponsorship are characteristic of all communities of single industry. Reference to this pattern suggests that sponsorship provides reasonably good employees, while it discharges an unwritten obligation of the company for loyal service from an employee. It is possible to practice this in a small town because families are all known either personally or by repute: "They know all the families in the town, they know who can do a good job, they know who have had tough breaks, they think they know who has potential, and so on and so on. This method of hiring by knowing the individual and his background is far more important than the actual qualifications which a person might have on paper." Another respondent explained it this way:

> In a small town almost all of these people in the plant have gone to school together, grown up together, met each other constantly in the community, were able to drive or walk to work, went to church together and the sum total of all this meant that they appreciated each other's problems much more than you would ever find in a large city situation. There is a real difference in feeling between people. This made it on the one hand very much easier to do all sorts of things, but on the other it created some difficulties too.
>
> Often the father went and used his influence to get his son into the plant. Often the father would be the foreman and would be sure that the lad got the job. Because the father had been an old and valued employee, sometimes this influenced management to have a son become a foreman, of all things. This certainly affected relationships in the plant.

Nepotism rather than ethnic conspiracy seems to perpetuate the system. This pattern can be disrupted if there is a drastic shift in occupational statuses, or a sudden expansion in job opportunities so that the jobs exceed the candidates. This is described by Carlton: "For the first time, through the scarcity of labour occasioned by the war, the French worker gained access to certain trades, such as paper-making, to the unions, some of which had been developing since the late nineteen thirties, and to the ranks of foremen in areas where the English had earlier established virtual tenure."[11]

11 Richard A. Carlton, "Differential Education in a Bilingual Community," unpublished PhD thesis (University of Toronto, 1967), p. 49.

That nepotism is not unheard of outside small towns is suggested by John Porter in *The Vertical Mosaic.*[12]

TRADE UNIONS

The trade unions provide institutions and organizations that are part of but separate from the company. But within a community of single industry the company is far more important than the trade union. In communities of single industry unions are seldom militant.[13] There are at least four indications of this lack of militancy.

First, although meetings are held according to the constitution, few members attend. "Our union holds a meeting a month but very few go. They don't care. This is our major problem. Everyone says 'Let the executives handle it.' We are lucky if we get five out of 100 at a monthly meeting. Everybody is interested at negotiation time - and that is when we get fed up - because it takes time and work to prepare material for negotiation." This rather sardonic remark by a trade union leader is characteristic of comments made in many communities of single industry.

12 John Porter, *The Vertical Mosaic* (Toronto, 1965).

13 "Seldom militant" does not brush aside seemingly notable exceptions. The bitter, protracted and violent strikes which occurred in and around communities of single industry, part of Canadian folklore, include the woods strikes in Newfoundland and Northern Ontario and the mining strikes in Quebec. The intensity of feeling and the shooting war exemplified in these conflicts suggest one reason why violent and militant conflicts occur so rarely. Imagine interpersonal relationships in an isolated community after a shooting war, when each person's affiliation is known and guilt of murder is rumoured about each protagonist.

Be that as it may, the bloody woods strikes of Newfoundland and Northern Ontario were not local affairs of a community of single industry although much of the conflict took place in and around these communities. In both cases, the issue was economic life and death for the protagonists; at stake was either the dominance of a small full-time efficient woods elite or of a very large part-time group of traditional amateurs earning "cash income" to support a marginal farm way of life. When a traditional way of life is threatened, shot guns appear and are used. All of this had little to do with the mill workers who processed the logs, regardless of their source.

The other notable exception to the general rule in a mining community in Quebec is far too complex to comment on here. See Pierre E. Trudeau, comp., *La Grève de l'amiante* (Montreal, 1956).

Second, the union seldom acts as an independent organization or institution within community affairs. This lack of self-consciousness as a meaningful corporate body is exemplified in the lack of donations to community enterprises or to the building and maintenance of facilities for use of union members or the community at large. In the hundred communities investigated, none had a union-sponsored recreation centre, recreation programme, or courses for adult education. The only dubious exceptions were the union bowling teams which took part in community leagues, and the sponsorship of short courses on union history and duties of the shop steward; these courses were basically sponsored by and originated from national headquarters.

Third, strikes are comparatively few and local strikes or wildcat walk-outs are rare. The loyalty of the men seems to be to their work role, the industry for which they work, and the community in which they live in isolation from the rest of the world. The close interpersonal relationships in the constant interaction within the community seem more important to the individual and his family than any ideological affiliation. Just as the production quota of the industry or unemployment is in the hands of impersonal and unknown national and international forces, the strikes and labour conflicts are linked with impersonal national and international trade union policy. Industrial conflict is not related to neighbours, working companions, and supervisors. There are grievances within industry, but usually these are handled locally and amicably.

If negotiations between workers and management are carried on within the community at all, they are with the aid of resource personnel from national or international headquarters. But even if these are hard fought sessions, the primary relationships within the community predominate over the conference table. As one local union leader stated: "Bargaining is fairly friendly. We all live here all the time. It is pretty hard to be enemies with someone you fish with, golf with and go to church with. This is all forgotten outside."

A fourth indication is that despite theories of elitism, class consciousness, notions of exploitation, and consciousness of self-interest, union leaders and workers in the industry do not use "we-group" terms and certainly never refer to themselves in classical class or working men's language. Nor in all the interviews, whether with wives, husbands, management, or labour, was there any indication of what might be called a "labour vote." "We have a number of labour members on the municipal council but these people are there as individuals and not as labour representatives" or,

> We are not interested in the community as a body – that is as a trade union – we are similar to the company management; our members, like theirs, are actively involved in community affairs but as people, not as representatives of the union. Union members are now active members of the service clubs, board of trade, etc., although for many years there was a line drawn and it was rare that you found a union member as part of one of these groups.

Or as another respondent said, "In all, there doesn't seem to be a definite labour vote – not one that you can count on. Occasionally there is what you might call a labour vote, but it is not at all clear. Actually there is more of a religious vote than a labour vote but this is not clear all the time either." Another respondent said,

> Is there a labour vote? The union is not active in politics as such; a person might get in because he is a union member but this is a very complicated situation. I think it is more that he gets in on religious or other sorts of grounds. Actually, I don't think labour is represented; for one thing, in the union we do not discuss politics. Constitutionally we are not allowed to discuss religion or politics, although we are expected to be citizens and vote.

Or, "We have two unions here but they do not vote politically along labour lines – definitely not. In fact, in many respects, the two unions have antagonistic interests even though they are linked in the same manufacturing process. But neither, in actual fact, vote in a political block." That this is so will come as no surprise to the NDP. Working men, whoever they are, seem to operate as citizens with affiliations within the community neighbourhood, and the family and industry take precedence over ideological notions of trade union vested interests.

Although unions have important functions, they do not seem to be a vital force in the local community. Some other force outside the community is seen to be in control of affairs. Whatever complaints are harboured, the local union does not feel that it can control the larger events.

Some factors that contribute to this phenomenon can be enumerated. It may be remembered that the interviews with management and trade union officials reported in the earlier chapters indicated *common* problems, such as a high level of turnover of personnel. The fact that trade union and management begin their relations in co-operation over a common problem rather than in conflict is not without importance. Second, it is clear that the local manager does not control the general policy guiding his administration any more than the local union leader controls his areas of jurisdiction. Third, as a rule, union jurisdictions are fragmented by craft considerations, so that there is no single union front. Fourth, the greater the extent that both the local manager and the local union leader become involved in their work-a-day associations, and their leisure-time companionships, the more the out-of-town "management," for each, becomes an impersonal "they" policy-maker, who operates with little understanding of local implications. The persistence of the references of local union leaders to their own headquarters as "management" supports this notion. Fifth, mine, mill and smelter towns epitomize masculine work in a male society.[14] This may be important, for Lockwood writes:

> The most highly developed forms of proletarian traditionalism seem to be associated with industries such as mining, docking and ship building: industries which tend to concentrate workers together in solitary communities and to isolate them from the influence of the wider society. Workers in such industries usually have a high degree of job involvement and strong attachments to primary work groups and possess a considerable autonomy from technical and supervisory constraints. Pride in doing "men's work" and a strong sense of shared occupational experiences make for feelings of fraternity and comradeship which are expressed through a distinctive occupational culture. These primary groups of workmates not only provide the elementary units of more extensive class loyalties but work associations also carry over into leisure

14 Goldthorpe and associates suggest that union affiliation does not have to have an ideological base to be strong. Instead union membership may be strictly utilitarian and pecuniary. In such cases affiliation does become somewhat more tenuous. See John H. Goldthorpe, David Lockwood, Frank Bechhofer, and Jennifer Platt, "The Affluent Worker and the Thesis of Embourgeoisement: Some Preliminary Research Findings," in Joseph A. Kahl, ed., *Comparative Perspectives on Stratification: Mexico, Great Britain, Japan* (Boston, 1968), pp. 115-37. See also Elizabeth Bott, *Family and Social Network* (London, 1957), p. 163.

activities, so that workers in these industries usually participate in what are called "occupational communities" ... Workmates are normally leisure-time companions, often neighbours, and not infrequently kinsmen. The existence of such closely-knit cliques of friends, workmates, neighbours and relatives is the hallmark of the traditional working class community. The values expressed through these social networks emphasize mutual aid in everyday life and the obligations to join in the gregarious pattern of leisure, which itself demands the expenditure of time, money, and individual striving "to be different." As a form of social life, this communal sociability has a ritualistic quality, creating a high moral density and reinforcing sentiments of belongingness to a work-dominated collectivity. The isolated and endogamous nature of the community, its predominantly one class population, and low rates of geographical and social mobility, all tend to make it an inward-looking society and to accentuate the sense of cohesion that springs from shared work experiences. (The one-industry town with its dominant occupational community would seem to produce the most distinctive form of proletarian traditionalism ...)

Shaped by occupational solidarities and communal sociability the proletarian social consciousness is centred on an awareness of "us" in contradistinction to "them" who are not part of "us." "Them" are bosses, managers, white collar workers and, ultimately, the public authorities of the larger society. Yet even though these outsiders are remote from the community, their power to influence it is well understood; and those within the community are more conscious of this power because it comes from the outside.[15]

Lockwood may be talking about "community" in the sense of community of interests, but, in this context, the community of single industry is a physical, geographical, demographic, and social en-

15 D. Lockwood, "Sources of Variation in Working Class Images of Society," in Kahl, ed., *Comparative Perspectives on Stratification,* pp. 100-1. In support of his various points, Lockwood cites: C. Kerr and A. Siegel, "The Inter-industry Propensity to Strike: An International Comparison," in A. Kornhauser, R. Dubin, and A. M. Ross, *Industrial Conflict* (London, 1954); University of Liverpool, Department of Social Science, *The Dock Worker* (Liverpool, 1954); N. Dennis, F. Henriques, and C. Slaughter, *Coal is Our Life* (London, 1956); R. Blauner, "Work Satisfaction and Industrial Trends in Modern Society," in W. Galenson and S. M. Lipset, *Labor and Trade Unionism* (New York, 1960).

tity (and consequently a community of interests). When talking about the community of single industry, Canadian style, the "we" is the townsfolk (bosses, supervisors and all) and the "they" are those who command general policy, union and management alike. Because of these and other factors, it is rare that there is open local conflict between union and management, or that unions have great meaning to the employees in the community of single industry.

Robert Alford concludes that class-based voting is lower in Canada than in the United States, Great Britain or Australia. He suggests that regional-ethnic and regional-economic concerns far outweigh any national class-oriented behaviour and work against the emergence of such behaviour.[16] In the case of the community of single industry, the interests have a community-economic base in addition to a regional orientation.

But we have to be cautious. The perceptive comments of Lockwood and Alford, like all broad generalizations, may or may not be valid; if they are valid (and it would be difficult to prove or disprove) do they apply to the Canadian community of single industry? It could be argued that citizens of single industry communities do have a "we" feeling; certainly, in Canada we have many regional "they" expressions incorporated in such terms as "Upper Canada," "down south," "mainlanders," "down east," "hog town," and so on. We might have expected antagonism to be expressed about financial interests beyond the nation, if we had listened to the "ownership of Canada" issue periodically raised by people with an academic interest in economics and political science.

In spite of the public declarations about the taking over of Canadian industry by interests in the USA, and the fact that many mining, pulp and paper, and manufacturing industries found in communities of single industry are known to be owned and controlled by shareholders in USA, no evidence was found to support USA "they" group feelings. There were no spontaneous references to US ownership in any of the 500 interviews; no one seemed concerned about the ownership and control of the industry for which he worked. One of the few rejoinders elicited by a direct question was, "We have a job, we live in this community; the rest is political stuff. It doesn't really matter who they say owns it." Clearly, this complex situation and its implications require far more research.

16 Robert R. Alford, *Party and Society* (Chicago, 1963).

In this chapter we have considered the organization of work in the single industry. The majority of the jobs are learned while working, and require little in the way of educational qualification or formal training; despite this the educational requirements are sometimes artificially inflated. Using Railtown as an illustrative example, we briefly reviewed the hierarchy, noting that the kind of work, the pay, the conditions of work and tradition impart a sense of worth to each job and a status to each employee.

The distribution of ethnic groups among the various levels of the occupational system usually begins by self-selection which in turn depends on cultural factors, time of arrival and historical accidents. The ethnic distribution, once started, is perpetuated by nepotism and ethnic sponsorship, usually informal. Justification, if needed, is found in ethnic stereotypes.

Within the community, upward mobility is based upon seniority for the most part. Upward mobility is sharply limited by barriers of region, specialization, skill, and union affiliation. The positions at the apex of the local industry are filled by officers who transfer from branch to branch. Their stay in the community is usually short.

Finally, the trade unions were considered briefly. Respondents felt that the trade unions, although important, were not crucial or effective forces in the community.

As we have seen, the single industry, because it provides the reason for the existence of the community, has widespread effects upon the population. Not the least of these is the influence that the industry has upon the stratification of the community. In the next chapter, we will consider this stratification.

7

Occupation, stratification and association

In the preceding chapter we considered in some detail the way work is organized in Railtown, and, indirectly, the social stratification of a large part of the community has been described, because the family takes its social status in the community from the position, wage, and prestige of the breadwinner. The position of each breadwinner is quite certain – there is no chance of a carman becoming an engineer – and the community is sufficiently small and isolated that each person knows the occupation of every other and where it fits in the hierarchy. In contrast, in the city, families may buy outward symbols of high status that have little relationship to income or job; a clerk may spend a large proportion of his income on rent and talk of the trust company for which he works, rather than his clerical job. To neighbours who know little about him, he may be accepted as holding a status quite different from that indicated from occupation and salary.

THE SECOND HIERARCHY

Where do shopkeepers, clergy, and teachers fit into the town's social system? Their positions are somewhat indeterminate, because although they have white collar occupations with regular hours, they are dependent on railway workers for their income; they serve, and in doing so, many do not earn as much money as railroad employees. Everyone in Railtown is quite sure that the doctors, the clergy, and perhaps a half a dozen others and their families are "superior." Everyone agrees, too that town labourers are the lowest, far below railroad labourers. Thus, the railroad workers form one hierarchy and non-railroad workers a second, with little evaluation of whether a taxi driver from one pyramid has a higher status than a yardman in the other. Diagrammatically, this structure might appear something like that in Figure 1.[1]

1 Clearly the stratification of Railtown is peculiar to Railtown, and other single-industry railway communities. The railroad engineer and conductor who live in urban areas, for instance, would be ranked differently in relation to other occupations. Railtowners, however, are not operating in a social vacuum. Their evaluation is not unlike that of the Occupational Class Scale developed by Blishen. In his table of occupations ranked and grouped by combined standard scores for income and years of schooling by sex, Canada, 1951, he reports the following scores which are pertinent to Railtown. Class 1: dentists, 82.5; physi-

FIGURE 1 A Representation of the Occupational Order of Railtown

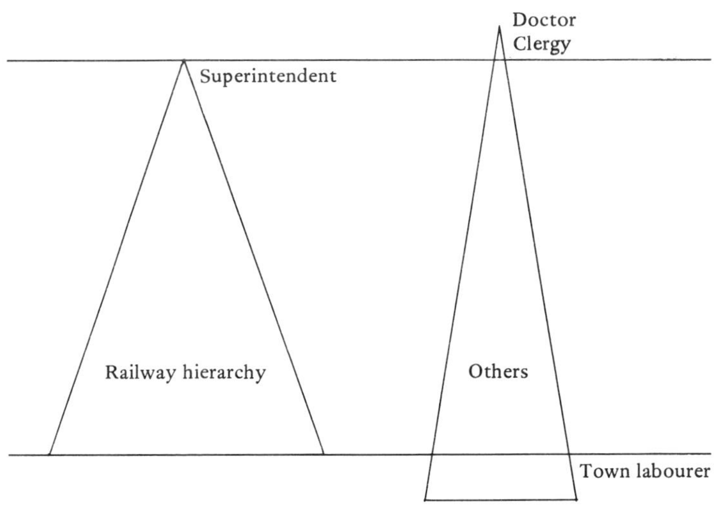

cians and surgeons, 81.2; lawyers, 78.8; school teachers (male), 62.2; clergymen, 61.0. This group constitutes the apex of the stratification structure of the non-railway occupations. Class 2: transportation managers, 60.1; dispatchers, train, 58.5. Class 3: agents, ticket station, 54.3; conductors, railway, 54.1; locomotive engineers, 54.0. This would be the apex of the railroad ranking. Railtowners would not agree on the ranking of ticket agents (relatively, it should be noted that stenographers and typists (54.1) have a score that is higher than conductors and locomotive engineers, and that window decorators (52.3) are in the same class). Class 4: telegraph operators, 51.6; locomotive firemen (apprentice engineers), 51.2; brakemen, railway (apprentice conductors), 51.1; and foremen, transportation, 50.7. Class 5: switchmen and signalmen, 48.2; mechanics, railroad, 47.2. Porters, 44.2; and sectionmen and trackmen, 41.4 (the bottom of the railroad hierarchy), are higher in rank than labourers, 40.8; janitors, 40.0; lumbermen, 37.4; and hunters and trappers, 32.0 (the bottom of the non-railway hierarchy). Considering the educational requirements and educational attainments of railroaders, it is amazing that there is such a close correspondence between the Railtown stratification and a score based upon income and years of schooling. See B. R. Blishen, "The Construction and Use of an Occupational Class Scale," in B. Blishen, F. E. Jones, K. D. Naegele, and J. Porter, *Canadian Society, Sociological Perspectives* (Toronto, 1964), pp. 449-57. In contrast, the railroaders hold a very different position in relation to the other townsfolk, in a more complex community structure such as that of Hanna. For a description of the relationships between business and professional men, farmers from a broad hinterland, and railroaders, see Jean Burnet, *Next Year Country* (Toronto, 1951), especially chap. 6.

The social stratification of the majority in the community is specified when the positions of the workers in the single industry are described. Each position in the industrial hierarchy specifies the amount of authority vested in the occupation, the wage, and the prestige accorded to it. Further, as each wage-earner is employed by the single industry or is dependent upon it, all of these facts are known by every citizen. A second and separate system of ranks is maintained simultaneously; this system incorporates all of the occupations and professions that serve the wage earners in the single industry. This second hierarchy has authority over the first, but it is also dependent upon it and subservient to it. Although few comparisons are made between the two, there is agreement that the apex of the professional hierarchy is "superior" to that of the industrial hierarchy, and that the lower echelons of the non-industrial hierarchy are beneath the lowest range of the industrial. Although the position, wage, and prestige of each wage earner in the industrial hierarchy are known to all citizens, the earnings of many in the non-industrial hierarchy are not known with any precision, and are more difficult to determine.

All citizens work and interact together constantly, so shared implicit definitions emerge. The shared knowledge of wage scales, type of occupation, and authority, rules out status indeterminacy, status pretentions, or the need to gossip to find out how much money someone "is worth." Speculation is limited to success on the stock market, the amount of savings, or the extent to which a family is living beyond its earnings.[2]

Further, the stratification described here is socially meaningful – not an abstract concept. The various classifications of occupation not only have common wage, occupational content, prestige, and authority, but have also common ethnic affiliation, working hours, language, and problems. The wage-earners of each classification and their families associate more closely with each other than with other occupational groupings.

2 See Alick R. Andrews, "Social Crisis and Labour Mobility, A Study of Economic Change in a New Brunswick Railway Community," unpublished MA thesis (University of New Brunswick, 1967), pp. 89-90. The preoccupation with finding out the worth of a person as described by Vidich and Bensman is unnecessary. This is not a community of capitalists and entrepreneurs. A. J. Vidich and J. Bensman, *Small Town in Mass Society* (Garden City, 1960), pp. 43-6.

Although club membership or community office holding and the like may enhance status, such activities do not change it. High status is accorded to the superintendent whether or not he participates in the community institutions; the lowest labourer remains that, despite his club memberships. Railtown, by definition, has not been in existence long enough to produce resident leading families of great wealth and lineage. Similarly in the absence of other systems of stratification such as political and military roles, the effective but simplified system of stratification rests basically upon the sole community industry.

The evaluations of residents suggest that partially differentiated occupational pyramids have developed. As Parsons has pointed out such a structuring of the social (and occupational) system tends to mitigate some of the strains inherent in the single undifferentiated pyramid.[3] This is especially important in a small isolated town where all are explicitly interdependent.

HIERARCHIES IN OTHER ONE-INDUSTRY COMMUNITIES

Railtown is not atypical of railroad communities,[4] and the railroad is not unique among industries. In pulp and paper communities, for instance, there are differentiations made in prestige and salary between woods and mill operations. Within the mill operation, differentiation is made between chief accountant and chief engineer, control superintendent and traffic manager, between the superintendent of maintenance and services and the superintendent of industrial research. These differences, a matter of skills, authority within the work structure and wages, are reflected in the community social prestige, ranking, housing.

In Minetown, the administrative personnel, headed by the general manager and supported by divisional superintendents, have precedence over the miners. Great differentiation is made between the men who work on the surface and underground miners. Once underground, again differentiation is made between those who remove the ore and those who supply the services for them. These men are grouped in categories that, aside from prestige, have meaning in terms

3 T. Parsons, *The Structure of Social Action* (Glencoe, 1949), p. 180.

4 The "running trades" are the "aristocracy" in Railtown; but they are also an elite in Andrews' study in a different province, and Cottrell's study in the United States of America. W. F. Cottrell, *The Railroader* (Palo Alto, 1940).

of social interaction. Each grouping tends to be made up of like categories in terms of educational accomplishment, ethnic background, and aspirations. Those on the same shift tend to associate together – not because of affinity but because they have little choice since their leisure and work hours happen to coincide. Activities in the town depend upon type of work obligation and hours of work. The interlocking social characteristics are suggested by a respondent in a mining community:

> The town has a very definite ... structure. First there is the business and professional group, and they have very little to do with the miners. The only place where the three groups ... all take part is in the Church as an organization. As a result, because of their ethnic background and the appropriate religious affiliation and the type of jobs that they go into, you find that you have certain characteristics of segments of the community, for instance, the labour group is Roman Catholic, the business and professional people are Protestant.

In Milltown, citizens made precise distinctions among the employees in the fabricating plant, research, the power dam, the shipping and other basic service departments. Each department was assigned a rank, and within each department, the position in the hierarchy was taken into account. Another respondent in a manufacturing town noted the same phenomenon:

> Everyone knows what everyone else's work is like, what they do and where they fit. However, we have been able to avoid the worst sins of stratification, mainly because the top echelons are scientists and engineers and they don't really push locally to try to achieve high prestige and high status. This is because they don't have to be recognized on a local level or in the local community. Their level of recognition is on a national and international level through their work.

Robinson states, in summary:

> There is a pattern of social stratification, based on the hierarchical ranking of employees in the company's organization. Social status corresponds closely to the position or job held by the employee in the industrial operation. The fact that almost all the residents are also employees of the same firm eliminates the subtle gradations

> and vagueness of social stratification prevalent in a more open society. Families are easily and rigidly classified according to what position the breadwinner holds with the company.[5]

Clegg notes the relationship between the company structure and community stratification and adds, "This is very evident in many single enterprise economies, because there are no other social hierarchies to diffuse into the community except that of the major enterprise. Your rank in the [company] structure determines your social position in the community. This stratification is reflected in the housing areas."[6]

HORIZONTAL AND VERTICAL MOBILITY

There is one other important implication of the organization of a one-industry town. Although it is possible to move upward in the hierarchy, the transition is usually slow. Promotion depends upon seniority of individuals who are well known, rather than on the impersonal competition of the larger urban centre; promotion proceeds within the department or skill channel which the employee enters, and to which he is relegated for the rest of his working life. So the bulk of the wage-earners remains in particular jobs for much of their lives. Some (depending on the stage of community development) occasionally move upward with some rapidity, but the distance they rise is limited. These limits are set by departmental divisions and ethnic restrictions.

The major barrier to upward mobility arises because the upper levels of the hierarchy operate according to a different principle and within a different flow of personnel. The upper echelons are part of an international, national, or company-wide system, rather than a local and community-bound system. The local manager or superintendent has been moved from another division or plant, and expects to be moved again. He, his wife, and his family are strangers in town;

5 Ira M. Robinson, *New Industrial Towns on Canada's Resource Frontiers,* Department of Georgraphy, University of Chicago, Research Paper no. 73 (Chicago, 1962), p. 84.

6 Edward T. Clegg, "A Regional Planning Analysis of a Single Enterprise Community of Settlements," unpublished MSc thesis (Community and Regional Planning, University of British Columbia, 1958), p. 122.

their loyalties are not bound up in local community affairs, but in the company as a whole and particularly on the next move. Their administrative techniques vary: some do not want to rock the boat, others are sent in to carry out a long overdue shakeup; but these people are not part of the community, and they know it and so do the inhabitants.

The problem is not one of absentee capital, ownership or management, in the sense that Warner discussed in *Yankee City.*[7] The very foundations of communities of single industry are built on absentee ownership and capital, so these communities have never had "leading families" who owned and managed the industry.

The horizontal movement of the upper echelons has a number of important implications for the community. First, there is constant change at the top, and one cannot rely upon the permanence of a particular local version of policy or discipline. Second, whether the changes in personnel are rapid or slow, the supervisor has a feeling of impermanence, and he carries out his duties and commitment to the town as though he were only going to be there for a year. Many executives have been in a community for thirty years, and have lived a life poised above suitcases that never had to be packed. Third, those with the highest wages, the most authority, the greatest influence, and the highest prestige, are the least likely to take initiative and participate in community activities. Thus those to whom most communities look for leadership are, in these cases, likely to be drones, if for no other reason than that it takes some time to learn the local social and political practices. Fourth, those moving up in the local hierarchy see little way of stepping on to this cross current channel of promotion. As a matter of fact, many of the men who move horizontally did arrive at this position by moving vertically within their department, but in a vast national organization, few have the opportunity to make the move. Many who have the opportunity refuse to take it.

Although the railway community experiences this constant shift in the upper supervisory group, railroading is one of the few industries that does not have an additional gulf of educational and professional career differences between the locals and the supervisory personnel.

7 W. L. Warner and J. O. Low, *The Social System of the Modern Factory* (New Haven, 1947). See also the discussion of this in M. R. Stein, *The Eclipse of Community* (New York, 1960), chap. 3.

In other industries, the engineers, scientists and administrators not only have different career lines and different interests and obligations in the local community, but also different levels of education and personal interest.

There is scarcely a respondent, management or worker, who does not spontaneously discuss the differences between the workers, and the engineers, scientists, and administrators. Respondents refer to the phenomenon with different vocabularies and concepts:

> Now it is *possible* to come up through the ranks to supervisory jobs – I have given you some examples – but it turns out, I think, that this will be less and less, and the move will be to develop more and more supervisory people with university training.
>
> The work force on the semi-skilled and unskilled level is drawn almost entirely from the local population. In other words, the local population was used for the main, basic, large proportion of workers; but the necessary specialists are imported.
>
> There is a certain amount of turnover here [at the supervisory level] in part because we have men who are here for training purposes. There is quite a turnover, because although engineers all earn a reasonably good salary, there are few highly paid jobs; engineers find they can move from here to jobs involving much more money.
>
> There is a power élite as there is in any community, and they live a fairly segregated life on a point of land, a residential area; you can have contact with these people through the officials of the company. Most of them are officials and professional people.
>
> English professional and administrative mill employees were recruited from an older group. Many came with families already established, sent their children to the schools in the south, where the latter eventually looked for employment, and the parents in due course retired or transferred out of the north.

SOCIAL IMPLICATIONS OF HORIZONTAL MOBILITY

Some of the implications noted by respondents include the lack of ties with the community on the part of engineers. This means that management personnel seldom own real estate and become part of the community, although they might remain in the community for life:

> A great number of the engineers and supervisory staff never do buy their own homes because they feel that they may be moved at any time, and that their stay here is temporary at the best. Most of the homeowners are at the next level – people who feel that they now have risen as far as they are able to and will retire from that position. I kick myself now because I have not bought a home. I always felt that I might be moved, but it has not turned out that way.

The reluctance to buy is more than the feeling of being temporary in a community of single industry:

> One of the problems of this place is the difficulty of getting the invested money back if I am transferred. For instance, our neighbours a few doors down have been transferred to an urban area. He has looked around there, and the sort of accommodation he has here is worth $40,000. This, of course, is the sort of money he hasn't got and he is trying to choose between a $40,000 house he can't afford and inadequate housing that he can afford. Meanwhile he is attempting to sell his own house here, and is running into real difficulties on down payment as he is moving away and needs capital to reinvest in some sort of house. He wants a $6000 down payment; however, all the interested parties who have come to look at the house have talked in terms of $2000 and this isn't very much. It means a second mortgage and, all in all, he is caught in a difficult position. This would be the sort of position that any of us would be in, if and when we wanted to sell and move.

Horizontal mobility is reflected in the reluctance of individuals to invest in community institutions; this is considered a problem in many of these communities:

> You've grown up in this town – it is your home town. No matter how long management people stay here, they are only here temporarily – even though they have been here for a long period. Most of them did not realize that they were going to stay as long as they have – but regardless, they say they are from Toronto, Montreal, or where ever it is – but never from here: it never becomes home town. If you are only here temporarily, if you do not have roots, if you do not belong, you are not willing to build a church because it is not your church. You are not willing to put a lot of money into a golf club because you will not be here in 20 years to use it.

After 25 or 30 years, when it is a community, you may be able to get people interested and vital, because it becomes a home community. If you were in a town two months, and someone came to your door and asked for $50 for a beautiful new recreation centre, you would say "no" and I would too. It would take four years to build, and by that time, you might have left, and your children would probably never use the place. Of course the same thing goes on here.

The following quotation gives one man's observations of how the stratification system, the differences in ethnic background, language and religion are worked out in personal relationships within Milltown:

Community interest of the people is dangerously low. I think that the basic reason that men don't take a more active part in civic enterprises in this city is that they are afraid of their bosses or of superiors who might be on the same board with them on some community project. They are afraid that if they argue with their boss or superior it will carry over into the work situation. And it is almost impossible to have civic boards or committees operate in this town without having some clash of rank within the job situation.

The Chamber of Commerce is a good example of that. There you have a good cross-section, not of local business men but rather of men in the company. Plant class tells here too. Involuntary as it may be, there is still conscious or unconscious class distinction. A better example is the Rotary. Here we had all the more important people from the plant – the general manager, the assistant general manager, myself, and some of the others were in it. We had our dinners but they were always very solemn affairs. Rotary is supposed to bring together people in fellowship, but there it was always "Mr" when speaking to the top men. There was that class distinction. No one was at ease. It was even worse for the French Canadians there. They had no "vacation" from English in the evening. They still had to keep speaking English. When the church asked us to withdraw we did, and it folded not long after that. I think the worst part about it though was seeing the same faces all evening after seeing them all day.

The trouble now is that the brains of the community are in the plant; the management people consider themselves only part of the passing parade and they won't lead the people. They simply consider themselves glorified transients with no feeling of public responsibility. They, and the rest of the city do have a public consciousness as far as charity goes. They will give unsparingly to any good cause, which leads me to believe that they could be made to do many other things besides just sitting around waiting to be transferred out of here. They waste five or ten years simply because they haven't been prodded enough. I'm going to try to change that.

TIME

The sole industry influences the work of the employees and their families, but it also affects time, which has social implications for each family and those with whom it associates. The nature of the industries characteristic of a one-industry town dictates either a continuous process or several shifts. Railroading, for instance, is a continuous process, twenty-four hours a day, three hundred and sixty-five days of the year; pulp and paper mills, smelting processes and a great deal of manufacturing are carried on as continuous processes; mines maintain either two or three shifts. The system of work allocation controls the distribution of time given to informal, formal and family relationships. In this way, the work institution influences the patterns and rhythm of community life.

Probably the most eccentric hours are maintained by the running trades in the railway industry. Regularly scheduled trains run at various hours of the day and night, and when there is considerable traffic, the hours at which the engineer, fireman, conductor, and trainman may be called for work may fluctuate widely. Thus one member of the running trades may return from a "trip" (to the next divisional point and back), get some sleep, and be called out again. The anticipation and prediction of work hours, in fact, may take up a great deal of the leisure time of these men as they go over to the "board" to see where their name comes in the list of rotating turns. Informal tips on the number of trains expected aid them to assess the probable timing of their next call. In days gone by, it was not unusual for the call boy to enter the church during service to call one of the parishioners for work duty.

A great deal of time is spent in organizing strategy in preparation for some special event. The individual can "lay off" a trip, or delay the celebration until the end of the month, when he might have a week off, having completed his month's mileage allotment. The planning of Christmas dinner, whether in the morning or afternoon, or on Christmas Eve or Boxing Day, depends on prediction of where the husband will be and at what time, for trains run on Christmas Day and so a great number of men must be at work.

The uncertainty of hours has a number of implications which affect the interpersonal relationships of both the man and his family. Working hours influence the relationships within the family and between the family and formal institutions, as well as the informal, more casual relationships.

The running trades keep eccentric hours, but the patterns of daily life maintained by their families have regular and different schedules. The school, the shops, churches, and formal organizations maintain traditional hours; leisure time activities take place in the evening and most of the populace sleeps at night. Meals are eaten in the morning, at noon and in late afternoon. The railroader is not only out of phase with the rest of the community, but he is also on a different schedule from the rest of his household.

Children at school, and a father and son working in the running trades present complex problems to the homemaker if she conscientiously prepares meals and packs lunches for all. Various other family roles are disrupted; regularized sex relationships are often disrupted; ordinary family activities are often curtailed because the breadwinner is sleeping during the day; the role of father is often restricted, leaving much more responsibility with the mother; family meals and ceremonials, often important to the social cohesion of the family, are sporadic; everyone's sleep is often disrupted by an early morning summons to work. Often there are physiological and psychological repercussions accompanying the uncertainty of time, and the difficulty of maintaining close family relationships.

WORK SCHEDULE AND ASSOCIATIONS

Meetings of the institutions of the town, Home and School Association, clubs and lodges, bowling and curling clubs, hockey games, and Church services are all held at regular hours. Participation of the breadwinner in these activities is considerably curtailed, for if he is not at work he may be awaiting a call to go to work, or sleeping after finishing work. This affects the membership and participation of railroaders in many associations, for it is unsatisfactory if some or all committee members are absent from meetings. The work schedule raises insurmountable problems for coaching a team or supervising a scout troop. It is costly to "lay off" a trip in order to participate in the responsibilities of one of the local institutions. This means that the railroader is often reluctant to run for public office. The institutions have fewer people upon whom they are able to call; it is not surprising that a larger than expected proportion of offices are filled by tradesmen, storekeepers and those railway workers such as shop tradesmen, whose work hours coincide with the regular business day.

The curtailment of formal activities affects the wife almost as much as her husband. Her participation is severely restricted when the children are young, and, without babysitters, it is as unpredictable as that of her husband. Activities requiring an escort are even more severely restricted. Work patterns, then, restrict the formal participation patterns of both husband and wife. The children have more freedom, but they can seldom expect both parents to attend a sports event, or a musical or dramatic performance, or look forward to weekends with all members of the family at the cottage.

WORK SCHEDULE AND INFORMAL RELATIONSHIPS

Informal relationships – the visiting of friends and neighbours – are only slightly less curtailed. In his off hours, the railroader often spends a few hours "over town" on main street, when he can stop and chat with other townspeople. There is a tendency however to associate with those who share the same work, the same vocabulary and problems. The lack of a predictable shift means that for long periods it is often impossible to spend an evening with close friends in the same occupations. A respondent reported an attempt to organize a date with another couple for an evening of bridge, and it was a month and a half until the two men were free during the same evening, so that the four could get together.

The uncertainty of working hours provides wives with an important topic of conversation. After the weather has been discussed, each wife reports on the hour her husband was called to work and what trip he is on and when he expects to return. During daylight hours at least, wives with small children are able to visit each other, shop together and talk over common problems, plans, and keep each other abreast of the news of the town. The play world of the children is little affected by the work time patterns except for the amount of permissible noise during the father's eccentric sleep periods.

TIME AND WORK

For railroaders, time takes on an additional significance; except for broadcasting and newspaper deadlines, there are probably few occupations that demand such precision. Express, local, special, freight, excursion and construction trains move up and down the lines, leaving the same stations and utilizing the same switches within a few minutes of one another. Speed, safety and efficiency depend upon punctuality. Cottrell noted: "A delay of thirty seconds in leaving a terminal calls for explanation; a delay of five minutes means an investigation; and one of a half-hour gives apoplexy to every officer from the superintendent to the lowest foreman."[8] All households try to keep their clocks at the correct time; the worker must be at his post at the exact time, if not before; during working hours exact time is the master of his every move. The characteristic gesture of the railroader is the removal of his large pocket watch to check the time.

Householders are aided and abetted in their quest for punctuality by the railway itself. Regular watch inspection is mandatory for members of the running trades. Citizens of railway towns are made aware of the time regularly by a series of whistles blown during the day. These whistles regulate the working day of those who work on regular day shifts in the railway shops and at other jobs with regular hours. Andrews describes this, in his study of a railway town:

> The institutionalized whistle calling men to work had always been part of the life of each person and home in the community. It served as a town clock, regulating meals as well as working hours. The number of whistles per day totalled nine, each with its own meaning: 7.00 am – wake up; 7.45 – leave home; 7.57 – ready for work; 8.00 – work commenced; 12.00 pm – lunch; 12.45 – leave home; 12.57 – ready for work; 1.00 – work commenced; 5.00 – final whistle, work day over. The steam whistle also served the

8 Cottrell, *The Railroader*, p. 61.

> community in times of distress as a fire alarm, reporting a person lost, or to give notice of a [train] wreck, which was four long blows at ten-second intervals.[9]

Although this might appear to be regimentation, it was not regarded as such. Time and the reminders of time were such an integral part of the lives of all citizens that the old steam whistle was regarded with affection rather than resentment: "The old steam whistle disappeared after the introduction of the diesels, but people retain fond memories of it. A new kind of whistle with another kind of tone has replaced it, but this the people regard with disdain. 'That new whistle they got is not half the one the steam whistle was. That one would really rattle the windows.'"[10]

SHIFT WORK

The influence of railway work, particularly that of the railway running trades upon the lives and the social interaction of the townspeople, is unusual and extreme in that a proportion of the community population maintains irregular working hours. Time becomes extremely important in other communities of single industry because, although a more regular rhythm is maintained, continuous production forces a proportion of the population to be at work at all times in the more traditional shift work.

Although the basic industries maintain shift work, the details of the arrangements vary somewhat. Most industries carry out continuous production, in three shifts; some, notably mines, maintain two shifts, sometimes with a third shift of a small work-force for clean-up and maintenance. In some communities each man works on a fixed shift. Others rotate, which requires each man to take his turn at each shift, with a larger force of clerical workers maintaining traditional working hours. The shift is usually a weekly one, but may be rotated every two weeks, or each month.

Whatever the particular arrangement, the working times impose restrictions upon the activities of the men and their families, and this in turn influences the institutions of the community. Whether work is organized as a permanent shift or a rotating one, the men find that

9 Andrews, "Social Crisis and Labour Mobility," p. 70.
10 *Ibid.*, p. 71.

their working and leisure time companions are the same, because there is no opportunity to associate with the men on the opposite shift.[11]

Ignoring the physiological and psychological consequences of shift work, each arrangement imposes a certain pattern. In the rotating shift, the family tends to plan, several weeks ahead, appropriate activities for each type of shift. If the man is on a fixed shift, the significance of the time restriction depends upon the particular shift on which he finds himself. On the day shift, he can participate in the community activities; on the evening shift, he associates with a group who are cut off from the great bulk of the community voluntary associations, meetings, entertainment, organized recreation, and leisure time activities. The significance of shift work[12] depends upon the age, marital status, and interests of the individual.

SOCIAL IMPLICATIONS OF SHIFT WORK

Although findings about the effects of shift work are basically the same the world over, in one sense, their significance for the life of the individual and the community are greatly accentuated in the smaller community. The individual is much more restricted in the types of recreation, restaurants and companions available to him than are people in a large urban area. The community of single industry is not large enough to maintain leisure time or even service facilities for twenty-four hours each day. Anyone who has attempted to buy a cup of coffee in a restaurant after midnight in a community of ten or fifteen thousand has convincing proof of this. One exception to this general rule is found in the company-sponsored recreation centre which caters to the various working hours of the men by scheduling such things as bowling, hockey, and restaurant services twenty-four hours a day; these exceptions are few, for such services seem to be

11 This fact becomes evident to the men themselves after, for instance, a mining accident in which working companions are killed. These same men had been the owners of neighbouring summer cottages and so the deaths affected both close working partners and leisure time companions.

12 The fuller and more detailed implications of shift work itself have been discussed in Paul E. Mott, Floyd C. Mann, Quin McLoughlin, and Donald P. Warwick, *Shift Work, The Social, Psychological and Physical Consequences* (Ann Arbor, 1965). See also J. H. Downie, *Some Social and Industrial Implications of Shift Work* (London, 1963).

maintained only in the early stages of the community's development, when single men are in the majority.

From the community point of view, institutions, clubs and associations are not able to call upon a large proportion of the population to fill particular positions and offices. Men on a fixed night shift are removed completely from activities; those who are on rotating shift are unable to attend meetings regularly. The work schedule reduces the extent of community participation, places a heavy burden on a few people and effectively concentrates the locus of power and influence upon a few in the community.

Discussion has centred upon the formal structure. Workers in one-industry towns, as everywhere, make special arrangements with fellow workers to miss a shift, to work a double shift, to trade days off and make other arrangements for special occasions; as a result, there is some flexibility to the arrangements.

Many workers and their families do not like shift work, but some find it fits their individual interests. The majority consider that it is an integral part of the work situation and accept it with fatalism and resignation.[13]

In this chapter, then, we have described the stratification of the population of single-industry communities in terms of the position held by the breadwinner within the sole industry. A second stratification system parallels the first, incorporating the professions and the non-industrial jobs held by those who provide institutional services for the industrial workers. The stratification system is in a sense prefabricated by the framework of the occupational hierarchy.

Two other characteristics were noted, and the impact of these were traced. The vertical and horizontal mobility patterns were seen as affecting the social interaction and community commitment within the community. The original differentiation based upon work, prestige and ethnic group was further accentuated by the influence of industrial time requirements. Shift work, and other variations on time allotment brought about differential association and affected opportunities to participate in community groups and associations. As we shall see in chapter 13 these patterns are somewhat modified by another variable, religion.

This, then is the structure of the community of single industry. In the next chapter we consider the interpersonal relationships that are carried on within this stratification system.

13 See Mott, *et al.*, *Shift Work*, p. 24.

8

Interpersonal relationships

During the stages of construction, recruitment, and transition, social interaction is fleeting and uncertain because no one is sure that he will remain in the community for any length of time. Once the community has reached the stage of maturity, however, patterned and distinctive social relationships appear among the permanent residents. The distinctiveness of these relationships arises from the common place of work and the common, small community base. People meet often, and unlike situations in which they work in one setting and live in another, information garnered from repetitive meetings is meaningful for and pertinent to all members of the family. Further, the more people interact, the more information is exchanged, the more values are shared and the more definitions of the situation become standardized. This means that most human encounters carried on by each member of the family is meaningful.

MALES

The majority of the males work for the company, and so during the course of their daily work they have many opportunities for informal chats. In Minetown the wash-house at the mine was a focal point of interchange of news and gossip for the community. Joking, horseplay, and exchange of information absorbed something like five hours of the miners' life each day, considering the change of clothes period in the wash house, the checking into the mine, the long journey to the coal face, the intermittent periods of enforced idleness in the mine, the long journey out of the mine, the checking out, and the period of undressing, showering, and dressing at the end of the shift. Obviously this was not the type of community in which the husbands returned from scattered jobs to hear news from their wives; rather the men as collectors and distributors of news in the wash-house went home and passed it on to their wives.

Minetown is atypical in the sense that few industries are built around a wash-house. But Railtown has its "call board" and its round house, not to mention the station where railway employees congregate; Milltown has its lunch rooms and rest rooms. All industries bring men together, and during their work, at their lunch break, travelling to and from work, the social interaction builds simultaneously interpersonal knowledge and general information. Wherever people meet, exchanges are commonplace, and their particular significance in the smaller community is the continual interaction day after day, year after year, and the relevance of the information exchanged. People in small communities have great knowledge of fellow citizens and this is particularly characteristic of the isolated one-industry town.

Information is relevant to the wife and children because they know the people involved and their wives and children. Gossip and teasing exchanged by males at work may be quite different from that exchanged by their wives; nevertheless, the news is of interest to the wives: "Talking to Bill – he says that Susie has had a miserable cold for a month – can't seem to shake it." "Oh, I wondered why I had not seen her lately."

FEMALES

Wives are generally credited with specializing in socio-emotional aspects of family life.[1] They are usually responsible for "keeping in touch" with the wives of friends; through shopping expeditions, they maintain exchanges with other mothers during the child-rearing period; during these activities wives pass along and collect a great deal of information. An article on a miner's family suggested the routine of one miner's wife:

> Almost everyone she meets in [the community] calls, "Hi, Rose," and many stop for a chat. People know Rose because she is on the [community] Ladies' Softball Team, is secretary of the bowling league, and teaches at the United Church Sunday School. On pay night she and Porky [husband] go with friends to the Rose Room of the [community] Hotel for cocktails and to listen to the electric organ. On Saturday nights they attend dances at the Union Hall, and every other week, while Porky is on night shift, a teenager stays with the Wheatley children and Rose sells tickets at the Roxy, [the community's] movie theatre ... "Sometimes I take my ironing next door to Pat MacRae's and watch TV with her" ... Other days she makes a tour of the neighbourhood, drinking coffee with friends; or they come to her kitchen to chat.[2]

1 See T. Parsons and R. F. Bales, *Family, Socialization and Interaction Process* (Glencoe, 1960), p. 3. Note the comments in Center for Settlement Studies, University of Manitoba, *Proceedings – Symposium on Resource Frontier Communities, December 16, 1968* (Winnipeg, 1968).

2 Edna Staebler, "Miner's Wife," *Chatelaine* (March 1962), p. 78.

Whether talking over the back fence, drinking tea in the kitchen, shopping, attending meetings, or talking on the telephone, norms are reinforced; definitions of the situation are shared – whether the weather, the single industry, or the latest birth in town – and information is passed from person to person. Some information comes from other wives, other news has been gleaned from husbands.

None of this news is irrelevant or seen as idle gossip by the male. For the husband, views on current issues and scraps of information help to account for the behaviour of a supervisor, a colleague, or subordinate. Other news is added to a growing fund of information about some social mystery which intrigues the wife or indeed the entire family.

CHILDREN

Children are carriers of news not normally passed from adult to adult, as any teacher in the junior grades is well aware. Many teachers give younger children the opportunity to share items of importance with the rest of their class, and many revealing pieces of information about family life are divulged. These are recounted at the meal table by each class mate. "Janie Black says her brother is getting married," or "Mr Brown is going to get promoted," or "Milley's mother is going to England next summer," or "Jimmy White is going to have a baby brother."

While this information is considered unreliable, it is then channelled through interaction networks, as unconfirmed information, "I don't know how true it is, but I *heard* ..."; and sooner or later the story returns confirmed, unconfirmed, or indeterminate.

Children have access to other people's homes in a way that their parents seldom have. Information about the house, the playroom, and the inhabitants of the house, not to mention the host's behaviour toward the child, is passed on.

CLUBS AND ASSOCIATIONS

There are many opportunities for face-to-face contacts in the clubs and lodges. In Minetown, for instance, there were eight fraternal lodges with their female counterparts, four mens' social clubs and three service clubs where liquor was sold. Primarily for the women there were church clubs, IODE, and organizations such as the Red Cross, Cancer Unit, Hospital Auxiliary, Mental Health Association, and St John's Ambulance Association, and these provided other opportunities for interaction and communication. There were three Home and School Associations. For the youth of the town there were the usual guides, scouts, cadets, and allied youth organizations in addition to a teenage dance each week. For adults there was also a weekly public dance. Beside the regular meetings of these organizations, some clubs had weekly bingo and card parties while others held regularly scheduled seasonal events which were open to the public. All these organizations provided many opportunities for face-to-face contacts, and in addition most of the population met in religious groupings once a week.

In a small community memberships of these clubs frequently overlap so that the network of interaction channels of communication is dovetailed. Both confirmed and unconfirmed news run the chance of being distilled, redefined, elaborated, and distorted many times from source to end.

In addition to this, of course, there are informal evenings among intimate friends. In the mining family, for instance, "In one corner is a round table where every week Porky and his pals play poker all Friday night and all day Saturday ... Joyce and Bill Boychuk, the Hogeans, MacRaes or Pollards – the men all development miners – often drop in to talk about various things."[3]

COMMUNICATION NETWORKS

In small single-industry communities the very structure of the community forces people to gather in the heart of the community in order to carry out the basic necessities of life. To pick up mail, to post letters, to shop, to take part in recreation, means going to the heart of the community because there are no subcentres. Each individual meets many others at one time or another in the daily round. Over time, citizens develop a nodding acquaintance with one another, and an intimate knowledge of many; a stranger in the community is conspicuous.

3 *Ibid.*, p. 80.

Citizens of communities of single industry are used to living within a web of primary relationships,[4] where walking down the street is an experience of personally greeting individuals they meet – knowing the person, his family, parents, loves, failures, and peculiarities. Each purchase or transaction is a relationship with a neighbour. To walk in the street of an urban centre with no one stopping to say "hello" or ever thinking or caring for the other is a bewildering experience for one who passes his life in a small community. "We are all very neighbourly. There is no discrimination here – our neighbours might be any race or colour or religion." Citizens rally to help when someone is in distress.

> If somebody is burned out, the whole community rallies around; it is a very neighbourly community. If anybody is in distress of any sort the people hear about it and do something about it. In fact, a lot of them go a long way out of their way to help someone else. By and large, every family is looked after by its friends and neighbours without community assistance as such.

It is in this setting that many ceremonies become community concerns rather than those of the individual or family. Although the entire community may not be involved, most of the people have knowledge of, and a great number play some active part in, the celebration of engagements and marriages. These are symbolized by attendance at showers, stag parties, and marriage ceremonies, as well as in the giving of gifts. Similarly, there is community curiosity about careers, and great interest in births. Concern at time of bereavement is symbolized by visits to the family, offerings of baking and assistance and the giving of flowers. It is rare in a one-industry community to find a ceremony, whether the celebration of a marriage or the final respects to the dead, that is not widely attended. A management engineer new to the community stated: "As far as the community itself is concerned, the people seem to be very happy. They are friendly and have taken us very much into their groups. This was far beyond our expectations. We did not expect to get kicked out, but we did not expect the people to be so friendly."

4 "Primary relationships" is used as a short term for the longer and more accurate statement that the relationships are closer to the ideal primary relationship than they are to the ideal secondary relationship at the other end of the continuum.

This round of leisure activity would describe fully the life of many urban dwellers as well as that of small town dwellers, except for the important difference that the people who share leisure in towns also share work, prayer, shopping, and life. Andrews describes the same phenomenon this way:

> The process of son following father in a particular job reinforced the image of the railway as a personalized, family-sustaining type of institution. Everyone who worked at the [railway] was a relative, a friend, a neighbour, in any case, one knew where the other fellow came from and where he had worked elsewhere. The same person, at whose side you worked all day, was at the lodge meeting that night, or "having a beer at the Legion" or buying his groceries at the same store. He even had a similar car, wore similar working clothes and, chances were, had a similar type of house.[5]

The descriptions of interpersonal relationships in the community of single industry provided by respondents suggests the "local influentials" described by Merton, "... *their influence rests on an elaborate network of personal relationships.* In a formula which at once simplifies and highlights the essential fact, we can say: *the influence of local influentials rests not so much on what they know but on whom they know.*"[6] To which it might be appropriate to add – *and what they know about whom.*

This continuing interaction has a number of implications, First, the frequency of interaction in an isolated world leads to a high level of shared knowledge, expectations, and norms. These common definitions have to be taken into account by the participants. A second implication is the high degree of personalization of relationships; the shared knowledge and the continuing biography make it difficult to treat parishioners, work-mates, or superiors impersonally. A third characteristic is the high level of observability – some have likened the small community to a goldfish bowl.

Previously, we discussed the informal way in which nepotism was carried out in the single industry. The industry will be considered further in terms of recruitment, patterned expectations, family relations within industry, discipline and personal discretionary power.

5 Alick Andrews, "Social Crisis and Labour Mobility, A Study of Economic and Social Change in a New Brunswick Railway Community," unpublished MA thesis (University of New Brunswick, 1967), pp. 100-1.

6 R. K. Merton, *Social Theory and Social Structure* (Glencoe, 1958), p. 400.

RECRUITMENT INTO INDUSTRY

The citizen knows that each person he meets is known by his habits, education, parents, and individual idiosyncrasies, and, more important, that these are taken into account. It makes a difference if you are Joe's son and that Joe is a good honest and reliable workman, a pillar of the church, and that you are assumed to be a chip off the old block, understood because of the totality of your behaviour and background. It is, as we have seen, under these conditions that respondents obtained jobs in the industry:

> I thought I'd like to earn my own way. My father was in the army [World War II] and I left school when I was in grade six. I was very young, not quite fourteen years old when I went to work. There didn't seem to be any trouble. They gave me the job. Of course, I lied – they asked me if I was sixteen and I said I was, although I didn't look anywhere near that; but they gave the job to me.

As we have seen in Chapter 7, informal qualifications for particular jobs are far more important than formal ones. In this case no birth certificates, no grade 8 certificates, and no formal evidence enters the contract. It was enough to know that the father was in the army, the mother was a "good woman" and the kid was "steady" and hard working.

In a single-industry community the company recruits, but recruitment is a two-way process. The company takes on employees but the employees take on the company. There are implicit obligations on both sides which go beyond the relationships usually associated with employment. One manager who moved from a plant in an urban area to a plant in a community of single industry noted:

> Differences between small towns and city work forces often show up in the absentee pattern and sickness incidence of an employee. In a small town you find much less absenteeism than in a large centre. But the small town slows people down. In the city people are more alert and productive. This can be offset; it is possible to have the machines set a pace. In a small town there is more understanding; the company plays a bigger role in people's lives.

SOCIAL EXPECTATIONS

Mutual expectations between people and between employees and employers become habitual. As we have seen even the ethnic character of the community tends to be preserved. Patterns of behaviour become stabilized and people are ambivalent about the community becoming diversified with additional industry and population. This was expressed by an executive who had moved from an urban heterogeneous work situation to that of a single-industry community. His comments were:

> At first I couldn't help thinking that you can get very comfortable here, very contented. Frankly you get to the point where you think that while you want new industry in here, you don't want to spoil "the land of milk and honey." You know that you might just get this basic Anglo-Saxon population changed if you get too much big industry in here, so you have to be careful. Mind you this tends to make you too damn secure; you can be this way in industry and it's not too good – but I don't know – I think that industrial competition keeps us from being too static. I suppose you can have problems with this when there is too much security in a plant. You know we have a very long term employment record. The workers get just as settled in and cosy as we do I guess. This can present some problems. There is a great deal of trouble when you bring in a new person to do certain skilled jobs, when one cannot find the proper personnel among the employees in the plant. But we seem to be able to produce pretty well. Maybe there would be more incentive if we were all not quite so sensible.

INDUSTRY AND THE FAMILY

Relationships at work become primary and often familistic in character. For instance, one executive of a mill that is part of a large complex stated: "But the large percentage of employees is local family labour trained in the family mill, as it were." Another person in an industry which had continued for almost a century in one community said:

> Within our organization practically all the labour force comes from the immediate community and the heads of the department and administrative staff are 95 per cent local people. Many of the workers have been here for three generations in the plant; actually rather than discouraging this we have the family ties preference as far as employees are concerned; this tends to sound paternalistic and there might be a tendency toward paternalism, but we think we have countered most of the difficulties that might be involved. We have little trouble with several members of the same family working in the same department at the business. This has never been a problem and all the years here we have only known of one department that was affected by this problem and this was not too serious.

This phenomenon of employing many members of the same family is not restricted to small firms. The same practices are found in large manufacturing concerns with a branch plant in a community of single industry.

> Now to many people our company would seem rather peculiar. They would say that there are too many family interconnections within the plant - there are too many brothers in one department. Actually if we didn't have this sort of thing we probably wouldn't have too many employees because people work as families. The other day it was brought to our attention that we had twelve brothers with 250 years' service or something like that within one of our departments.

INDUSTRIAL DISCIPLINE

These primary relationships within the single industry have benefits, but also have costs. It is difficult to enforce impersonal and rational industrial discipline when relationships are warm and personal. In one large industry, for example, the problem of industrial discipline seemed to involve the blueberry, but actually it was concerned with family relationships:

> The disciplining and the adapting of the men of the area to industrialization had been quite a problem. Even as few as six years ago we would have a tremendous loss of personnel during the summer.

> We would have 300 or 400 men all leaving in the late summer to go to pick blueberries. It seems odd that they would try to make money picking blueberries, but they would have a partial holiday – they would have a tent and their wives and children with them, combining a holiday with blueberry picking. At the same time they would make quite a bit of money in a short time doing this.

Lack of industrial discipline, the bane of industry in underdeveloped countries, is not uncommon in Canada. For instance one industry found great difficulties in keeping shift work operating seven days a week, but slowly, work arrangements affected family patterns:

> Still in French Canada family life is the most important thing. But industrial life has broken this down considerably too. All throughout this area on a Sunday the old folks probably have twenty visitors: all the brothers and sisters and cousins and all the rest of the relations descend upon them, and woe betide the household who doesn't have a food supply for the group. This is an old tradition and men are terribly concerned and terribly interested in the accomplishments and the life of their cousins and their brothers and so on. Industrialization has reduced the number of opportunities to do this sort of thing; when you [the industry] work a seven day week, you just haven't the time and the inclination to follow up these sorts of relationships.

When departments include sets of family relationships in addition to sets of work relationships there are problems in distinguishing between family and work obligations. One respondent noted these conflicts when he said:

> One major difficulty is to find a good foreman. The main reason here is that in this community everyone lives together and if someone is in charge of his wife's brother or someone else there are personal relationships set up so that they hate to be tough. This means that you have reluctance on the part of the lower levels of management to discipline the work force or to insist that a good job be done.

Therefore the family intrudes into the plant; but these relations are reciprocal for the industry intrudes into the family. As a result, there is an integration of the families in the community, each maintaining mutual obligations. This was well expressed by an informant:

> I am very glad that I was not raised here. There are two or three hundred young men who have grown up here, who are accustomed to be snugly content within the family womb – they think they have a right to have a job, they have a right to have a living in the town. Even though there are no jobs available for them, they wait around. I think that most of the trouble that we are having at the moment is the cumulative effect of paternalism. Paternalism also encourages nepotism – here we have a segment of privileged people who live in this community. In the communities around us there are people who are also employees of the company but who look upon the youth of this community with loathing. This is understandable from their point of view, because the people here are spoiled children.

Personal knowledge can introduce strains of another kind into interpersonal relationships. If familiarity leads to disdain rather than to affection it becomes next to impossible to withdraw contact at work or play. One respondent, for instance, described his boss in the following way:

> In my estimation he is a two-timing, insincere, suave, oily, greasy, politician. Somebody has to handle the politics of the company and he is it. He is not well liked and I don't think he is very efficient nor is he overly smart. My impression is that he has bungled badly and tends to fumble around in his policy quite often, getting into more difficulty than he needs to and then once he gets into difficulty, then there is a lot of hullabaloo before he gets out.

Despite this attitude, the respondent was obliged to associate with his boss in activities on and off the job, except in informal friendship groups.

PERSONAL DISCRETIONARY POWER IN INDUSTRY

These personal relationships when introduced into the plant add further responsibilities to the management. Problems of discretion and compassion, usually dealt with through impersonal rules and regulations, become personal discretionary problems faced by individuals:

> We do have some trouble with the older workers. It depends a little bit on the section they work in – some are not able to continue with their work. We are able to move them to other occupations without too much trouble. We had one man who was having a great deal of trouble with his back, and he was 64½. Well, we thought he should stick it out until his pension, so he moved into a reasonable job – he is an elevator operator and this doesn't take any physical effort. Now he is 65 at the end of October and he has applied for a six-month extension – so this is the kind of thing we tend to do.
>
> But, on the other hand, the introduction of new machinery also raises problems. We have a new machine which involves a new technique and is very fast; the men are afraid of it. Actually it is a pushbutton control – very little effort is needed here – but if something goes wrong and if the operator pushes all the buttons together it fouls up the machine. Now this has been going on for six months, and it is raising a real question as to whether he will ever learn this machine – it looks as if it will take a couple of years, if he ever does. To remove him – what would we do with him? This is under discussion at the moment.

In the preceding chapter we noted that the structure and work of the single industry deeply affected the community at large. The position of the breadwinner and his family in the stratification system was established throughout the industry along with the appropriate level of work and status accorded to each ethnic group in the community. In this chapter we have noted that family life and local values intrude upon the industry. Considerations of nepotism, gossip and beliefs, which are supposed to have so little part in the rational structure of modern mass-production, affect the interpersonal relationships and the very structure of the industry. The two worlds interpenetrate; in any community in which the main work force earns its livelihood in a single industry, and yet must live within the same small community, there can be no meaningful separation of work from non-work. No event within the community, wherever it takes place, is irrelevant to anyone.

Nevertheless, work and the daily round of community activity continue. Urban people may work with those whose values they do not share, but they are relieved of these relationships after work. The citizen of the small community of single industry is not able to play segmented roles with such ease.

SOCIAL OBSERVABILITY

It has been established that because of the size of the community, the structure of the work organization, and often the geographical isolation, the citizens of the community are subject to an unusually high level of observability[7] which persists over long periods. Some degree of observability is a precondition for social control; it is impossible to sanction behaviour if people are unaware of it. On the other hand, constant observability requires the individual to meet strict requirements at all times, as any worker can tell us, if his supervisor is "breathing down his neck." Social life normally assumes and permits leeway; strict conformity becomes taxing.

It is well recognized, for instance, that even in primary relations, role observability is limited and intermittent; when abnormal circumstances such as unemployment force family members into fuller role observability for prolonged periods new patterns of behaviour emerge to counteract this increased visibility.[8] In situations of enforced close contact[9] such as northern weather stations, submarines or even one-industry communities, mechanisms and diversions develop or are introduced to insulate individuals' activities.

In all these cases "the autonomy of the person is experienced as threatened by having no private, that is to say, wholly separate and secret life immune to observation by others."[10] Behaviour which is at odds with the expectations of some of the other members may proceed without undue stress if there is some immunity from observation. Normally, however, insulation which permits degrees of privacy is an integral part of the social structure. In a community of single industry such traditional insulating mechanisms as intermittent

7 George Simmel, *The Sociology of George Simmel,* translated and edited by Kurt H. Wolff (Glencoe, 1950). Merton, *Social Theory and Social Structure,* pp. 319-22, 336-40.

8 E. W. Bakke, *Citizens without Work* (New Haven, 1940); *The Unemployed Man* (New York, 1934).

9 For examples of extreme cases see N. M. Burns, R. M. Chambers, and E. Hendler, eds., *Unusual Environments and Human Behavior* (New York, 1963); R. A. Lucas, *Men in Crisis: A Study of a Mine Disaster* (New York, 1969).

10 Merton, *Social Theory and Social Structure,* p. 343.

or sporadic interaction and segmental role playing are less easily maintained than in larger urban communities.

A further complication is introduced because within single-industry communities there is a greater likelihood that more normative expectations are held in common by more of the population than is found in an urban area. This means that communities of single industry are characterized by a high level of common knowledge as well as a high level of observability. High role observability compels conformity of behaviour to normative standards; common knowledge removes most of the ambiguity from these standards. In these circumstances two possible sources of behavioural leeway have been removed; on the one hand, lack of insulation forces uncompromising behavioural conformity, and on the other hand, lack of ambiguity forces uncompromising normative conformity. Further, the isolation of the majority of one-industry communities literally seals them off from other alternatives for great periods of time.

There is an additional source of discomfort. We have noted that in a small one-industry community the frequency of interaction and the high degree of observability over a long period is highly conducive to reciprocal knowledge embracing the totality of the individual. Together the high degree of involvement and the observability tend to lead each man's observations beyond the superficiality of role playing to find out more than the other person reveals to him voluntarily.

STRUCTURED EFFECTS OF ROLE OBSERVABILITY

There are two pertinent areas to be explored. The first is the differential effects that observability introduces. We cannot assume that role observability and the accompanying problems will affect all people in the community in quite the same way. Second, because intense role observability is uncomfortable, we would anticipate that mechanisms of social insulation would be built into communities of single industry.

1. Importance of the Role

We have suggested that the strains of the high level of role visibility are experienced differently; to a large extent this differentiation depends on the role played. One attribute of the role is its importance to the community. This means that the superintendent, general manager, and his family, for instance, are under extraordinarily close scrutiny because some decisions of this man, and, for that matter, his wife, have great implications for all in the community. Particularly when the supervisor of the single industry first arrives in the community, all citizens attempt to classify him by age, religion, ethnic group, and other pertinent social characteristics so that his institutional interests can be assessed. All citizens add bits of information to a common fund – what he said to a workman, whether his wife turned up at a missionary society meeting, what a caller found inside the house (both its furnishings and its cleanliness), what grades the children are in and how intelligent they are and, even more important, although it takes a little more time, what experience individuals had had in the community from which the man and his family came.

2. Moral Commitment of the Role

Full observability and intensive social control also deeply affect those roles seen by the townspeople as involving particular moral obligations. The school teacher, in a small community, for instance, is often expected not only to perform public duty during school hours but to be a paragon of virtue in off-duty hours. The plight of an unmarried female teacher in a small town who is being courted by a local male is notorious. Townspeople and students all know where the swain's car was parked until what hour the night before, or what they did on Thursday evening and at what time the teacher came home. Although many schools have regulations about teachers smoking during off hours on school property, it is only in a situation of high visibility that one finds teachers hesitating to smoke or drink in public places. Public scrutiny tends to be especially sharp when considering the children of married teachers; their progress in school, their marks, and achievements are assessed with considerable care; if they do poorly, this information is used to support other dullards or to criticize the system itself, but high academic standing is attributed to favouritism.

Clergy face an even more difficult task because of expectations that they should not only preach the gospel, but also act it out in real life. Slight deviations are severely criticized whether in dress, speech, jokes, or off-the-job activities. The clergy even more than the teachers are not expected to have periods off duty; the role is seen as a total one. The children of Protestant clergy are expected to act as role models of achievement in school, excellence in manners, and virtue in behaviour.

Particularly the doctor's role is seen as total, and although most admit that expectations are unreasonable, it is still thought that the doctor, by nature of his skills and his role, should be on duty twenty-four hours a day, seven days a week. In a one-doctor community this pattern of behaviour is indeed forced upon the doctor. The expectations surrounding his work also restrict the type of recreation he can take part in. In other words, many professional people in small communities are expected to play total roles.

3. The Socially Vulnerable

Role visibility has differential impact within the community outside these highly specialized roles. Possibly the easiest way of summarizing the differences is in two very broad categories. The first are those people, by far the majority of the population, who have a lot to lose by being sanctioned negatively. These are the people who wish to maintain economic and social security, namely, "that there is an excellent chance that his work career and income will be steady and adequate to meet his standard of living. This is the kind of security ..."[11] Davis describes these people as working "like beavers and having an insistent conscientiousness. They have the craving for respectability to drive them and the hope of a better home, or better job, or higher status for their children to pull them."[12] Homans noted "a feeling that a man was not a fully self-respecting citizen unless he had a job, the desire for the prestige outside the factory that comes from working up to a job within it ..."[13] In other words, the vast majority of citizens would suffer considerably if negative sanctions were imposed by friends, neighbours, and fellow citizens. Hence, this potential sanction forms a major basis of social control and this in turn is enhanced by high role observability.

11 Allison Davis, "The Motivation of the Underprivileged Worker," in William Foote Whyte, ed., *Industry and Society* (New York, 1946), p. 105.

12 *Ibid.*, pp. 105 and 106.

13 George Homans, *The Human Group* (New York, 1950), p. 95.

4. *The Socially Invulnerable*

All communities of single industry have people who live on the fringe of the work world, and the institutional structure of the community. Davis has called this group the underprivileged workers and discusses the emotional, cultural, and economic determinants of their way of life: "He lives in a social world where visceral, genital, and emotional gratification is far more available than it is in a middle class world. Recreation, relaxation, and pure laziness from Friday night through Sunday night are extremely satisfying experiences."[14] Individuals and families in this category have little to lose by negative sanctions imposed by the majority; high levels of observability and ensuing sanctions do not affect them to the same extent as others. This is not to suggest that these individuals have no norms, but rather that a subculture develops which produces variations upon the major normative themes. Basically these illustrations indicate that social observability and its ramifications have differing effects for people at various positions within the stratification hierarchy.

SOCIAL INSULATION

We would expect the pressure of observability of all conduct and unrestrained enforcement of the letter of the normative standards to be literally unbearable in any social situation. Some limits on full observability of behaviour are required for effective operation of a social system. The kinds of expectations and the degree of observability which we have considered up to this point describe a social situation which is difficult to maintain without strain. Lacking certain structural mechanisms such as role segmentation or variations in role involvement which normally insulate members one from another in larger and more complex communities, we would expect other mechanisms to limit complete observation. Because all citizens are involved to some degree in the problems brought about by a high level of observability one would expect structured repetitive mechanisms of insulation in addition to unique individual improvisations. It is important to note that the mechanism is no less effective and in fact may be more effective if its use is not explicitly recognized and

14 Davis, "The Underprivileged Worker," p. 103.

talked about. In other words the consequences of social insulation need have little to do with the motivations people have. These insulating mechanisms also serve as barriers in the communication networks discussed at the beginning of the chapter.

1. Withdrawal

The classical and most widely-used mechanism to produce social insulation is withdrawal. The availability of social withdrawal depends upon many factors; we will consider a few of these. One is the relative ease with which citizens are able to leave the community; if there are good roads individuals or families can move out of the orbit of social observability. When a neighbouring community is available for shopping, eating, and a wide range of other activities the extreme social observability is reduced. It is not, however, eliminated because there is always the chance that the individual meets his neighbour there; however, silence may be preserved by a conspiracy of the guilty. This is alluded to by Hall.

> In so far as the new community is planned, in the "good" sense of the term, it may have no room for the disreputable activities which are typical of recreation and leisure in a modern community. These questionable activities are likely to migrate to one or more of the towns on the periphery of the new community; the peripheral town becomes a sort of a moral garbage heap for the planned community.[15]

The activities that are carried on beyond the community are many and varied and have different significance for each individual. For instance, in the study of Coalville, one physician explained that he did most of his social visiting and entertaining in a neighbouring town rather than be seen drinking too much by a patient. Magill notes that eight of the eleven professionals in his sample reported that most of their interaction patterns were outside the town. He suggests role conflict: "On the one hand, community expectations demanded that everyone perform his role on a particularistic basis; on the other hand, however, the professional role demands that 'clients are treated

15 Oswald Hall, "The Social Consequences of Uranium Mining," *University of Toronto Quarterly* (Jan. 1957), p. 234.

according to universalistic obligations.' The conflict could be resolved by picking friends outside the community."[16]

Priests have been known to have a standing arrangement with a taxi company to bring them safely back from the occasional spree which takes place outside the community. On the other hand, the men in the top administrative group within the company make little use of these facilities if for no other reason than that their jobs require them to do extensive travelling far from the community. The journeys provide the opportunity to mix pleasure with business. Housewives take an opportunity to shop with reasonable anonymity. Teenagers utilize the lovers-lanes of the neighbouring community rather than their own. The pleasures and activities can range from a simple "evening out" away from "shop-talk" to activities that are more disreputable in the eyes of the townsfolk, such as a visit to a prostitute. Under these conditions each community accommodates the citizens of the neighbouring town by providing a range of activities away from social observability. The author of "Miner's Wife" comments:

> The new highway has given the citizens of [the community] access to the world; they don't feel shut in any more because in a few hours they now can drive to [a large community]. Rose and Porky sometimes get a sitter to stay with the children and run down for a weekend of shopping and night clubs ... "It's good to get out and see how other people live," Rose tells her friends.[17]

The need to get to "civilization" was noted by many respondents quoted in the chapters on the various stages of town development.

Railway towns without road connections used to depend upon the railway passes[18] which provided free transportation to whatever community people selected for this wide range of important activities. The problem, however, is quite different in the isolated community with no ready access to the outside except by air; the doctor has no neighbouring community to utilize; the priest has no nearby location where he can relax; the housewife has no out-of-town shops; the teenager has no foreign lovers-lane. In this situation the administrative group in the single industry have the advantage because of their

16 Dennis W. Magill, "Migration and Occupational Mobility from a Nova Scotia Coal Mining Town," unpublished MA thesis (McGill University, 1964), pp. 26-7.

17 Staebler, "Miner's Wife," p. 78.

18 For a description of the pass system, see Andrews, "Social Crisis and Labour Mobility," pp. 83-5.

periodic travels while the rest of the population can withdraw only once or twice a year.

Despite the problems there are long traditions of smoking behind the barn, of making love in the hay-mow, of finding liquor in a dry town, or even of secret masturbation within the snug confines of the family; man has a propensity for building social insulators. One important source of insulation is the self-contained house. Stable communities of single industry have high percentages of home owners. These communities are not characterized by semi-detached houses, row houses, or apartments. Planners in the Arctic find that individuals insist upon self-contained houses despite the difficulties of heating, weather, distance, and cost. The self-contained home permits family life with minimal observations from outside.

In isolated communities a substitute for roads is often found in water transportation; many families have a boat or canoe and in parts of the country a large proportion have a cottage or a "summer camp." Although the summer cottage cannot in any way supply the range of alternatives that are found in a neighbouring town, it provides some social insulation through withdrawal. The men's annual hunting and fishing trips serve in the same capacity.

Withdrawal is possible, of course, while still remaining in the community. Sometimes it is deliberate:

> As far as I am concerned I just will not visit my neighbours because they always talk about jobs. When I am off work I want to get away from the troubles of the day. In the two years I have been here, my two visits to neighbours have been for the express purpose, on the part of my neighbours, to talk over his job situation. So I just don't go out any more.

It is even more complicated for someone with company responsibilities to work and play with the same people.

> The great difficulty in this town and in all company towns is that you cannot get away from the company – you must play with your fellow workmen. I will not be friendly with a lot of people, partly because I want to have my own quiet time and partly because it harms them to be a friend of mine. If someone gets a good house – then the tongues begin to wag. It does them a lot of harm.

For others insulation is unpremeditated:

> Some people don't mix well. If the person is quiet and retiring, well, he can be alone. There is a community spirit here, but it is apt to be cliquish. Everyone has their own fine time, and it is often a little difficult to break in. If the person is a little retiring, and if he does not happen to get in in the first few weeks, he will be unhappy. But, here again, I think a lot of that is personal attitude, and there is nothing the company or community can do.

Whether intentional or not, withdrawal disrupts the communication networks, thus reducing the amount of common information and knowledge, and provides insulation from observation.[19]

2. Age, Ethnic, and Interest Groupings

Small isolated towns of single industry are quite often defined as being "a good place to bring up children." This suggests that parental supervision is shared by the entire community. If there is no way of leaving town, and if all the people know all others, then no matter where the teenager goes he is under supervision. However, limited relief from constant surveillance is achieved by the simple mechanism - one used by the parents, as well - of segregation by age and sex. A group of teenagers can meet regularly in recreation rooms with a certain amount of privacy. Likewise, their parents can meet in various club, lodge, and formal groupings, some characterized by formal vows of secrecy rather than implied confidentiality.

The many cliques within the community obviously serve many functions, but basically provide for regular private meetings among friends. The doctor deprived of friends in a neighbouring community finds a companionable crony who will share in activities that are not discussed outside of the group; the priest meets a school teacher or a parishioner with whom he can talk informally. These activities may

19 Insulation is a common social (or anti-social) phenomenon. It takes over particular cultural characteristics. Insulation is being referred to when we state that the Englishman's home is his castle; we observe insulation when we see the hedges of Britain. It is said that in crowded Japan the people have developed "internal" mechanisms of social insulation. The Japanese do not see, hear (or react to) what they should not see or hear. Thus paper walls become socially sound proof and visible puppeteers are not seen at a puppet show. For examples of social insulation in an extreme social situation see Lucas, *Men in Crisis*, chap. 5.

take many forms including such rituals as Saturday night bridge. Although these meetings are extremely important the social insulation is limited because recipients of confidences are fellow townspeople and workers; there is always the danger that confidential information will be shared with others and so become common knowledge.

Railroad engineers tend to associate with railroad engineers, and Porky entertained fellow development miners.[20] The reason is not hard to find – those sharing the same occupation have a common vocabulary and experience. Their wives share this, and regardless of other differences, common attitudes, knowledge and association provide a basis for social exchange. One respondent noted occupational and stratification differences when he said:

> I enjoy golf. There you've got a fine class of people. No, there are no men from the production line in the club. They would go there and drink beer and make a fool of themselves. Anyway, it isn't the type of recreation they want. What they need is a spectator sport like baseball where they can sit and comment on the game with their friends. Golf is primarily a game for intellectuals.

Social exchanges and observability depend upon a common communication system, so that when there is a language difference, interaction is sharply curtailed:

> As far as my neighbours are concerned, they are all on a similar level of occupation and rank in the company. We mix socially, of course, but it is not too satisfactory because the wife of one of them cannot speak a word of English. I speak some French, but my wife does not know a word of French. We hesitate to ask her in to bridge or to a party because we do not want to embarrass her. So this restriction does hamper spontaneous social life.

Another respondent made the same point. "My wife does find that the language barrier is a little difficult. She finds it difficult to shop sometimes and to talk to people." Even when the language barrier has been surmounted, ethnic differences in manner, food, and way of life provide barriers to unselfconscious and informal interaction.

20 Lockwood's comments are pertinent here. D. Lockwood, "Working Class Images of Society," in J. A. Kahl, *Comparative Perspectives on Stratification* (Boston, 1968), pp. 98-114.

GAMES

In addition, there are types of social interaction which in themselves contain walls of social insulation. These are not unique to communities with single industries by any means. They are used widely throughout the world. One example is the social insulation inherent in bridge-playing, a common pursuit in the single-industry community. Lynd's insightful analysis of bridge-playing suggests the bridge provides

> ... the best inexpensive guarantee our culture has discovered against a "dull evening" when friends "drop in." Social talking presents far more risks to a hostess, and it is a much more personal type of relationship liable to run on the rocks of monotony, vacuousness, gossip, or outright antagonisms ... Bridge [is] the hostess' best friend and the universal social solvent: safe, orthodox, and fun. Men and women who are not interesting talkers can still be good bridge players ... [Bridge is] fun-in-small-social-groups ... an unparallelled device to avoid issues, to keep things impersonal, to enjoy people without laying oneself open or committing oneself to them and to have fun in the process.[21]

The Lynds go on to describe the games of the non-bridge-playing population which include pinochle, tedro, knock-rummy, and poker. The same insulating qualities can be attributed to dancing, canoeing, the formal ritual of lodges, listening to pop records, watching movies, and to many organized activities.

The final type of game that will be considered in this illustrative list is the "wild party." Isolated northern communities are notorious for heavy consumption of liquor. Used in some ways, liquor can be considered as a form of social insulation; used in others, it can be seen as introducing a new range of permissibility within any set of human relationships. The Christmas office party illustrates the activities that can go on when it is understood that everyone is sharing in a normative holiday.

In communities of single industry important occupations emerge which act as insulation for clandestine activities. The taxi driver

21 Robert S. Lynd and Helen Lynd, *Middletown in Transition* (New York, 1937), pp. 270, 271.

is an example. It is he who is phoned to make the trip to the bootlegger or, for that matter, the liquor store. War time restrictions on procuring liquor flushed out many housewives who were unsuspected alcoholics. They had remained undetected because the taxi driver was responsible for the fetching and carrying of the liquor.

Although in a mature community of single industry almost everyone in town knows something about everyone else, some know more about particular people. Many of the forms of insulation that have been discussed are forms of differential association, which is, of course, influenced by propinquity.

As noted earlier, Rose, the miner's wife, took her ironing next door for company. Despite the telephone, neighbours usually have more contacts than non-neighbours. Certainly the frequency of interaction between families on the opposite sides of the town is considerably less than between those who live nearby. All other things equal, over time, the infrequent interaction will lead to less concern, less observability, and less knowledge.

Commitment to the community also influences both knowledge and insulation. The scope and intensity of the involvement of citizens with each other is related to the expected and actual duration of the stay in the community. This has been well illustrated in the previous chapters. Over and over again respondents have noted that people who felt transient in the early stages of the community development or, for that matter, the construction workers themselves, were not willing to invest time or energy in either the community or personal relationships with their fellows. Again it was noted that the members of the supervisory group, whose horizontal mobility differentiated them from the population, have a preoccupation with their jobs, but for many the temptation is to remain uninvolved in the community.

It can be seen then that mechanisms develop which serve to reduce the intense observability in these communities. The intensity of observability varies from community to community depending upon the social isolation and it varies with the types of roles played within the community stratification structure. It should also be stressed that these insulating mechanisms do cover some deviant behaviour (according to community definitions) but basically permit perfectly legitimate activities such as shopping trips "away from the neighbours for a change."

In summary, then, we have noted that the males, females, and children are all in positions to be news gatherers and distributors.[22] Because of the single work and community base, news and information are relevant to the activities of each member of the family. Clubs and associations provide additional information networks,[23] but they also represent barriers to communication to the degree that they reflect language, ethnic, or occupational differences. As a result all citizens have an ongoing account of the activities of many people in the community. This information, and the personal relationships involved, affects all patterned relationships within the community, including those at work. It is suggested that there are strains set up by excessive knowledge.

It was noted that a high level of observability had different implications for individuals located in different parts of the social structure playing particular types of roles. Some of the types of social insulation that protected citizens from excessive observability were described.

All of this suggests that we should consider the related problems of social conflict and social control. But, before this can be usefully discussed, it is necessary to consider other types of patterned and persistent relationships, as exemplified by the institutional structure of the community. In the next chapter, our attention will be taken up by the leisure time pursuits of the citizens of communities of single industry.

22 In *Small Town Stuff* (Chicago, 1932), Albert Blumenthal recognized the difference between "news" and "betrayed confidences," but called them both "gossip" (chap. VII). I have chosen to use formal and informal news which keeps citizens informed on a word of mouth basis as quite distinct from gossip, or betrayed confidences, which are considered in Chapter 14. In James West's *Plainville USA* (New York, 1945) and Arthur J. Vidich and Joseph Bensman's *Small Town in Mass Society*, "gossip" is used in the derogatory sense, but one senses that the gossip contains confirmed and unconfirmed news.

23 For a detailed account of voluntary associations in nine Canadian single-enterprise communities of various sizes, see Institute of Local Government, Queen's University, *Single-Enterprise Communities in Canada* (Ottawa, 1953), pp. 169-73.

9

Recreation

People living in communities of single industry, like people everywhere, spend a major proportion of their day away from their place of employment; this part of the day is conventionally called leisure. Many participate in leisure time activities. Recreation had and still has a moral dimension. This is well illustrated in the common sense phrases so frequently heard in every day life. People are urged to use their leisure time constructively; others decry the increase in spectator activities rather than in participation. A busy round of activities is "a good thing"; drowsing in front of the television set with a bottle of beer is felt to be morally inferior to taking part in sports or hobbies. Courses are for "self-improvement." The shorter work week is alleged to introduce the "problem" of leisure time; some urge that people be educated for the use of leisure. The retired are advised to take up a hobby "for something to do."

RECREATION AS SOCIAL CONTROL

Many of the post industrial revolution leisure time activities were explicitly set up so that young workingmen would be saved from the grog shops, taverns, and beer parlours. Organizations were set up to benefit "mind, body, and spirit." All of this suggests that implicitly and explicitly leisure activities are to keep people from other pleasures or sins. And the seven deadly sins of 1711 are quite complete: pride, envy, sloth, intemp'rance, av'rice, ire, and lust; after those, what else is there? The basic "sins," sex, liquor, drugs, and gambling have been around for a long while. S. D. Clark catalogues the moral indignation concerning drinking, gambling, fornicating and opium-smoking from the earliest settlement of Canada until World War I, from Louisburg on the east to the Yukon on the north and west.[1] From the beginning, officials, churchmen and moralists were concerned in stopping "sin." In many ways sobriety and piety became connected. "Satan finds some mischief still for idle hands to do."

> Two contrary assumptions about sobriety and piety dwell comfortably side by side. On the one hand, they are considered, like thrift and industry, as characteristics of the country rather than the city. The freedom, diversity, anonymity, and excitement of urban life are thought to encourage hedonism, while the rural

1 S. D. Clark, *The Social Development of Canada* (Toronto, 1942).

pattern of living, with its stress on hard work, strong informal social controls, and lack of opportunity for dissipation is believed conducive to self-denial and restraint. In Canada the surveys of the Canadian Institute of Public Opinion dealing with attitudes towards Sunday observance and the drinking of alcoholic beverages substantiate this view. On the other hand, qualities such as sobriety have been linked with the Protestant ethic, and hence with urbanism and capitalism; their exercise in one's own calling and their imposition on others are considered to have played a part in providing the modern entrepreneur with a clear conscience and disciplined work-force.[2]

Perhaps the linking of leisure time and moral and religious commitment is responsible for the ideological fervour which underlies so many leisure time activities. To many it has become an obligation: "all work and no play (approved play, that is) makes Jack a dull boy." In contemporary society some would add "apathy" to make an eighth deadly sin. The pace maintained by suburban families to taxi their children to their various activities connotes the implicit moral obligation. In any isolated northern community of single industry when asked about the large families in the community, many respondents reply "the winter nights are long up here," with all of the implication of time on one's hands. Sports are seen as building "character" and participation in team sports is often required as a qualification for the work world, possibly because team athletes learn "sportsmanship – the art of cheating while pretending not to."

Army officers keep their men busy at basic training camps, councillors at summer camps fill the day with constant "activities." Respondents, in an earlier chapter, stated that it was important for the men to work long hours during construction so that they did not have time to talk. Parents "organize" birthday parties for six-year-olds (otherwise they would fight – and have a nice time). Isolates, now, as in the days of Plymouth Colony, are suspect. All of this leads to the conclusion that social control is one of the functions of recreation.

Although social control is undoubtedly important, voluntary associations perform other functions, whether or not they are recognized

2 Jean R. Burnet, "The Urban Community and Changing Moral Standards," in S. D. Clark, ed., *Urbanism and the Changing Canadian Society* (Toronto, 1961), p. 70. This paper illustrates the moral indignation and action in urban areas.

by the participants. Some of the typologies developed suggest some of these functions. One classification, for instance, is in terms of "performance," "sociability," "symbolic-ideological," "productive" – each of these as seen by the participants.[3] Another classification distinguishes between "instrumental," "mixed," and "leisure" types.[4] Another is, "expressive groups," and "instrumental groups."[5] A still further typology is based upon "accessibility of membership, status defining capacity of the association, and the function of the organization for the participant defined as instrumental and expressive."[6] Others have usefully distinguished between the influence of voluntary organization activity upon the integration of the personality system (social-psychological) and on the integration of the social system (sociological).[7] One other author sees voluntary organizations in terms of "goal attainment," "social integration" in the criss-crossing of memberships, "pattern maintenance" in the reaffirmation of shared values, and in the "facilitation" of other functions.[8] Generally speaking, most authorities consider voluntary associations to be crucial to a "late liberal" philosophy; they are seen as best exemplified in the small town, and somewhat threatened in the city.[9]

Nevertheless there is no agreement on what items or combination of items constitute the most desirable leisure time activities. The multitude of activities, active, inactive, group and individual, some requiring elaborate facilities and equipment, presents great problems to any small town; few towns can maintain the range of activities necessary to please all tastes of all age groups.

3 C. K. Warriner and J. E. Prather, "Four Types of Voluntary Associations," *Sociological Inquiry* (Spring 1965).

4 G. A. Lundberg, *et al.*, *Leisure, A Suburban Study* (New York, 1934).

5 A. Rose, *Sociology* (New York, 1965).

6 C. S. Gordon and N. Babchuk, "A Typology of Voluntary Organizations," *The American Sociological Review* (Feb. 1959).

7 N. Babchuk and J. N. Edwards, "Voluntary Associations and the Integration Hypothesis," *Sociological Inquiry* (Spring 1965).

8 D. H. Smith, "The Importance of Formal Voluntary Organizations for Society," *Sociology and Social Research* (July 1966).

9 See the discussion of this point of view in D. W. Rossides, *Sociology as a Functional Process; An Introduction to Sociology* (Toronto, 1968), especially part V. Rossides links the idea of leisure to the early Greeks. "Leisure to them meant a richly stimulating but congruent social and moral order. Implicit throughout their conception of leisure [or the good life] is the idea of *aretê* or versatility combined with excellence." (P. 287.)

An almost obsessive quality has been attributed to recreational activities, voluntary associations and formal organizations in communities of single industry by Derbyshire, Robinson, and Walker.[10]

> A visitor to one of Canada's resource towns is immediately struck by the number and variety or recreational amenities available – swimming pools, artificial ice arenas, golf courses, recreation halls, parks and playgrounds, to mention but a few – and the high degree of participation in off-duty recreational programs, be they athletic, welfare, fraternal, church, youth cultural, educational or social. Our four cases are no exceptions. The nature and extent of recreational facilities and of residents' participation in active clubs and organizations go far beyond what is found in ordinary communities of the same population size elsewhere.[11]

If, however, one moves beyond the superficial view and asks townspeople about recreation – what recreation members of the family participate in, facilities that are available and used, facilities that are missed – seemingly contradictory statements, often in the same interview, are consistently found. Respondents maintain: (i) there really is nothing to do in the community, (ii) the community is over-organized, (iii) they are very busy, and small-town life is most rewarding, and (iv) people are apathetic. In order to explore these statements, it is necessary to examine the complex field of recreation in more detail.

NUMBERS OF ASSOCIATIONS

One community studied maintained 125 organizations. Few people there have more than one or two club affiliations, and the entire population – men, women and children – numbers fewer than 1500 people. This means that there are about ten people per organization, assuming that every person joined one organization. In Minetown

10 Ira M. Robinson, *New Industrial Towns on Canada's Resource Frontier*, Programme of Education and Research in Planning, Research Paper no. 4 (Chicago, 1962), pp. 87-9; Edward Derbyshire, "Notes on the Social Structure of a Canadian Pioneer Town," *Sociological Review*, 8, no. 1 (July 1960), pp. 63-75. Institute of Local Government, Queen's University, *Single-Enterprise Communities in Canada* (Ottawa, 1953), chaps. XI and XII.

11 Robinson, *New Industrial Towns*, pp. 87-8.

(adult population 3000), a count was made of the meetings and entertainments provided by clubs for adults during a six-month period (November to June). It was found that male fraternal lodges held 44 meetings, female fraternal [sic] lodges held 22 meetings, male church clubs held 16 meetings, female church clubs 20, men's service clubs 22, other female clubs 17, other male clubs 9, and miscellaneous clubs with mixed male and female membership held 40 meetings. This amounted to 175 meetings, and of these 157 were basically devoted to entertainment. In addition, one fraternal lodge held 22 public bingo parties, another men's club held 20 public bingo parties, and there were eighteen public dances.

Railtown, a community of 3000 (total population), maintained 150 voluntary associations. Robinson notes that one of his communities (then in a very early stage of its development) had "about 60 social, cultural, recreational, political, ethnic and fraternal organizations ..."[12] In another Canadian study, nine communities had from 19 to 103 groups.[13] In still another community (less than ten thousand), there was a roster of 96 very active organizations. But this did not give any indication of the activities (this community is hardly typical because the organizational details were in the hands of a recreation director):

> In an ordinary town you have about 14 per cent participation in the recreation programme; here it is 95 per cent. It takes about 400 volunteers, leaders, to keep this programme going. For example, the library requires 40 volunteers to operate it. The youngsters are looked after in their team sports, not by one team – we have 35 teams; and the coaches and leaders of these are changed every eighteen months – in other words, parents take turns.

It is difficult to interpret statements such as these, or, indeed, rates of participation, because of the poverty of Canadian research material. Hausknecht has compiled material from two national studies in the United States (reputed to be a nation of joiners) and has come to the following conclusions which are relevant to our discussion: only about 35–55 per cent of Americans belong to voluntary organizations; membership correlates directly with income, education and occupation, and inversely with size of community; membership by

12 *Ibid.*, p. 88

13 Institute of Local Government, Queen's University, *Single-Enterprise Communities in Canada,* pp. 169-76.

age represents a normal curve slightly skewed toward the upper age ranges; married individuals are more likely to belong than single, widowed, and especially divorced and separated individuals; home owners are more likely to be joiners than are renters; native versus foreign born seem not to be associated with membership in voluntary associations; Protestants have significantly higher membership rates than Roman Catholics even with religious commitment kept constant; sex, age, race, religion, political identification, size of community, homeowners versus renters, and socio-economic status all affect the type of association one is likely to belong to.[14]

SOCIAL DIMENSIONS OF APATHY

The recreational association of Milltown distributed a "Recreation Interest Survey" asking the respondents to check the activities which interested them most. Of the 70 activities listed, 36 were printed in bold type, indicating that these 36 were already organized. This survey was first published in the company paper and later distributed to 2000 families who were water tax payers. From the company paper distribution eight replies were received, and from a later house-to-house distribution forty replies were returned.

The rate of reply was interpreted locally as an indication of a low level of interest (apathy), but a further consideration of the questionnaire probably clarifies the issue. It is doubtful if individuals who already participate fully in the activities of the town would submit their interests again: to them, there would be no need. This leaves the individuals who are interested in participating in an activity not

14 M. Hausknecht, *The Joiners* (Totowa, NJ, 1962). Other studies relevant to the subject are: N. Babchuk and A. Booth, "Voluntary Association Membership. A Longitudinal Analysis," *American Sociological Review*, 34 (Feb. 1969), pp. 31-45; T. Caplow and R. Forman, "Neighbourhood Interaction in a Homogeneous Community," *American Sociological Review*, 15 (June 1950), pp. 357-66; L. Kuper, *et al.*, *Living in Towns* (London, 1953); L. Reissman, "Class, Leisure, and Social Participation," *American Sociological Review*, 19 (Feb. 1954), pp. 76-84; R. C. White, "Social Class Differences in Uses of Leisure," *American Journal of Sociology*, 61 (Sept. 1955), pp. 145-50; M. Young and P. Willmott, *Family and Kinship in East London* (London, 1957). The implications of recreation are discussed in Center for Settlement Studies, University of Manitoba, *Proceedings – Symposium on Resource Frontier Communities, December 16, 1968* (Winnipeg, 1968).

currently organized (provided there are "enough" people interested to make it financially self-supporting). Many activities, such as boxing, ceramics, puppets, or weight-lifting, have such limited appeal that the basis for a club is questionable. Then, there are a series of activities which, although popular, are not usually performed in a group – bicycling, fly-casting, music instruction, sewing, etc. A third category of interests has a limited appeal and, to be meaningful, they require competition: volleyball, soccer, or rugby. Some sports have so little chance of finding an opposing team that the high expenditure in equipment is barely warranted.

Each organization has a small number of vital members. From time to time, some activity becomes popular, and for a brief time acquires a large active membership. Others, however, such as the chess club, the square dancing club, and other specialized activities seldom have more than a handful of ardent members. It is difficult for these organizations to be self-supporting, even if only a modest rent is asked for their premises. It is also obvious that no one club will have a permanent, large and enthusiastic following; it is impossible to have them all thriving. Hence, to each individual club president, the citizens may seem apathetic. Apathy, an over-used and misleading word, usually means "no one else is interested in what I want to promote."

But the accusation of "over-organization" is equally appropriate because those interested in specific organizations are actively recruiting new members; from the point of view of any one individual and potential recruit there are too many demands upon non-working time. A considerable amount of work is required to keep each organization operating.

From the point of view of the volunteer leaders, and those who attempt to participate in a wide range of activities, the community is over-organized because many calls are made upon the time of the keenest participators. A community can be characterized as over-organized or apathetic at the same time, depending upon the point of view. The busy people find the interpersonal contacts involved in these activities rewarding.

In what sense is there "nothing to do?" The short answer is that there is nothing *new* to do. The same old faces and the same old activities are fine, but there are occasions when it would be pleasant to "have a change of scene" or see a play, or perhaps, just for once, go to a night club. In other words, despite the high (some would claim, the frenetic) level of activity in the community, there are a number of activities that are not there and never will be. Each of the four statements about community apathy, over-organization, social reward and lack of things to do, is quite accurate in a certain sense.

A more detailed consideration of recreation may help to amplify these points. First, social leisure time is spent in two ways: in informal casual primary groups (a number of friends in for bridge for the evening), or within the more formal arrangements of the voluntary association (team sports, amateur theatre). The more formal voluntary organization will be considered first. Unlike the less formal, home-based social intercourse, the formal voluntary group has no ready-made facilities.

RECREATION FACILITIES

A number of basic facilities are required for any elementary form of community recreation; these include some sort of hall for bridge parties, meetings, dances, teas, and some sort of sports area. Facilities may include this basic minimum or an elaborate set of plants providing a recreation centre, stadium, skating rink, gymnasium, swimming pool, curling rink, playing fields and golf course augmented by restaurants, snack bars, taverns, bars, night clubs, bowling alleys, and billiard rooms.

The problems faced by a community of single industry, with a population less than 30,000, involve the distribution of the costs of these facilities, and decisions on necessities, priorities, and the range of facilities. The building may be undertaken by the company, community, school, churches, unions, or the clubs. The agency that undertakes the capital and maintenance costs affects the use of the building. It makes a great difference socially, for instance, if the only available hall was built and maintained by the Orange Lodge, the town, the company, the union, the school, the Roman Catholic Church, or a business entrepreneur.

Usually a division of labour emerges, so that a variety of facilities under a number of sponsors is available. The people of many communities of single industry have fallen heir to some sort of facilities erected by the industry during the early stages of the town's development (often as a temporary expediency). One example is noted by this respondent in Milltown:

> The recreation centre has quite a long history. Originally, a number of people from the plant and from the office wanted some sort of recreation. Some wanted to wrestle, box, and so on. So they formed an Athletic Association. The company helped them out a little, and they thrived or languished from time to time according to the mood. Then, when wartime expansion came along, we were very crowded: people living in construction camps, boarding in town and so on. They had to have some sort of recreation. So the recreation centre was built as a temporary building. The Athletic Association and the company took over and the company decided to take over any deficit. The building is still there, [but] now the place is a little dead. It provides some recreation and does a good job. But part of it is going to be replaced.

Another respondent warns about the difficulties involved in this sort of arrangement:

> Handouts are not a part of the company's function. They are the worst thing you can give these people. The company should handle the initial investments like golf courses or gyms, etc., but for the use of these, people should pay. They should be made to realize that they must be part of the activities in the town and the only way to feel such a part is to make some of the burden theirs.

As we have previously seen, those companies that feel they must provide minimal facilities in early development are anxious that the community take over these responsibilities at later stages. This process of disengagement introduces friction and disquiet.

Robinson suggests that the characteristic social activities are due to the company policy:

> Much of the responsibility for this "busy, busy" free time must be ascribed to the sponsoring companies. The companies have felt that in order to have a stable and contented labour force in the industrial plant, the employees and especially their wives and children, must be happy in their leisure hours. An employee who is actively engaged in sports or hobbies, they reasoned, has no time or excuse to grumble, and is, therefore, likely to be happy at his work if he is happy at his play and home life. Hence, the companies encouraged organization of and participation in recreation acti-

vities, and in many instances provided such facilities themselves during the early stages of the town's growth.[15]

Aside from ascribing a corporate motivation to a company, and overgeneralizing, there is some truth in this statement, for employees do have leisure time and they require facilities outside their homes. One respondent noted the difference that a curling rink made to holding engineers in Milltown, a fairly isolated community of single industry:

> That is something that the company could have had here 20 years ago. It is something that would have kept many people here. Something as simple as that. We have about 100 playing. Perhaps 15 of those wouldn't have stayed the last six years if they hadn't had something like curling to keep them occupied during the winter time. Fifteen may sound like a small number, but when you have a trained man and you multiply him by fifteen, then those fifteen saved, pay for the rink in no time. But the company hemmed and hawed and waited and produced grandiose schemes for stadiums seating 20,000 and other impractical ideas instead of doing something concrete about the situation. There was actually nothing fifteen years ago to stop them from putting up a sheet or two sheets as they have today. Ten or twenty thousand dollars spent that way will save the company one or two hundred thousand dollars in manpower in terms of qualified and experienced engineers.

SPONSORSHIP AND RESTRICTIONS

Another described a community in which the company transferred the responsibilities for facilities which it built, very soon after their completion:

> A number of social and recreational activities of course are private – the skating rink is private, the golf club is about 18 miles from here, where grass will grow, and it was built by the company originally, at great cost, and is now given over to its private membership. There is no yacht club – there used to be one but it was a drinking club rather than a yacht club and it has gone into dis-

15 Robinson, *New Industrial Towns*, p. 87.

> use. There is some talk of reorganizing it very soon. There is a swimming pool.

As noted above, however, the company is not the only or even chief culprit. Each sponsoring institution imposes some restrictions upon the use of facilities:

> As far as recreation is concerned, we really don't do enough about it. Kids are looked after to a large extent by the school which has playgrounds. We have organized playgrounds attached to the school. Unfortunately the School Board has taken down all the equipment for the summer, although we agreed to monitor the playgrounds for the children's entertainment. We contribute to the recreation centre, which is a separate organization and administered by the shareholders, or members, or the people who contributed to it. The recreation centre is free to all children but a charge of $15 per family is made for adults and [they are] encouraged to bring their children in on this family membership.

Each institution then imposes a distinctive type of restriction upon the use of the facilities. The effect does not stop there, however, because the programmes often come under the direct sponsorship of the owner of the building. The owner of the building provides a subsidy for the organization using it; rents, if any, are nominal. Thus a church auditorium may, on one hand, be restricted for the use of members of the denomination, thus segmenting the social activities of the town, or the church may exercise some control over the use to which the auditorium is put – some denominations do not permit the use of the hall for dancing or card parties, or bingo, or theatrical performances. Many schools have stringent regulations concerning their property. Catholics are unlikely to attend activities in the Masonic Temple. To the extent that the facilities and sponsorship restrict participation, leisure time activities inhibit social integration and enhance in-group values.

On the other hand, commercial enterprises are rare, particularly while the population is small or in the early stages of community development. It is felt to be far too hazardous to open a first-class restaurant and bar, bowling alley or amusement park, not to mention a theatre for stage plays. As each sponsor has notions of appropriate facilities, most communities of single industry lack services such as night clubs which, though not necessarily essential to daily living, are accepted parts of the urban scene.

HOTEL, DINING AND DRINKING ACCOMMODATION

In fact, many communities do not have a hotel; others would not have one if it had not been built or subsidized by the company. These hotels are curious institutions; originally built to accommodate important guests of the company, they are usually utilized to house new management personnel while they are getting settled, and at the same time they provide some services to the community; they become expensive tangles of incompatible aims. One company hotel was attempting to provide simultaneously a "show place" for the district, living quarters for some of the young, unmarried management personnel, a luxury hotel for company executives and guests of distinction, a social centre for the community, a tourist resort, and a location for plant, social and business functions.

It is easy to see that these various functions are incompatible. By making some functions feasible, the hotel immediately sets up conditions by which other functions are inconceivable. For instance, it is not possible to have the main part of the hotel taken over for a local dance while important guests are resting. It does not seem wise to foster easy informality among the permanent guests while entertaining world-renowned figures. The type of furniture and decorum expected by an ambassador may not be appropriate to a labourer. On-the-line workers often feel uncomfortable when a farewell smoker is held in a luxurious setting.

A recent newspaper story noted the closing of one such hotel which had been operated for forty years.

> ... No buyer for [the] landmark has come forth and the citizens of [the town] are worried about the hotel's plight. One company official said high operating losses had made it impossible for [the company] to continue in the hotel business. The inn has always been a deficit operation for the company. The 120-room hotel employs 35 full-time workers. The inn is the town's most beautiful building. It stands on a hill that rises from the river and it overlooks groves of white birches, green elms and ash and green pines.

> Perhaps the inn's proudest occasion was when Queen Elizabeth and Prince Philip registered there in 1961. The inn was built in 1928 to provide accommodation for company employees and visiting officials and customers. Very few guests register at the inn and there are few boarders. On Saturday night, the plush bar is quiet. The [company] hopes the building will be bought and used, but high operating costs may scare off potential buyers.[16]

Interviews suggest that from time to time people become bored with the daily routine of work and the evening routine of amusing themselves with all the work and organizing that self-entertainment entails. This lack of break in the normal routine, even in the form of a visiting circus, is the most difficult thing that a young family faces: "It's tiresome for the wives also. There is no place for them to go. There is no shopping district to potter around. So that when you come home at night they want to go out. Where do you go? A movie, perhaps, but it's no excuse for a theatre." Another respondent said:

> We have nothing to fall back on here. There never has been a bar. We have tried to get one. There have been three referendums and the bar down below was built when we were fairly sure that it would come through – but it didn't. I think the company is quite anxious that it should. During construction they did not want it – because it would be very troublesome. But it would add revenue for us, and make the place much more pleasant – cocktails before dinner, and so on. It would cut down drinking in the rooms appreciably. But I do not know when it will come, if ever.

OFFICERS OF VOLUNTARY ORGANIZATIONS

In a small, isolated community of single industry, the citizens become aware of the limitations of their human resources and talents. Participation in voluntary associations, clubs, hobby groups, sports, and so on rests to a considerable extent upon the abilities of fellow citizens to organize and administer; often the existence of the group depends upon someone's specialized skills. Lack of a wide range of

16 *The Globe and Mail* (Toronto, May 23, 1968). See also the discussion in: Institute of Local Government, Queen's University, *Single-Enterprise Communities in Canada*, pp. 140-2.

activities is often spoken of as "apathy"; this term raises the interesting question of whether a "leader" organizes, sparks and "leads" a group, or whether a number of enthusiasts band together to form a group and find a "leader." A number of respondents noted the upsurge in particular activities when, for instance, a new clergyman or teacher comes to the community; the clergyman might begin a young people's club, or revitalize women's activities in the church; the new teacher might be a soccer enthusiast, or reintroduce extra-curricular drama into the school.

But the main weight of responsibility for voluntary organizations falls upon the citizens of the community. It is well known that institutional office and voluntary association responsibilities are accepted by a comparatively small group of people in any community: "You get a few people, a good few, who spend a great deal of time and effort on various specialized activities. People here are rabid supporters of one thing or another. You cannot attend everything. Your time is not long enough. Then there are those that do not do anything. You find them everywhere." This activity and interest is usually cyclical, depending to some extent upon age and other related family responsibilities the individual maintains.[17] When the population is small, the range of interested and vital people is limited. In addition, the community of single industry is subject to a high level of mobility and feeling of impermanence among those at the apex of the single industry and the stratification hierarchy. The importance of this mobile group lies not only in their numbers and their position in the social structure, but also in their education, recreation and sports background, as well as experience and skills useful to the community.

DEPENDENCE ON SPECIALIZED SKILLS

Respondents note the drastic effects when a voluntary leader with special skills moves out of the community or becomes ill. One respondent, for instance, discusses the absolute dependence upon local talent for some sorts of activities:

17 For an example see: Richard A. Carlton, "Differential Educational Achievement in a Bilingual Community," unpublished PhD thesis (University of Toronto, 1967).

> We have a drama league – English and French. We provide facilities, actually we rent the church basement for them, give them guidance. We have music, choral and ballet, or rather, we have had it from time to time. Actually our programme is very low as far as the arts are concerned. This is partly because we have to go with the trends and fads and partly because we are restricted by the talent at hand. If we haven't got the people to teach ballet and haven't got the people to lead choral, then there is nothing very much that we can do about it. Most of the groups are fairly active, depending on the leadership. At the moment I would say about 25 per cent of our programme is very active and carries on with continuity. The Choral Society, for instance, is the one that is bogged down at the moment because their director is ill. She is pregnant and is going to be ill for some little time.

Another respondent made the same point about a different community:

> A good example of the sort of thing that happens – we had a very good theatrical group here, it went into a big boom and then it suddenly died. The people who were interested in directing moved out of town and the impetus just wasn't there. It has been recently revived because some of the people who have moved into the town are great enthusiasts and we have had three one-act plays running for three nights and getting 1200 people there. So it is on the upswing. Badminton, on the other hand, was really thriving with 80 people, and now it is down to 30 and it will probably go down further, until another natural group leader turns up ... The younger people have no interest in the town affairs. All they want to do is please themselves. Fishing, hunting and playing softball; they are all for that. But when it comes to meetings of any sort, you don't see them.

Or,

> The merchants and railway officials, who are considered to be part of the upper social echelon of the community, as well as the "outsiders," for example, the teachers, are blamed as well: "The merchants and railway officials don't help the town out much. Even the teachers don't take part in any community activity. Their atti-

tude is that they are only here for a short time, so the hell with the community. Most of these people who come in are just here to grab the money."[18]

Many activities of a very specialized nature cannot be supported by a small population. Often it is difficult to find enough active members for these activities, in a large urban area. This inability to find members and maintain a membership holds, whether the activity is subsidized or not:

> As far as community spirit is concerned, the community is just what you make it. There is enough diversity here, enough people here, to be able to find a group with whom you are compatible, if you want to play bridge, if you want to play poker, go to a show [movie], golf, etc. It is all here. It depends on the individual and nothing else. My interests? Poker; summer: golf, garden; winter: read, magazines, radio, library, bridge, etc. As far as recreation is concerned, there is pretty well everything here. But I can't name a single organization in town that is really vital and that completely finances itself. They have all been subsidized. The golf club? Yes that is expensive, but most people feel that it is expensive anywhere. It is vital and it would be a great deal more expensive if it were not for the company. They looked after the construction – which was done at the time of plant construction, some charged to the government, and some to expense account and so on.

THE ROLE OF THE RECREATION DIRECTOR

In those communities with a recreation director, no one is sure whether he should act as initiator or merely as an administrator. When he does act as initiator, the project does not always succeed, as noted in this account:

> The recreation director has done a good job. He is a sincere man; I don't know how he is getting along. He pushes a great number of things – for instance the playgrounds – for supervised play. He thinks it is a good idea and so do I. That was done by public sub-

18 Alick R. Andrews, "Social Crisis and Labour Mobility, A Study of Economic and Social Change in a New Brunswick Railway Community," unpublished MA thesis (University of New Brunswick, 1967), pp. 49-51.

> scription. He came round to the house one year – I did not have any children at that time, but I thought that there was a good idea behind it, so I gave him $5. The next year I did the same. I understand that it has been abandoned this year, due to lack of interest and support. But that is something that he has pushed strongly.

Recreation directors based in a recreation centre, although few in number, do provide among other things continuity of leadership and facilities, a central source of information, and a focal point through which new programmes are initiated. They are able to co-ordinate and assist local leaders and coaches. With a full-time employee, it is possible to bridge gaps between the local fads and flurries of activity, and make it possible for a new organized activity to emerge when appropriate:

> At the present time, as I said before, we are no longer promoting new activities and we do not encourage the perpetuation of old ones, in fact none of these clubs are inactive. As soon as they are inactive, they go out. We now ask, as we said before, that there be a need or a concern about something before we will do very much about it. The non-joiner does all right for himself. You have a number of people who just don't do anything in group activities, yet they have beautiful gardens, or you have others who will go out and golf but will golf at dusk when there is no one around. These people are respected, they are fine, they want to choose it that way. We have one curler who goes down with his team and he will go down and curl for two hours with his team once a week and he will not say a word to anyone from the time he comes in until the time he leaves. I don't know what he is doing, he may be thinking chemistry problems all the way through this.

FADS AND FASHIONS

Individual enthusiasms, collectively, pass almost unnoticed in the city. In the small community, however, disaffection or disinterest among a very few people soon makes itself felt and the activity is temporarily doomed:

> Now get this! I was phoned to ask if I would help out in a plan to organize a ball team for the kids – that I would only have to turn out, with an assistant, every two weeks. I said "sure." It seemed to be well organized – pick up the balls and the bat from the recreation director's house, take them down, and the kids would be there; spend a couple of hours supervising and then return the equipment. I said "sure" and the two of us went down to the field at 7:00. There was one person there – a little girl. Where were the thirty to forty others?

Or:

> There is little that we can do as the crowd is very unpredictable and this place was hardly built to be a teen centre. In the same way I have tried to have table service in the grill, but one day two people go down and the next thirty. One lady tried very hard to get the young people together in the Anglican Church – an AYPA – but she got so far and the thing fell through. From time to time they have fads here. First it was square dancing. Everyone danced for a year, then it was reduced to 30, and now it is one yearly Klondike party. That is the way everything goes.

THE COMMUNITY AGE CYCLE

Shift work interferes with the services that the individual is able to contribute to the community. But other factors influence the interaction; the extent of the participation of adults in community services depends upon their age and stage of life. During pregnancies and when children are very young, the wife, and usually the husband too, retires from community activities. When the children enter school and take their part in recreational groups, the parents become involved. They are either shamed into it, or are in active competition with other parents, or they need the sheer assurance of supervising their own children when they are absent from home. Once parents become involved in kindergarten or Wolf Cubs, they seldom remain in this position, for ten years later the same parents may be found coaching hockey or chaperoning a high school dance. Parents are drawn into active community participation through their children:

> There is lots to do – there are clubs galore. I took my turn, and I did a lot in the Boy Scouts and so on – for years. I gave it up a few years ago. When I retired, I called a meeting of parents for the last meeting and said that a lot of boys were outgrowing the Scouts and anyway they needed a different type of recreation beside the scouts, and I suggested baseball. The first thing mentioned was – "Let's approach the company!" I said: "No. Either we look after it ourselves for our children or we will let it go." No one was interested.

This directing of adult activities toward their children is reflected in another phenomenon – the cycle of the community. The stages of the development of the community have been noted earlier; once the community has reached maturity, the cycle of retirement, employment of young people, the raising of families, and the lack of employment opportunities and forced migration for youngsters continues. Any child who is born and brought up out of phase, as it were, has fewer recreational activities. The children who grow up out of phase are those who "have nothing to do," because the majority of parents are preoccupied with the development of life of a different age group. This problem may be illustrated by a letter to a newspaper editor written by a youth who left his community:

> In one part of your paper I see where a "great number of the town's young people are being deceived." That's too bad! It could, of course, be because the young people of the town have never had enough to do with town affairs – not been allowed to express their desires as to the needs of the town, enough for older, more sensible people to know whether they are capable of thought or not ...
>
> Why can't the people get together, and if they want something to scrap about and insult each other about, make it something useful ... like a new rink, a diving tower at the beach, rugby teams, etc. in the high school – along with boxing, wrestling, and other sports, in a well-equipped gymnasium – which is, needless to say, something I never saw until I left my home town ...

In an urban setting this correspondent might have been able to carry out his interests more easily. The small single-industry community can seldom cater to minority interests.

COMPARISONS OF RECREATION INTERESTS OF YOUTH

That these are minority interests is indicated in a study of youth made in 1966. The sample involved 96 youths; 24 from an Ontario urban area; 24 from Ontario communities of single industry; an additional 24 respondents were from a Quebec urban area and 24 were from Quebec communities of single industry. Each group of 24, all superior students in grade 11, was made up of 12 girls and 12 boys. These students were given a list of leisure time activities and asked whether they participated regularly, occasionally, or never. Only three activities were participated in regularly by 50 per cent or more of the students: reading (61 per cent), sports (50 per cent), and cruising (promenade) (57 per cent).

There are interesting differences even among these leisure time patterns; for instance, reading is an urban phenomenon – almost twice as many urban students claim to read regularly than small town students. Sports, on the other hand, seem to be more popular in small towns, and Ontario and Quebec girls cruise more regularly than boys: perhaps it is part of the female role to wander round to see and be seen!

As might be suspected, most activities fell into the "occasional" category: movies (78 per cent), hobbies (53 per cent), dancing (57 per cent), television (50 per cent), meeting friends in restaurants (52 per cent), parties (80 per cent), clubs (47 per cent), political clubs (39 per cent), and participation in the arts (42 per cent).

Almost 35 per cent of the students did not have a hobby; the replies suggested that urban students participated in hobbies more than small town students, and more Ontario students had hobbies than Quebec students. On the other hand, a disproportionately large number of urban students report that they had never danced – perhaps there are many more alternatives available. Television watching was selected almost as many times as a regular activity as an occasional one. All Quebec students reported that they went to restaurants to meet friends, but almost 20 per cent of the Ontario students claim never to have participated in this activity. In all, 11 per cent claim they had never gone to parties.

Social club activities were much more widely participated in by students from Ontario. Generally, team games were male preoccupations, but 42 per cent of all the students never participated; the proportion was even higher in Quebec. On the other hand, the arts seemed to be the preoccupation of urban females; 40 per cent of the students never participated. It is also clear that at the high school level the students were not actively preoccupied with political clubs (UN, Model Parliament, etc.): 40 per cent occasionally and 15 per cent regularly took part.

The students were not all active in executive work in various organizations: 40 per cent of the students were not serving on any executive (and this was evenly distributed in urban and small town student population, Quebec and Ontario). Among the 56 who were serving, 60 per cent were on the executive of one organization each; 4 students were on four or more executives of school, church or other types of clubs.

In general terms, the major leisure time activities of these young people were informal and social, including movies, parties, cruising, and meeting friends, or solitary activities such as reading and individual sports; there is less interest in organized activities. This small sample suggests that despite differences in available facilities and differences in the social setting in which they live, there are relatively few major differences between the leisure activities of small town youth and those of the urban areas.

EXPECTATIONS OF CITIZENS

Many citizens, who are able to, leave the community on every possible occasion, to enjoy recreation "outside."

> There is still an exodus from town at the weekends although it is not as great as it used to be – now mainly the mobile single people go. But most of the professional staff do a lot of travelling in relation to their work. Of the other people some have summer cottages, but relatively few, as it is mainly the staff who want to get away from the telephone. They find it necessary to have a summer cottage somewhere where no one can reach them. Of the 5200 people in town, however, 375 are young, unmarried people. These include professional staff, young professional staff just out of college, and teachers. About 30 per cent of the teachers are unmarried.

Regardless of sponsorship, there are particular recreational facilities that are not found in small communities. In many ways, the citizens have more facilities and programmes within easy reach than many suburban families; but the local human resources and talents are limited; activities are high on párticipation and low on skill, appreciation, or spectator characteristics. Further, many of these activities, whether within voluntary associations or in informal cliques and friendship groups, rotate within the same orbit, with the same people working for the same company. There is no way to move to a new crowd, or to lose oneself in the anonymity of the Forum or Maple Leaf Gardens. This being given, the attitudes toward this type of life depend to a large extent upon the expectations of the individual.

Contrast the views of this young lady with those in the succeeding quotation! The native-born states:

> Yes, I was born here, and have lived here all my life. Oh yes, I love it. We have lots to do – it is quiet but we enjoy it very much. In the winter we skate and ski – it is very quiet in the winter. But in the summer there is swimming, tennis, parties and in the summer the students are all home.
>
> The tennis courts are not very good. We do play badminton in the winter, but it is not very good either. The ceiling is too low. Now the construction people are here, it is really lively. They like to come to our parties too – are you staying long?
>
> They have a dance in the neighbouring town in the Recreation Centre every two weeks or so, and guests can go. They have dances at the golf course too. Here we have had a few dances but they are not held very often because someone got tight once and they did not like it.

The recent arrival, however, notes:

> I like to live here for a short time, but I would not like to live here for the rest of my life. I miss concerts, music, good reading, I miss a lot of things which I believe are necessary for a happy cultural life. This is helped by many things here – there are a few concerts a year – three or four a year only; nevertheless they are important. The show [movie], well, we go fairly often; it is not too bad. We do resort to the radio, reading books and that sort of thing.

Other respondents are aware that those who grew up in small towns and are familiar with the patterns of life fit into life in a small community of single industry with more ease than does the individual born in a city.

> Actually there is only a certain group who really likes this town. A lot of the young engineers hate it. This is because they have nothing to do – especially if they have been city dwellers. Newlyweds are not a good bet, they like a very gay life and are not happy, especially the wife who is alone all day. The wife is the important factor. No husband can stay, no matter how content he is, if the wife is nagging and discontented. It is no place for the wife who is a cultural enthusiast. If her life is symphony orchestras, ballet, etc., then she should not be here. I think that the best bet is a young, small town couple with a young family.

Contrariwise, the small town youth has difficulties in adjusting to urban life, as one respondent points out:

> This is a good place to bring up kids. School is the best in the province. But this is true only to a certain age. They go as far as grade 11. Then for 12 they have to go out to some other place to get their last year before going to university. This is very expensive.
>
> Another problem has arisen on this point. These kids have been brought up in isolation and they have never seen bright lights. And once they get away the experience is very difficult. They have been raised in a vacuum and the shock is very hard on their academic study. There are a number of examples of boys who did very well in school here and went away and failed miserably. The only way you can account for it is their discomfort and preoccupation with new, complicated surroundings.

But, according to one informant, it is all worth the price: "However, everyone seems to be very happy with the recreation. I think it is one of our great achievements. In fact the stores would like to use a lot of High School boys on the weekend for extra help, but they find it very difficult because the boys are all involved in leagues and recreation and teams and this sort of thing."

INFORMAL RELATIONSHIPS

The great majority of relationships in the community are carried out within the family and small informal friendship groups.

> Many of the wives congregate in small groups for afternoon tea and morning coffee. The most popular pastime is bridge – both in clubs [almost exclusively female] and in casual games [mixed]. Many of the husbands either bowl or curl in the winter or golf and play tennis in the summer. Both husband and wife attend the moving pictures when there is a good one, and usually they attend any special events such as a Gilbert and Sullivan operetta, or a play. Many of them claim that if they attended all the activities sponsored by the various clubs and associations, they would have more than they could possibly handle. The majority of married adults' activities take place in small circles of friends.

One respondent describes the weekly and seasonal activities:

> In our leisure time we have friends in to play bridge. There are a lot of bridge clubs, both afternoon and evening. Not many mixed clubs; my wife plays every second week and I play poker every second week. We alternate week about so there is someone home with children. We have a tremendous number of social evenings: Two nights curling, during the season, the odd show [cinema], whenever there is a concert or play, we go to that. Around Christmas there are a lot of cocktail parties and that sort of thing.
>
> In summer, bridge drops off and people go to the tennis courts, play golf, swim, have picnics, do gardening and see less of their neighbours. There is a wonderful spirit here – but a clique spirit. You are in the group or you are not. Each has a fine time but it is restricted. Not much point trying to mix incompatible people.[19]

Another notes:

19 See W. Michelson, "Space as a Variable in Sociological Inquiry: Serendipitous Findings on Macro Environment," prepared for discussion in a seminar session on "The Spatial Environment and Social Functioning," at the 1969 American Sociological Association Meeting. Michelson investigates systematically the seasonal differences in activities in suburban Toronto. See also the discussion in: Institute of Local Government, Queen's University, *Single-Enterprise Communities in Canada*, pp. 140-2.

> We have social life but not of the organized type like you'd find at the Rec. Centre or in sports. I've given up the golf club because I want to save some money this year. Most of our social life centres around three or four families, but even that has fallen off in the past three or four years. I think the main reason for that is that nobody can afford to. No one has the money to entertain, well, shall we say, royally. I hate to give a cocktail party because I think it's a cheap way of getting out of social obligations that have accrued. So what do I do? Don't entertain, don't go out. Oh, we have our own small group where there is no necessity to worry about returning parties, etc. Talk at these gatherings usually turns to company talk. It's almost inevitable.

Another more transient member of management notes:

> We play a lot of bridge and enjoy it, and we go out to friends' houses and ask them back. This has recently been curtailed because my wife is expecting her first baby and does not feel too well. Still I am not a part of the community, still a stranger, and I know that I am not going to remain here long – two years at the most – a short training programme. I find the isolation, both psychological and actual, very great. It would not be so bad if I had a car, but I haven't got one. I never expect to have one, or at least not for a long time.

A single male member of management who lives in the company staff house describes his activities:

> There are organizations which I belong to. There is a great amount of lethargy. There are chronic gripers, cynics, and those who are perfectly happy to do nothing. I lay this down to personal differences. After an evening party at the staff house, several have said "that was fun, isn't it nice to *get together.*" There are a lot of parties but these go from room to room. A lot of drinking is done. But I have made a great attempt to get some of the cynics to get out to participate.
>
> I have also been in the St Mark's players, and there we have had a lot of fun. We put on two plays and the turnout for them was quite good. That takes up quite a bit of my time.
>
> Then I play badminton, which is quite good although the ceiling is far too low; but we have a lot of fun. I also play golf in the sum-

> mer, play tennis, use my car a lot, and this year I also attended art classes.

One account gives much of the mood of the social life of this particular town:

> But I like living here – there is lots of good fishing. There are many who hate it. My wife likes it. As soon as I am off to work she will get on the telephone, and there are the other young wives who will talk to her for hours. Then everyone will scurry round and do their work and go out with the baby carriage and do their shopping – and walk two abreast, chatting again. She is very happy. I am very fond of music and I do miss that here. The radio reception is very poor and you cannot pick up anything during the day and at night very little.

RECREATIONAL INTERESTS OF AGE GROUPS

Many respondents point out that the social and recreation requirements are quite different for differing age groups. This is so everywhere, but in a community of single industry the recreational patterns and emphasis tend to follow the age cycle. The next two accounts, for instance, talk about the plight of children who have been born and are living out of phase, as it were, with their contemporaries: "My children have found it extremely quiet and they get quite restless here. I think it is a shame that a city of this size can't provide any more in the line of recreation." And:

> They can't play tennis after five. They can't go to the recreation hall because they are too young. Take those two away and what have you got? There is talk among my daughter's crowd about leaving. The majority, if not all of them, talk about getting out of town. They feel tied down here. They find no means of working off excess energy, so that there is constant talk of leaving. Personally I'm not worried about her leaving. She may.

In contrast, another respondent admitted that his interests were modest, and certainly he was not very concerned about the recreational problems of youth. "Of course I am an older man and your interests and leisure and everything else is always changing. The preferences of an older person are different from those of a younger one.

Perhaps some of the younger people are not as content as I am because when you get to my age, you are more interested in slippered ease."

Another respondent felt that times had changed and, although he did not understand the problems of youth, they gave him a feeling of virtue:

> What was there to do when I was a child? Nothing. There was no recreational centre. We played a bit of hockey. Money was hard to come by. Our main recreation was fighting French kids. We had a very dull time. One thing which stands out in my mind was the work done by Mrs X who organized a dancing class when we were 13 or 14. She charged 25 cents per month and donated her time. We did not have to have any money – she taught us social poise and how to dance ... this went on for several years and among that group we had houseparties, which gave us something to do on Saturday night. That stood out as one of the brightest pictures of my childhood.
>
> The younger generation – they have a different set-up. I have a kid brother 15, he plays tennis – much cheaper than it used to be; he plays golf, goes to the restaurant, sips cokes, etc. He always seems to have something to do, whereas I had less.

A female respondent said: "My observation of small towns was that they were much better for boys than for girls. Boys, through sports and so on, often got attached to the community. Girls had to get out." Other respondents noted that occupation of the individual and age both made differences in the experienced recreation needs:

> The miners themselves don't take a big part in our programme. They like to go to the lakes and fish, etc., because that gets them away from the mines and out of the whole area. Their families of course come here and join in our programmes but, after all, the men work a hard eight-hour day in the mines and then go home – and that is the end of their day as far as they are concerned.

SPONTANEOUS ACTIVITIES

There are close links between informal recreation and formal associations. Respondents report that, periodically and quite spontaneously, they decide that it would be most enjoyable to spend the evening bowling or curling. They are not able to do this on the spur of the moment, because the facilities are taken up by bowling and curling leagues. In order to participate the player must join a team and follow the playing schedule, which means playing regularly whether he feels like it or not. If he drops out too often, he incurs the anger of his team mates.

In much the same way, several middleaged male respondents reported smelling autumn in the air and wishing to "toss a football around" and have a "real workout," or, on a soft spring evening, having an urge to "get out and play a bit of baseball" and recapture the rapture of youth. Team companions, preoccupied with daily chores, were hard to come by. One respondent reported that in a burst of enthusiasm, they made up a baseball team, and entered a local league. He described the disenchantment of having to play on schedule, whether in the mood or not. He then described the end of the season when the team played every night of the week, all day Saturday and Sunday to make up games that had been rained out during the schedule. He ended the long recital with the words: "We'll never try that again!"

Whether urban or small community, it is more and more difficult for an adult to participate in sports (other than solitary hobbies or sports) without becoming a part of the structure and obligations of a formal association.

It may be said, in summary, that communities of single industry have a large number of associations, clubs and special interest groups, so many that they cannot all be supported all the time – this lack of support is called "apathy" by the club leaders. The facilities required for some activities are extensive, and it was noted that the sponsor of the activity and the owner of the facilities made a considerable difference to the interaction patterns in the community. If all recreation is centred in a community- or company-owned recreation centre, the resulting interaction is quite different from that of a community where recreation is sponsored by various denominations.

One distinctive quality of all recreation in communities of single industry is that it is active and participatory rather than inactive, spectator- or appreciation-oriented. There is little commercial recreation; these are communities in which "you make your own fun." This type of activity, however, raises the problems of skills and leadership. Pottery-making groups, theatre groups, and sports teams need active and skilled voluntary leaders. The quality and quantity of leadership at any given time has a great influence upon the amount of activity in itself as well as on the area in which this activity is directed. The age cycle of the community and changing recreation fads also influence the amount of activity in particular areas of recreation. The smaller the community the more likely it is to have informal recreation; a very small community may be organizationally dormant.

It is just as impossible to satisfy a spontaneous urge to go bowling or curling in a small community of single industry as it is in the urban areas. A great many activities have become institutionalized into league, club and team structures requiring schedule discipline.

To the extent that there is active participation, recreation activities are effective agents of social control. The sponsors of the activities and available facilities affect the degree of social integration that takes place. Church sponsorship and church facilities limit accessibility to the programmes, incorporate, by implication, symbolic ideological aspects, and reinforce shared values. The lack of criss-crossing of memberships limits the integrative qualities of these activities. In general, although the recreation activities imply social control, the extent of the reaffirmation of parochial group values limits the reinforcement of shared community values.

Recreational activities described and discussed by the respondents in this chapter are characteristic of half the population of Canada. The major variable affecting the activities is the size of community. The sponsorship offered by some industries is an additional bonus or liability, depending on how one wishes to evaluate it.

In the next chapter, our concern is with those who supply the goods and personal services to employees and their families.

10

Goods and services

Buying and selling seems to have caused social friction from the beginning of man's most elementary division of labour. Throughout history there have been regulations concerning fair prices, fair measures, quality of goods, and the cornering of the market. As each family becomes increasingly less self-sufficient, buying and selling becomes a repetitive activity; commercial exchange probably accounts for more social encounters than any other activity outside the home. In contemporary North America, there are few who order what they want, regardless of price, but for the majority there is little room for the old world tradition of haggling. The standard fixed "advertised" price excludes meaningful price discussion and bargaining.

In modern industrial societies, the marketing process has become so complex that, although everyone complains, no one can find a sure villain. The farmer claims he does not get enough for his produce, the consumer feels he must pay too much, but everyone in the elaborate chain between the two disclaims any responsibility – he is becoming bankrupt too! To add to these complexities, marketing is deeply influenced by advertising. As a result, both buyer and seller are involved in elaborate games of semantic fiction. So, people "save" money by buying now, pay cash-and-carry stores to act as their own clerk and delivery boy; while they claim that they buy what they want, more usually, they buy what the seller wants. Under these conditions, where facts are few and emotions run high, great care must be taken with the data. There are many attitudes, but whether these attitudes are based upon reliable data is of little concern here; our concern is with the social consequences of these attitudes upon the interpersonal relationships in the community.

CONFLICTING INTERESTS

In communities of single industry, the storekeepers and their employees form the bulk of the second, non-industrial, stratification pyramid. There seems to be a social ambivalence on the part of individuals in the major hierarchy of the town toward those who supply the goods and services. Although local store owners are given fairly high prestige, it is not without some reluctance. The worker often seems to resent the fact that the store owner does not wear work clothes, and he somehow feels that he, the worker, is being exploited. In various ways the storekeeper is reminded that he is the servant of the wage-earner. Prices are constantly compared with those of other communities and those advertised in city papers.

The ambivalence shown toward the store owners and entrepreneurs was referred to in Chapter 2. The role of the shopkeeper is to serve the requirements of the population of the community. To some extent, and for some goods and services, he dominates a captive clientele. Housewives complain about the prices, and feel that the storekeeper is taking advantage of the restricted competition. To counter this, the housewives order a number of articles from the mail-order offices of urban department stores, and go on at least one annual shopping expedition to the city. If geographically possible, housewives search neighbouring towns for bargains.

These activities alarm and annoy the store owners who maintain that they support community endeavours, and that the large urban departmental stores do not. They point out that the small store can order similar or superior goods, not stocked locally, and have them as quickly as those ordered through the mail-order catalogues. Many local stores extend credit to their customers, and often maintain a large stock to attract and keep local customers. The storekeepers usually group together as a Board of Trade or Chamber of Commerce to promote local development and hold campaigns to encourage people to buy locally. These activities are usually looked upon with suspicion by the townsfolk. The profit of the local storekeepers is usually thought of as being basically incompatible with the best interests of the town and its population.

One union leader saw the businessmen of his mining community as deliberately creating an economic boom there so that they could profit and then pull out:

> The present building boom in the community is completely out of line with its economic base, and is an exploitation of the workers. There seems to be no other explanation why a union member would have been signed up for a contract of $92.00 a month for 25 years. There is not going to be any mining here in 25 years – if there is any here in five years – the officials of the mine company agree.
>
> There is a concerted effort on the part of the Chamber of Commerce and the commercial class to maintain an optimism, and this optimism is unfair to the people; it is unfair to ask people to invest and put faith in an area that cannot possibly maintain itself.

> The North is a wonderful part of the country, but it certainly doesn't attract any industry. I just returned from Colorado yesterday, and there I saw with my own eyes, ghost towns that at one time had 7000 people and now have 73 people. The businessman is behind this sort of thing because the miner who has been earning around $3000 a year in the end has nothing – even if he buys a house he won't be able to sell it – whereas the merchant in the town has been renting premises and he has nothing to lose and when mining begins to fold he will move out to another community.

THE STORES AND THE DEVELOPMENT OF THE COMMUNITY

The position of the shopkeeper in relation to the rest of the population shifts as the community moves from one development stage to the next. Bradwin, for instance suggests that in the construction days of community development the merchants are not particularly sympathetic to the underdog: "... directly or indirectly, the merchant is dependent on the money spent on the line. It is not in his interests to ostracize trade by criticizing any methods of the contractors or their subs. His business sense requires no prod."[1]

The kinds of problems that citizens and particularly wives talk about depend considerably upon the isolation of the community and the stage of community development. At stage II (recruitment) for instance, there is an incomplete shopping area with many unavailable goods and services. One isolated community, for instance, had no liquor store. Another larger community, adjacent to other shopping areas, lacked local services: "We badly need a good restaurant, a liquor store, a tavern, more diverse clothing stores, a hardware store and a

1 E. W. Bradwin, *Bunkhouse Man. A Study of Work and Pay in the Camps of Canada 1903-1914* (New York, 1928), p. 263; Institute of Local Government, Queen's University, *Single-Enterprise Communities in Canada* (Ottawa, 1953), chap. 10 is devoted to a discussion of the company owned store as well as the privately owned store. See also, Center for Settlement Studies, University of Manitoba, *Proceedings – Symposium on Resource Frontier Communities, December 16, 1968* (Winnipeg, 1968), Center for Settlement Studies, The University of Manitoba, *Aspects of Interdisciplinary Research in Resource Frontier Communities,* pp. 63-75. For an account of the company store in western USA see James B. Allen, *The Company Town in the American West* (Norman, Oklahoma, 1966), chap. 10.

dime store. A shopping centre might be a help. I have never seen a town of this size with such a small and incomplete shopping centre." Another respondent in the same town said,

> Seventy per cent of the trade that would normally belong here is taken out of town to neighbouring communities because the family goes out of town to buy beer and liquor, and there they do their other shopping at the same time. Many of the men like to spend their Saturday afternoons over a "beer" in the neighbouring taverns and their wives do their shopping while their husbands drink beer. These additional shoppers here would increase trade, and the increased turnover would influence the cost of goods.

Once there is a complete set of services in the transitional stage (stage III), however, the next focus of complaints is the lack of competition. Shoppers are unhappy with a monopoly situation. One respondent had just become used to the luxury of a new chain grocery store,

> The new chain store is a great help. Up until it came, prices were outrageously high. However, although the chain store can undersell the smaller credit groceries, it does not approach Montreal prices, as it has no competition from other chain stores. Further, the local chain store does not keep up the high standard that it holds in the city, either in cleanliness, service or prices.

Interviews with housewives in Milltown, which was in the maturity stage (IV), were arranged through housewife hostesses who invited a group of friends in for morning coffee and to talk to the interviewer. Invariably, the discussion of the stores was most heated; the contributions were characterized by conflict and vindictiveness; most of the respondents, quivering with anger, arrived with batteries of evidence to prove that they were being exploited by merchants – usually clippings from the town paper and the city papers indicating price differences for similar items on the same day in the same grocery chain. The intensity of the feelings and the importance of the topic may be judged by the fact that one small group of housewives had grocery store advertising clippings from Vancouver, Winnipeg, Toronto, and Montreal papers, with only a day's notice of the interview. The evidence did seem to indicate that there was a mark-up of from one to five cents on canned goods. The main focus of indignation was the price of groceries:

> We are pleased with the chain store, but they have no opposition. As a result, we sometimes pay a price which is twice as high as Montreal for an article. One hundred per cent profit is too great – but this is made on many small items ... fresh vegetables particularly – an item costing 5 cents in Montreal costs 10 cents here.
>
> Food is expensive. It is more expensive than it is in Toronto even. But the chain store has done a good job of holding prices down. The other stores were really making an awful rake-off on us.

Part of the reason for this may have been that there were fewer available alternatives for grocery shopping.[2] The housewife felt trapped. Clothing and furniture and other expenditures could be saved up for an annual shopping venture in the urban area or could be purchased through the mail-order catalogue. "We do not like the stores as far as clothing is concerned. We go into Montreal occasionally and do other shopping through the catalogue. Catalogue shopping is a new experience, but we find that it is fairly satisfactory as long as you are not in a hurry, and do not mind substitutes, or the delay involved in exchanging things."

Prices are only one problem noted by the respondents; quality of goods, and selection are also mentioned. The following is a fairly dispassionate account of the local shopping facilities and the problems involved:

> The town has changed a lot in the last ten years. Particularly important I think, is that the shopping facilities downtown have expanded considerably. At least we have a 5¢ and 10¢ [sic] store here now. The grocery chain is in new and improved quarters and this is good for basic grocery shopping. We have a department store here and this is a help, but I am very disappointed in it. I expected great things. However, they must have looked around at the other sorts of stores in the area and stocked accordingly because their goods are quite shoddy and they certainly do not carry a selection. When you go in and see a snowsuit – size 4 and size 10 and you think they are rather nice – they don't have it in size 6 or size 8. The other drapery, yard goods and clothing stores I don't go into,

2 Complaints about high prices are probably universal. In communities of single industry, the prices are blamed on lack of competition and freight rates; in urban areas, high prices are attributed to hidden monopoly, unreasonable markup, trading stamps, loss leaders, and the like. Wherever the buyer is located, he seldom has a price theory that leaves the merchant blameless.

> but although it isn't necessary to go outside for everything as you used to, most people do the major part of their shopping outside where they have a much better selection. Certainly most of the stores here have taken the townspeople for everything they are worth. There has always been a hardware store and one thing I will say for it – they usually have a large stock. Pretty well anything you go for, they have one, but at a tremendous price. It is now a big help that we have semi-competition. Someone has opened a combination of sports store and hardware store. It doesn't carry the range but in some things it does present competitive prices. The department store carries a little bit of hardware and of course the dime store has a hardware department and things like this – and we are now getting down to competitive prices.

Staebler quotes her miner's wife as saying, "'It's good to get out and see how other people live,' Rose tells her friends. 'And you should see the difference in prices! We pay far more for things in [the community] than they do in any places we've been. That blue dress I bought for sixteen dollars was only ten in Toronto. We pay thirty-two cents for milk and they pay twenty-three.'"[3]

As far as the storekeepers are concerned, higher prices are universally attributed to increased cost of transportation of the goods to the community of single industry.[4] If this is accepted by the customer, it is only with great reluctance. "The stores say the higher cost of living is due to transportation costs, but I can't accept this because railroaders have calculated the cost of transportation between here and the city and say that it does not account for the increase." Another respondent said: "They all screamed that the cost was due to transportation. Well, that good road has been open for two years, but there was never any lowering of prices due to good road transportation."

The relationships between the entrepreneur and the customer involve something more than an economic transaction. Often, for instance, ethnic and cultural differences between buyer and seller become involved in the relationship and the attitude. On the part of the customer respondent, this is often inadvertently disclosed by terms such as "Jew store." From the seller's point of view, this com-

3 Edna Staebler, "Miner's Wife," *Chatelaine* (March 1962), p. 78.

4 Freight rates have always been a traditional Canadian "problem" – on the national political level, in the regional context, and in the local community.

plexity of relationships may be illustrated in this interview with a man who controlled a regional retail and wholesale empire.

> All the stores in the area are *Canadien*. You see, *Canadiens* cannot go into electricity, they cannot go into manufacture, because they have not enough money, or know-how. They can only go into commerce. So they have owned the stores here. At first they charged a lot, but now that has been changed. We try to bring our prices down to the same as in Montreal. But, we do not allow an English branch to move in. At least the commerce is *Canadien*, and we can show that we can do as well as in any other city.
>
> You have heard about high prices no doubt? Well, it is not so! I will give a reward of $150,000 for anyone who can show prices that are 3½ per cent higher than the average Montreal price. Prices here are fair. We follow Montreal pretty well. In groceries the prices are a little higher, but that is understandable. But in other things it is just as well.
>
> In fact, we have to watch Montreal pretty carefully. In Montreal, a furniture house advertises 40 weeks to pay, so we allow 40 weeks. Then, they began to advertise 48 weeks. We followed suit, and finally it reached 60 weeks. That is what we use.

The proposed remedies for high costs and lack of variety vary. Ironically enough, some respondents were desperate enough to suggest that the company should control the stores, reverting to the old notion of the company store: "If it is a company town, and it is, with all its disadvantages, then there should be some control of the stores in the town. Either have it as a company town or do not have it as a company town, but do not have the disadvantages of both – with outrageously high prices. In another community: "Several of the citizens have written to competing chain stores from urban areas to ask them if they would be interested in coming here. Beyond that, housewives feel that they are in a situation which they are helpless to remedy. A buyers' strike is impossible, we have no alternative store, and we do not know how to attract competitors into the town."

The vast majority buy their groceries in the town, and carry on their shopping for clothing, furniture and appliances outside the community: "We seldom buy clothing and furniture here. We buy either by catalogue, or by waiting until vacation time, and buying all we need then, for the coming year. The prices are extreme in their differences. The store owners attribute such high costs to the price of transportation, but I'm sure that we are being gouged by real profiteers."

SOCIAL IMPLICATIONS OF SHOPPING

Shopping, however, is much more than an economic exchange between buyer and seller. It is a social event, and within a single industry community, the social event involves interaction between shoppers as well as between buyer and seller. For this reason the ecological location and distribution of shops, the policy of paying cash or "charging" purchases all have wider implications within the family, among families, and between family and merchant.

The ecological distribution of shopping areas affects shopping patterns. If the weekly shopping is done in a few hours on Thursday evening at a large shopping centre, there are few social contacts and very little interaction and shopping becomes a weekly chore. If, however, the shopping district is strung along the central Main Street, and it becomes part of the afternoon routine each day for mothers pushing the baby carriages down Main Street while shopping, then it becomes a social occasion, where housewife meets other housewives; it also provides entertainment – window shopping is a traditional and inexpensive form of recreation. Both of these ecological distributions are quite different from the housewife and mother who is used to sending the child around the corner for a loaf of bread. The neighbourhood grocery store is still not obsolete, and fits into the expectations of many people.

These social implications of shopping can be illustrated by comments made by respondents. The social aspects, for instance, are implied in this comment: "But the thing I am really perturbed about is what we can do with the town to bring it to life. A shopping centre might be a help." In other words there is not much point of going out to interact with others if others are not attracted to the area. Staebler notes:

> Rose loves to go downtown to look around for bargains. Broadway, the main street of [the community] is paved and has cement walks and stores on both sides – two well-stocked modern super-

> markets, a gift shop, a new [department] store, several dress shops that satisfy Rose's fashionable tastes, and a drug store where she buys fascinating shades of eye shadow, nail polish, and lipstick.[5]

These social activities are not restricted to women, as Andrews' description of the activities on the main street of a railway town illustrates:

> The activity of the retired railroad men is vividly enacted upon the main street of the community. Many of the retired men, those who are relatively healthy and active, have taken upon themselves many of the functions formerly done by the females of the household. These men run the various errands such as limited shopping and picking up the mail, perhaps working around the house. Approximately 120 such retired men are in the town, with nothing much to do except finding ways of being sociable, and it is not uncommon to see dozens of them in the business area during any part of the day. Many of them still wear the traditional and treasured apparel associated with the railway image: for example, the striped, peaked cap is in evidence most of the time.
>
> It is not surprising to visit a store and see six or seven of these old timers doing the shopping and, perhaps, not a woman in sight. One can hardly fail to note how these men tend to dominate the daily scene upon the main street.
>
> This section of the population tends to follow a daily routine of visiting the post office in the morning for the mail pick-up, doing some shopping and having "a little talk while meeting with some of the boys." This routine continues again during the latter half of the afternoon when the daily newspaper arrives at the post office. This area is a gathering place where joking, arguing, and general conversation are the order of the day until the newspaper arrives, which may be any time between 4:30 and 5:30 pm.[6]

There are still many who place friendly, personal relationships above chain store efficiency. These people want the personal touch in their buying relations:

5 Staebler, "Miner's Wife," p. 78.

6 Alick R. Andrews, "Social Crisis and Labour Mobility, A Study of Economic and Social Change in a New Brunswick Railway Community," unpublished MA thesis (University of New Brunswick, 1967), pp. 20-1.

A French Canadian is used to the community atmosphere of a small town. He wants his restaurant where he and his cronies can sit and talk, and a butcher shop where the butcher is able to pass the time of day. He wants his shop just around the corner, where the people of those streets can congregate. He does not feel at home there. He does not like the shopping at the chain store. He would rather pay a cent or two more and feel at home.

Others see the corner store in a utilitarian way: "The shopping centre is far away. If my wife is in a hurry she will go to a little market. Here she pays twice as much as she does at the chain store. She uses it only if she is in a hurry." Many respondents identified window shopping as part of the shopping routine. Here, for instance, is one comment:

As far as wives are concerned, they do a lot of shopping outside of the community. They do shop here, it is much better now than it used to be, we have a departmental store and a wide variety of speciality shops, but they also like to go out and they go to the bigger centres nearby, and certainly I don't think there is a family here that doesn't make two expeditions a year out to an urban area for shopping – a lot of it is window shopping, but this is a fairly important item.

So, although housewives seem to resent monopoly, they also resent lack of facilities for comparison shopping, which is partly window shopping, partly entertainment, and partly a focal point for interaction with other shoppers. Shoppers do not always buy the best bargains:

The wives used to complain about shopping, they used to complain about mark-up in groceries like green vegetables and this sort of thing. This is a lot less now we have a selection – they can do some comparative shopping. We have three shopping centres; usually the wife complains about a store, but she compares prices and usually stays on at the store she originally complained about.

The cash-and-carry chain store is a new experience to some. They find shopping this way enjoyable and inexpensive, and find that this is one method by which they are able to budget their income.

We buy most of our canned goods at the chain store but we don't buy our meat there. I think that buying for cash as we're doing now is a wonderful way of doing it. It should be explained to everyone that they won't be digging themselves into a hole if they try it. We buy everything for cash, so that when the end of the fifteen days comes up we may be running short and don't eat quite as lavishly for the last two or three days at the end of the period. If you buy on credit then you buy just as well for the last few days as you do for the first few and you just don't notice that you're spending more than you should because you are putting it on the slip. That way every two weeks you're running into debt a little and it's surprising how fast and how much it adds up. I used to work in the grocery business and it's amazing how much credit some of these grocers carry, $400, $600, $800, for a lot of these people.

The recent experience of the cash-and-carry chain store for this respondent has made him quite aware of the differences that buying for cash, rather than for credit, make in the routine of life both outside and inside the family.

We can conclude that, whatever the community or the industry, there is a great deal of manifest hostility on the part of the employees of the single industry toward those who supply the goods and services in the community. The hostility is greatest in those areas where the shopkeepers have the greatest power, and where the customer has the fewest alternatives, basically in day-to-day grocery shopping.

This suggests that in North America, the culture is such that the individual is unhappy if he feels he is being victimized, and has no alternative or no counter weapon. Freedom to assert oneself and make one's own decisions seems important to the urban housewife who is willing to spend a great deal of cunning, money, time, gasoline, and car depreciation in order to save three cents on a "special" at a distant supermarket. This suggests that these activities are a type of sport, a method of one-up-manship (or one-up-womanship) in relation to other housewives; it may serve as proof that she is doing her job with dispatch, enterprise and intelligence. The three cents may be important, but the situation suggests that shopping status may be more crucial. It is inappropriate to ask what the family does with the twenty-three cents "savings" from an expedition to the supermarket on Monday morning to buy "reduced" "stale" bread which is put into the freezer for later use. Somehow, an enemy has been defeated or outflanked. This and the "I can buy it wholesale" syndrome suggests a fruitful (or breadful) field of consumer sociology.

On the other hand, non-imperative goods such as clothes and major appliances (which have far less hostility associated with them) operate in reverse. The lack of bargains, range of choice, or quality of material justifies a trip "outside."[7] One can wait; when one does buy, the rewards are manifold. There is the trip itself; the report of it to friends; the delectable goods put on display; the opinions requested; the guessing games on the cost. This suggests that a monopoly situation is not resented because it is a monopoly as such, but because of the status deprivation that it enforces upon the individual shoppers concerned.[8]

The hostility involved in these negotiations suggests one of the reasons why the industrial hierarchy and the non-industrial hierarchy are not integrated in the stratification scheme in the minds of the citizens. The storekeepers feel abused, and the customers feel exploited. No one is sure who is master and who is servant. This introduces all manner of strains into the interaction: the very indeterminancy of it all is disturbing. Any arrangement that does not permit both parties to feel that they are the victor prolongs these difficulties and distinctions.

THE NEWSPAPER

Almost every community has some formal mechanism for communication; it may be a few mimeographed sheets with badly drawn advertising, a printed weekly (with at least half of the centre pages devoted to imported "filler"), a company-sponsored news magazine, or a major weekly newspaper. Many single-industry communities are

7 "Outside," of course, is a relative term. For those a community of single industry "outside" is the nearest market town, or a major city; for the resident of the major city, "outside" is a metropolitan area, or "across the border." For Canadians "outside" is the United States of America; for citizens of the USA it is Canada.

8 This analysis does not imply that prices are too high or too low, that there is or is not a monopoly, or that a monopoly is or is not appropriate. Certainly, the activities just described are not restricted to shoppers in communities of single industry. The attitudes and activities have added significance in the community of single industry because shopper and shopkeeper are closely associated over a long period of time.

not large enough to support an independent newspaper. Most small town weekly newspapers survive as an off-shoot of a profitable printing business. It takes a community of considerable size to support this type of service.

Whatever the form, the newspaper tends to emphasize "personals" on the belief that people like to see their name in print. The paper serves as the notice board for the community, and also carries the town council notices. If the editor is lucky, he carries the advertising of the local stores. If he is unlucky, the local stores advertise their "specials" with handbills. Whatever the arrangement, the position of the paper is so precarious that the editor is seldom a "fighting editor."

This is especially so during the early years of the community: "The weekly paper in new towns is similarly circumstanced. It has but a meagre circulation and struggles hard to get on its feet. The printery depends largely on job work, much of which comes from the offices of the builders of the road. How, then, can it speak out? Why kill the goose that lays the golden egg?[9]

The paper recounts the comings and goings, birthdays, marriages, births, deaths of the citizens. Stories that boost the community are played up, and derogatory stories are played down, or not mentioned at all. The editor is vulnerable to the blandishments of the merchants and the power of the single industry. By necessity, he is a home town booster. Clearly there are exceptions to the general rule. Occasionally controversy is aired in the paper; if it were not so, some important data would be unavailable for this study.

These general statements about the content of the weekly newspaper in a community of single industry, are verified in a content analysis of such a Canadian newspaper made some years ago. The "Minetown Informer" had a rare "fighting editor" who was not fatalistic about his community, despite great community difficulties. Regardless of the atypical situation that was being studied, the content analysis of a year of publication revealed the following:

Throughout the year, when all the sections of the newspaper were combined, it was found that the subjects written about most often were the people, institutions, and groups *within* the community ("We"). Of all the items in the newspaper (excluding filler and advertising) 67 per cent were about "We." Approximately 30 per cent of the

9 Bradwin, *Bunkhouse Man*, p. 263.

relevant items were concerned with people, institutions, and groups *outside* Minetown who in some way affected the town ("They"). Only about 3 per cent of the items were about "uncontrollable facts," that is, things over which people had no direct control.

Certain values within both "We" and "They" were stressed more often than others. The items on the ways in which people contributed to and reinforced local values and perpetuated the community made up 76 per cent of all the items about "We," while the items on the ways people negated local values or in some way failed to contribute toward the perpetuation of the community, made up the remaining 24 per cent. Items on the people outside the community who reinforced the community values made up 85 per cent of the "They" items, while 15 per cent were devoted to people outside the town negating local values.[10]

This analysis suggests that in addition to providing for the communication of certain types of information, the newspaper does reflect and formalize values held by a large proportion of the citizens. In this respect, it can be seen as augmenting information channels, adding to shared knowledge, maintaining community norms and, to some extent, increasing role observability.

LAWYERS

Bradwin noted that: "The lawyer found in a small construction hamlet has two alternatives: he can work with the big interests, or he can, in turn, handle the petty cases of complaint for the workers against the company. The former is the most lucrative course and is generally adopted."[11]

In a sense, Bradwin's comment is an over-simplification of the case. Circumstances seem to conspire against the lawyer in a community of single industry. First, the local industry is a branch of a large national or international corporation; legal work for the local industry is handled at headquarters. Second, the union is a local branch of a much larger organization, and its legal work is carried out by city lawyers. Third, communities of single industry have very little turn-

10 Laura E. J. Stultz, "Definition of Alternatives in a Critical Social Situation: A Content Analysis of a Newspaper," unpublished thesis, BA Honours Sociology (Acadia University, 1960).

11 Bradwin, *Bunkhouse Man*, p. 263.

over of real estate; certainly they lack the rapid speculative sales characteristic of a rapidly expanding city that some lawyers have found so lucrative. Fourth, communities of single industry lack an agricultural hinterland. In contrast a small (1800) community with a complex economic base is able to boast two lawyers.[12] Fifth, it is seldom that the community is the centre of boom town speculation, such as mining claims. Sixth, the local institutions are few in number and small in size requiring very little legal work.

This means that the lawyer in a community of single industry has very little upon which to base a practice other than the most routine drawing up of wills, contracts, an occasional real estate sale, and what civil cases there might be. As far as civil suits are concerned, the lawyer, unlike the doctor and dentist, cannot be the servant of all the people. If he represents the company, he cannot represent the union; if he represents Joe in a case, he cannot represent Joe's foe, Harry.

It is not surprising that few small communities of single industry have a lawyer. The citizens of the majority of these communities have incomplete professional services.

In the next chapter we turn our attention to the peculiar role-playing problems that emerge in the healing arts of the community. We will discuss patients, physicians, dentists, nurses, and hospitals.

12 Jean Burnet, *Next Year Country* (Toronto, 1951).

11

Healing arts

Recently a major urban daily paper had a number of news items and a feature story about a one-doctor town that had no doctor. The reason that this story was of interest to the newspaper is clear from the report sent back by the staff writer; he notes that a boy

> was bleeding and torn after being mauled by a big dog but they couldn't even give him a sedative to ease the pain when he arrived at the hospital here. It was a hospital without a doctor – so the eleven-year-old boy had to endure a jolting and painful three hour ride by car over pot-holed and twisting roads to hospital at [a neighbouring community] . Doctors there did what they could to repair his arm, they sewed some of the torn flesh together and grafted skin over a hole where a three-inch square of flesh had been torn away by the dog. That was ten days ago and this ... community of six thousand, already baffled and frustrated over its doctor shortage, grew angry when a man injured in an accident had to go to hospital 84 miles away to have his head sewn up. Then a worried young woman expecting her first boy was rushed to the same hospital. The townspeople got a doctor from [a community 350 miles away] to come to the hospital to handle the emergencies last Monday.[1]

The feature story continues and enlarges upon the problem:

> One doctor lives and practises here but he went on holidays ... He arranged with another doctor to take over his practice for three weeks but could not find anyone for the final week ...
>
> [The doctor] is probably the most overworked man in town, they say, answering calls anytime in the day or night when he is available. But he is often out of town, at other communities or at lumber camps and just not here for emergencies. Even when he is in town he has to call in another doctor [from eighty or more miles away] to give the anaesthetic so he can operate, or transfer the patient to another hospital.
>
> The angry people of this community say it is not good enough. They are demanding that someone – they don't say who – must find at least one more doctor. A spokesman for the Canadian

Parts of this chapter have appeared in Rex A. Lucas and Alexander Himelfarb, "Some Social Aspects of Medical Care in Small Communities," *Canadian Journal of Public Health*, 62, no. 1 (1971), pp. 6-16.

1 *Toronto Daily Star* (April 22, 1968).

> Medical Association said today a town the size of [this one] should have at least two general practitioners and a specialist. The national average across Canada is one doctor for every 825 persons but this includes doctors engaged in research and teaching in allied fields.[2]

THE MEDICAL PROFILE OF A COMMUNITY

In the history of the relationships between physicians and the citizens of another community we find that shortly before the turn of the century a young doctor, Dr White, came to the community soon after his graduation and practised medicine in the town for over forty years. At that time the community, with a much smaller population than that found today, boasted two other doctors. Dr Grey acted as Dr White's assistant and looked after most of the out-of-town work, which involved fulfilling contracts to supply medical services to isolated lumber camps and mines in the area. In addition, a second practice was maintained by Dr Black. The community built a well-appointed hospital and all three doctors had hospital privileges. Dr White was head surgeon throughout his lifetime, and was served by a faithful hospital matron. Dr White's reputation as a surgeon was excellent and there was great confidence in the hospital. In addition to his reputed excellence in surgery, he carried out his work in a way which comes very close to that of the idealized country doctor. This was the doctor who delivered thousands of babies and presided over the illnesses of three generations. He practised in an era when babies were delivered in the home as often as in the hospital. Dr White was very reassuring, never an alarmist; he made home calls; all of his prescriptions were made by his own hands in his pharmacy behind his consulting room; he had never in his entire practice sent a bill for his professional services. It was reputed that patients had to insist on finding out how much they owed. On the other hand, virtues are also seen as liabilities in a small community. Although Dr White was never an alarmist, people thought that this was often to the detriment of his patients.

Meanwhile, Dr Black carried on his second and smaller practice. There was a conviction in the community that Dr Black was an alcoholic. Many patients had little faith in his reliability and the towns-

2 *Ibid.*

people kept track of errors. Babies born with injuries were living reminders of errors that their mothers attributed to the attending physician. Many were reluctant to accept Dr Black's services if neither Dr White nor Dr Grey were available. Dr Black predeceased Dr White by some fifteen years and his place was taken by Dr Brown who stayed for four years, who in turn was replaced by Dr Green who stayed about six years. Dr Green was the first doctor in the community to send prescriptions to the drugstore. All his predecessors had been their own pharmacists.

During World War II Dr White died of a heart attack brought about by overwork and two days after his funeral his family left the community. Shortly after that the unpresented and unpaid bills of a lifetime practice were put into the hands of a collecting agency by the estate to an amount reputed to be $800,000. Much to everyone's astonishment someone had been keeping accounts. The community discussion of this development was considerable.

After the death of Dr White, the father figure of the community, Dr Blue, a young graduate and a home town boy made good, returned to his native community to practise. He has remained for 26 years, and 28 doctors have come and gone in the community during this time leaving Dr Blue responsible for some 6000–8000 people in the community and its far-flung hinterland.

Dramatic human interest stories in newspapers reflect the concern expressed by royal commissions and more recently by the Ontario Committee on the Healing Arts about the distribution of medical services in non-urban areas. The long-standing concern of the federal and provincial governments has been intensified recently by medical insurance because citizens who lack nearby medical aid pay the same premiums as those who can choose among many specialists.

For many years provincial governments and private industry have sponsored medical care for those living in isolated communities. In Ontario, for instance, the government has required employers of bush workers, miners, and mill workers in isolated places to have medical assistance available.[3] This was accomplished through a medical con-

3 E. W. Bradwin, *Bunkhouse Man. A Study of Work and Pay in the Camps of Canada 1903-1914* (New York, 1928), pp. 170-210. Medical services in the Yukon gold-rush were quite different. See S. D. Clark, *The Social Development of Canada* (Toronto, 1942), p. 333.

tract system.[4] Many resource-based industries maintained their own medical department and hospital as a necessary part of their operations. More recently, the Ontario Department of Health has offered bursaries to medical students on condition that they serve in a designated unserved area for as many years as they receive educational aid.[5] As a further inducement, practising physicians are now guaranteed a yearly income of $26,000 if they serve in an isolated and doctorless community.[6] Recently, there has been talk of supplying pilot lessons so that the physician has freedom to come and go from his isolated community. The distribution of medical services is important to patients, doctors, governments, and the various medical associations.

Although the existence of great disparities between urban and rural medical services has been thoroughly documented in gross statistical terms, little research attention has been paid to the more detailed implications for physician and patient. The Committee on the Healing Arts, for instance, states, "while we have not studied in depth the

4 The Ontario medical contract provided for the following:

1. The contract physician covenants and agrees to: (*a*) visit the camp or camps of the employer as often as may be necessary to give adequate medical and surgical care and treatment to the employees, (*b*) render medical and surgical care and treatment to every employee; (*c*) report in writing to the Minister of Health once a month all cases of sickness and non-industrial accidents suffered by employees during the previous month, and (*d*) notify the Minister of Health in writing of the name and address of any other medical practitioner engaged to perform any services under this contract other than consultant services. 2. The employer covenants and agrees to deduct from the wages or earnings of each employee the sum of $... per month, in respect of all employees who have worked during the month for the employer or his contractors or sub-contractors, and to pay the total amount deducted without rebate or deduction to the contract physician within one month after the money is deducted, as provided in section 23b, sub-section (*a*) of the regulations.

The distances and problems involved are well illustrated in Government of Ontario, Department of Treasury and Economics, *Design for Development: Northwestern Ontario Region, Phase 2, Policy Recommendations* (Toronto, 1970), Fig. 4.

For a history of the medical services and the contract system in Northern Ontario see Bradwin, *Bunkhouse Man*, pp. 165-210. Also S. D. Clark, *The Developing Canadian Community* (Toronto, 1942) and Institute of Local Government, Queen's University, *Single-Enterprise Communities in Canada* (Ottawa, 1953), pp. 202-5.

5 *Report of the Committee of the Healing Arts*, vol. 2 (Toronto, 1970), p. 63.

6 *Toronto Daily Star* (April 11, 1970).

problems of making provision for health care in under-served rural areas, villages and small towns, or for that matter in some parts of cities, the existence of shortage of services in many areas has come to our attention."[7] Grove reports:

> Generally the small town and rural communities do badly and in some places when the sole doctor has retired or died or moved away, or merely "had a coronary," there is great difficulty in replacing him ... Unfortunately we lacked the time and resources required for a detailed study and proper assessment of the situation – that is to say, from area to area throughout the province. Our impression is that grave shortages may exist in places of which the public hears little, while in others, minor deficiencies may be exaggerated by vocal residents and/or the local medical community.[8]

These important macro level studies have not dealt with the immediate day-to-day social situation. In the macro studies, communities of single industry are smudged together with rural areas into a "non-urban" category or are grouped by size of community rather than by social characteristics. In this chapter the quantitative data concern single industry communities in Ontario (illustrative of the nation as a whole) but the qualitative data are drawn from interviews and observations throughout Canada.

THE COMMUNITIES

An eleven-year medical profile was drawn for all 240 Ontario communities of single industry with a population of 30,000 or less. These 240 communities range widely in size; some are small sawmill towns or power station outposts with a population of perhaps 150; others are large well-established communities of 15,000 or more, but in each community the citizens draw their livelihoods from the one industry and its service components. The inhabitants of these small isolated communities have desired and, with prepaid medical insurance, will insist on adequate, if limited, medical services.

According to the formal census definition of the 240 communities, seven had a population in excess of 10,000; 13 were between 5000

7 *Committee of the Healing Arts*, vol. 2, p. 183.

8 J. W. Grove, *Organized Medicine in Ontario* (Toronto, 1970), pp. 8, 246.

and 9999; 17 were between 3000 and 4999; 65 were between 1000 and 4999; 50 were between 500 and 999; and 88 communities were 500 or less.

Some communities of 2000, as defined by the census, have a population hinterland of 4000 people living as trappers, railway workers, prospectors, bush workers, mine developers and the like, widely scattered and formally listed as "unorganized." Hamlets of a few hundred often represent concentrated centres for large, widely distributed populations. Clearly it would be possible to locate hundreds of additional communities with a population of 500 or less, but the number of these communities, by whatever definition, are irrelevant to our purposes. The 240 communities under consideration have a population of 444,394. The population listed as "unorganized" in the Districts of Algoma, Cochrane, Kenora, Manitoulin, Nipissing, Rainy River, Sudbury, Thunder Bay and Timiskaming, alone is 96,488.

All of these communities lie in Northern Ontario, that huge resource-studded part of the province lying north of Lake Superior, and in a line drawn through Sudbury and North Bay southward to Ottawa. Basically, the communities are located in Ontario Economic Region 9 – Nipissing, Timiskaming, Cochrane, Sudbury, Manitoulin, Algoma – and 10 – Thunder Bay, Rainy River, and Kenora.[9] The geographical and demographic character of this area is characteristic of the greatest expanse of the nation. The problems of providing medical services are staggering; the physician-population ratio of Manitoulin is 1:2235, and Kenora has 4377.7 square miles per physician.[10]

The number of doctors in each community in 1968 was established. The first most obvious point is that medical service is affected by size of community. Table 1 illustrates this relationship.

The table suggests that there is a relationship between the size of community and health services. Although this holds generally, there are several qualifications that should be kept in mind. The first is that the census and formal definitions of community can be misleading; a very small community may be the centre of a large hinterland. Two of the four communities with a population of 499 or less that have a doctor come under this specification. The second is that some

9 For the relationship between health and economic regions in Ontario, see R. D. Fraser, *Selected Economic Aspects of the Health Care Sector in Ontario* (Toronto, 1970), Appendix 2.

10 S. Judek, *Medical Manpower in Canada* (Ottawa, 1965), pp. 323-4.

TABLE 1
Medical services by size of community, 1968

Size of community		No doctor	One doctor	Two doctors	Three doctors	Four or more doctors
499 or less	(88)	84	4	0	0	0
500 - 999	(54)	49	3	2	0	0
1000 - 2999	(61)	33	13	5	6	4
3000 - 4999	(17)	6	3	0	4	4
5000 - 9999	(13)	4	0	0	1	8
10,000 and more	(7)	0	0	0	0	7

companies influence doctors to enter the area: this is the case of the two other one-doctor communities with a population of less than 500 (they have a hinterland). The third qualification is that fairly large communities are unable to attract a doctor although there is more than enough population to support a practice. This is apparent in the 1000–2999 group, where there are four communities with four doctors each, but 33 without any physicians. Finally, there are four "communities" of over 5000 with no doctor; this rather startling finding is partly created by definition of community. These are scattered populations which appear as a political community organization by formal definition. With these qualifications of definition in mind, the data indicate that the larger the community the less likely it is to be doctorless, and the more likely it is to have a larger medical team.

In addition to the 1968 distribution, the number of doctors for each preceding year to 1958 was established for each community. Each community profile, then, is made up of the doctors serving in each community within an eleven-year period; it provides us with a picture of the nature and distribution of current medical services, the past situation, and the turnover rate of doctors during the eleven years.

There are four distinctive profiles: in each the main category refers to the state of medical services in 1968 – communities without a doctor, communities with only one doctor, communities with an incomplete medical team, and communities with a more complete medical team. The sub-categories refer to the eleven-year medical history of the community.[11] Both the present and past medical distribution influence the continuity of service, patient expectations, and the quality of professional-client relationships.

1. Communities without a doctor (176+). (a) Communities which have been without a doctor for the past eleven years (163+). (b) Communities without a doctor which have had one at some time in the past eleven years (13).

2. Communities with only one doctor (23). (a) Communities with only one doctor, served by the same physician for the past eleven years (14). (b) Communities with only one doctor served by a series of physicians during the past eleven years (9).

3. Communities with an incomplete medical team (38). (a) Communities served by several physicians over an eleven-year period (16). (b) Communities served by a single physician for the eleven-year period, with one, two, or three additional doctors for short periods (15). (c) Communities served by two or more physicians, none of whom have remained in the community for the eleven years (7).

4. Communities with a more complete medical team (3).

These four community profiles and their sub-categories shift our attention from the usual demographic variable of size of community to the characteristics of medical services brought about by social-medical variables. Before moving to a consideration of these communities, it might be well to describe some of the characteristics of these doctors. First, contrary to popular stereotype, the communities under consideration are not hosts to many alien doctors. In all the communities, a total of 70.3 per cent of the doctors were trained in Canada.

11 These figures distort slightly the picture of medical practice for four reasons: first, any physician who left his practice or retired in 1959 would be included in the analysis as having stayed for only one year even though he may have completed a twenty-year practice in the years preceding 1958; second, at the other end of the time period, those doctors who have recently arrived (23 new doctors arrived in 1968) would be included in the count as remaining for one year although some may indeed practise in the community for the rest of their lives; the third inflation of short term tours of service is the result of the doctors who have moved from town to town, after a stop of one or two years; and the fourth (and to some extent counteracting the others) consists of doctors who have made two moves in one year, one of which would not be accounted for in an annual directory. The Canadian Medical Directory was used as the basis of the compilation; spot checks indicated that the data were accurate.

The remaining 29.7 were distributed in the following way: 19.8 per cent from Great Britain, 8.5 per cent from Europe, and 1.4 per cent from other parts of the world. Interestingly enough none of those from the other parts of the world settle in communities with one or two doctors.

In terms of age, we have 5.2 per cent under thirty, 30.2 are between 30 and 39, 32.5 per cent are between 40 and 49, 16.5 per cent between 50 and 59, and 15.6 per cent are 60 and over. The greatest proportion of the last age category are concentrated in the one-doctor and incomplete medical team communities. The bulk of doctors with five or less years of service are concentrated in communities with more than one doctor; the largest percentage of doctors with long term service (eleven or more years) is concentrated in the one-doctor community category.

COMMUNITIES WITHOUT A DOCTOR

Of the 240 communities of single industry, 176, or 73 per cent were without a physician in 1968. Communities without a doctor and which have been doctorless for the past eleven years predominate; of the 176 doctorless communities in 1968, 163 (93 per cent) have had no doctor for an eleven-year period or longer. Some communities are too small to maintain a medical practice; however, others are large enough to support at least one physician.

Medical services are available "outside" (the distance varies from twenty to 200 miles). In an acute emergency, transportation can be improvised to move a physician to the patient, or more usually the patient is transported to the closest medical aid by a "mercy flight." This term refers to a harrowing experience on the part of the patient, such as is demonstrated by the following descriptions, "so the eleven-year-old boy had to endure a jolting and painful ride by car over pot-holed and twisting roads to hospital,"[12] or "for 40 nightmare miles [the mother] held her haemorrhaging two-and-a-half-year-old son in her arms, terrified he would not live until she got him to a doctor ..."[13]

Citizens lack the assurance that aid is always at hand; in contrast the urban dweller knows that in the absence of his own physician,

12 *Toronto Daily Star* (April 22, 1968).
13 *Ibid.* (April 11, 1970).

others are available and that aid is always ready at the emergency department of any metropolitan hospital. In a community without a doctor uncertain pregnancies and complicated births become major problems unless the patient is able to move to a city for diagnosis, assessment and supervision.

The additional cost of health services in money and time is great. Any serious medical problem entails the cost of return travel to a medical centre. When the difficulty of making contact with a new and complex medical world outside the community, and the period of absence from family and friends when one is hospitalized in a strange city are considered, it is clear that illness under these conditions involves social and psychological costs also. After the trip home, the patient faces convalescence without medical supervision.

But the acute emergency forms a very small part of the services performed by the physician and an insignificant part of the total patient-physician relationship. In the doctorless community many of the activities usually reserved for the North American physician are taken over by others. Traditional patent medicine cold cures, for instance, take on much greater significance in this type of community. The purveyor of patent medicine takes over an informal advisory role; he recommends the nostrum that is successful in "curing" coughs. Informal folk remedies are passed from family to family; ailments are treated with mustard plasters, salt solutions, hot toddys, Kruschen Salts, backache and kidney pills, baking soda, cod liver oil, tonics, liver pills, and liniments. These communities are the preserve of the patent medicine almanac. Further, the citizens of the doctorless communities share with their urban brothers the modern equivalent of snake oil and the cure-all potion, for they too have access to the headache tablets, cold cure pills, indigestion remedies, laxatives, and nasal sprays – all advertised on television.

In mature communities, grandparents and kin who have raised children replace the pediatrician. Problems of acne, pregnancy, menstrual cycles, and menopause – the crises of the cycle of life – are referred informally to those who have experienced the full cycle. What they do not know can be found in the home medical encyclopaedia.

The nurse is the most important health authority in a doctorless community. Most small communities boast of at least one housewife who was at one time a nurses' aid, midwife, practical, or registered nurse. In a doctorless community she uses a range of skills that under urban hospital conditions are seldom called upon. In an emergency she sutures a wound, presides over childbirth, gives injections, and maintains death vigils. She is called upon to disinfect and bind injuries, diagnose chickenpox, and give special nursing care to post-operative patients who have returned from urban hospitals. Often it is her decision that sends the patient on the long journey to consult expert medical advice. Even formally untrained women who have nursed informally have "expert" practical medical knowledge, and are willing to share it.

The clergy, the school teacher or even the manager of the local industry take over some of the activities of the psychiatrist; what they lack in psychiatric theory is often more than compensated by their knowledge of the patient and his background. These, then, are the permanently doctorless communities in which others take over informal responsibility for many tasks usually reserved for the physician.

Among the communities that had no doctors in 1968, there is a smaller category of communities, which although doctorless now, have had one or more doctors in the last eleven years. These communities are unable to attract and hold a physician permanently; 13 communities have had on-again-off-again medical services. In a certain sense these communities with gaps in their medical services are not as well off as the permanently doctorless communities. The community that has never had medical services has a complex, unorthodox, but reasonably efficient system of maintaining health services at a minimum level; in contrast, the community that has a trained expert allows the informal folk medicine network to fall into disrepair. Immediately after the departure of the doctor, there is a great and acknowledged gap in community services; the citizens' feelings of insecurity about health problems and emergencies are intensified.

THE PHYSICIAN'S ROLE

Before examining the second category – the community with only one doctor, the role of the physician will be considered briefly. A great deal has been written about the subject; for our purposes, a few words about several essential characteristics will suffice. The extremely complex set of expectations on the part of physician and patient have been built up by the few physicians and the many patients over many years. Although there are subtle changes over time, the doctor-patient role is part of our cultural heritage. In our society, for instance, it is not common to find childbirth in the home with the assistance of a nurse, midwife, or grandmother, or the death of the aged in the ancestral bed surrounded by the family and clergy. Generally traditional remedies handed down through generations have been replaced by expert opinion, new drugs and therapy directed through a professional-client relationship.

Although the doctor's role is varied, his work includes preventive medicine through innoculation and the yearly check-up. The doctor reassures his patient in addition to dealing with his health problems. This epitome of all professional-client relationships moves far beyond the passing on of expert information; the relationship involves faith on the part of the client, and the receipt of confidential and privileged information by the physician; it involves the physician's strange combination of impersonality and warmth.

The idealized professional-client relationship is built upon the case that, "the doctor finds each case unique, if not in symptoms, then in the attitudes and anxieties the patient brings with him, the presence or absence of concern on the part of the patient's family, the degree to which the patient will follow instructions, and the likelihood of success of treatment."[14] The doctor must have specialized technique, or "knowledge-about," as well as "knowledge-of-acquaintance," as William James[15] put it; or high technical skill and an intimate knowledge of the patient and his history. Further, "a special relation of confidence between professional and client or patient is involved ... the client must respect and like him as a person ... Since the client reposes such confidence in a profession, he must be the epitome of virtue and entirely beyond reproach."[16]

Many aspects of the physician's role are changing in contemporary society. The family doctor who looks after the health of several generations, who is able to cope with all emergencies, is being replaced by specialists; the more complex division of labour compels the general practitioner to refer many patients to medical experts. The independent practitioner is challenged by highly sophisticated and specialized medical teams of doctors and nurses, backed by diagnostic and therapy technicians.

Despite all these changes there is still an idealized and perhaps mythical notion of what the professional-client relationship should

14 Edward Gross, *Work and Society* (New York, 1958), p. 77.
15 William James, *The Principles of Psychology* (London, 1890), vol. I, p. 221.
16 Gross, *Work and Society*, p. 78.

be. In part, this persists because "the professional is the man who knows. He has power precisely by virtue of being a repository of knowledge. The client is ignorant."[17] To maintain this knowledge in a rapidly changing world the doctor must maintain communications with colleagues to keep abreast of innovations, and to maintain, as Hughes calls it, "a professional conscience and solidarity."[18] In addition to the patient's belief that the physician should have complete and personal interest in his welfare, he is convinced that the physician should always be on call when needed; at worst there should be an alternative expert available at all times.

Although the patient usually thinks of the doctor-patient relationship as a professional dyad, it is clear that both patient and doctor are part of a very elaborate role-set; "that complement of social relationships in which persons are involved simply because they occupy a particular social status."[19] This role-set is most apparent to the patient when waiting to see his physician at his office; he becomes aware of fellow patients, nurse, receptionist as well as the doctor. In hospital, the patient notes a wider array of social relationships – physicians, nurses, social workers, medical technicians, dietitians, and so on.

The relationship between the doctor and each patient is greatly influenced by the range of seen or unseen role partners involved. The interaction may involve simply a doctor, a receptionist, and the patients, or many doctors, nurses, technicians, as well as receptionist and other patients. The role of the physician is difficult and taxing under the best of conditions. In the following sections, the difficulties of playing the role of physician within role-sets imposed by the small community of single industry will be examined.

COMMUNITIES WITH ONLY ONE DOCTOR

Twenty-three of the 240 single-industry communities had a lone doctor in 1968. The fact that the community in isolation is served by one doctor has implications for both the physician and the patient. First, we will turn to the physician, the only doctor. An occupational

17 *Ibid.*

18 Everett C. Hughes, "Dilemmas and Contradictions of Status," *American Journal of Sociology*, 50 (1945), pp. 353-9.

19 Robert K. Merton, *Social Theory and Social Structure* (New York, 1968), p. 42.

hazard of any doctor is the difficulty of maintaining his expertise.[20] There is much talk of medical men being twenty years behind in their knowledge. No doctor, of course, wants to find himself in this position and most try to avoid it. Normally, one solution involves group decisions on diagnosis and treatment, when each man learns from the others. This routine, quite obviously, cannot be maintained in a community with one doctor. The lone doctor in an isolated community not only misses colleagues for consultation, but also the informal shop talk and exchange of medical case histories which are so important in the informal continuing education of medical practitioners. Further, the practice of medicine has to be carried on without the benefit of the all important medical team, elaborate facilities, and supporting services.

In some cases the doctor is present in the community because of the influence of the single industry, and he is torn between industrial obligations, his auxiliary private practice, and service to the far-flung hinterland. In a study of a pulp and paper community, for instance, Carlton notes: "Doctors were only there because the company hired them and they were not likely to travel miles into the bush to minister to patients."[21]

Despite the awesome responsibilities of the one doctor and the difficulties he faces in carrying out a practice and keeping up with his field, some physicians choose a practice in a small community for other compensating reasons. Some, for instance, make this choice "to get away from the turmoil and the rapid pace of the larger cities ..."[22]

> A wish to return to their home towns played a major part in determining the location of practice of approximately one-third of the doctors [in a sample of general practitioners] both in Ontario and in Nova Scotia. Other less frequently mentioned reasons were that they liked a small town ... or that it was away from "well-established regions," and that this was "a good place to live."[23]

For a short time, at least, there are a number of attractions in this type of practice for the young graduate, because he can accumulate a great deal of experience and high earnings in his early days of

20 K. F. Clute, *The General Practitioner* (Toronto, 1963), p. 455.

21 R. A. Carlton, "Differential Education in a Bilingual Community," unpublished PhD thesis (University of Toronto, 1967), p. 41.

22 Clute, *The General Practitioner*, p. 53.

23 *Ibid.*, p. 55.

practice; in a small community the only doctor escapes many of the uncertainties associated with setting up a solo practice – he does not lack patients. This practitioner also escapes from direct observation or supervision by colleagues and superiors. Under these conditions it has not been unknown to find that a physician took the opportunity to practise rather elaborate surgery, for which he had had no specialized training; Clute, for instance reports, "Two others [respondents], also interested in surgery, settled where they did because the local hospitals did not demand specialist qualifications for those undertaking surgery."[24]

Despite these advantages, the physician's work is complicated when he lacks colleagues. But, if physicians have problems, so do their patients. There is a preoccupation with medical matters in small communities of single industry; people voice insecurity about medical services; residents express fear of an illness which would entail a move to the city for specialist's care; some dread an emergency requiring a specialist to come to the town. Informants have a fund of illustrations of medical debts and obligations from the past.

The essence of this most important life and death professional-client relationship is confidence and faith. The plight of the patient is serious if he has no faith in the only doctor. This does not mean to say that the layman has any objective criteria upon which to base his judgment; it is well known that patients choose their physicians on non-rational grounds. An individual in an urban area, for instance, who must undergo major surgery may choose between all of the experts in the community, in theory; in fact, he is referred to a specialist by his physician who in turn was originally selected by the patient, not on the number of successful or non-successful cases or any other objective criteria, but on the recommendation of friends. Nevertheless, when the urban client finds the relationship unsatisfactory, he always has alternatives or, at least, he thinks that if things go from bad to worse he will be able to move to another doctor.

The relationship between physician and patient is different when the patient has no alternative. The patient is not an expert in medical matters, so on one hand, he may have great confidence in medical services which according to expert opinion are inadequate, and on the other hand, he may have no confidence in highly skilled services. Often the relationship is damaged because a number of residents of small

24 *Ibid.*

towns are convinced that small town practitioners are inadequate, otherwise they would be in the city.[25] Similar logic is used in the armed forces. This basic health insecurity built into the community definition by citizens of isolated communities, is more closely related to the lack of alternatives than to the competence of the physician.

Although the difficulties faced by both the physician and the patient are characteristic of all communities with only one doctor, there are two variations on the theme, each with its own peculiarities. The variations centre about continuity of medical services. The first is the community which has been served by the same physician for the past eleven years. There are eleven of these communities. Most of the doctors graduated more than 20 years ago, some more than 30 years ago, and one more than 50 years ago. This type of medical career, with its dedication to patients, a giving of one's life to a community, illustrates a particular type of role and medical practice. The work and responsibility are great; the rewards are the warmth of personal relationship and the esteem in which the practitioner is held by the townsfolk. Most authorities doubt that when these doctors die or retire (47 per cent are over 50 years of age), they can be replaced by anyone willing to maintain the same type of practice.

The longer the physician remains as a solo practitioner in a single-doctor community, the more certain patterns become accentuated. If it is a challenge for any physician to keep up with his field, the long-term lone practitioner finds it extraordinarily difficult. For one thing, his very close relationship with his patients and his feeling of responsibility for them works against refresher courses or even vacations. The physician usually has a case which disturbs him and which he feels he must see through to its conclusion. In this sense, at least, the lone physician is cursed with the feeling of indispensability; although much work is routine, a proportion of it involves awesome responsibility.

25 *Ibid.* Jean Burnet discusses professional men:

> Those preferring small-town life or practice are exceptional. The attraction of the big city is strong. It lies in part in the living conditions, including opportunities for attending concerts and art galleries and associating with people of similar tastes and outlook, in part in the professional advantages of libraries, equipment and colleagues at hand, in part in the greater prestige and greater income of the big city professional.

Jean Burnet, *Next Year Country* (Toronto, 1951), p. 114.

For evidence that health problems are a major preoccupation, see: J. S. Matthiasson, *Resident Perceptions of Quality of Life in Resource Communities,* Center for Settlement Studies, University of Manitoba (Winnipeg, 1970).

There are two other unanticipated consequences that arise out of the relationship between the lone doctor and the patients of the community; first, the longer the physician practises in an isolated community, the more likely he is to have primary and personal relationships with at least some of his patients. The knife-edge balance between warmth and impersonal distance tends to be disrupting; additional strains are placed on the physician when he must preside over the death of a close friend of forty years' standing.[26] The second unanticipated consequence is that the longer the doctor serves in the community and the closer his relationship with townspeople, the more difficult it is for a new doctor to enter the community and set up a competing practice. Often patients resist the introduction of a younger doctor into partnership.

In addition, the physician is involved in a practice that is larger than he can handle, often including medical contracts and mercy calls from a large hinterland; he acts either informally or by appointment as the community's medical health officer, coroner, physician, psychiatrist, gynaecologist, surgeon, and anaesthetist. Major cases, of course, he refers to specialists in urban areas. Even the maintenance of professional contacts between himself and these experts becomes a major administrative problem.

Finally, the physician is usually the best educated citizen in the community; his civic services are in great demand for school boards, voluntary associations, politics, and other community activities. His counsel carries great weight, but these civic demands often become so burdensome that he is happy to move to the relative anonymity of the city. There, no one knows whether he is being a good citizen or not.

The rewards are great. Despite the limitations and frustrations, this type of practitioner knows that he is indispensable, that he provides assurance to many hard working citizens, that despite limitations, he saves lives, and sometimes performs miracles. The patients, despite the snipers, recognize his role in such words as "He's our saviour ... he's one in a million ... always there when I need him ... I pray for him every night."[27]

26 Not all physicians are able to resolve this conflict between particularistic and universalistic expectations by selecting friends outside the community, permitting a formal secondary professional role, as noted by Magill in Coalville. D. W. Magill, "Migration and Occupational Mobility from a Nova Scotia Coal Mining Town," unpublished MA thesis (McGill University, 1964), pp. 26-7.

27 *Toronto Daily Star* (April 11, 1970).

The community with a lone long-service physician contrasts with the community with one doctor, served by a series of physicians during the past eleven years. There were nine communities with one doctor in 1968, but not with the same doctor found eleven years earlier. The doctor in 1958 has been replaced by recent graduates or by doctors from outside Canada. The one characteristic of medical practice in these nine communities is the short stay of each replacement; most young doctors stay for only a year or two. This lack of continuity in medical services raises types of problems in relationships which are quite different from the long-term close and intimate professional-client relationship found in those communities that have a doctor who has spent his professional life in the community. The rapid turnover makes impossible any continuity of treatment or long-term understanding of a continuing case history. Seen in relationship to the community that permanently or periodically lacks a doctor, however, these citizens are fortunate. Patients who lack confidence in the incumbent, can hope that the next man in the rapid turnover might suit them better.

ROLE VISIBILITY

The basic characteristics of a lone-doctor practice in a community of single industry have been discussed. The physician's life in a small community is made even more difficult by the type of role visibility in his role-set. Although role visibility is found in the other communities to be discussed, it is clearest, and its repercussions are more deeply felt, in a community with only one doctor. The physician's work is complicated by the informal news channels which circulate laymen's informal amateur appraisals of his work. In the one-doctor community each patient knows all other patients; all deaths and lingering illnesses in the community are known and discussed. In the city, few fellow patients know each other and physician's errors are seldom known by all patients and the general public. Further, as Clute points out in his study of the general practitioner, each doctor has his own favourite diagnosis and therapeutic treatment;[28] this bias is common to all occupations, but medical practitioners are especially susceptible because of the indeterminacy of symptoms. As a result,

28 Clute, *The General Practitioner*, p. 232, *passim*.

some practitioners are very conscious of tonsils, others sensitive to the appendix, still others test constantly for diabetes, and so on. These preoccupations become known; it is easy for a townsperson who knows all the patients to note an epidemic of tonsil operations when a new doctor comes to town. All of these illustrations point to the difficulty of maintaining the confidence of the patient under conditions of public role observability.

R. K. Merton was concerned with the problems of social relationships within a role-set when the various role players had differing expectations. He directed his attention to the mechanisms which led to the observability of norms and of role performance; this observability leads to the articulation of the role-set.[29] In his study, *Men in Crisis*,[30] R. A. Lucas explored the rare situation in which there is almost complete role observability. In this situation, the members of the role set invent mechanisms of insulation that enable them to play their roles. The delicate balance between observability and insulation affects many roles, none more so than those of physician and patient in a small community of single industry.

Doctors in a big city are insulated from their patients. In a one-industry town, however, the doctor is insulated from his colleagues. This means that the pressure of role observability in the town exposes the physician to his patients' biases rather than to the expert appraisal of skilled colleagues.

This observability produces a different type of setting in which to work; it contrasts sharply with that of a physician affiliated to an urban hospital. The difficulty of maintaining confidence in a physician who has a community reputation for making errors can be illustrated in the following comment: "We've got a surgeon up here and actually he is referred to in party conversation as 'Mistakes.' When you mention that, everyone knows who you mean. Now how can you have confidence in such a man. When he sets a leg you're not sure he can even do that right." The informant was discreet enough not to mention that the same doctor was also the district coroner.

On the other hand, for the individual who has confidence in his doctor, life is made all the fuller for the relationship, as suggested by another respondent:

29 Merton, *Social Theory and Social Structure*, pp. 41-5.

30 Rex A. Lucas, *Men in Crisis: A Study of a Mine Disaster* (New York, 1969), chap. 5.

> If there is a vital doctor, it is the spark that lights the community and spreads down through all areas – everyone depends upon this person for their health. Everyone will be sick at one time or another. But it is the social medicine that is the most important. You don't have to have the best specialist in the world in a town like this, you need someone who is vital.

Not only the doctor's professional work-life but also his private life and leisure time activities are observable to all citizens. In the study of Coalville, for example, one physician when asked if he spent most of his free time with friends in Coalville or outside the town, replied:

> That's hard for me to say. You see, in a small mining town like this you can't do everything you want. If you go to a party and you have taken a few too many, the person you have to operate on or whose children you deliver may be watching. You have to be selective about your friends. Because of this I have only a few friends here; we do most of our visiting and entertaining in [a neighbouring town].[31]

The physicians who live in communities without neighbouring towns have no opportunity to escape from the observability of their social life as well as their work.

But, observability is a two-way process. While the physician and his work and play are being observed by the untutored but often perceptive eyes of the citizenry, their own lives are open to the educated scrutiny of the doctor. Unlike his urban counterpart, the small-town physician knows a great deal about his patient and the patient's family and activities. One doctor pointed out that practice in his home town was made easier by his detailed knowledge of the background of patients.[32]

In any role-set, the amount and location of observability and insulation is crucial; the case of the physician in a small single-industry community illustrates the social consequences of a particular combination. Every role-set has strains of one sort or another; the role-set involving the doctor in a small community has inherent strains that affect both physician and patient. These strains are not the same as those involved with urban doctor-patient relationships.

31 Magill, "Migration and Occupational Mobility," pp. 26-7.

32 Clute, *The General Practitioner*, p. 55.

COMMUNITIES WITH AN INCOMPLETE MEDICAL TEAM

The third broad category is the one-industry community with more than one doctor, but not enough physicians to make up a basic balanced health team. These 38 larger communities could maintain a small hospital, but the range of services and specialization is limited. The physicians lack the new machinery, the laboratories, and the technical specialities[33] that serve and enhance the practice of the urban physician with hospital privileges. In the smaller hospital the duties of anaesthetist, laboratory technician, and pharmacist, are distributed, supervised, and regulated in a different way. Nevertheless, these practitioners have colleagueship and their patients have more services available. In addition the patient has alternative sources of medical assistance.

The sixteen communities which have had the long-term services of two or more physicians in the community since 1958 have had a far more stable and complete medical service than any of the communities yet considered. This service makes possible assistance in times of emergency when the attending physician is absent; it provides alternative professional help for the citizens; this professional help is available with continuity; the physicians have assistance available if consultations are required; with the co-operation of two or more of the physicians, more sophisticated medical practice and surgery is available in the community.

The more complicated situation of communities served by a single physician for the eleven-year period, with one, two, or three additional doctors who stay for a short period, is characteristic of fifteen communities. They have had one doctor who has been in the community for the eleven-year period from 1958 to 1968 along with a number of other doctors who stay in the community for a year or two. In theory, the older man can be of assistance to the young practitioner by sharing with them his lifetime of medical experience. The older doctor also benefits by being brought up to date with new techniques that the younger man has learned.

From the patient's point of view, the stability of the one physician and the rapid turnover of the others does raise problems of profes-

33 These "behind the scenes" services are not as apparent to the patient. See Oswald Hall, *The Paramedical Occupations in Ontario* (Toronto, 1970). Particularly note chap. 11 and the Appendix.

sional-client relationships and client ethics. There is no problem if the patient is a long-term client of the older and permanent physician. If, however, the patient is not pleased with this relationship and changes his doctor only to find that his new physician leaves, then the patient may have to return to the older physician. This tacit admission of lack of faith strains the role playing for both the physician and patient. "Although this community is basically a one-doctor town, from time to time there are two, three, or four doctors. 'Don't quote me,' most of [the residents] say when questioned. 'I've got to live here and he is our only doctor.'"[34]

There are seven communities which have two or more doctors, none of whom have been in the community for the full eleven-year period. Characteristically these mobile physicians are recent graduates or doctors who have been trained outside Canada. To use perhaps an extreme example, one community had three doctors in 1968; two of them graduated less than ten years ago, and the third is a doctor who was trained outside Canada. One has been there six years, one for one year, and the other arrived in 1968. If the past experience in the community is any indicator, it is unlikely that these three doctors will stay long because between 1958 and 1968 this community has had 16 doctors; most spent less than five years there.

MOBILITY OF PHYSICIANS

It is quite clear that there is a high level of mobility of medical practitioners in communities of single industry, particularly in the last two sub-categories. It may be recalled that 176 of the 240 Ontario communities of single industry under 30,000 had no doctors in 1968 and have not had a doctor for the past eleven years. When account is made of individual doctors who have practised in the remaining 77 communities, we find a total of 505 physicians in practice over the eleven-year period. Only seventeen per cent of these doctors remained in any one community for the eleven-year period. In contrast, 37 per cent of doctors have remained either one or two years; a full 64 per cent have remained in the community for less than five years. This is a remarkable rate of mobility. When a mere seventeen per cent of the doctors have remained consistently in practice in a community for

34 *Toronto Daily Star* (April 22, 1968).

an eleven-year period, continuing physician-patient relationships are severely curtailed. These fragmented relationships have social as well as medical implications.

The answer that these mobile physicians are moving from small towns to general or specialized urban practices is an oversimplification. While some doctors undoubtedly move to urban areas, these profiles show that a number of doctors move from one small community to another; some moved as many as five times in eleven years but kept within a region and always practised in communities of roughly the same size. Clute suggests some clues for these moves:

> One doctor left a large city because the area in which he lived was "down at the heels"; he later made two more moves, from one small village because of "the dead winters" and from another because there were "too many old people."
>
> The moves made by five of the doctors who had practised in more than one Ontario community were necessitated by lack of enough practice to produce a reasonable living. Some of these men had to move several times before they found communities in which they were able to establish satisfactory practices. On the average, these five practitioners had had two-and-a-half years of practice before they settled in the communities in which they were located at the time of the survey. The average duration of these practices, since the last move, was approximately 22 years.[35]

This reported search for an ideal small town may seem somewhat superficial. The practice of medicine can be highly competitive; Grove, for instance, notes the habit of robbing Peter to pay Paul – he cites instances in which community officials, when faced with a departing doctor, recruit from a community of much the same size, and the officials of the "raided" town, in turn, try to recruit a doctor from another town.[36]

But the profiles indicate that some mobile doctors move to progressively smaller communities.[37] One possible explanation for the action of these doctors may be found in the medical contract system or its new equivalent. Many small communities of single industry

35 K. F. Clute, *The General Practitioner*, p. 53. It should be noted that the doctors in Clute's sample were not highly mobile. He reported "a feeling of permanency," and an average duration of practices of twenty-two years, pp. 54-6.

36 Grove, *Organized Medicine in Ontario*, p. 246.

37 *Ibid.*

have a far-flung hinterland of woods camps, small mines and the like. Looking after the health of woodsmen could well become a well-paying type of specialization, and one that is very attractive to the doctor who is fond of hunting, fishing, and the outdoors. Statistics lend some credence to the link between the small-town doctor and local industry because "the only specialty that has a significant number of doctors in places under 2000 is occupational medicine."[38]

COMMUNITIES WITH A MORE COMPLETE MEDICAL TEAM

The final category of medical service associated with communities of single industry is the more complete medical team. It might be argued that none of the communities have anything like a complete medical team, for none of the communities have an anaesthetist and there was only one psychiatrist practising in 1968.

Three communities of the 240 have a large enough medical force to provide a more complete diagnostic service and perform major operations. None of these communities has a population of less than 5000 and one has a population of over 15,000. Not only do these larger communities have more doctors, but they stay much longer. Most of the doctors practising in these communities in 1968 were there in 1958; few stay less than three years.

The communities in this category have a sufficiently large population to support a hospital and a number of technicians to augment the individual medical practice. The hospital provides a set of working relationships with colleagues as well as providing facilities. The additional doctors and the low rate of turnover make it possible for them to have consultations, to learn from each other, and to spend leisure time within a group of colleagues.

One community whose population is just over 30,000, which has grown from a single-industry community to a regional commercial centre, illustrates the different complexion of medical practice in the larger centre. This community had 25 doctors in practice in 1968; seventeen of these (almost 70 per cent) were practising there in 1958; only two of the doctors that arrived after 1958 have left before spending three years in the community. In all, then, 70 per cent of

38 Fraser, *Health Care Sector in Ontario*, p. 242.

the doctors in this community have remained for the eleven-year period as compared to 17 per cent in the other communities just discussed. While most of the doctors in this larger community graduated from medical school thirty years ago or more, the few young doctors (recent graduates) who have practised or were practising in 1958 stay much longer here than do the young doctors in smaller communities. Of the ten doctors in this community who graduated twenty years ago or less, none remained in the community for less than five years and five have remained for eight years or more and are still continuing practice. The other characteristic that distinguishes these medical practitioners from those of the other communities is the specialist degree. In this community 56 per cent of the practising physicians hold some specialist degree. Seventy per cent of them have been able to provide their clients with a continuing professional relationship and specialized services, as well as assistance in time of emergency.

HOSPITALS

Forty-two of the 278 communities under consideration have a hospital of some sort; 236 communities have no nearby facilities for those who are ill. The forty-two hospitals that are available vary tremendously in their size, staff, and type of equipment; they range from the small Red Cross outpost hospital to the modern well-equipped hospital of 150 beds. Some were built by the single industry when the community was begun; others were built with money raised by public subscription, and still others have been built more recently under the various intergovernmental arrangements. Some communities are not considered to be large enough to support a hospital, others have never built one: "Oddly enough with all the city activity - and there is a lot of it - and with the participation of the company we have never had a hospital, and any hospital cases must be flown out." Other hospitals are small and inadequate: "One of the big problems here has been the lack of hospital facilities. There never have been adequate hospital or medical facilities; there have always been too few doctors and if you need [additional] medical service you have to go 150 miles."

Although there are 42 hospitals in the 278 communities, two of the communities with hospitals have no doctors and 4 communities have one doctor; this suggests the limitations on the medical services available. There are limitations on what one or even two doctors can accomplish. As a result some hospitals have modified their functions from diagnosis, surgery, and therapy to those of a community old-age home. Elderly patients who have no home care available are given nursing care, room, and board in the local hospital. Other hospitals are merely way stations between the patient's home and the long trip to adequate medical facilities. Even the larger hospitals have problems in getting adequate staff; only three communities had a sufficiently large medical population with some degree of specialization to be able to provide broad medical diagnosis and treatment. There was no anaesthetist in any of the 278 communities. Few have laboratory technicians, and as one indignant letter writer to an editor said recently:

> The one and only laboratory technician is leaving this month [from the small modern hospital which is well equipped] and seemingly [there is] no effort to replace her. This is a false economy. As a result of no laboratory test, the doctors will have to hospitalize the patients for a longer time – an expensive proposition. Diagnosis will be made more difficult by the lack of laboratory tests; also, determination of a patient's care in some cases will be delayed. A well-equipped laboratory sitting idle is a waste of thousands of dollars of equipment not to mention the inconvenience of the medical staff and the time factor.

Even the larger and well-equipped hospitals, however, are not necessarily a complete answer. The citizen must have confidence in the competence and care provided by a hospital; like the relationship with the doctor, the act of putting one's body and life into the care of others assumes confidence and faith. Gory hospital stories are well known, but if the listener is convinced that the fault was due to the incompetence of one unrepresentative nurse among the thousands of nurses in the city or, if he feels that there are alternative hospitals nearby, these horror stories are grotesque but humourous. When, however, these stories and experiences are attributed to a small permanent staff of the only hospital available then there is hesitation to use or re-use these facilities. One respondent, for instance, said:

> I'd like to talk to you about the hospital. It's in fantastically bad shape. I can get you signed statements from at least 20 men about "incidents" that they have had at the hospital. On my level of the

company, at least, there is no confidence in the hospital at all. Whenever we have to have something done we go to the city. It isn't only the question of inadequate staff, it's primarily a case of low morale among what little staff there is. But it is incredible the situation that exists there now. I'll give you a few examples. I can take a pencil and run it around the wash bowl of the bathroom and pick up a whole mess of hair. When my wife had one of the babies her nursing time came and went. No one answered her insistent ringing. I came in over an hour later and went into the nursery, no nurse. I finally found her in a little room at the end of the hall drinking ginger ale with the doctor. Another time my wife was nursing and she asked for a breast shield. They gave her one which was pretty sloppy and sticky when she got through, but they simply put it back in the drawer. The next day she asked for one and they gave her the same breast shield still sticky and dirty. She did not ask for a clean one for fear that they would go and wash it in that dirty wash bowl I told you about.

Another respondent talking about hospitals stated:

I have had a very unfortunate experience with the hospital. When my last child was born, the delivery was perfectly normal. My wife stayed in the hospital for five days. When she came home she was in great pain as she could not stand or sit comfortably, or lie down. After three days of this we called the doctor and he found she had a temperature of 104. He could not understand this and finally my wife broke down and admitted that she had not had her temperature taken during her entire stay in the hospital. We took her back and the doctor called for her chart and it had been marked normal every day. He blew a gas jet, but, of course, there is a limit to what a doctor can do; he cannot act as a nurse too. The doctors are okay but the service and the nursing service is very very poor indeed. This little incident meant another 3 weeks in the hospital; we would not use the hospital again for any purpose.

In another community a respondent said,

It's unfortunate, but there is laxity in the hospital; here it's a laxity that comes from the top. The head doctor perhaps is capable, but there is a definite need for much more discipline and supervision. You will undoubtedly talk with many people who are dis-

> appointed with the hospital who had confidence in the personnel. Much of what I know has arisen because they are under-staffed. Nobody seems to give a damn whether the patient eats or not, there is no emphasis on helping the patient get well; the patient is there and that is all there is to it. There is no dietitian.

When these sorts of specific illustrations are circulated among people in a small, one-industry community, eventually people distrust the hospital and its services. The definition of inadequacy becomes diffuse as for instance in this comment: "Hospital facilities are very inadequate. There is a very limited staff. It's an extremely poor setup. Now, I don't know why I said that exactly. I think I'm reflecting the attitude of the doctors, as what they say certainly doesn't inspire confidence." Or another respondent said, "My wife has not been too impressed with the hospital. Everything turned out all right, as it happens, but as she said, she is thankful that everything was all right, because if there were complications it would have been just too bad. This is perhaps unfair, but then it is the way she feels. I myself know very little about it."

Many feel that the low level of medical services is due in large part to the nursing staff: "My wife has been hospitalized several times and I have been in one or two days myself, and I found the nurses are a very demoralized bunch; they are another unhappy group in this town who have my sympathy." The recruitment of nurses is difficult, and the kinds of limited facilities offered by a one-industry community makes it even more so. Many of the hospitals draw upon part-time help from nurses who are married and raising their own families in the community.

The majority of the population in communities of single industry, then, has no nearby hospital facilities; for those who do, they are often scant comfort. The distrust of the local institution varies considerably with the position of the individual in the hierarchy. The bush worker, for instance, is far less critical of the services that are provided than is the company executive. Many, if not most, of the population, must go to a larger medical centre for hospitalization or surgery. This has wide implications including the fact that the patient is far away from kin and friends during the period of illness. Often the patient is discharged from the urban hospital and is forced to return home when there are few adequate facilities for convalescence.

NURSES

As we have seen, respondents find it almost impossible to discuss the hospital without discussing the personnel and the nurses in particular. Aside from the valuable work done by the religious communities, there are at least three patterns of nursing role in communities of single industry.

The first pattern is "the nurse" role, characteristic of doctorless communities, and it was discussed to some extent earlier in this chapter. Obviously this is an important, distinctive, and prestigeous role. In northern, extremely isolated communities information about the resourceful and perhaps eccentric nurses of the past seems to take on the quality of folklore. Several informants in one community told the story (with various embellishments) of the eccentric British woman who appeared one day with a packsack on her back, from where no one knew. She found a room and was the only source of medical aid in the area, and gradually she took over many roles: mother confessor, arbitrator in disputes, and a hard, firm, and fair authority-figure in the tough, brawling, emerging community. Eventually telephone connections were made to the outside world, and within the community. One of the stories told of a panic call to the nurse, saying that she must come right away, because there was about to be a fight to the death between two well-known local protagonists who were sworn enemies. The nurse answered with calm authority: "You tell them that they cannot begin their fight until I get there, for I refuse to patch anyone up hours after an injury." She then calmly went about her interrupted business, and several hours later, packed her medical bag, and walked over to the scene of the proposed fight, and announced calmly, "Now you may start your fight." Needless to say the fight did not take place. After playing her key community roles for three years, she appeared one day with packsack on her back and sweeping her eyes over the dilapidated shacks in the wind swept snow, said "Today I am leaving; this community has become too civilized. You now have telephones, you do not need me. I am needed on the frontier," and she disappeared as suddenly as she had come and was never heard of again.[39]

39 A delightful story told many times – and doubtless many of the exploits are based on fact. It must be noted, however, that she could hardly appear and disappear quite as suddenly as claimed because the only way in or out of the community was the plane that served it three times a week.

The second persistent pattern of nursing service in communities of single industry concerns out-of-town nurses, of which there is characteristically a very high turnover. The city personnel departments of many industries located in isolated regions, while not promising marriage, do point out the number of lonely and unattached young engineers on their staff, as well as the high rate of nurse's pay. In one such community the turnover of nursing personnel was 60 per cent each year. And they left unmarried. With the universal demand for nurses, it is not surprising that many "try the north for a while," and then leave. Some find a very rewarding life in a community of single industry, but many stay for a short while only.

The third persistent pattern is that many of the nursing services are performed in communities of single industry by nurses who are married and living permanently in the community. Some work regularly, others "fill in" in time of emergency, others periodically serve in "special" nursing, or home nursing, and one may take on the task of the school or public health nurse if the community has one.

The role of the nurse-citizen-neighbour in the hospital can be quite complex. Seen from one point of view, the nurse is working at a high level of community observability. This may well encourage her to carry out her assignments with meticulous care because she knows that any neglect of her patients will have social repercussions. It makes a difference if the patient tells her friends that Mrs Orange "was wonderful," or recounts a tale of neglect: this social control is wielded by the patient rather than by the profession or superiors.

On the other hand, a number of patients pointed out they they were unhappy when ministered to by a nurse who lived down the street and who shared the same close social life: "I know her too well." Under certain circumstances, such as childbirth or at a time of excessive pain, the patient feels exposed and vulnerable in the company of an acquaintance. With the usual public role-playing in abeyance, the patient feels that he or she has lost face, and furthermore that the loss of face might be reported to others later. There are social circumstances when the impersonality of strangers is preferred to the solicitude of neighbours. Under these circumstances, it is known that excessive knowledge is not held by someone with whom the patient will have to interact in the future.

The patient is never quite sure whether the excessive knowledge will be shared. The oath of the physician provides assurance that the knowledge he commands will not be shared, except with colleagues.

Nurses' ethics are important, but the neighbour-nurse of the community of single industry is placed in a difficult position because she has a range of knowledge which she is expected to exchange in conversations with friends. It is difficult to refuse to answer the question of a concerned friend, "And how is poor Mrs Purple?" Each cue is picked up by the person who asks the question, and inferences are made about each disclosure or lack of disclosure, and this is passed into the informal community communication network. In small communities it is not possible for the nurse to discuss impersonally (as she may do with impunity in urban areas) "the interesting case we had to-day." In the community of single industry, the interesting case is an identifiable individual. This role-set also lacks insulation.

It may be significant, and perhaps prophetic, that what has remained informal and unrecognized for many years is now becoming recognized and formalized. The following newspaper account may predict things to come:

> A committee of doctors and nurses has found that nurses have been able to diagnose and cure half of the cases of illness in Northern Canada.
>
> The committee's report was given to Health and Welfare Minister John Munro last October and released yesterday at a national conference on assistance to physicians. The committee suggested that a nurse with extra training and able to ask a physician's advice could probably handle 99 per cent of the cases. It recommended that nurses working in the North be given a six-month training course with two to three months of that period spent in apprenticeship in a Northern nursing station.
>
> Such a course should teach a nurse to decide correctly on treatment on her own initiative or on a physician's advice, describe symptoms to enable the physician to know the state of the injured or ill person and take life-saving measures when a physician cannot be consulted or transport cannot be arranged.
>
> The committee visited areas in Northern Quebec, Manitoba, and the Northwest Territories.[40]

40 *The Globe and Mail* (April 9, 1971). A number of experimental programmes has been instituted in various parts of the country. One example is the mental health programme in northeastern Ontario. P. H. Melville, "The Raven's Eye': The Regional Mental Health Programme at Northeastern Psychiatric Hospital" (mimeo, 1970).

DENTAL SERVICES

In much of North America teeth are considered sacred by many; it is commonly accepted that one must keep one's teeth as long as possible. This is usually accomplished by periodic visits to the dentist for a check-up, fillings for decayed teeth, and X-rays to detect hidden trouble. If this cannot be accomplished, then there is dissatisfaction and anxiety. In addition, many wish to call upon specialized services for the straightening of growing children's teeth.

In the 240 communities there are 59 dentists. In all, 35 of the 240 have dental services available; most of the population has none. Those who are in the upper echelons of the industrial hierarchy spend most of their summer vacation at the dentist's:

> My wife and I are a good example of that, we are both from Toronto [and] we go home every summer for our vacation period. Do you know what I do when I get down there? Take care of my teeth. My wife sometimes leaves a week early and goes down to the city with the kids because they can't have theirs done in one week. It's awfully expensive, but what can we do? That is how we spend our vacation, that and shopping. The big problem is that there is no preventive work here.

A recent feature article in a daily newspaper commented on the lack of dental facilities for many communities (including communities of single industry) in Ontario. The community singled out for illustrative purposes is the same one used to illustrate the doctor shortage. The article states, in part:

> The 1450 school children of [the community] have been without dental inspections for three years, Mayor --------- said yesterday.
>
> A dentist who lives at [community A] drives 84 miles to [the community] to practise two days a week, otherwise residents have to drive 170 miles [to community B] or 130 miles to [community C], the mayor said. Such trips require overnight stays.
>
> "We've been doing everything we can to get a dentist but without much luck. We have been down to see the Health Minister and the Royal College of Dental Surgeons."
>
> [The community] has a population of 3700 persons. "But there is a total population of 8000 in the area who have been without dental care since our old dentist left," Mayor --------- said.

> There are 20 other communities in Ontario that need dentists, according to a survey by the Royal College of Dental Surgeons of Ontario ... [some] are centres of population of about 150,000 people who lack dental services ... About thirty other towns have been supplied with dentists through the project, which is based on a system of bursaries. Dental students have been given grants of $1500 a year, if single, and $2000 a year, if married, provided they agree to go to a specified small town to practise and remain for one year for each year in which they obtained bursaries ...
>
> It is true that some graduates do not stay in these towns longer than they have agreed, but another graduate has usually moved in right behind to continue the service, he said.
>
> ... Whereas it is difficult for a graduate born in a large city to settle in a small town, men raised in rural areas were usually willing to go back to them, [the registrar] said.[41]

The great majority of communities of single industry have no dentist, and so the people in these communities lack one more set of professional-client relationships. The oil of cloves in the hands of the local nurse provides an emergency service of a sort. The cost of dental care is high for those people who are as far as five hundred miles from the nearest dentist. The travelling dental clinic on the major railways in Northern Ontario is effective for many children in the communities visited, but this system cannot deal with the more complicated problems of tooth and jaw abnormalities.

Many communities have one dentist. Here the problem is similar to that of the one-doctor town. A professional man is available, but if the patient has no confidence in him, this strains the relationship. In some cases the lack of continuity of dental care creates some difficulties.

The communities that boast of two or more dentists are most fortunate; but the more sophisticated services of such specialists as peridontists are universally lacking in communities of single industry.

Although the citizens of a community without a dentist feel deprived, they find it beyond their powers to obtain a dentist. As the newspaper article points out, neither the Health Minister nor the Royal College of Dental Surgeons is able to intervene directly. Again, while they lack a vital set of professional services, there is no clear-cut locus of blame or focus for action.

41 *The Globe and Mail* (Oct. 24, 1968).

THE HEALING ARTS

It is clear that one of the problems of the healing arts is the distribution of available physicians. This difficulty, recognized by the citizens, the physicians, various medical associations and governments, is particularly severe in Canada because of the distribution of the population. The communities described were all in Ontario, a province with a large number of communities of single industry, but the findings would probably be even more telling in other provinces.

Rowat suggests that modern municipal services depend on a base of 30,000 inhabitants and ideally 40,000.[42] The evidence just reviewed suggests that a population of over 30,000 is required to maintain basic institutional services in the healing arts.

The extent of the problem is indicated by the fact that there are far more rural than urban units in Canada. "Statistics show that the average population of the more than 4000 local governments in Canada [excluding the second-tier counties] is only about 3000. The large cities pull up this average and the vast majority of municipalities actually have populations below 3200."[43] The health service complications are obvious. The awareness of the government of Newfoundland of the impossibility of maintaining basic services for small isolated communities is reflected in the programme to encourage people to move from the small outports.

Some people blame the medical associations and the structure of medical practice for the uneven distribution of medical personnel. It is interesting to note that the USSR, a country geographically like Canada, but unlike it in the structure and organization of medical practice, experiences the same difficulty of distribution of personnel.[44]

42 See Donald C. Rowat, *Your Local Government* (Toronto, 1962), p. 133.

43 *Ibid.*

44 Mark G. Field, *Soviet Socialized Medicine; An Introduction* (New York, 1967), p. 72. The feldsher, or physician's assistant, is used extensively in the USSR. Given the size of the territory in the USSR and the reluctance of physicians to practise in rural areas, other measures had to be devised to provide some modicum of medical assistance for the rural population. It is in this connection that the role of the feldsher comes into focus as a possible solution and perhaps a model worthy of examination and emulation by other societies facing the same general problem.

The feldsher is a semi-professional health worker, officially known as a physician's assistant. Feldshers (from the German *Feldscherer,* or field barber

Citizens of small communities of single industry, then, have incomplete institutional services in the healing arts, and the services that are available tend to take on significance and characteristics different from those found in larger heterogeneous communities. But, as the articles and interviews illustrate, the citizens find that there is nothing that they can do about it. Further, the various "theys" - local governments, medical associations, provincial and federal governments, are able to do little about the situation. Health services, like so many other aspects of life in a community of single industry, seem to fit into the limbo of "that's the nature of things." Unlike urban citizens, few residents of the small community of single industry feel that they control many of the factors that affect their health and well-being.

The services and role relationships described in this chapter are those experienced by over 8,000,000 Canadians. Clearly the important variable affecting medical services is the size of the community.

or company surgeon) were originally introduced into Russian armies by Peter the Great in the seventeenth century and served primarily in the military. In the nineteenth century civilian feldshers, mostly retired military feldshers, began to practise in the countryside, where they provided the bulk of medical attention available to the peasantry. While the Soviet regime intended to eliminate feldsherism (in essence a second class of medicine), this has not proven possible or practicable because of the demands for medical personnel and particularly the shortage of physicians in rural areas. Staffing the countryside with feldshers apparently does not pose the same problems as trying to use physicians. Many feldshers are of peasant origin themselves and therefore are not too reluctant to return to the village with the added prestige of the educated person. Openings for feldshers are more limited in the cities, since there already are enough, and sometimes too many, doctors. Moreover, the general educational system is such that it tends to channel rural youths into feldsher schools rather than into the medical schools, because the medical schools require the kind of secondary education not as easily available in the countryside as in the cities.

In theory, of course, the feldsher is only a doctor's assistant and Soviet health authorities emphatically deny that he is entrusted with medical functions and medical decisions. The fact of the matter, however, is that under conditions where there is no physician around, or when no physician is available, the feldsher will fulfill many medical functions, except, perhaps, for routine surgery. A complaint often voiced in the Soviet medical press is the presence of feldshers in positions demanding doctors. In some respects, the feldsher's functions in rural districts resemble those of the public health nurse in the more isolated districts of the United States.

Field, *Soviet Socialized Medicine,* pp. 126-7. This system has formalized what in Canada has been carried on informally and unofficially for years.

In communities of single industry the company has played an important role by providing for some health arrangements. Some of the larger industries engaged a company doctor, others used the medical contract system; in conjunction with government, all companies have taken responsibility for some sort of medical services for their employees. With the introduction of universal medical insurance, this responsibility has been shifted to the provincial governments. This change may compound the inherent problems – it was one thing to be without medical services, but it is another thing to be without them but have to pay for them.

12

The school

Three basic precepts underlie systems of education in Canada today. The first is the right of each province to exercise control of education within its own borders; the second is the division of responsibility between the provincial Department of Education and the local school boards; the third is that, as far as possible, educational opportunity should be equalized from elementary through secondary to higher education, whatever the social, geographical, and financial position of the student.

This having been said, we know that educational opportunity is not equalized. The fact that education is under the jurisdiction of the provinces introduces regional, cultural and provincial differences; in 1961 British Columbia had 68 per cent of its 15–19-year-olds in school, while Quebec had only 50.1 per cent.[1] We know that only 6 per cent of the 25–34-year-olds in Canada have attained a university degree.[2] We also know that those who go on to university are not necessarily the most intelligent.[3]

The type and amount of education that a child receives are influenced by the region in which he lives, its culture, its value system, the economic conditions, and perhaps more importantly by his parents' position in the stratification system. Educational achievement and IQ are strongly related to income, father's occupation, education of parents, and other social factors not embraced by the child by his own volition. The number of rooms in the home, the size of family, the father's income per family member, the parents' education, and living with one parent all are related to IQ range.[4] The Dominion Bureau of Statistics indicates that there is a remarkable disparity between the school attendance of the children of parents in various occupations and earning certain incomes. Families making under \$3000 per year had 12.0 per cent of their 19–24-year-olds in school; families with an income of \$7000 and over had 50.0 per cent of this

1 J. Porter, *Canadian Social Structure: A Statistical Profile* (Toronto, 1967).

2 Economic Council of Canada, *Second Annual Report,* Table 4-5, p. 84; the table is reprinted in Porter, *Canadian Social Structure,* Table G8, p. 120.

3 O. Hall and B. McFarlane, *Transition from School to Work,* Report no. 10, Department of Labour (Ottawa, 1963).

4 See Daniel W. Rossides, *Society as a Functional Process: An Introduction to Sociology* (Toronto, 1968), p. 262. The discussion is based upon data collected by John E. Robbins, "The Home and Family Background of Ottawa Public School Children," in B. R. Blishen, *et al.,* eds., *Canadian Society,* 1st ed. (Toronto, 1961), pp. 501-4. See also John Porter, *The Vertical Mosaic* (Toronto, 1965), chap. 6.

age-group in school. More telling, physicians and surgeons had 73.6 per cent of their 19–24-year-olds in school, whereas non-farm labourers had 9.8 per cent of their 19–24-year-olds in school.[5]

The relationship between occupation and ethnic group and religion is well established, not only in Railtown, but on the national level. Blishen shows that there is a continuous association between high prestige occupations and British ethnicity, and a continuous association between low class and other ethnic groups in Canada.[6] Porter does not see much change in this relationship between 1931 and 1961.[7] This then means that there is an association between religion, ethnicity, and amount of education.

These general trends hold not only for Canada, but also for most countries in the Western world. They have serious implications for Canadian youth, families, industry, and communities because in Canada there are few well-marked alternative educational routes. In Great Britain, for instance, there is a well-developed apprenticeship system which serves to provide an alternative to formal school training. Further, this route can and does lead to the ranks of professional occupations. The apprenticeship system has been poorly developed in Canada.

APPRENTICESHIP

Canada has not gone through the century-long transitional period between manufacture by organized craft and contemporary mass production. A study undertaken by the Department of Labour expands this point.

> In the survey sample, the proportion of non-Canadian trained workers in each trade with apprenticeship training invariably exceeded that of the Canadians. This heavy incidence of apprenticeship training among the non-Canadians was especially apparent in

5 Dominion Bureau of Statistics, *Reports of the Census of Canada, 1961*, Bulletin 7.1-10 (Ottawa, 1965), Table X. See also *University Student Expenditure and Income in Canada, 1961-62* (Ottawa, 1963).

6 Bernard R. Blishen, "The Construction and Use of an Occupational Class Scale," in B. R. Blishen, *et al.*, eds., *Canadian Society*, 2nd ed. (Toronto, 1964), chap. 31.

7 Porter, *The Vertical Mosaic*, chap. III. In view of the nepotism discussed earlier, this is not surprising.

the sheet metal trade. In this occupation, all but one of the non-Canadians had undergone training by completing apprenticeship, whereas only 12 per cent of the Canadians had done so.[8]

Industrialization developed rapidly in Canada in a period when precision work was being transferred to machines, requiring less skill on the part of the men who operated them. The great surge of industrialization during and after World War I involved speed and mass production with the great need for semi-skilled workers. In addition, for many years the major industries of the country were characteristically extractive, rather than precision manufacturing.

What apprenticeship there was reached a low point during the depression of the thirties when even skilled workers found it difficult to get jobs. Although the industrial demands of World War II revived interest in apprenticeship, again, the greatest demand was for semi-skilled workers. Hence, not only has there been a lack of an apprenticeship tradition but the high level of mechanization at the time of the first and second waves of industrialization with the concomitant requirement of few skilled workers meant that apprenticeship as a formal method of training did not advance.

Most workers received informal on-the-job training, "sitting beside Joe to do what he does." To quote the Department of Labour survey, "The reality of the situation is that many Canadian tradesmen acquire their skills either through informal means alone or through a combination of formal and informal training."

With this general background, it is not surprising that highly skilled tradesmen were not an elite in the work world. Further, to become an apprentice meant working at a low wage for a considerable period, forfeiting immediate high wages. "At 1947 wage rates, it would have taken an apprentice toolmaker approximately eighteen months to reach the wage level of assembly-line worker."[9] Rather than becoming apprentices, then, youth chose to move into highly paid semi-skilled jobs in factories. Those who continued their education (and apprenticeship programmes are restricted to young persons who have a high minimum education) directed it toward academic study leading to white collar work. It is little wonder then, that one respondent said it is "prestigeous to go to university but not to a lesser institu-

8 Department of Labour, Report no. 4, *Acquisition of Skills* (Ottawa, 1960), pp. 8-18.

9 E. Chinoy, *Automobile Workers and the American Dream* (Garden City, NY, 1955).

tion ..." The trades have never been highly revered, "The acceptance of vocational training by the community at this stage appears questionable."

The educational system tends to separate theoretical from practical skills. This means, for instance, that engineering training is carried out in a faculty (applied science) within a university. The vast majority of engineers in Canada have reached their position by receiving a Bachelor of Engineering degree at university (with negligible practical experience); very few have become engineers by accumulating technical skills through formal apprenticeship study and experience within the plant works. With this avenue closed the tradesman's job becomes an end in itself.

Every factory, however, must have a nucleus of highly trained technical men, if only to keep automatic machines in working order. A few industries have maintained an excellent apprenticeship system, and tradesmen have come from the technical schools or polytechnical institutes in the country, but in Canada immigrants have been a major source of skilled tradesmen. The backbone of the skilled trades in Canada is made up of men who have been trained in the United Kingdom or in Europe. To quote the Department of Labour survey again,

> About 35 per cent of all tradesmen interviewed in the five trades had received the great part of their training outside Canada. This high proportion reflects the heavy reliance of Canadian industry on immigration as a source for skilled workers, at least up to the period of the survey in 1956 ... The extent of immigration was closely related to the level of skill, that is, the more highly skilled the trade or occupation, the greater was the dependence on immigration as a source for skilled workers.

This survey also showed that the armed forces training made a considerable contribution to the training of technicians. Many factories, then, have filled the greater part of their needs for skilled workers from the ranks of persons who have already acquired their skills elsewhere.

In a national sample, only 14 out of 104 companies had formal apprenticeship training of any kind. Of these, only 7 firms can be considered as making a major contribution in terms of apprenticeship education. Respondents commented:

> Management is not usually prepared to take the responsibility and time for training. Industry is, of course, influenced by the highly successful traditional pattern of academic achievement as a sorting tool; many employers believe they can do a more effective and more economical job of providing specific training and that the higher the level of academic achievement, the more trainable is the young person.

It is obvious that Canadian industry places heavy reliance upon the formal school system, and the vocational and technical education provided by it. Great significance must be placed, therefore, upon the data and comments concerning school drop-outs, lack of vocational schools in the community, and related phenomena. If young people drop out of school before advancing to the higher grades, or without going to vocational school, they are almost certainly destined to end up as unskilled or semi-skilled labour; there is little apprenticeship to offer alternative education and promotion.

THE SCHOOL

The school is a complex organization and carries out many functions. Sociologists usually look at it as a major institution for the transmission of the culture or, more properly, selected aspects of it. Officially the school provides children with the tools of language and literacy, and introduces the child to a selection of accumulated knowledge and problem-solving techniques. At the same time, step by step, the student is provided with credentials for various positions in society. Thus, the school is seen as identifying talent, and providing some students with scholastic credits that permit them to move upward in society. It also provides custodial care for those who are not able or willing to accumulate credits, yet are compelled to remain in school. The school is so organized that religious and often language subgroups maintain their separate traditions, as seen in religious school segregation.[10]

10 An over-all view of education can be found in D. A. Goslin, *The School in Contemporary Society* (Glenview, Ill., 1965). See also Robert R. Bell and H. R. Stub, *The Sociology of Education: A Sourcebook*, rev. ed. (Nobleton, Ont., 1968); Neal Gross, "The Sociology of Education," in R. K. Merton, L. Brown, and Leonard S. Cottrell, Jr., *Sociology Today, Problems and Prospects* (New

In a formal sense, education is free, compulsory, and standardized, and represents a major intrusion of government into the community and home. Actually, education is anything but free, and despite the universality of the rules within any one province, each school is a social world of its own with its own peculiar characteristics. One reason for this is the influence of the local external system upon the school; geographical location, size of community, wealth, ethnic and racial makeup of the population, age structure, organized pressures, the types of industry, and so on, all influence it from the outside because they provide its socio-economic setting, and from the inside, because the nature of the community has much to do with the attitudes and approach of the students to it.

Another reason why each school takes over individualistic qualities, despite the formal curriculum and classroom, is that the school is a complex of interaction and role playing. Each student interacts with his teachers, and his peers; each encounter helps to define particular roles and relationships. This informal system is bound to influence the formal grading and selecting procedure. Conflict between teachers and between teacher and pupil, and courtships between students, all become part of the complex set of interrelationships. But, in some respects, the interaction is biased, for teacher-pupil interaction does not incorporate status equality. The child is expected to change behaviour to conform to the norms of the teacher, however unreasonable they may seem to the child. This does not mean to say that the relationship is not reciprocal, for students certainly change the behaviour of their teacher, no matter how imperceptibly.

Several characteristics of the local school system create particular problems in a community of thirty thousand or less. One is the range of educational opportunities available, and a second is the recruitment of teachers.

COURSE AND TRAINING ALTERNATIVES

In urban areas, with a large population and an elaborate division of labour, the over-all offerings are wide and varied. In the smaller com-

York, 1959), pp. 128, 152. For Canadian material see Porter, *The Vertical Mosaic,* and B. Blishen, *et al.*, eds., *Canadian Society,* 3rd ed. (Toronto, 1968), part III, and the special issue (Sociology of Education) of *Canadian Review of Sociology and Anthropology,* 7, no. 1 (Feb. 1970).

munity with a smaller school system, and thus a more limited division of labour, the types of training which go beyond the academic, university-oriented course are restricted.

In a survey conducted in 1962 there were twelve communities (24 per cent) of the 50 in the sample of single-industry communities that had no provision for vocational or technical training. These twelve communities all had a population of less than 15,000, too small a number to be able to economically sustain diversified and specialized training. In addition, nine of the twelve communities were isolated locations several hundred miles from the nearest vocational training centre.

Some respondents lived in communities which were so small that there was no provision for the small number of youth who require the advanced grades of high school. Many of the other respondents discussed communities in which there was a full high school training available, but little or no vocational training. When vocational or even university training is many hundreds of miles distant, the cost is high. The lack of availability, and the increased cost both tend to discourage qualified students from completing their education as these remarks suggest:

> University education or equivalent is expensive; vocational training is available on a very limited basis only.
> There is a lack of vocational and educational training, lack of good openings with a future, lack of vocational guidance.
> No educational choice, i.e., no vocational or technical schools.
> It is 500 miles to the nearest vocational institution.
> There are no local universities or trade schools.
> Unemployment from lack of vocational training.
> Securing the means of a higher education.
> Lack of employment opportunity: only a small percentage of local youth can be absorbed as permanent employees by the company. The majority must look elsewhere and are at a disadvantage because of lack of local vocational or trades training facilities, and also because of a certain lack of breadth and sophistication in outlook – this latter a result of the parochial atmosphere of a former frontier town which has tried to hang on to its "frontier spirit" too long and has thus become ingrown and hypersensitive to criticism.

Raymond Breton has shown that the organization of curriculum and the programme of study influence the students' educational intentions.[11] J. W. Peach found that "occupational aspiration levels for students in single-enterprise communities are similar to those of high school students in other Canadian and American rural and urban communities."[12] Few communities of single industry provide practical vocational and business courses for those with low aspirations or special courses for the gifted student.

The lack of facilities and variety in course offerings is sometimes due to the size of the community, but at other times to policy. One respondent noted:

> Because society (influenced by parental pride) demands the prestige of a university entrance course for all, there is no other choice for local youth, except for an incomplete commercial course for girls. As a result 77 per cent of high school students drop out before completing matriculation because they are unsuited to it. The company and other influencers of public opinion have failed to exert a constructive force on the school system so that a wider choice of courses could be available for those not equipped to go on to university. For example, when the new General Course was introduced it did not get a trial here because the company and re-

11 Raymond Breton, "Academic Stratification in Secondary Schools and the Educational Plans of Students," *Canadian Review of Sociology and Anthropology*, 7, no. 1 (Feb. 1970), pp. 17-34.

12 J. W. Peach, "Predictors of Occupational Aspiration of High School Students in Single-Enterprise Communities," in Center for Settlement Studies, University of Manitoba, *Aspects of Interdisciplinary Research in Resource Frontier Communities* (Winnipeg, 1970), pp. 35-62. See also, Center for Settlement Studies, University of Manitoba, *Third Annual Report, 1970* (Winnipeg, 1970); J. S. Matthiasson, *Resident Perceptions of Quality of Life in Resource Frontier Communities*, Center for Settlement Studies, University of Manitoba (Winnipeg, 1970); Center for Settlement Studies, University of Manitoba, *Proceedings - Symposium on Resource Frontier Communities, December 16, 1968* (Winnipeg, 1968); Institute of Local Government, Queen's University, *Single-Enterprise Communities in Canada* (Ottawa, 1953), pp. 185-90. See also, Ronald M. Pavalko, "Socio-Economic Background, Ability and the Allocation of Students," *Canadian Review of Sociology and Anthropology*, 4, no. 4 (Nov. 1967), pp. 250-61; Ronald M. Pavalko and David R. Bishop, "Peer Influences on the College Plans of Canadian High School Students," *Canadian Review of Sociology and Anthropology*, 3, no. 4 (Nov. 1966), pp. 191-200.

> sponsible citizens refused to endorse it. Frustration in the high school destroys the incentive to train for a useful place in the working world.

The single industry is sometimes passive in the educational situation. In other cases it wields great influence by building schools, promoting local technical schools, and encouraging youth to remain in school. Support for a proposed programme could well influence the school board and authorities.

TRANSIENT TEACHERS

In addition to the range and type of training available in the one-industry community, there is the problem of teaching personnel. All communities of single industry which are isolated pay teachers on a scale comparable with the pay scales in urban areas. This has come about through sheer economic necessity; in order to attract qualified teachers, these salaries must be paid. This usually means that young graduates from teachers' college select these high-paying jobs, as a prelude to teaching in a different area with similar salary but with a broader range of social amenities. As a result, there is an all-important group of teachers who are oriented toward horizontal mobility in the provincial education system, rather than toward a career in a particular school and community.

The following comments of the younger staff express this outlook toward teaching, and detachment from the community in addition: "I came here for the money, but I won't stay. Next year I'm going back to [a southern Ontario town] ... all my friends are in the south; I'm too far away here. I never heard of the town before I came here, but I came because my husband [also a teacher] got a job here. We're moving to [a southern Ontario city] next year." Another teacher stated:

> I came here because the north always appealed to me; I was looking for a different outlook, a frontier spirit ... something more simple with less pressure. I'd like to remain in the north, but not in this town ...
>
> I came here to see a new type of life; I'd always lived in southern Ontario. I stayed because of inertia. Now I'm moving to [a southern Ontario city] for my professional advantage ... there's a new school.

> I came here because of the opportunity offered in the setting up of the technical wing; but I won't stay. I've found the distance to Toronto too great ... for night courses, for example . I'm getting further behind academically and there's a good opportunity at a new school in [a southern Ontario city].
> I came here because of the opportunity for a departmental headship and for the salary, but I would have to move in order to advance my career: there are young men here already ...[13]

The school board is concerned with such matters as hiring a full complement of staff, and erecting and maintaining buildings within the restrictions of its budget. With limited buildings, funds and teachers, the board is concerned with courses and streams. As one board member explained:

> From time to time there has been a lot of pressure put on us to teach typing, commercial courses, and home economics in the school. Home economics and that sort of thing requires too much equipment and is far too expensive – the pupils can learn that at home. We did have commercial for a year or two – with a special teacher, but with our small enrolment, that is not worthwhile – and we discontinued it. Not enough demand for that sort of training, I think.

In the Canadian tradition, board meetings tend not to be open (officially or unofficially) and board members are seldom elected on a community-wide basis. In one community, the annual general meeting was held on New Year's Day: "The board usually nominates a replacement to be voted upon at a general meeting. This meeting is held on New Year's Day with little publicity. It is only rarely that the townspeople attend the meeting as it is held at such an inconvenient time. Many are not aware that such a meeting is held, or that it is open to the public." The trustees of many schools were not representative of the community's population.[14]

The school board's main concern is the upkeep of the school buildings and the final examination results of the pupils – their school's record. Just how this record is accomplished concerns them little, and this problem, along with the majority of the educational prob-

13 Richard A. Carlton, "Differential Education in a Bilingual Community," unpublished PhD thesis (University of Toronto, 1967), pp. 298-9.

14 A. B. Hollingshead, *Elmstown's Youth* (New York, 1949), p. 125.

lems themselves, was left in the hands of the principal. In a manufacturing town: "The salary is very good – we have to pay a good salary to attract good teachers and the salary is the same as in Toronto. Our principal was getting around $12,000; I think it is around $15,000 now, which is a darned good salary" (1965).

In a pulp and paper community:

> Turnover and enlargement of staff have also been a source of difficulties: the present staff totals only thirteen, but in the last three academic years, twelve new teachers have been introduced. Unable to locate, attract or hold qualified staff, the board has, on occasion, lured housewives and high school students into their classrooms. From all accounts in the community, both French and English parents believe that academic standards are far from the expected level.

The same phenomenon is noted in a mining community: "We have 60 teachers in town and the turnover is about 20 per cent each year." Teachers tend to be nomadic, especially during the early years of their careers. The mobility may be more excessive in the small, isolated community of single industry, but, in any event, we are concerned, not with whether the pattern is typical or atypical of teaching careers, but with the implications of these patterns in the community of single industry.

High turnover of teachers in a single-industry community suggests that the communities are paying a high price for inexperienced teachers and the teachers are mostly inexperienced. These teachers do not and are not able to take on major roles in the community outside school, if for no other reason than that the day-to-day preparation for classes, and the marking of assigned work, is more than a full-time job for a new teacher. We already have noted the high observability associated with the teacher role. As a result, the community knows a great deal about the teacher, but the teacher finds it takes time to know much about the community or the students whom he or she teaches.

THE FAMILY AND THE SCHOOL

Clearly, neither the statistical trends nor the scholastic record of any community of single industry can be attributed to the school alone. The record of students has something to do with the facilities and type of courses offered. Further, the student's persistence has something to do with the home he comes from, his friends, the occupational opportunities (as alternatives to school) as well as the school and its teachers. The future of the student is not predestined, but circumstances tend to conspire against some students. Not all sons of labourers are destined to become labourers, and not all sons of doctors become doctors or even go on to university. If facilities, parents, the peer group, the occupational opportunities and the attitudes of teachers all point up or down, it is likely that the student will follow the appropriate course. If, on the other hand, one of these (or even some other variable, such as the opinion of the clergy) should point in a different direction, then there can well be an exception to the pattern (be it a "drop-out," or an unusual accomplishment).

All young people are born into a culture, and take over its general forms of procedure and ways of looking at life. At the same time, each youth is born into a family, and that family, though it passes on the basic ideas of the culture, does so with variations peculiar to its own life experience. As a child grows up in his family circle his occupational range is narrowed. Some families stress short term goals, others encourage deferment of immediate gratification in order to achieve long term goals. Youth may be encouraged to look for security or to take risks; to remain in school or to drop out; or youth may get next to no guidance from the family.

> Local youth have rather a distorted view of the world due to the quite high level of local prosperity. They are inclined to assume that this prosperity is "par for the course." Even those who have had limited opportunities of travel have not been exposed to the less fortunate economic areas. It is therefore difficult to convince them that education is of greater importance than it was to their parents at the time those parents immigrated here.

Thus, though most nations attempt through compulsory education to equalize youth's opportunity to secure training, that equality is profoundly modified in homes that are far from equal. The world opened to the young man depends on whether his father has knowledge of a few or many occupations and it may make a decisive difference to a youth's goals if in his family circle he associates with successful lawyers, salesmen, or miners. It is mainly in connection with the occupations of his father and his father's friends that the child is likely to receive occupational models:

> [The father faces] the problems of ensuring that they receive adequate educational preparation for future jobs which will provide them with a good living; overcoming the handicap of being spoiled and given too much license by their parents. The majority of youngsters today have not been prepared to face the realities of living – they have been sheltered and coddled both at home and in school and have never been properly taught the meaning of responsibility, self-discipline and other important elements of strong character. Too many youngsters have the problem of facing a very difficult and complex world with the attitude that the world owes them a living and they are here to collect – the problem arises when they find that they must fend for themselves and they don't have the equipment to do it.

Some families provide their children with sharply defined educational goals, others have faith in education, others have no confidence in it, and still others discourage it beyond the minimum age level. The variety of viewpoints is illustrated by interviews in Railtown. These attitudes were related to ethnic background, which of course was in turn related to occupation and socio-economic and status level in the stratification hierarchy.

All 83 parents interviewed in the British group thought that education was "a good thing." All but ten of the adults interviewed felt that their children should achieve more in life than they had. Ninety per cent expressed a desire that their children should go to college or some type of training beyond high school.

Most of the British parents knew quite precisely the type of occupation they wished for their daughters, based on a short, inexpensive, post-high school training to provide some skill and a sense of independence. Only two felt that it was appropriate for their daughter to remain at home without an occupation. The boys seemed more difficult to direct; a profession should be followed, but the parent was not able to narrow the goals to anything more specific. The ambivalence of goals is shown quite clearly:

> I really don't know what John should do. It is so difficult nowadays to know what is best. What do you think he is suited for? He doesn't seem to know, and we don't want to push him into anything he doesn't like. We hope he will be a doctor or something like that, but he doesn't seem to be too interested in school. I sup-

pose he could always go on the road [railway], but we had hopes that he'd do better than that.

Among the Indian group, few of the parents have ever been to high school. The child leaves the house each day, and whether he appears at school or does homework is of little interest to the parent. The child is encouraged to do part-time seasonal work. Few Indian families urge their children to continue to go to school, or to set a goal for them to strive for beyond school.

> Our two oldest boys quit school. Sonny, the oldest left in his last year at public school. He failed his year twice, and didn't seem interested. Our second boy went on to high school. We didn't mind. Then, one morning he said he wasn't going back to school. He got a job on the extra gang. He was out of work for the next year, and just hung around the house. Both of them have a trap-line in the winter – which brings them in a little. They don't give anything to us for board though. Henry, the next boy, is in second year high school, and seems quite interested. He gets along with the teachers better than the other two did. He may go on to school for a while.

Many French-speaking parents displayed a similar lack of understanding of and interest in high school education for males. "What is the use of that kind of stuff. Louis is 'going on' in the shops next year. I talked to the foreman, but he is still too young, and so he'll have to go to school one more year."

Some parents repeatedly reaffirm their faith in education, but cannot assist their children by guiding and encouraging them through the initial steps. "Education is a good thing. If I had good school, I would not be where I am today [town labourer]. I keep telling my kids: get lots of education, and everything is easy. I want my boy to be a doctor – then we'd be proud of him. I never had that chance." The following excerpts illustrate contrasting parental views:

> Education is not such a good thing as we are led to believe. If a boy has the rudiments of education and a good trade – he'll do OK. The trouble now is that they teach them such useless stuff in school. What is my boy going to do with Latin? He comes home with problems in algebra and he can't even add properly yet. A good trade's the answer. Tradesmen will be working when you University graduates will be starving. On top of that the principal seems to have it in for my boy, so the sooner he gets out of there the better.

Jim is going to get lots of education. As far as I'm concerned lack of education is why I am where I am today [fitter]. If I'd had more mathematics and general high school education, I could have a darn good job. I'm restricted, but he won't be. He should go ahead and get a university education. Then he will *show* the other fellow what to do and not do it himself.

THE PEER GROUP AND THE SCHOOL

The family, however, is not the only influence upon the schooling of youth. A number of respondents attribute the school drop-out phenomenon to the influence of the friendship group of youth. They are pointing to the fact that within the school and in the community youth find their own friends – their peer group. This important group, a cross-section of the next generation, has great influence on its members. This is the group which brings up-to-date, as it were, the ideas and behaviour of parents and teachers, adapting these values to the world as they see it.

It has been stated that one function of ambition is to discipline present conduct in the interest of a future goal. Thus the youth who wishes to achieve a high-status occupation will commonly resist the temptation of quick money in the interest of the larger occupational rewards for which he hopes to qualify later. This usually implies a good deal of self-discipline, both in spending and behaviour, in favour of the steady pursuit of a long education. These self-imposed restrictions are in sharp contrast to "impulse following" behaviour.

While a young man's family and teachers influence his ambition, the peer group is very influential in his choice of immediate goals. Such things as occupational choice, leaving school, making quick money in a dead-end job to buy a car, finding acclaim in achieving high school grades, getting married early, are all strongly influenced by what the youth's best friend does. These crucial choices are sometimes due to the most casual and fleeting dissatisfaction or to the lure of a passing opportunity; often the basis of it is unconsciously laid in an unhappy home situation or a vindictive teacher.

Often youths leave school, at the urging of their friends, to take what they think is a "temporary job." Usually this job turns out to be a delusion. Research has shown that for the vast majority, a man's first job is indicative of his subsequent work life. Although there are exceptions, and some are promoted, generally the worker tends to remain close to the job level of his first job; though workers change jobs, the movement is usually horizontal. Thus, if a youth enters a semi-skilled job from school the chances are very high that he will move from one semi-skilled job to another, remaining at or near this level of work and wages all his life.

Respondents, then, talk of short term gratifications: "There is a low sense of responsibility with no inclination to defer consumption to make possible greater consumption later. In many cases (particularly older families, though not so much in 'ethnic' groups) there is a lack of self discipline to learn, or get education. There is no tradition here as to the value of education, though this is now coming to be understood." Material gain is preferred to other values: "A car is more important than a real purpose in life."

In some communities youth seems to wage a war against school: "I thought I'd like to earn my own way ... I think I lost interest in school. I wanted to get in on the money. I was looking ahead to when I could drive a car – that seemed to be the big thing then. Well, the last year I went to school, it wasn't very exciting. I didn't like that: I wanted to get a job ..."

But, even in communities where school is respected, there are a number of perils, as these respondents suggest:

> Being accepted as young adults; they have a terrible burden to overcome, that of being a teenager or young punk. We, as adults, cannot accept them for what they are.
>
> Too many outside activities to distract young people from their studies.
>
> Indiscriminate use of alcoholic beverage perhaps due to easy access to money.
>
> Youth's reluctance to accept personal responsibilities in all phases of community life, leading to trouble areas such as delinquent attitudes in community and highway traffic laws.
>
> Problem of developing a practical philosophy on life; set high standards and objectives for themselves, have to realize that these can seldom be reached, but this should not discourage them or diminish their efforts.
>
> Failure to get the much needed schooling because of family needs in some cases, and in others, the desire for the "fast buck."
>
> The problems of a materialistic world put pressure on youth to

accept a wrong set of values – material gain above service.
Choosing between furthering one's education or leaving school for what seem attractive wages while still young. Predominance of low-skilled jobs in the community encourage school drop-outs. Inducement of "big summer money" encourages teenagers to drop out of school.

INDIVIDUAL ORIENTATIONS

The influence of family and friends, and individual differences, introduce quite different goals, orientations, and aspirations on the part of individual students. This is illustrated by three contrasting views by Railtown youth: Bill, son of a town labourer, said:

> I'll continue in school until grade 10 if I get through my first year of high school. I won't go to university because it isn't necessary. I don't want to spend my life here because there's no place to get a good job. There's more to do in the city and better places to get a job, and there seems to be more chances to get a job in the States. I don't want to do what my parents have done because they have worked too hard.
>
> I suppose if I finished high school I can have an easy job, but I don't like school. I think I'll be a mechanic or a truck driver. This was suggested to me by my brother-in-law.

Ann, daughter of the high school principal, stated:

> I consider that higher education is necessary for a girl wishing to have a career which will support her in comfort or luxury. I do not wish to remain in Railtown because it offers few opportunities to educated people, and I have observed that professional people returning to their home town lack the respect of the people who knew them as children.
>
> I would like to live in the USA because it offers great opportunities for Canadian-educated professional people. If I lived in a city, opportunities of meeting people of my own type would be greater, and choice of employment is greater.
>
> I do not want to follow the occupational line of my parents (both teachers) because the salary is too low. Furthermore one may

easily become settled in some small town and stay there indefinitely.

Ample money is essential to happiness, and the professions are likely to supply it; I have formerly considered entering high school teaching, engineering, journalism, or advertising, but my present choice is medicine. My parents suggest teaching or nursing.

My two greatest problems at present with regard to my career are certainly as to what I definitely want, and worries over financial difficulties. Although I have decided upon medicine, as a profession, I am not sure I would make a good doctor. Also I am positive I would not be satisfied as a general practitioner, and my parents' financial status will make it difficult for me to specialize.

Joseph, son of a first-generation Italian railway labourer, stated:

I would like to go to university, but I might be too old by the time I get there or I might have to quit school first, the way prices of things are to-day.

I don't want to work at the same job as my father. He is a sectionman and he told me never to work on a section for there is no future. He told me that he will let me go to school as long as he can afford to, but not for very long for prices of things are so high. But you really don't need any more education than this (grade 9). I hate to see my father work so hard for me to go to school and fail. I hope not.

I would like to get a job or my own business place where I can be sure that I will not starve. I would like to be a bank manager for up to now, I am trustworthy, honest, but not a 100 per cent smart pupil yet. For in my life I would like to have a full university career ending in a profession. But my father is a hard-working man, and there are six of us being fed and clothed by only his two hands, and still to-day things are not cheap. I would not like my father to do any more for me now, or to ask for any more.

If I can borrow money (and pay back) while I'm going to university for better education, I would be very pleased and thankful. For this may be my last year of school, if I can't help it by being a successful pupil. But many people whom I've met have told me to get lots of education, that I won't be sorry in the future. I will try to follow this as far as I can help it. I would like to help my parents for it is very hard for them.

THE SCHOOL AS A SORTING AND SELECTING INSTITUTION

A number of studies have seen schools as selective institutions.[15] This means that students entering the system are sorted out. Periodically, individuals leave at various levels. The ones who emerge at the top are qualified to enter university and various levels of the work world. Native ability is not the single criterion for advancement through the educational system.[16]

Teachers use other norms to select those students who are to continue their education. The criteria are derived in great part from the ideas and values that are widely held in the town in which the school is located. This enables the school to fit into the machinery of the particular community's social order.[17]

Leaving school can be accelerated by the attitudes and actions of the teaching staff. Methods of encouraging the pupil to leave school are in general use. First, the teaching staff inflicts sarcasm and detentions upon the student to such an extent that he wishes to leave school. Second, the principal and teaching staff make continual reference to the appropriate role and place the student should assume. The third method is direct tampering with marks, or making arbitrary decisions on marginal cases.

While sitting in the corner copying school records in one high school, it was impossible for the writer not to overhear the determination of marks at the final staff meeting. The issue was focused upon two marginal students with an average of 47 per cent. Of one student, a girl who was, in the words of a female teacher "cheap, frivolous, smokes, stays out with boys to all hours of the night and is precocious" it was decided, "I think another year in grade 9 would do her a lot of good." The other candidate, although "slow" was seen as "a little gentleman who tries very hard and comes from a nice family." He was passed; "I think we should give him the benefit of the doubt."

15 W. L. Warner, *et al., Who Shall Be Educated?* (New York, 1944), p. 50.
16 *Ibid.*, p. 46.
17 *Ibid.*, p. 45.

THE TEACHER

The role of teacher tends to be quite ambivalent; there are pressures that force role playing with students to be both diffuse and specific, both particularistic and universalistic. Students should be treated fairly, all in the same way, but individual differences should be taken into account; the teacher is there to teach skills, but he also teaches manners and assists the child facing a crisis.

However, the teacher who stays in the community of single industry for a brief period has little understanding of the problems faced by the pupils or their families. This is the main thrust of Carlton's argument in his study of a community of single industry.

> For perhaps a majority of younger teachers, life in the northern community is a busy round of activity within a narrowly circumscribed area. Heavy work load at the school keeps the teacher out of the mill and out of the commercial heart of the community during the work day; moreover, academic and related tasks generally account for a substantial number of evenings and weekends, particularly at examination time. For the rest, school events - sporting, dramatic, musical or social - offer occasional interruptions in the cycle of lively colleague-group partying. Golfing or curling are professionally acceptable pursuits, helping to fill the time between trips to southern Ontario during special holidays, or the mass exodus at summer recess. Many of these teachers have only the most superficial awareness of the history, structure, and problems of the community, or of their impact on the students whom they face daily.[18]

One major implication of this lack of knowledge of the local community and its population concerns the social definitions that become part of the ongoing educational process. These definitions include ethnic expectations, appropriate behaviour, occupational selections, distinguishing the "late bloomer" from the "lazy arrogant" student, and other sorts of subtle distinctions. The new and inexperienced teacher is more likely to apply universalistic and perhaps highly idealized standards to the students. These definitions might well be unjust to the student.

18 Carlton, "Differential Education in a Bilingual Community," p. 299.

THE PERMANENT TEACHER

The teacher of long standing – whether by choice, inertia, or inability to move – by becoming part of the community, tends to incorporate and perpetuate community definitions within the school system. The streaming of students, and their encouragement or discouragement and guidance, takes on the nightmarish qualities of a perpetuated cycle of self-fulfilling prophecy. Indians are inferior because they cannot get through school, and they cannot get through school because they are inferior. One teacher who remains in the school system for some years is sufficient to perpetuate the social structure of the community because he passes on to the new and inexperienced teacher the local bases of social evaluation. He comments on the families with "bad blood," or "too much interbreeding," or which elementary school produces students who always fail in high school, or the capabilities of each ethnic group, the members of the school board who have children in school, and the children of the management of the industry. In addition, the tradition of separating Roman Catholics from Protestants in the various provincial school systems influences these decisions; all except two of the communities under consideration have segregated schooling, at least on the primary level. More complications ensue when Roman Catholics are French-speaking. All of these factors are of great significance in the small community. A few illustrations will suffice. In a pulp and paper town: "Mr --------- raked another teacher over the coals for not slamming the Catholics harder in a history course; I guess he feels the kids are brainwashed and he wants to counteract it. The teacher thought she had been fair; she tried to present both sides of it. Mr --------- is very anti-Catholic!" Another department head expressed a similar image of the French Canadian:

> There's no justification for the [claims of Quebec] – they've made their bed and they must lie in it. The French Canadian didn't get into the picture in time, suddenly awakes to find himself landless and powerless, and it comes out as cries against Anglo-Saxon dominance. They're victims of progress ... Oh yes, I teach that. I throw out controversial questions for debate in grade 11. I say: "Don't you think all the French Canadians in Northern Ontario are mentally deficient?" There were sixty thousand French Canadians at Confederation – this led to inbreeding and mental deficiency. The

general consensus of opinion is that the average French Canadian is mentally less stimulated – I don't want to say "inferior."[19]

In a mining community:

As far as the school is concerned, the incoming students come from different areas, not only within the community, but also from a number of outlying areas which have no high school. They come in with widely differing abilities and we attempt to group them according to basic testing. On the basis of these tests, I can make some pretty good generalizations about the students. Those who go to the Separate School, who are also Catholic, also Labour, come in with about thirty-fifth percentile in verbal skills and about fortieth percentile in mathematical skills. On the other hand, the students coming from Protestant schools or the public schools who are Protestant, sons and daughters mainly of the professional, commercial and mine managerial group, enter with a fifty-fifth percentile on verbal tests and fifty-fourth in mathematics. This means that, without any question, the people from the Separate School, the Catholics, and the immigrant people, or the sons and daughters of workers, who are also immigrants, definitely have demonstrably less ability. This is reflected in a number of things.

One principal confided:

You can't trust the Indians. You can't blame them, as it isn't really their fault – they just haven't had a chance. Look at the home they come from and the part of the town where they live. None of the boys get far, and the girls are good for – well, you know what!

Then, remember, there's that Indian bunch that lives down there in Lower Town with them. They're a wild bunch – bootlegging all the time. The Italians provide it and the Indians drink it – and you can't trust an Indian when he drinks. Well it is that type from Lower Town who sit here in school, year after year. What am I supposed to do with them? Now I ask you – what can I do? They just won't work and they do not finish school. They just sit and make trouble so that all our time, attention and energy is taken up with this scruff instead of putting it on some worthwhile pupils.

I hope you don't think that I am prejudiced. To prove that I am not – look at the jobs these lads are working at when they quit

19 *Ibid.*, p. 305.

> school. Not one of them is doing anything worthwhile. They are not dependable and they will not work.

The last informant presided over the future of the community's youth for thirty years, as high school principal. Once the stereotype is established, and once it can be illustrated by marks received, grades passed, test percentiles, jobs held and family life lived, it is easy, by nuance of inflection, or outright expulsion, to guide the career line of the student, and mould his self and social image. The sarcasm, the detentions, the nagging and the differential treatment encourage the students to flee from the unpleasant experience. Notions about behaviour appropriate to ethnic, religious and occupational groups are superimposed upon definitions of appropriate interaction with the two sexes.

In one school the teaching staff claims that it is much easier to teach girls than boys – that girls are more co-operative and easier to handle. The majority of the girls get higher grades; and girls almost inevitably stand at the head of the class. Girls, they find, are less apt to lose interest in school work. They continue to higher grades, attend school regularly, complete assigned homework and are more receptive in general to the efforts of the teaching staff.

> We always have more trouble with the boys. I don't know why, because I don't think they are less intelligent than the girls. They just have less interest in school work. The girls appreciate all that we on the staff do for them but the boys have to be kept at the grindstone all the time. We almost have to force them to work. Our greatest disappointments are when boys who really *have* something drop out of school at the end of grade 10 or 11 and go to work.

As a result of the tendency of the males to be less interested in their school work, the teaching staff continually exert more pressure on the males than on the females. Harsher discipline, added detentions, and strict insistence upon rules and regulations are forced upon the boys. Girls are treated with greater respect because they are females and because they co-operate and take their school work seriously. Many of the teachers were undecided what the results of such measures were; they tended to think that these harsh methods forced some of the males to continue at school and increase their work, but that many more were driven from school. Their unhappy surroundings in the school reinforced their disinterest; hence they left. The teachers felt that this was one way to "separate the sheep from the goats," a legitimate way of differentiating between "poor" and "worthwhile" students.

> Moreover, the school is a feminine world in the vocational sense. It prepares girls admirably for their careers in the work world. The skills they learn are immediately transferable to the job world. Especially is this true for those who continue to university, those who prepare for school teaching and nursing, and those who enter clerical occupations. The skills learned in school seem ideally adapted for transfer to the job; with little time delay.
>
> For the boys it is otherwise. Those who drag along to senior matriculation are in many cases unfitted for university work. If they choose school teaching, they find themselves in a girls' world. If they head for a strictly masculine type of work, the skilled trades in industry, they find that their jobs have little connection with their prior schooling. There seem to be few places where skills learned by boys in school, even in vocational school, can be applied to a specific job. The contrast between boys and girls is indeed startling. The graduate of a stenography course can start work immediately as a full-fledged stenographer. The graduate of a four-year course in mechanics starts as an apprentice.[20]

Peach's multiple regression analysis carried out on data collected from students in five single-industry communities suggests that community factors such as isolation or dependence on the single industry do not influence the occupational aspirations of students. He also found a difference in the best predictors of occupational aspiration for boys from that for girls.

> The best predictors of the occupational aspiration level for high school males in single enterprise communities were intelligence, number of school grades failed, father's occupation, socioeconomic status, and number of extracurricular activities in which the individual participated. For high school females in single enterprise communities, the best occupational aspiration level predictors were intelligence, socioeconomic status, number of extracurricular activities, and leadership rating.

20 Hall and McFarlane, *Transition from School to Work*, p. 65.

Differences between responses of boys and girls and the corresponding differences in factor loadings are intriguing. The appearance of a fourth factor which identifies that attraction, for some boys, of these communities may not be surprising. Simple observation indicates that single-enterprise communities are more of a male than a female preserve. Although the factor accounts for the least amount of variability, the high loading of the two variables shows its importance. Because this factor did not emerge from the female data, it is apparent that these communities do not have the same appeal for high school girls as for high school boys.

Another difference between boys and girls is the relative strengths of the external and internal motivating forces. Earlier the argument was advanced that community isolation and community size might spur adolescents to higher educational achievement in order to give them better opportunities of moving from the community. If education acquires an instrumental value, the internal motivation will be greater than the external motivation forces. Factor loadings tend to indicate that education will have acquired a greater instrumental value for boys than girls.[21]

PERSONAL RELATIONSHIPS

Within the small world of the community of single industry, it is very difficult to maintain the detachment required to evaluate students' performance in a dispassionate way. The urban teacher often has this detachment because he or she does not know the child's family, usually not his brothers and sisters. The intermingling of urban teacher and pupil and pupil's family during the ordinary routines of life are usually kept to a minimum. We noted earlier that the school system does much more than pass on special technical skills in its training-selective process. The question then is whose values form the basis of the social skills? Whose decision is it that boys' hair must be short, or that girls cannot wear slacks? Within the school system of the single-industry community, these values are recognized within all but the most marginal of the community families. Only occasionally do the values propounded in school conflict with those learned at home, in the day-to-day interaction within the community, and at work.

21 Peach, "Predictors of Occupational Aspiration of High School Students in Single-Enterprise Communities," pp. 55-7.

For the student and parent who get into difficulty, there are no alternative schools. This means that the pupil is faced with conformity, dropping out, or the prohibitively expensive recourse of studying at school in some distant city. There are a few exceptions; often the children of the top management are sent to private boarding schools (for their roots are not in the community), or, if the school's academic record (the number of students who pass senior matriculation) has sunk to an alarming level, some parents may send their children off to a boarding school for their last, crucial year. Otherwise the system seems to be considered as appropriate. For those who think it inappropriate, there seems to be little that can be done. One community attempted to organize a home and school association; the principal was not anxious to have one:

> You know, a lot of these workers have no grey matter. Most of them make loads of money and just waste it. There's been talk of a parent-teacher association, but, outside of a handful of people, there's no-one here with enough grey matter to offer anything constructive. Take old -------- now what could he suggest? – and he'd talk too if we had one of these associations. He's got a son in the school – spending his third year in grade 10. They just have too much money.

But a letter to an editor presents the other side.

> The parents pay well in both money and sacrifice to see their children properly educated, and must insist on a clarification of existing conditions.
>
> True, each year we have a graduating class of five or so, many of these having repeated their year. What has become of the large number who enter high school each year? These pupils enter high school after competing in the same [entrance] examination. True, there will be a certain percentage who, for one reason or another, do not intend to complete the course, but surely there should be more encouragement and co-operation in seeing that a greater percentage reach their goal.
>
> What possible objection could reasonably be given to a parent-teacher organization? This method of discussing school and home problems has been adopted through the province.

But the establishment of a home and school or parent-teacher association does not provide much of an answer, because, within the context of the community, discussion of abstract problems of education becomes an attack on a neighbour (if not a friend), and at the same time places the pupil in a vulnerable position. The parent-teacher association in Milltown had run into a set of problems which are common to many small towns:

> We feel that any criticism of the existing teachers or teaching is misconstrued to be a personal attack on a personality level. Because of this, we are hesitant to speak at a meeting for fear of reprisals upon our children. Several cases of this sort of thing were reported, and, as there is no alternative school in the town, it means that these children had to go out of town for their high school education. Because we feel that criticism is not possible the teacher association is not vital.

MOBILITY

One of the most important functions of the educational institution is to assist in the social mobility of the individual. Educational symbols achieved in the school permit both horizontal and vertical mobility. By supplying symbols of qualification, the educational institution has great power over the pupil and his occupational orientation. In a community of single industry it provides the youth not only with upward mobility, but also with one of the most useful emigration routes from the community. The data presented, however, suggest that all youth have not equal access to educational qualifications.

> The schools ... function importantly in the operation of the system of status and social class of the societies in which they exist. Where a society contains disadvantaged groups, education is one of the possible means of mobility for them, just as it is one of the means by which members of the dominant group maintain their status ... the ordinary operation of educational institutions, quite apart from deliberately discriminatory measures, tends to cut down the amount of mobility opportunity the schools provide.[22]

22 Howard S. Becker, quoted in Carlton, "Differential Education in a Bilingual Community," p. 335.

Studies completed in the USA and in Great Britain suggest that the educational process becomes a self-fulfilling prophecy.[23] When the barriers of attitude, values and interaction are considered, it is no wonder that the national educational statistics considered by Porter[24] and others persist.

But the educational qualifications of youth are inching up (perhaps not at the rate of technological advances). In a sample of 92 students from grades 11 and 12, it was clear that they were educational pioneers; 45 per cent of the fathers of these students attained a primary school education or less. An additional 32 per cent achieved secondary school standards and a further 23 per cent had university training.

In this chapter we have considered the course offerings, educational facilities and alternatives. The main emphasis, however, as in all our considerations, has been upon role relationships; these were considered in terms of transient and permanent teachers, each maintaining distinctive relationships within the sorting and selecting process.

We now turn to a consideration of the final major community institution, the church.

23 S. M. Lipset and Reinhard Bendix, *Social Mobility in Industrial Society* (Berkeley, 1962), pp. 197-8; Allison Davis, *Social Class Influences upon Learning* (Cambridge, 1950); Patricia Sexton, *Education and Income* (New York, 1961); O. N. Holly, "Profiting from a Comprehensive School; Class, Sex and Ability," *British Journal of Sociology*, 16 (1965), pp. 150-8; Brian Jackson, *Streaming: An Education System in Miniature* (London, 1964); John S. Coleman, *The Adolescent Society* (New York, 1961).

24 Porter, *The Vertical Mosaic.*

13

Churches

"This town is run by the Orange Lodge and the Masons," one Roman Catholic respondent said indignantly. In another community, a Protestant said, "This is a priest-ridden place." The frequency of spontaneous derogatory religious references in interviews suggests that the long tough roots of sectarianism are found in Canadian small towns.

These roots do not begin during the construction stage, when religion is not crucially important in the lives of the workers. Bradwin, for instance, states: "The Church has never properly appraised the campman. Even until very recent years a whole hinterland is placed under one superintendent. He is expected to cover an area bigger than France and Germany put together."[1]

Once wives and children move into the community, however, some provision is made for permanent church and schooling. One by one churches are built as sufficient people from each denomination gather. The importance of differences in belief, creed, form of service, ritual, church architecture, Bible, prayer and fundamental assumptions are illustrated in the rarity of a community church shared by all Protestant denominations, even in the smallest community, and equally vividly by the rules of endogamy and exogamy maintained by Roman Catholics and Protestants. Assertions of firmly-held fundamental abstract principle are at work here, not convenience nor rational and logical arrangements.[2]

An additional reason for the accentuated sectarianism in small communities of single industry probably stems from the varied roles the churches play. In an urban centre, with a plethora of activities under a wide range of sponsorships, segmented roles and opportunities for anonymity, the over-all importance of particular churches is not as discernible.

1 E. W. Bradwin, *Bunkhouse Man; A Study of Work and Pay in the Camps of Canada 1903-1914* (New York, 1928), pp. 265-66. S. D. Clark comments on the indifference toward the church in early mining camps and the inability of the established church to adapt to instability: S. D. Clark, *The Social Development of Canada* (Toronto, 1942), especially p. 373 and p. 216. For a discussion of the relationship between churches and cotton mills in North Carolina, see, Liston Pope, *Millhands and Preachers* (New Haven, 1942).

2 Religious differences and conflict have had a long and continuing history in Canada. This topic has been one of the continuing interests of S. D. Clark. S. D. Clark, *Church and Sect in Canada* (Toronto, 1948); *The Developing Canadian Community*, 2nd ed. (Toronto, 1962); *The Social Development of Canada.* Documentation of conflict and seeds of conflict are found on pages 222, 306 and 375-9 of the last mentioned.

THE SCHOOLS

Most small towns, more conspicuously than cities, have their schooling split along religious lines. This means that families associate with different school systems and the youth of the community are brought up in separate, distinct, and often rival, educational systems. This major and significant cleavage in the social life of Canadian communities has not been given adequate attention. There are infrequent crossings of religious lines for educational purposes, transfers are discouraged on both sides of the religious fence and often severe sanctions are imposed. Carlton notes one example:

> [Catholic] parents who sent children to the public school were on occasion denounced by name from the pulpit or were denied communion. A French Catholic woman dwelling on the outskirts of [the Community] with a family of six found herself on relief following her husband's desertion. In order to avoid the high cost of the separate school education which included the purchase of texts she transferred her children to the public school. At her next confession she was told by the priest that she might not receive communion and that she was to consider herself excommunicated. This woman has not since attended church. (This is not a unique case. The researchers encountered several cases of such discipline and were informed that the sanction of ex-communication had been regularly invoked during the period in question.)[3]

The most extreme form of religious segregation of schooling in both fragmentation (in denominational schools) and rigid institutionalization of the arrangements is found in Newfoundland. The religious supervision of schools, of course, has a long history in the province. In 1843

> The Act defined the educational districts, put each district under a board, and ordered that these Boards would be either Catholic or Protestant as the population in each district was preponderantly one or the other ... In 1850 as a further sign of progress, the first steps were taken to establish in St John's three academies, Roman Catholic, Anglican, and Wesleyan, which have ever since occupied an outstanding place in Newfoundland's educational development.

3 Richard A. Carlton, "Differential Education in a Bilingual Community," unpublished PhD thesis (University of Toronto, 1967), pp. 60-1.

By 1948, the enrolment

> by denominations was 24,477 Roman Catholic; 20,526 Church of England; and 17,215 United Church of Canada. There were 4350 children in schools run by the Salvation Army and 4235 in amalgamated Protestant schools. It has been shown in the historical review that education developed with state aid along denominational lines. The denominational system has often been criticized. In fact, however, the degree of duplication and overlapping of facilities in small communities is much less than may be thought. That is because of the denominational homogeneity to be found in the majority of the Island's many settlements. There are even towns of considerable size in which almost every family belongs to the same religious faith. Its chief weakness lies in subdivisions since any denomination that has reached a certain minimum percentage of the provincial population may be recognized for educational purposes. At present, three of the major denominations make up about 90 per cent of the population. These are the Roman Catholics, the Church of England, and the United Church of Canada. But three other religious groups, the Salvation Army, the Seventh Day Adventists and the Pentecostal Assembly, are also recognized and operate their own schools. It is also a fact that the tendency towards Protestant amalgamation is increasing. A high educational authority estimated in 1956 that about 15 per cent of Newfoundland settlements, for the most part, relatively small, are adversely affected by the multiplication of denominational schools.[4]

To complicate the situation, in Labrador, the Moravians and other missionary groups compete educationally with the other six denominations. When, in a small and poverty-stricken Newfoundland community, one observes six competing small schools, with six sets of children, six sets of (denominationally pure) teachers, and six sets of determined parents who attend six separate churches, one suspects that religion is important. The logical thing to do would be to combine all in one new school, with more competent teachers, at considerable saving; but religion is not logical. The amalgamated school in Newfoundland is the invention of the management of companies in

4 A. B. Perlin, *The Story of Newfoundland* (no date and location of publication provided), pp. 75-9.

communities of single industry. It was brought about in the old days, when the company built and controlled the community, and in the process, built and controlled the school. Amalgamation was forced on the community by sheer authority vested in the company in days gone by. As the responsibilities of the community are transferred from the company to the citizens, new denominational schools spring up.

THE BASIS OF RELIGIOUS CLEAVAGE

It is unclear what great threats are involved in this community cleavage, so delicately balanced with unwritten and often unspoken rules. During interviews direct questions elicit stories of the out-group which, although local, represents national or international grand conspiracy. It seems enough to mention some social sin committed by a "dogan," while hinting at a conspiracy in the Roman Catholic marriage regulations designed to swallow up the Protestants; on the other hand Catholics are not quite sure whether the economic dominance of the Protestants is connected with schemes of the Orange or Masonic lodges or some other nefarious group. The activities of youth are often segregated on moral grounds; there are enough differences in the religious and social attitudes of Catholics and Protestants to justify this. The lack of a blue-law conscience on the part of Catholics, permitting them to dance or play bridge on Sundays, is anathema to fundamentalist Protestants; easy physical contact among youth at dances alarms many priests. Indistinct notions of confession, confirmation, total immersion at Baptism and such practices, all augment the shared lore that the in-group has about the out-group. In addition the religious denominations incorporate competing ethnic groups.

Catholics are seen as reproducing at a greater rate, marrying earlier, and posing a population threat to Protestants. Many Protestants resent the alleged claim that there is no salvation outside the Roman Catholic Church. They feel that the supernatural power of holy oils, water, candles, medals and relics is at best mumbo-jumbo, and at worst a cruel racket. The same can be said of mass money for the souls of the dead. The more sophisticated are concerned with the infallibility of the Pope. The transubstantation of bread and wine of the Eucharist, the immaculate conception, the assumption of Mary into Heaven, and the role of priest either as intermediary or confessor are looked upon as alien.

Freemasonry is seen by Roman Catholics as conspiratorial, atheistic, and aggressively anti-Catholic. The Bible in the hands of anyone introduces the anarchy and blasphemy associated with some of the fundamentalist Protestant sects who recognize preachers with no theological training. The controversies regarding The Jehovah's Witnesses are well known.[5]

Although seldom made explicit, such notions as "the battle of the cradle" or one group being "swamped" by another are shared among those of the in-group. Jessie Bernard, for instance, discusses "battle for the babies" as an issue of denominational conflict among Protestants and Roman Catholics in the United States, but not in her following chapter entitled "Jews and Non-Jews."[6] In Canada, there is considerable reluctance to discuss these issues publicly except in some of the more aggressive fundamentalist Protestant pulpits. Traditionally the birth rate and the rules concerning mixed marriages are contentious issues among the Protestants, while immigration policy is an issue among the Catholics, particularly French-speaking Catholics.[7]

5 For a fuller discussion see: Watson Kirkconnell, "Religion and Philosophy: An English-Canadian Point of View," and T. R. P. Louis-M. Regis, o.p. "La Religion et la philosophie au Canada français," in Mason Wade, ed., *Canadian Dualism* (Toronto, 1960), pp. 41-77. Related works include Clark, *Church and Sect in Canada;* R. C. S. Crysdale, *The Industrial Struggle and Protestant Ethics in Canada* (Toronto, 1961); Jean-Charles Falardeau, "The Parish as an Institutional Type," *Canadian Journal of Economics and Political Science,* XV (Aug. 1949), pp. 353-67; E. C. Hughes, *French Canada in Transition* (Chicago, 1943); H. Miner, *St. Denis* (Chicago, 1939); John Charles Falardeau, "Role et importance de l'Eglise au Canada français," *Esprit,* 20e anée (Paris, 1952), 2e semestre, pp. 214-29; S. D. Clark, *Movements of Political Protest in Canada, 1640-1840* (Toronto, 1959); W. E. Mann, *Sect, Cult and Church in Alberta* (Toronto, 1955); Hugh Herbison, "Doukhobor Religion," in H. B. Hawthorn, ed., *The Doukhobors of British Columbia* (Toronto, 1955), chap. 4; John A. Irving, *The Social Credit Movement in Alberta* (Toronto, 1959).

6 Jessie Bernard, *American Community Behaviour,* rev. ed. (New York, 1962), chaps. 17 and 18.

7 For a summary statement of the extreme French Catholic view, see William Peterson, *Planned Migration: The Social Determinants of the Dutch-Canadian Movement* (Berkeley, 1955), pp. 119-38, particularly the views of Henri Bourassa.

INTERMARRIAGE

Differences of theological belief and practice have existed for centuries, and people have become inured to them by and large. But there are current issues, and these are important because they affect role relationships directly.

> The attitude of the Roman Church to mixed marriages is, to Protestants, a scandal. If the marriage is not performed by a Roman priest, the Church declares it void and invalid; the parties are living in sin and their children are illegitimate. The civil law says otherwise; but in marriage the Church claims a higher authority than the state. The mental anguish of the Catholic partner may be imagined. When, however, the Protestant partner agrees to have the marriage solemnized by a Catholic priest, he must make a number of serious concessions: a dispensation must be bought; the wedding cannot take place in church and there can be no music or any other sign of rejoicing; the Protestant partner must sign a witnessed document that all children of the marriage must be brought up as Catholics, even if the Catholic partner dies; the Catholic partner must sign a promise to try to win the Protestant partner to Catholicism; and the Protestant partner must agree to take religious instruction from the priest.[8]

It is not surprising that there has been a tremendous resistance to marriage between Protestant and Roman Catholic. Parents discourage close social association between Protestant and Catholic children; they are particularly unhappy if a Protestant and Catholic start "going steady." Budding romances are watched with great interest by all concerned and the engagement and marriage of such a pair is considered as a tragedy by many in the community. On occasion, feuds begin, families do not speak, and the couple marry without benefit of parents' blessing. If youth follow these rules of endogamy (and exogamy) the number of potential marriage-mates in the community is cut considerably.

An extreme example illustrates that religious fervour dies hard even within marriage. In this case, a daughter of a leading Roman Catholic

8 Watson Kirkconnell, "Religion and Philosophy: An English-Canadian Point of View," in Wade, ed., *Canadian Dualism*, p. 54. These regulations have been slightly modified since this was written; the stigma still remains.

family in a community of single industry married a Protestant man. The events were discussed in the community with great glee, for not only had general community norms been broken, but the basic principles of both families had been contravened. The couple married, settled down, and carried on married life under the observant eyes of the community. The wife attended her church, the husband occasionally attended his. The union was childless. While the couple was away on a holiday, the wife was hospitalized, and the husband died of a heart attack. As the wife was immobile in the hospital, the body of the husband was returned to their home community, where it was interred by his family in the Protestant cemetery. (It seems particularly important that people be buried denominationally.) Eventually the Roman Catholic wife recovered and returned home. Her first act was to have the body of her husband disinterred and moved to the Roman Catholic cemetery.

ETHNICITY AND RELIGION

> The fact remains, however, [that] the English Canadians are predominantly Protestant and the French Canadians are overwhelmingly Roman Catholic. Hence it comes about that the Protestant English Canadian tends to think of the French Canadian as the Canadian Roman Catholic *par excellence.* In 12th of July oratory, it is the French rather than the Irish Catholic who now tends to become the target for theological thunderbolts; while to the French Catholic, *les Anglais* are characteristically English-speaking Protestants.[9]

Ethnic differences add to the threat of religion when, for instance, Catholic stands for French instead of Irish. Religious opposition becomes augmented with cultural and linguistic rivalry. Under these conditions one group feels severely threatened by the other. In many small communities the Anglican Church is known as "the English Church," the Catholic Church as the "French Church." Somehow, then, the future of the family, the culture, the way of life, is felt to be threatened by the opposing religious out-group. These threats are made quite explicit in the family and are perpetuated in the Church;

9 *Ibid.*, p. 41.

many parents say "Of course I hope you will choose the man you love, but I do hope he will be of our religion."

There are a few situations in which the religious groups come together. One is often the golf course; in a small community a nine-hole golf course is a luxury and all golfers, Protestant, Catholic, priest, or clergyman are welcomed. One of the few times that all the clergy of the town assemble in one place is when support is needed for a vote on the wet/dry issue. The clergy co-operate similarly to warn each other about, for example, an underaged local couple who are trying to get married; desperate youths will often go from one member of the clergy to another, regardless of denomination, in the hope that one will perform the ceremony.

PROTESTANT DENOMINATIONALISM

So far, our consideration has been focused on the split between Roman Catholics and Protestants. This however, is an over-simplification. The Protestants are divided into a number of denominations, Anglicans, United Church, Presbyterian, Lutherans, Baptists, Evangelical, Salvation Army, and so on. There are at least two Protestant denominations in most communities.[10] Experiments with a Protestant community church are usually short-lived. An example illustrates the difficulties involved:

> Regarding the church – the Roman Catholic church – it is a very important factor in community life. I think its importance is lessening, but it is a very important factor. As far as the Protestant church is concerned (are you a Protestant?), originally the first Protestant church was an Anglican church and the clergymen in the very early days tried to get a church organized, but he was "high church." Most people were not very interested in that type of religion. In the early days I myself tried to get some of the men in the camps interested but with little success, and finally the minister left. Then a United Church man came to the district and

10 In a community as small as Hanna, Alberta, the churches included: Roman Catholic, Lutheran, Church of England, United Church, Salvation Army, Calvary Tabernacle, Church of Christ, Seventh Day Adventist and Pentecostal. Jean Burnet, *Next Year Country* (Toronto, 1951).

> started a church and he had a small and simple little church which the people built – the worshippers – and it was used as a community church. There were Baptists, Presbyterians, United, high Anglican, low Anglican, and everyone else.
>
> All this went very well until five years ago when this church burned down, and it was decided to rebuild it. I was on the building committee of the church, and the finance committee. A problem arose because there was a group of very rigid and narrow high Anglicans who were bound and determined to use this opportunity to establish a church of their own. They had the Bishop out here a great number of times – and you know how Bishops are, they are essentially politically minded. They find what the people want and then back them up. I am a low Anglican – my father was an Anglican minister. I had always used the United church and I was in favour of a Congregational church; I was not in favour of two churches which I knew would cut our community in half. I did my best to get the two groups together. I spoke to the Bishop and said "Is it not true that they are trying to do their best to get the Anglican and United church to amalgamate?," and he said, "they will amalgamate only if the Anglican church can absorb the United church." He stated that he felt more at home, as an Anglican, in a Roman Catholic church than in the United church. There was a great deal of bad feeling. So it was impossible to reconcile them. I told them that I would support one church, the Community church, and if they split, I would support neither. Now both have a small congregation and are barely able to support their two elaborate buildings.

Each Protestant denomination then has its own church buildings and organizations for its own congregation. Each denomination forms an in-group which is in competition with all other Protestant denominations, as well as Roman Catholics. But there is more feeling of kinship, albeit distant, among the various Protestant denominations than between each Protestant denomination and the Roman Catholics.

Even though each denomination provides an in-group, each of these, in turn, splits internally. So within the Anglican Church, high Anglicans disagree with low Anglicans on the singing of responses and the choral order of service; in the United Church the ex-Methodists disagree with the ex-Presbyterians on the order of service and the activities appropriate for young people; the Baptists split between "hard shell" Baptists and the liberal Baptists, and so on. These feuds are carried on within each church family, as it were, and are often much more acrimonious than the cleavages between denominations in the community.

Religious differences in the community become structured through social usage in such a way as usually to prevent open conflict. In contrast, the disputes within the church family, like all families, are more open and are prone to arise at any time. Two important occasions permit the drawing of lines and the joining of battle. The first is the annual congregational meeting when reports are received and policies discussed and questions asked; the second is the choice of a new clergyman. The choice of a new clergyman is most important because his background, whether conservative or liberal, high or low, influences the development of the church during his tenure in office.

The largest congregations assemble when a new man is "preaching for a call." It is clear that the clergyman and his family are important to the congregation and to the community. Each clergyman has his own particular area of expertise and concentration – each feels that there must be additional work done among young people, or the women of the church, or the young marrieds, or some other group. So the programmes carried on by a particular church change with a new clergyman. Just as obviously, no professional person can be all things to all people. As the clergyman continues in office, certain individuals drop out of active participation in the congregation. They claim that the clergyman is "insincere" or "we do not feel at home with this type of service." The wife of a clergyman has great influence through her interest and activity or inactivity in the church and its organizations. These very important functionaries have difficulties because of the problem of the balance between primary, personal and secondary, impersonal relationships with members of the congregation. Unlike the urban church, it is not possible for the clergyman to restrict his activities to Sunday service and official functions of the church. The clergyman in a single-industry community is a full member of the community with a wife and children whose activities are known and observed. The problems surrounding the clergyman and his denomination provide great sport and become the basis for much conversation and speculation. Stories of conflict and dissension within one congregation are recounted with glee by members of the others.

Similar difficulties assail the Roman Catholic church although the conflict within a parish is usually along ethnic lines. The Roman

Catholic church often incorporates a wide range of ethnic and cultural groups – Irish, French, English, Italian, German, and so on. When a parish is made up of both French and Irish Catholics there is considerable conflict; under these conditions it makes a strategic difference if the priest is French- or English-speaking. Controversies regarding lay teachers versus members of the teaching orders in the Catholic school, the maintenance of a convent, the physical upkeep of the church, the model of car, and living arrangements of the priest, and whether the vacations are appropriate to the salary of the priest are all discussed by parishioners. The ethnic divisions within the church probably will take on more significance with the shift to the vernacular mass. The Latin mass provided neutral territory for ethnic and linguistic groups within the church services at least.

The role of priest is complicated by two-way role observability. The priest knows the parishioner-confessor, and the confessor knows there is only one priest; despite public civilities, each knows that the other knows. The confessional takes over different significance in a small town where the parishioner may meet his priest in town many times during the activities of the week. The priest is unable to play the impersonal religious role appropriate in an urban area.

SOCIAL ACTIVITIES ASSOCIATED WITH CHURCH

Community cleavages are accentuated because the church is the focal point of much social activity in a community of single industry; under its umbrella many voluntary associations serve various age groups. Although there is some crossing of religious lines, it is infrequent, and related to the amount of religious content of the programmes. Thus a great number of the activities for the town's young people, much of the choir music, women's organizations, teas and suppers are carried on under religious auspices. The churches provide a ready made in-group, as well as the all-important physical facilities for club activities. In this way, then, the members of a denomination are brought together in active interaction; cliques of friends and close associates form along denominational lines.

Religious auspices take in activities that are usually considered non-denominational, such as girl guides, brownies, boy scouts and wolf-cubs. Even when these groups hold their meetings on "neutral" territory – that is, town property rather than a church basement –

Catholic children are often asked to withdraw by their own religious authorities. Sports teams, because they arise out of school or church organizations are split denominationally. Recreation centres, even when built by community enterprise and directed by a professional recreational expert, have encountered great difficulties because of religious cleavage:

> The team programme runs amok of the religious denominations; something isn't approved by the Catholics, other things are not approved by the Protestants, so there tends to be less teenage work than there might be; but they are free to participate in the general programme even if there is no special programme for them. The recreation centre is in conflict from time to time with the Roman Catholic Church about social life and what is considered right for the social programme; there are, however, few undesirable teenagers. The recreation department operates its facilities and co-operates with all groups.

The opting out of community activities by the Roman Catholic Church often has gone as far as the annual memorial service at the Cenotaph in memory of the war dead of the community.

In addition, the churches are of importance in the one-industry community because they routinely sponsor activities to "raise money." The activities – whether variety concerts, shamrock day teas, June garden parties, AYPA plays, rummage sales, or sales of cakes and fancy work – all have the additional function of bringing people together to work in groups. These co-operative efforts are not unstructured, and each person takes his appointed place. Members of other denominations ritualistically attend these affairs. The time, effort, and materials donated by the sponsoring individuals usually exceed the returns from the money-raising bee, but the social cohesion encouraged by co-operative activity remains. Individual churches, part of a much larger ecclesiastical organization, sponsor local activities that are part of a regional or national programme. In a community where there is seldom "anything new," where there is little recreation apart from the do-it-yourself variety, the church takes on an important role. A missionary from Bolivia who has been supported in part from the local church funds is a new person in town who talks about a world far from home; to meet this person, to discuss his or her adventures, and to have tea, provides a respite.

Roman Catholics and Protestants alike, find that a major goal, such as building a new church or paying off a mortgage brings the congregation closer together. As one priest reported,

> One of the things that helped to integrate the Roman Catholics in this area was our building campaign; this helped to break down the intragroup feeling because they all had to get together and stand together to organize the community and make the sacrifice to build this building. Eighty per cent of the pledges that were made have been realized; the people certainly have been greatly integrated because of this project.

CHURCH AFFILIATION

It is no wonder then that one of the first questions asked about a newcomer is "what Church?" It makes a difference whether the newcomer is on our side or their side. Therefore, the religious conviction of each high school teacher is of more than passing interest. The most significant religious affiliation is that of new members of management who enter town. The new manager and his family lend prestige, financial support, and perhaps even active participation to one church. When a Presbyterian arrives in a town with no Presbyterian church, there is interest in whether he will settle into the Anglican Church or the United Church. The person without official religious affiliation, or the person who belongs to one of the more esoteric religious denominations not represented in the community, is looked upon with some consternation. There is a considerable attempt to integrate this individual into some part of the over-all religious structure.

> I am a Christian Scientist – non-orthodox. We found that the recruiting on the part of the clergy was a little too strong. We do not feel part of any church; we go to the United church occasionally but we do not feel particularly happy there. We would be much happier in a Congregational church – a community church, where there was more compromise all the way around.

The non-conformist, then, cannot fit into the community religious structure; at the same time, from the individual point of view, the non-conformist and his family are cut off from a great number of social activities that are carried on under the auspices of, and in the meeting rooms of, one church or another. Some sort of nominal adherence is usually achieved through the children of the non-conformists who want to join Girl Guides or a young people's association. It is not uncommon then to have children of a Jewish family attending Anglican young people's activities or the children of a non-church-attending atheist going to the United Church CGIT. Needless to say, the religious denominations of the physicians in the community are of importance if for no other reasons than the conflicting views about birth control and the priorities of obligation in case of difficulties during childbirth.

The churches then provide a regrouping which is different from the structuring of the company hierarchy. They also provide the bases for a social life and cliques that go beyond either association within occupational level, neighbours, or community-sponsored recreation. Although the churches provide in-groups and out-groups, social life is so structured that there is seldom open conflict.

Religious cleavage tends to be a product of local citizen demands, rather than of the dictates of the particular denomination. There are many possible illustrations of this point, but none more effective than an interview (in French) with a French-Canadian Roman Catholic Bishop, reputed to be "liberal." During a courtesy call discussion, he turned to the writer and said,

> Tell me, what are your impressions of the area. I must confess to you that I do not know what is going on in my diocese. You must remember that local farm boys go into the priesthood. They are local and rural, they attend the local seminary, they reinforce their local ideas, and become local parish priests. They distrust me because I came from outside the district. No one ever tells me anything. I am a prisoner in my own palace. I know that the information they give me is erroneous. How do you, as a social scientist, view what is happening in the area? I know that the priests are bound to be conservative, but what else?

POLITICAL ACTIVITIES ASSOCIATED WITH CHURCH

In over 100 communities of single industry, in which interviews were carried out, there were no indications of a union vote, but respondents in every community noted the religious vote. The significance of voting along religious lines depended a good deal upon the proportion of Catholics and Protestants in the community. As long as one group had a considerable majority, voters tended to vote along religious lines permitting either a token or reasonable representation for the minority. When, however, the percentage of Catholics and Protestants ranged between forty and sixty the issue was much more difficult to resolve. Many found themselves, as voters so often do at provincial and federal elections, torn between the man as an individual and the group that he symbolized. In these cases, an informal and tacit agreement on a religious division of labour on the town council emerges. One comment illustrates this:

> As far as a religious vote is concerned – shall we say that religious feeling is always there, but it is usually dormant? But it does not take very much to raise an issue so that voting and all sorts of activities go along religious lines. We have all sorts of tacit agreements. If there is a Catholic Mayor we have a Protestant Deputy Mayor selected from the aldermen or with a Protestant Mayor we have a Roman Catholic Deputy.

Or, as another respondent explained, "in our town in one riding we have had two Protestants and one Catholic for 20 years; there has only been one exception."

This close relationship between religion and political voting has been noted in other Canadian research. Grace Anderson, for instance, concludes:

> ... religious affiliation of the respondent is more influential in voting behaviour than any other variable tested; the present study thus confirms Robert Alford's findings for nine public opinion surveys conducted in Canada, in which "the differences between the religions within similar strata were consistently larger than the differences between classes within the same religion."[11]

11 Grace Anderson, "Voting Behaviour and the Ethnic-Religious Variable: A Study of a Federal Election in Hamilton, Ontario," *The Canadian Journal of Economics and Political Science*, XXXII, no. 1 (Feb. 1966), p. 37; Lynn MacDonald, "Religion and Voting: A Study of the 1968 Canadian Federal Election in Ontario," *Canadian Review of Sociology and Anthropology*, 6, no. 3 (Aug. 1969), pp. 129-44; Robert Alford, *Party and Society, the Anglo American Democracies* (Chicago, 1963), p. 276.

S. D. Clark long ago related religion and politics in Canada's development.[12] Alford reminds us that this process is still going on;[13] Engelmann and Schwartz suggest that the political relevance of religion has always existed throughout Canada's history: "Of all the factors dividing Canadians in their political outlook and behaviour, religion is uppermost in importance. Yet there has never been a specifically religious party in Canada, such as the Christian Democrats, nor one dominated by anti-religious sentiments."[14] Part of their explanation is that "Religious issues do not normally become national, since the areas in which they are most likely to arise – child welfare, the solemnization of marriage, divorce, and education – are all under provincial jurisdiction."[15] It is in the community, particularly the small community, where the religious issues become significant, not so much in terms of principles but in conflicting norms and daily interaction. Alford suggests that religious influence is waning:

> ... social rather than theological content of religion has become important. And while memberships in different groups will always be divisive, it is a different kind of divisiveness than that based on beliefs and values. In Quebec, the pervasiveness of the Catholic Church shows signs of weakening. Greater participation of the laity, loosening Church control over education, evidence of self-criticism, and even the emergence of an anti-clericalism dormant since the decline of La Parti Rouge, suggest a weakening of Church influence over all facets of life. This is now an era of ecumenism and if different religions can begin a dialogue, then we might anticipate that political parties will be influenced by this as well. Finally, we would suggest that practical politics will be an ever increasing consideration in contributing to the decline of religious-based political cleavages.[16]

The trends seen by Alford may well be emerging on the national scene and even in the city, but the evidence suggests that it will be a

12 Clark, *Church and Sect in Canada,* and *Movements of Political Protest in Canada 1640-1840.*
13 Alford, *Party and Society,* p. 230.
14 F. C. Engelmann and Mildred A. Schwartz, *Political Parties and the Canadian Social Structure* (Toronto, 1967), p. 58.
15 *Ibid.,* p. 59.
16 Alford, *Party and Society,* p. 231.

long time before the importance of sectarianism disappears in the smaller community. There are several reasons for this. Many religious principles have little significance until they are worked out in interpersonal relationships. Despite the social rather than theological emphasis noted in church activities, the participants are part of a subculture with many distinctive and basic values.[17] These basic assumptions, these implicit "givens" concerning individual rights, spiritual authority and the like, are challenged when members of two subcultures contemplate intermarriage. Rules of endogamy and exogamy are basic to most cultures, groups and families, and are not lightly put aside.

The second major reason for predicting that religious differences will continue to be very important in the small community arises out of the first. The value differences lead to patterned activities, so that the community becomes structured along religious lines. The institutionalization of religion in such structures as the school and church leads to its perpetuation. When a great number of social activities are carried out along denominational lines, the religious structuring of the community becomes much more pervasive. Unlike city-dwellers, the citizens have few alternative activities, even if they seek them. Religion has great salience as reflected in the fact that it, rather than position in the stratification system, is reflected in local voting.

This in no way implies that the beliefs within any denomination are held tenaciously. It does not assume that denominational theological beliefs, such as a literal acceptance of the New Testament, a fiery hell, life after death, are accepted without question; it does not assume that the devout go to church regularly or say grace at meals. Indeed research indicates that these theological beliefs and religious activities are changing.[18] Basic and implicit assumptions that affect interpersonal relationships are more fundamental.

17 For a discussion of churches and cemeteries in communities of single industry, see Institute of Local Government, Queen's University, *Single-Enterprise Communities in Canada* (Ottawa, 1953), pp. 191-200.

18 See Donald R. Whyte, "Religion and the Rural Church," in W. A. Tremblay and W. J. Anderson, ed., *Rural Canada in Transition* (Ottawa, 1966), chap. I. Also Pierre Berton, *The Comfortable Pew* (Toronto, 1965); Vernon W. Larsen, *The Minister and the Church* (Saskatchewan, 1964); Crysdale, *The Industrial Struggle and Protestant Ethics in Canada;* and R. C. S. Crysdale, *The Changing Church in Canada: Beliefs and Social Attitudes of United Church People* (Toronto, 1965); Clark, *Church and Sect in Canada.*

Seen from a much broader point of view over a long period of time, religious conflicts can be seen as religious and social movements. On the day-to-day activity level of the community of single industry, however, the broad sweep of social movements becomes lost in the religious complexities of personal relationships. The heritage from outside is made up of the beliefs, stereotypes and assumptions associated with each denomination. The kinds of religious differences just described are of great importance because fully half of the population of Canada lives in the religiously-charged context of communities of 30,000 or less. The small religiously homogeneous community is rare, and will become more so. A homogeneous community such as Miner's St. Denis may still be found in rural Quebec, the "French Shore" of Nova Scotia, small fishing villages or (Baptist) agricultural villages in the Annapolis Valley, but homogeneity is incompatible with industrialization.

This, then, concludes our consideration of the role relationships characteristic of the institutional organization of the community of single industry. The patterned relationships associated with the company, union, stores, recreation, associations, healing arts, school, and the church have been discussed. Although much could be said in summary, it seems more profitable to consider these organizations in terms of social conflict and social control. This is the subject of the next chapter.

14

Social conflict and social control

We have considered the stages of development of the community of single industry, the organization of work, the stratification system, the interpersonal relationships, and the patterned interaction characteristic of such institutions as school, church, recreation, medical organization, and stores. One major question has been implicit: how is the system articulated? We now ask two sub-questions: first, how is social conflict retained but contained; second, how is social control maintained?

Prolonged violent controversies and major feuds such as those noted by Coleman on such issues as racial desegregation, fluoridation, or loyalty oaths introduce great strains into any community.[1] Such conflicts do not have to be restricted to desegregation of schools, or fluoridation, but may erupt over labour-management conflict and other issues. These community-shattering controversies are unusual in Canadian communities of single industry; but they are not unknown, as evidenced by the Asbestos strike, and the woods workers conflicts in Newfoundland and Northern Ontario.[2] Deaths are not soon forgotten.

Major controversies that split the community into two warring factions would make life unbearable in the isolated community of single industry; intra-community conflict serves to unify groups, while inter-community conflict unifies the communities. Looking at the community as a whole, the problem is how conflict is sustained but kept within bounds. This question does not imply that people spend their time purposefully promoting conflict, and then carefully dampening it down if it seems dangerous. Rather, social control is basically self control; it is also implicit and emergent in ongoing human relationships. The patterns of these relationships have a good deal to do with the type of social control that emerges.

Coleman describes part of the divisive process that takes place in community conflict:

1 J. S. Coleman, *Community Conflict* (Glencoe, 1957).

2 On the Asbestos strike, see Pierre E. Trudeau, comp., *La Grève de l'amiante* (Montreal, 1956), and Jean-C. Falardeau, ed., *Essais sur le Quebec contemporain* (Québec, 1953). Comparable technological change involved in the violent woods workers strikes are described by Gerald Fortin and Emile Gosselin, "La Professionalisation du Travail en Forêt," *Recherches Sociographiques* I:I (1960), pp. 33-60, and Marc-Adelard Tremblay, "Les Tensions Psychologiques chez le Bucheron: Quelques Elements d'Explication," *Recherches Sociographiques*, I:I (1960), pp. 61-89.

As in an argument between friends, a discussion which begins with *disagreement* on a point in question often ends with each *disliking* the other. The dynamics which account for the shift from disagreement to antagonism are two: "involuntary," and deliberate. Simmel explains the involuntary process by saying that it is "expedient" and "appropriate" to hate one's opponent just as it is "appropriate" to like someone who agrees with you. But, perhaps there is a stronger explanation: we associate with every person we know certain beliefs, interests, traits, and attributes. So long as we disagree with only one or a few of his beliefs, we are "divided" in our feelings toward him. He is not wholly black or white in our eyes. But when we quarrel, the process of argument itself generates new issues; we disagree with more and more of our opponent's beliefs. Since these beliefs constitute *him* in our eyes, rather than isolated aspects of him, his image grows blacker. Our hostility is directed toward him personally. Thus two processes – the first leading from a single issue to new and different ones, and the second leading from disagreement to direct antagonism fit together perfectly and help carry the controversy along its course. Once direct antagonism is felt toward an opponent, one is led to make public attacks on him.[3]

As participants in a dispute become psychologically "consistent," shedding doubts and hesitancies, they shun friends who are uncommitted, and elaborate their associations with those who feel the way they do. In effect, the psychological polarization leads to social polarization ... The outcome of course, is the division of the community into two socially and attitudinally separate camps, each convinced it is absolutely right. The lengths to which this continually reinforcing cycle will go in any particular case depends on the characteristics of the people and the community involved.[4]

We now turn to a consideration of those characteristics intrinsic in communities of single industry that keep controversy below a certain intensity, and inhibit psychological and social polarization.

3 Coleman, *Community Conflict*, p. 10. The discussion which follows leans very heavily on Coleman's work.

4 *Ibid.*, p. 13.

INHIBITORS OF INTENSE CONFLICT

One characteristic of communities of single industry, of course, is that all citizens are interdependent. Although this answers all questions, it solves nothing; citizens do not set out to love their neighbours as themselves so that divisive controversies do not arise. Perhaps it might be well to enumerate some patterns subsumed under the general term "interdependent."

1. Isolation

The single industry community, by its isolation, its distinctiveness, its lack of hinterland, assumes an identity and a distinctive feeling. There is a distinct sense of inside and outside on the part of most of the population. This notion of community identity and belonging blunts the edge of conflict. This high level of involvement, Coleman suggests, has two conflicting implications; people will fight to have the kind of community they want, but are constrained so that the community will not be disrupted.[5]

2. Lack of Immigration

The lack of incoming residents means that the population remains fairly homogeneous; there are no wholesale and sudden expansions or ethnic invasions. Teachers and clergy enter the system and introduce new and challenging ideas, but these individuals are unusual because they *are* new; due account is made of their actions, as we shall see.

The rare communities of single industry that undergo a large expansion of the industry and of population are vulnerable to intense social conflict. A new wave of population is often difficult to absorb; there are newcomers and old timers, usually characterized by differences in ethnic characteristics, age, housing location, and opinion.[6]

3. Emigration

One way to resolve conflict is to leave. As we shall see in the next chapter, many young people leave the community. Some leave eager-

5 *Ibid.*, p. 21.

6 An example of these differences is found in D. E. Willmott, *Industry Comes to a Prairie Town* (Saskatoon, 1962).

ly and others with reluctance. Presumably there are some selective forces at work, so that those who are hostile to the system, its norms and its people resolve their hostility by leaving. This escape hatch is always available to older people; intense hostility may encourage families to leave.

It is difficult to say to what extent emigration is utilized to resolve conflict; the possibility of emigration has important implications for those who leave and those who stay. Those who stay have made a commitment implicitly. Leaving may be unrealistic in terms of job alternatives outside, house equity and other practical matters, but by remaining, the individual demonstrates that "practical" matters are more important than any principle upon which conflict arises. Some teachers have moved because of principles; others, implicitly committed, have remained often to become principals.

4. The Single Industry

The fact that a large proportion of the population is brought together daily at work is important. Employees are forced to interact; the more often they interact the more they share common values.

The members of each ethnic group take their appointed place in the work hierarchy through a system of nepotism; superordinate-subordinate relationships are institutionalized in a work system. Although all groups become part of the system there are different interaction rates among them; the men have more to do with their work-mates than with those who work in a different department. Work, then, integrates and segregates simultaneously. Further, various inequalities become legitimated, patterned, a part of the normative system and integrated into the sets of mutually-shared expectations. Unsuspectingly, ethnic and other differences, potentially sources of serious conflict, become patterned and so blunted.

5. The Citizens Live and Work in the Same Community

There is a great deal of interaction, and ultimately, the majority of citizens share many of the same values. This comes about through a long process, culminating in the period of maturity (IV). These shared values depend upon the fact that all work and live in the same community, in contrast, for instance, to the suburban commuter who lives in one community and works in another. When men work at diverse tasks without association, values often diverge imperceptibly; often in suburban areas, the values of the neighbours are not known. In these situations it is possible to live beside someone with sharply contrasting views, without knowing it until a local issue arises. Suburbs have been notorious locations for deep divisive community controversies; the conditions that make this possible are seldom found in a community of single industry unless there is massive immigration (point 2) of "newcomers" who challenge the "old timers."

6. *Personalization*

Controversies that divide the community concern matters of principle. We have seen, however, that one major characteristic of life in a community of single industry is the extreme level of personalization. Individual and family concerns are taken into account in industry, the school, and other institutions. One of the outcomes of this is that the individual habitually views life in terms of individuals rather than abstract issues.

7. *Clubs and Associations*

People living in a community of single industry not only work together but play together. The increased interaction provides for increasing normative agreement, while personalizing the relationships even further.

As we have seen, recreation serves as an agent for social control. Because participation is defined as morally desirable, there is considerable pressure upon isolates to associate with their fellows. To the extent that the organization of recreation surmounts ethnic and religious lines, it provides auspices for additional interaction. Each community of single industry has a plethora of voluntary associations, clubs and groups. In any community characterized by a high level of interaction, there are few chances for the psychological and social polarization discussed by Coleman to take place. The network of work, shopping, and club associations is such that if social polarization begins to emerge, it is broken by the interaction required for daily living and playing.

8. Individual Cross Pressures

When an issue emerges, the tendency in communities of single industry is to "do nothing." Some people suggest that this is refusing "to rock the boat." This may be so, but "doing nothing" is characteristic of a person who is subject to cross pressures. A variety of loyalties and obligations inhibit his action. Voting studies have shown that individuals caught in cross pressures are slow to make up their minds about the candidate for whom they will vote, and so they often do not vote at all.[7]

The individual who has many relationships within the community, is likely to find himself effectively neutralized politically in community issues. If one group of associates feels one way about an issue, and another group feels differently, he tends not to take sides, particularly if he can see points on both sides. This results in his retiring from the fray or reluctantly taking a side; neither alternative characterizes an impassioned protagonist.

9. Institutional Cross Pressures

The organizations, clubs and institutions of the community of single industry are involved in a set of interdependencies, although some of these may well be antagonistic. The policy decisions of the officers of the various institutions are subject to two kinds of pressures. The first is internal; when the members disagree on an issue, or when the majority of members is individually neutralized through cross pressures, it is difficult for the institution to take sides. The likelihood of the membership being affected in one of these ways is very high. The second pressure is from outside the institution. The institution is a part of the community structure with its implied dependencies on support and antagonism. The institutional officers usually see that the balance is not upset. If the relationships were seriously disrupted, it could have widespread consequences both internally and externally. The interdependencies that grow up in a community of single industry are such as to constrain institutions, as well as individuals.

7 For a bibliography on voting behaviour, see S. M. Lipset, P. F. Lazarsfeld, Allan H. Barton, and Juan Linz, "The Psychology of Voting: An Analysis of Political Behavior," in G. Lindzey, ed., *Handbook of Social Psychology*, vol. II (Reading, Mass., 1954), pp. 1124-76.

In many ways, what we have described in this chapter is antagonistic co-operation. "It consists in the combination of two persons or groups to satisfy a great common interest while minor antagonisms of interest which exist between them are suppressed."[8]

10. Avoidance of Confrontation

Despite the interdependence, someone contravenes the implicit norms occasionally, or, more often, a newcomer who does not understand local ways challenges the system. Then, "if in doubt, do nothing." Coleman notes that one of the classical ways of dealing with issues, is to deal with them privately, and informally, rather than publicly and formally. Those within the system tend to work privately and informally; it is the outsider, the newcomer, the uninitiated, who challenges publicly and formally. This is well illustrated in a non-battle waged in the weekly paper of a community of single industry. It began with an editorial:

> In the columns of this paper this week we publish a signed communication from one of the teachers of the High School. This document purports to show that there are conditions existing at the school which should be remedied and the writer advocates the calling of a public meeting to discuss openly some of the points brought out in his letter ...

The letter, from a new teacher in town, accused the principal and board of forcing the resignation of two teachers for insufficient and illegal cause. A week later the following editorial appeared:

> There have been no replies from the Principal, the High School Board, or any interested ratepayer to the communication of last week.
>
> We do not intend to unduly prolong this controversy. However, if any interested ratepayer has any comment to make in relation to the above question, they will have the privilege of so doing through the columns of [this paper]. Failing any comments from any of the ratepayers, who ultimately pay the bill, we see no purpose in further prolonging the discussion ...

Several weeks later:

8 L. Coser, *The Functions of Social Conflict* (Glencoe, 1956), p. 140.

> I had the idea that last week we would have had some form of communication from the school authorities in reply to the scathing letter of the previous week; but no show.
>
> I am not particularly interested in the matter one way or the other, but people will talk and with the complete ignoring of the matter by the Board, people are asking if these accusations could be so true that they could not be refuted. And they also ask if the Board has been so lax that these things have been going on which they apparently know nothing about should now come before the public in such a manner that to ignore them is the only thing they can do without losing face.
>
> These, gentlemen, are the reports making the rounds of the town.
>
> By hearing only one side of any question one cannot form any opinion.

The stranger made the public accusations. Neither the board, the principal, or the public made any move to resolve the situation. No meeting was called. There was no public confrontation. The reason for the newcomer's objections was that the original decisions had been made informally and privately. (The teachers involved left the town at the end of the school year.)

The effectiveness of the avoidance of confrontation as a procedure is important, regardless of which side is "right" or "wrong." The lack of response reflects, in part, the knowledge among the townspeople that the letter writer does not understand local usage or the private and informal way in which decisions are reached. A newcomer to a faculty, for instance, often asks public questions and makes public objections which are based on legitimate claims; the other department members, however, have "got used to the system," that is, incorporated the informal norms and patterned procedures, so that the problem is no longer a problem. Often the comment is made, "He'll learn." Community usage works in much the same way. What seems incredible to the stranger is quite acceptable to those who are part of the system.

There are many who claim that the private informal procedures are characteristic of Canadian life in general. Many boards and commissions and bodies meet in camera, and assume that the public has no right to participate or object. That the informal procedures are not restricted to Canada is illustrated in Coleman's comment on school boards in the USA:

> ... it is interesting to note that when a member of a school board, or someone else highly involved with the community, makes a derogatory charge against a teacher, he seldom makes it publicly, but forces the teacher to resign through board pressure. When some community member on the outside has such a charge he often makes it publicly, creating a controversy in the community.[9]

Basically, then, conflict is controlled by not having problems. When problems become issues, there is no issue because nothing is done. Nothing dies faster than a one-sided issue:

> Identification with the community thus interrupts the process of degeneration of conflict at the critical point: where it turns from disagreement to direct antagonism. It is this antagonism, together with the personal attacks which go along with it, that leaves scars on a community, creating lasting cleavages and increasing the likelihood of future conflicts. Community identification helps preserve the form of controversy, restricting it to those procedures necessary to resolution of the problem, and inhibiting those which create lasting bitterness ... In communities, and other kinds of organizations, the norm "unity above all" is employed often to dispel criticism of authority, quell uprisings, and defeat those who oppose the status quo. Identification with the community seems to act as a *conservative* influence on the content of the outcome. Whether this is "good" or "bad" in any particular case depends upon one's perspective. The effect of the *form* of the outcome, by contrast, is good by any standards; the controversy is inhibited from deteriorating into an unrestrained fight.[10]

11. Absence of a Focus of Hostility

We have considered the interpersonal and social characteristics of the community of single industry that inhibit divisive controversy. Many communities have been split down the middle by economic issues, by questions of power and authority. Without doubt, the logical focus of attack would be the single industry that controls the lives of its employees.[11] That community controversy is seldom concentrated

9 Coleman, *Community Conflict*, p. 21.
10 *Ibid.*
11 *Ibid.*, p. 6.

on the industry requires an explanation. What are the qualities of the single industry that inhibit divisive controversy?

(*a*) *The Location of Decision-Making*

Respondents in every community of single industry talk about, complain about, and bitterly criticize the single industry. This industry controls the economic aspect of life, the environment, the stratification system, often the housing, as well as many other facets of life. The company, then, seems to be a natural focal point for hostility and open, divisive conflict. The hand that feeds often has been bitten.

There are, however, a number of mitigating factors. The respondents document quite clearly that many local decisions are made locally. Local recruitment, for instance, is carried on according to local norms within each small social system. The transient manager can act only on the advice of the local authorities according to local tradition except where these decisions run contrary to the general guidelines laid down by head office. We have noted that the structure of the industry itself is such that these guidelines must be broad in their nature. This means, then, that the local manager cannot be blamed for the local structure.

In other matters, such as the laying off of men, he cannot be blamed, for he is following instructions from above, and outside. The local manager is clearly a servant of the same company as the rest of the population, and is not responsible for the policies he carries out. He may be seen as carrying out these instructions badly or well, but, good or bad, the local population knows that he will not be in the community for his lifetime. All of this means that there is no clearly discernible local focal point for blame, hostility or conflict.

Hostility is directed toward an impersonal and undefined "they." This, then, directs attention to the next level – the level of head office. In a certain sense the citizens of the community of single industry are subject to the decisions of an absentee owner; but although decisions affecting their welfare are made by people they never see, this authority structure was incorporated in the ground rules when the community was established.[12]

12 This is basically a different situation from that described by Warner and associates in the Yankee City series. The problems described there were a result of the *change* from a system in which the factory owner was a local citizen, sub-

It is important to note, then, that the railroader, the pulp worker, the miner, are aware that decisions are not made by the local superintendent; they are equally aware that they are not made in head office. Railway workers, for instance, know that the decision on how many trains will run through their divisional point has nothing to do with some little man or some corporation board wielding absolute power in Montreal. They know that the amount of work in the community depends on many factors: the world demand for wheat and the state of the prairie wheat crop; the shipment of beef cattle from the west to the east; the changes in technology; the invasion that trucking has made on way-freight; the inroads that cars and airplanes have made upon passenger traffic. Oldtimers remember the excitement when the local crew took its turn in the relay to speed the special "silk train," with its valuable cargo of oriental silk, from the west coast port. They are aware that their daily round depends and always has depended upon decisions in all parts of the world over which they, the superintendent, and the board have little control. They are not unaware that government policies have something to do with their destiny. They also know about "acts of God" which presumably have something to do with moisture, frost, and winter on the prairies, and directly affect their pay cheques.

The gold miner knows about high and low grade ore; he knows something about government subsidy of gold-mining; but he also knows about the world price of gold, President de Gaulle, South Africa, and many other influences far beyond his ken. The Nova Scotia coal miner knows something about freight rates, competition, and changes in fuel technology; he may blame Upper Canada for his plight, but it is difficult for him to do anything about Upper Canada except join it. Similarly the pulp and paper worker in Newfoundland and the steel worker in Ontario know that when the mill runs at eighty per cent capacity the edict may have come from head office, but that the decision did not originate there. The citizen of the single-industry community does not feel that he controls his own destiny, but at the same time it is not easy to finger someone for the blame. In his eyes, power, control and authority are diffuse.

This does not mean that he does not complain; he certainly is not adverse to selecting a scapegoat, depending upon his ideology, his

ject to local norms, to one in which the decisions were in the hands of an absentee owner. W. L. Warner and J. O. Low, *The Social System of the Modern Factory* (New Haven, 1947).

mood, or his position. But workers seem much more sophisticated in their view of power than most university students and many of their professors, who still search for the locus of power.

(b) Distribution of Control

One of the facts of life in Canada is the institutionalized distribution of power. Nowhere is this more apparent than in a small community. We have made a great deal of the importance of the single industry, but it is the local branch of a larger industry. It is not owned by a local leading family; instead it is managed, in trust, by a transient manager. Further, there is no community of single industry in Canada in which a single leading family owns the local industry, or the bank, the radio and TV outlet, the paper, the real estate firms, the loan companies, the stores, the undertaking establishment, and indirectly the church.[13] The only communities which had anything like this concentration of authority and control are now extinct – small family owned fiefs without banks, maintained in the wilderness away from the main lines of the transcontinental railways. In these, during

13 It is structurally impossible in Canada to have an "X family" as described by an informant in the Lynds' *Middletown in Transition*:

> If I'm out of work I go to the X plant; if I need money I go to the X bank, and if they don't like me I don't get it; my children go to the X college; when I get sick I go to the X hospital; I buy a building lot or house in an X subdivision; my wife goes downtown to buy clothes at the X department store; if my dog stays away he is put in the X pound; I buy X milk; I drink X beer, vote for X political parties, and get help from X charities; my boy goes to the X YMCA and my girl to their YWCA; I listen to the word of God in X-subsidized churches; if I'm a Mason, I go to the X Masonic Temple; I read the news from the X morning paper; and if I am rich enough I travel via the X airport.

Robert S. Lynd and Helen Merrell Lynd, *Middletown in Transition* (New York, 1937), p. 74.

In chapter 3 the Lynds go on to document this opinion by noting that the X family had great influence upon how men were getting a living through control of the banking, legal talent, industry, and retailing. The X family was influential in the control of making a home, through real estate control; the training of the young, through the presidency of the school board; spending leisure, because it involved X family philanthropies, religion, and government. The X family was instrumental in caring for the unable through good works. In addition, the X family had a powerful stock interest, described as "controlling" the morning paper of Middletown, thus controlling information. Under these conditions there is a focus for any discontent.

the depression years, the only outside agency was the post office, and this was manned by company employees.

Canadians are often accused of having a branch system mentality; if they don't have one, they certainly should. Their bank is a branch of one of a number of nation-wide banking systems; their grocery store is a branch of one of a number of regional chains; their loan company is one of a number of regional systems; their insurance company is a branch of one of a number of national, foreign, or international insurance systems; their local merchants compete with branch mail order offices maintained by one or more of a number of nation-wide retailing organizations; their radio is linked with the local station or local repeater station of a national radio network, instead of (or in addition to) a local station; their television is linked to several national networks; their churches are local branches of national or international hierarchies or federations.

All of this has a number of important social implications. First, decisions about all facets of life are not vested in one man or one body. The industry does not control the bank, and the bank does not control the industry, and neither control the local loan company or local stores. Second, the policy laid down by any one of these crucial organizations is not the decision of the local incumbent in office. Each institutional officer has carefully prescribed areas of discretion. Other than niggling decisions, the control of policy and decisions is in the hands of forces outside the community. This fact has many implications, but it is clear that it influences the locus of local discontent, and control.

But, if all of the community institutions are considered, these decisions are made in a number of head offices. Those analysts and politicians who subscribe to the elitist theory point to a dozen, or fifty, or five hundred men who run Canada by virtue of interlocking directorates. Those who make this type of claim are not familiar with what happens at annual, semi-annual, or rarely, quarterly, meetings of boards. It has been said without malice, and not without perception, that the appointment of a woman to the board of directors of a major Canadian corporation ruined the poker game traditionally played the night before the board meeting. The board meeting is not the locus of hard work, detailed consideration or basic decision-making; much of the work of the board is ritualistic.

This suggests that power by its nature is diffuse. It has something to do with thousands of workers, their productivity, their reports, their suggestions, along with information coming from many departments including accounting, and (rarely in Canada) research. The top executives handle the cumulative decisions and plans of the company. The view of a board, with limited expertise, presiding over the destiny of the nation, in isolation from the industry they are directing, is naïve in the extreme. This is not to say that the board does not have potential power – otherwise the top echelons of the organization would have life appointments; but power is as restricted as that of an eleemosynary hospital board which presides over the very special functions of that specialized institution and its experts. To suggest otherwise commits one to a political ideology or is a product of analytical reification.

This discussion of the location of authority and the distribution of authority suggests two things. The first is that it is very difficult if not impossible for the citizen of a community of single industry to locate a source of authority. It is difficult to direct intense conflict against an enemy you cannot find.

Secondly, the citizen of a single-industry community has the feeling that he has no control over his destiny. He knows, and publicly admits, that he has no control over the number of doctors in the community or his own hours of work, and level of employment. And Coleman maintains, as one of the conditions for divisive community conflict, that "the event must be one on which the community members feel that action can be taken – not one which leaves the community helpless."[14]

Lacking intense conflict, then, there are a number of possible ways of coping with the situation. The most common is probably fatalism, disguised by a veneer of grumbling. Inexperienced researchers who interview men who lost their jobs through technological change, and eventually found others involving lower pay and a longer journey to work, were incensed that the workmen were fatalistic rather than indignant. But the respondents persistently replied that even if they had to add four hours of travelling time to their work day, they were happy because the new place had a "good bunch of boys." This general outlook may well partly explain the lack of militant unionism in most of these communities.

14 Coleman, *Community Conflict*, p. 4.

Finally, a great deal of the financing of the local community comes from the provincial and federal government.[15] Major community decisions are made outside the community according to regulations imposed by higher levels of government. This trend further removes the citizens from control over their own destiny.

SOCIAL CONFLICT

In the first part of this chapter, we considered the various social patterns that inhibit divisive controversy in the community, preventing social and psychological polarization. This inhibiting process does not, however, rule out social conflict.[16] In many senses people in small communities are divided, differently located in the social structure, and in conflict with one another. Through time, however, mechanisms arise that localize and limit excessive social conflict. We noted earlier that most relationships were highly personalized, and so conflict became highly personalized as well. There is a major exception to this. The one area in which there is an elimination of the personal elements is, of course, religion. Here conflict is in terms of impersonal principles, of dogma and creed.

1. Religion

Religion is an involvement in abstract principle rather than in deeply personalized relationships, and it changes the nature of the potential conflict. Coser, for instance, notes:

15 Vidich and Bensman make much of this, and for a very good reason. They point out: "The effects of state aid are openly apparent insofar as the granting of aid is conditioned upon the regulations and requirements which define how and under what circumstances it shall be spent by the local agency." A. J. Vidich and J. Bensman, *Small Town in Mass Society* (Garden City, NY, 1960), p. 202.

16 It has been noted that conflict performs many functions, and that the absence of conflict has to be interpreted with care:

> The absence of conflict cannot be taken as an index of the strength and stability of a relationship. Stable relationships may be characterized by conflicting behaviour. Closeness gives rise to frequent occasions for conflict, but if the participants feel that their relationships are tenuous, they will avoid conflict, fearing that it might endanger the continuing of the relation.

Coser, *The Functions of Social Conflict*, p. 85.

> Conflicts in which the participants feel that they are merely the representatives of collectivities and groups, fighting not for self but only for the ideals of the group they represent, are likely to be more radical and merciless than those that are fought for personal reasons.
>
> Elimination of the personal element tends to make conflict sharper, in the absence of modifying elements which personal factors would normally introduce. The modern Marxian labour movement exemplifies the radicalizing effects of objectification of conflict. Strict ideological alignments are more likely to occur in rigid than in flexible adjustive structures.[17]

The number of religious references in the accumulated data is significant. We noted earlier that the small community in Canada was the hotbed of sectarianism. The implications of religion within communities of single industry are many. Differences in creeds and ideologies separate acts of worship. Religion divides the educational system. There is a religious vote. Religion becomes the basis of separate voluntary associations, groups and clubs. Religion provides the rules for endogamy and exogamy. Further, it is next to impossible to keep aloof from the churches because so much of the social life of the town is church-centred or church-sponsored. Religion is so important that it is not seen as an appropriate basis for good-natured teasing and joking.

No matter how we look at it, religion becomes a crucial area of hostility and conflict, and the resulting division is maintained on the basis of abstract principles. But this hostility is institutionalized. It is an integral part of the structured interpersonal relationships of avoidance and reserve. This means that it is normatively accepted by all contenders. Further, religious differences leave none the loser because all have the "right" answer. And even these differences are not local differences, for the convictions, rituals and creeds are shared by the denominations in all other communities in all countries of the world.

Although religion divides, it also unites. It provides for in-group solidarity within a meaningful set of quite complex relationships. Each church has within it potential for conflict, again on the basis of im-

17 *Ibid.*, p. 118.

personal principle (high or low Anglican service, or theological principles among the Baptists); but this internal strife, although divisive, is ultimately controlled, for the same impersonal principles provide the contestants with few alternatives other than separation. To join an opposition church is unthinkable. Thus, Church A provides a community of interests for its adherents in antagonism to Church B, and at the same time provides an arena for conflict within its own walls; but the conflict within Church A, between Aa and Ab, has its own governor in that this dispute, though important, is insignificant when compared with the differences between Church A and Church B.

The relationships between the congregations within the community are governed by yet another set of institutionalized practices. The balance and representation of political interests in the community are symbolized by the religious vote. If for some reason there is a gradual change in the proportions of religious affiliation in the community, the political structure is soon adjusted; first, there is heightened competition and conflict (unspoken, outside each denomination) until the battle is won. But, it is a battle that is impersonal, secret, and according to strict election rules – in a word, institutionalized. Then, when the adjustment is made, there follows either a gentleman's agreement, or a formal arrangement. One such agreement is that when there is a Catholic mayor, there must be a Protestant deputy mayor, or vice versa; another is that there should always be one French Catholic on the council.[18]

18 Conflict consists in a test of power between antagonistic parties. Accommodation between them is possible only if each is aware of the relative strength of both parties. However, paradoxical as it may seem, such knowledge can most frequently be attained only through conflict, since other mechanisms for testing the respective strength of antagonists seem to be unavailable.

Consequently, struggle may be an important way to avoid conditions of disequilibrium by modifying the basis for power relations ... conflict, rather than being disruptive and dissociating may indeed be a means of balancing and hence maintaining a society as a going concern.

[There are] ... three different ways in which conflict creates links between the contenders. 1, it creates and modifies common norms necessary for the adjustment of the relationship; 2, it leads each party to the conflict, given a certain equality of strength, to prefer that the other match the structure of his own organization so that fighting techniques are equalized; 3, it makes possible a reassessment of relative power and thus serves as a balancing mechanism which helps to maintain and consolidate societies.

Coser, *The Functions of Social Conflict,* p. 137.

Although the communities in question were not communities of single industry, Aileen D. Ross' study of the Eastern Townships is pertinent. She traces the changes in economic, political, educational, and religious institutions that came about with the invasion of French-speaking Roman Catholics into an area that had been English-speaking and Protestant.[19]

While Normanville is not a community of single industry, either, John D. Jackson's study of French-English relations suggests four hypotheses which are directly related to the thrust of this chapter: "I The institutionalization of the relations between conflicting parties reduces the level of militancy exhibited by both parties ... II Conflicts within a basic consensual framework tend to exhibit a lower level of intensity than conflicts over a basic consensus ... III If the institutionalization of the relations between conflicting parties is reduced, the level of militancy will increase in both types of conflict – those over and those within a basic consensual framework ... IV If conflicts over a basic consensual framework take place in a situation where the relations between the parties remain at a relatively high level of institutionalization, the degree of intensity will tend to increase while the degree of militancy will tend to remain at a low level."[20]

Jackson's concluding paragraph could well describe communities of single industry in Canada: "A final word on Normanville: today it appears as a placid, friendly town. And indeed it is. But the intensity and militancy of Franco-Ontarian-English conflict is currently at a low level because the relations between the groups are highly institutionalized – in school, church, and town hall; because the current issues take place within a basic consensual framework; and because the degree to which major conflict fronts are superimposed is low. This does not, however, suggest that the conflict itself has disappeared – that "we have no problems here."[21]

19 Aileen D. Ross, "French and English Canadian Contacts and Institutional Change," *Canadian Journal of Economics and Political Science*, 20 (Aug. 1954), pp. 281-95.

20 John D. Jackson, "A Study of French-English Relations in an Ontario Community," *Canadian Review of Sociology and Anthropology*, 3, no. 3 (Aug. 1966), pp. 128-9.

21 *Ibid.*, p. 131. See also, Richard J. Ossenberg, "The Conquest Revisited: Another Look at Canadian Dualism," *Canadian Review of Sociology and Anthropology*, 4, no. 4 (Nov. 1967), pp. 201-18, and Donald P. Hayes, Ernest A. T. Barth, and Walter B. Watson, "Community Structure and the Mobilization of

2. *Entrepreneurs*

A second area of intensive but controlled conflict and hostility characterized every community, without exception. This was distrust and conflict between the employees of the main industry and the local entrepreneurs.[22]

This conflict is contained by a number of factors. In the first place, mutual interdependence restricts the conflict. It has never come to the point that the townspeople boycotted all of the stores. Limited warfare is carried on through the mail order catalogue. This forces the storekeeper to fight back, to regain and retain his customers. Impulse buying, convenience, competitive prices, and the like reduce the extent to which the customer goes elsewhere for goods and services. As noted previously, the level of hostility is greatest in the areas in which the customer has few alternatives, particularly in grocery buying; there are fewer ways in which the customer can take effective action.

Nevertheless, even these hostilities and conflicts become patterned and repetitive as illustrated in the social distance maintained and the prestige withheld, exemplified in the stratification system. There are, on both sides, insiders and outsiders. The recognition of this is incorporated in joking and teasing relationships between customer and entrepreneur. Although conflicting interests and hostility are intrinsic in the relationship, they are limited by the nature of the relationship.

3. *The Referendum*

Another common form of controlling conflict is the use of the referendum. It was noted that religious differences – matters of principle – get worked out within the political structure through institutionalized voting. Other sets of abstract ideology are voted upon from time to time; the campaign and the vote, however, is contained within rules of the voting procedures. The most popular issue in most provinces of Canada is whether or not to permit citizens to drink alcoholic beverages by the glass in public places.

Support," *Canadian Review of Sociology and Anthropology*, 4, no. 2 (May, 1967), pp. 87-97.

22 The intensity of the hostility was illustrated at some length in Chapter 10.

The wet-dry referendum has been part of community life in most provinces for many years. It almost seems to be a ritualistic procedure which incorporates conflict, and at the same time, realigns community forces. In many communities, the wet-dry referendum brings together the various denominations as allies against an evil which surmounts differences in creed. This is an institutionalized occasion for "blowing off steam." Once the "wets" win, it is difficult to say what issue, if any, can take its place.

4. Gossip as Conflict

We have noted that in a community of single industry, there is a tendency to operate personally rather than in terms of impersonal issues. It is not surprising, then, to find that conflict is also personalized. The major category of social conflict in a small community of single industry is gossip. But gossip by its nature is private, informal, personalized, and unlikely to lead to community conflict or the splitting of the community into factions.

Gossip, informal and confidential as it is, is a superb weapon for personal conflict and hostility. It is possible to carry out guerrilla warfare behind the facade of propriety. Gossip can incorporate personal revenge or group antipathy equally well; it can be an all-consuming activity; it is shared with the listener. It can be effective without endangering the larger community or its complicated web of forces.

Our considerations in this chapter have included the inhibition of divisive controversy, and the institutionalization and channelling of conflict. Put the other way around, we have been talking about social control. Gossip is a case in point; as we have just noted, gossip can be seen as social conflict, but it is also an important mechanism of social control. At this point, then, we turn our attention to the mechanisms of social control, and then to the role of gossip in this process.

SOCIAL CONTROL

In our discussions of role observability and the differential effects of this observability we alluded to social norms and social control without specifying their implications. As our interests are concerned with communities of single industry in general, we are not interested in specific norm content but rather with the nature of community normative patterns. For instance, the longer the community remains in the period of stability, the more clearly defined these normative expectations become and the more widely they are understood.

Norms, of course, are a very general category subsuming the traditional notions of law, mores, and folkways. Within the normative structure, there is control exercised over the formulated rules (law) which are common to all communities. These rules are institutionally enforced by the police, as representatives of society, and the due process of the law, which includes the court case and the decision of the judge or jury. The application of the rules is often, if not usually, guided by local norms so that the laws are applied to some citizens and not others. The policeman's discretionary powers are at an informal level. Occasionally, this level of discretion becomes formally and explicitly known. The following letter which appeared in a newspaper in a single-industry community illustrates this point:

> I have been a reader of your column for some time and note that you say what you think about any subject – irregardless [sic] of who's [sic] toes you step on. Well, something happened a week or so ago which I would like to have your opinion on. The police were looking for something in a car the other night and stopped a car on the Main Street; they searched it and in that car they found an open case of beer. Although the police were looking for liquor they had stopped the wrong car and still made a score!
>
> You did not hear about it? Neither did anyone else because it was hushed up and the papers did not get hold of it *because the man in question was a railway man.* If he had worked for the stores in town, in the bush, or on the highway, he would have been pulled out in police court for everyone to see.
>
> Now, do you think that any form of employment should be classed *below a railway man*? Is it fair to a large number of men in other jobs who have no protection?

The second level of normative expectation consists of the less formal and tacit understandings of patterned expectations which are supported by sentiment and commonly held by all. Within this area are a number of deviant acts, including pre-marital sexual intercourse. The third level, the folkways, are the routine expectations which are less commonly supported, including assumptions that people will attend church and look after a range of community obligations.

All of this makes one wonder to what extent behaviour which deviates from these expectations is permitted. Although many people do conform to the ideals of what "ought" to be done, there is a relatively wide range of permissible behaviour. As one respondent said, "I find that I can get away with all sorts of things in my position provided that I keep within reasonable bounds." What are "reasonable bounds"? What are the social consequences of strict adherence to the rules of local expectation? What are the consequences of slight deviation from these expectations or a very wide range of deviance from them? The answers to these questions are not clear in the early stages (I and II) of community development, when there is less consensus on the norms.

GOSSIP AS SOCIAL CONTROL

Negative sanctions may take the form of a sentence in a court of law, isolation by friends who do not approve, or teasing by work mates, but one of the most effective means of social control in a small and isolated community of single industry is gossip. Earlier we traced the communication networks along which confirmed and unconfirmed news passed; this news may or may not have foundation in fact.[23] Citizens spend most of their day in formal role playing and so are subject to the range of knowledge held by their role partners, much of it gleaned from informal information passed along from person to person. It is important to the citizen, for instance, to know whether or not his physician is an alcoholic.

Vidich and Bensman in their comments on the etiquette of gossip state:

23 *Small Town Stuff* by Albert Blumenthal (Chicago, 1932), is built around gossip in Mineville. In his chapter (VII) on gossip he notes that he has taken gossip to include the definitions of the townspeople, which include both "informal news" and "derogatory stigma." I have chosen to separate the word of mouth news channels and the "derogatory stigma." Clearly, the two areas overlap from time to time, but the social consequences of news and derogatory gossip are quite different.

> In a way, then, it is true that everyone knows everything about everyone else, but, because of the way the information is learned, it does not ordinarily affect the everyday interpersonal relations of people; in public view, even enemies speak to each other. When the victim meets the gossip, he does not see him as a gossip and the gossip does not let the privately gained information affect his public gestures; both greet each other in friendly and neighbourly manners, and perhaps talk about someone else. Because the people of the community have this consideration for other people's feelings (we like to think of ourselves as considerate and kind and not out to hurt anyone ... that's one of the main reasons you live in a small town). Relationships between people always give the impression of personalness and warmth.[24]

The point made by Vidich and Bensman that the public encounters between victim and gossip do not reveal the content of accumulated informal knowledge is quite correct. What the authors do not explore is the fact that a good gossip knows what gossip is about. Everyone is a good gossip at one time or another and any citizen in a small community of single industry knows that a wife "is on a binge again," or that a husband is perpetually banned to the cellar where he smokes his pipe into the furnace rather than "fogging up the house," or that a husband goes home after a day's work to do his wife's laundry. The gossip also knows that this knowledge is shared with others.

Each person, then, knows that the victim of gossip loses "reputation," whether formally called loss of status, or loss of face, or stigma; each person knows that this informal knowledge will affect the victim's personal relationships with all others in the community.

The effectiveness of gossip as a mode of social control then, involves, in the words of Homans,

> both actual and virtual changes; what does happen if a man departs from his existing level of obedience to a norm, and what would happen if he did so, although in fact he does not. In everyday social life, virtual changes are the more important of the two, for through them intelligence takes part in control ... The members of the group are obedient to its norms not only because they have actually disobeyed and been punished in the past, but also because they

24 Vidich and Bensman, *Small Town in Mass Society*, p. 45.

see what would happen if they did disobey. They may not think of the relationships of the social system in the same way that we do, but they are nevertheless effectively aware of the relationships and are therefore able to anticipate the consequences of breaking a rule.[25]

Thus to return to the three types of norms discussed above, all citizens knew the identity of the railroader who was stopped by the police; if anyone did not know, he would make it his business to find out after reading the letter to the editor. This informal knowledge influences the relationships that all citizens have with that individual and his family. But this would not show in a manifest concrete way during public meetings between the victim and the knowledge holder. Or, in the case of the mores, school children learn that some high school senior "has to get married," the news of the plight of the pregnant girl and the father of the unborn child passes through the informal communication channels, and all citizens have excess knowledge. This does not mean to say that the new mother will not have a white wedding with elaborate mock-chaste splendour, and certainly townspeople will attend the wedding reception afterwards; it does not mean that the townspeople will necessarily view the situation with compassion, glee or even with some vindictiveness; but they know what happened and the victim knows that they know what happened and the victim's family knows that everyone knows.

This means that knowledge provides power and influence and secret knowledge provides a weapon in interpersonal relationships. At best, it introduces a condescending superiority into relationships – the pleasure of using the double entendre when talking to the bride's mother, the bride herself, or the groom. Ultimately stored away, this information becomes a more potent weapon for the future, if it is necessary to use it. Many politicians have been defeated by whispering campaigns about long past indiscretions.

But, as in international affairs, the arsenal can be used offensively or defensively. Usually, the ammunition is used defensively, for when a person is caught out, and is publicly confronted with gossip-gleaned knowledge, the counter attack utilizes ill-gotten knowledge stored by the victim. This is when the "put down" is prefaced by the phrase, such as, "well at least my son didn't ..."

25 George Homans, *The Human Group* (New York, 1950), pp. 292-3.

But in addition to this control, gossip serves to dissipate immediate issues by means of confirmed or unconfirmed news (the building of a biography of those persons who can be trusted and those who cannot) through private and personal means. Gossip also provides for the systematic accumulation of the great weapon of interpersonal conflict – the ultimate put down." Whenever an issue requires it, the individual has a store of ammunition.[26]

Although each person would like to store ammunition against others, he would prefer that fellow citizens had no unsavory information about him. But there are countervailing forces at work. Secrets are very difficult to keep, and when in trouble, the individual often seeks counsel. All people have close friends, confidantes, or members of that intimate in-group, the family. Gossip, then, has its roots in intentional or inadvertant betrayed confidences. And for the reasons that sacred confidences are betrayed, we turn to Blumenthal's perceptive analysis:

> (a) There are irresponsible information purveyors – persons who must tell.
> (b) While people are on intimate terms they normally confide in and otherwise learn a great deal about one another. When their relations are temporarily or permanently broken, the situation is ripe for wholesale breaking of confidences.[27]
> (c) The desire to appear interesting to others often causes indiscretion to the point of violation of confidences.
> (d) Persons are led into disclosing confidential information in order to prove points in arguments.
> (e) There are "accidental slips" which are not realized as broken confidences until after they have occurred.
> (f) Many confidences are broken because as time passes people are likely to forget that they received the information concerned in confidence.
> (g) Some people care less about privacy than others and so they easily disregard what are to them the excessive requests of others for secrecy. The leading female gossip of the town, as has been indicated, secures her disrepute largely because of telling about others that which she does not care if others tell about her.[28]

26 See Coleman, *Community Conflict*, p. 10.
27 A very good reason for not discarding friends!
28 Blumenthal, *Small Town Stuff*, pp. 139-40.

Certainly, gossip is prevalent wherever people meet, but the significance of gossip in small towns is much greater than in urban suburbs because of the interdependence and lack of role insulation of the citizens. But, the fact that everyone has the goods on everyone else inhibits out and out personal battles or ruthless community conflict. It is far too dangerous a game to be played loosely. Ghosts of the past have a habit of rising to haunt the individual. In a certain sense, then, gossip by its nature, tends to inhibit public confrontations.

The effectiveness of gossip as a mechanism of social conflict and social control depends, to some extent, upon the position of the person in the social structure. As we noted in Chapter 8, some people are in socially vulnerable positions; others feel that they are vulnerable. Gossip simply keeps the biography of those who are invulnerable up to date, but this knowledge affects the character of the relationships carried on with the vulnerable. Ultimately, of course, one of the methods of dealing with gossip is to make maximum use of social insulation; if indiscretions are hidden and not shared, gossip is reduced. Thus people find means of playing one role and hiding another. Some call this Canadian, others hypocritical, but it might more accurately be called institutionalized evasion of gossip.

15

Marriage and migration of youth

Occupational choice is affected by the nature of the community in which youth grow up. Isolated one-industry towns or communities surrounded by a sparsely populated hinterland impose structural constraints which limit the range of available occupations; these constraints are social as well as physical and geographical. Entry into occupations anywhere is restricted, to some extent, by sex, age, physical fitness, formal education, and skills, and often by ethnic affiliation and religion; the limitations in a community of single industry are even more pronounced.

MALE OCCUPATIONS IN THE COMMUNITY OF SINGLE INDUSTRY

Within the town there are two job alternatives for males. The first is to work for the basic industry. Interviews from Minetown illustrate this:

> I thought I'd like to earn my own way. I left school when I was in grade six and I was very young, about 14 years old, when I went into the mines. I think I lost interest in school. I wanted to get in on the money. I was looking ahead to when I could drive a car, that seemed to be the big thing then.

Another respondent said: "Well, the last year I went to school, it wasn't very exciting. I didn't like that; I wanted to get a job and the mines were the only thing. Well, at least, at that time we thought it was quite a thing, and a job was a job." Still another said: "I think myself, it [mining] was all that was around here."

Magill found similar trends in Coalville. One respondent reported: "Mining was the only thing available. In other words, I didn't decide on it. There was only one thing facing us ... the mines. Everyone looked forward to the mine. As far as education was concerned, it was a lost cause. You could see it with the young people at that time; they just thought 'we can always go into the mine.'"[1]

The cultural perspective, determined primarily by the family, largely defines these job horizons. The family contributes specialized

1 Dennis W. Magill, "Migration and Occupational Mobility from a Nova Scotia Coal Mining Town," unpublished MA thesis (McGill University, 1964), p. 22.

knowledge of particular occupations. To enter mining was easy because the candidate knew the language and the work, had the necessary personal relationships with miners and the officials in the mine, and could maintain his position within the social relationships of the town. The same is so whether the industry is a mine, a mill, or a railway.

There is, however, one severe qualification to this first alternative: an absolute restriction on the numbers that are employed in the mines. There are periods when it is impossible to get work. Then, many are compelled to wait and some are forced to migrate.

The second alternative is to supply a service to those in the single industry. Compared to mining this is not attractive to the majority of the males: "I went into the mines because there was no other work here – you could have got a job in a store but you never know how long it is going to last or when they don't need you, so I went down to the mine."

In Coalville, much the same feeling was reported: "At 15 I worked for the milkman, helping him on the truck, delivering milk. Worked about a year, and then started in the mines. I lived across the road from the pit and I went over and put my name on the list ..."[2] Professional opportunities within the communities are few and have high educational requirements.

FEMALE OCCUPATIONS IN COMMUNITIES OF SINGLE INDUSTRY

With the notable exception of textile mills, most industries in such communities exclude females from all work except office routine. In the community institutions, offices and shops, the majority of sales clerks, typists and secretaries are females. The plight of girls, then, is more serious than that of boys because there are so few jobs for females in communities of single industry. The most useful skill is seen as typing and shorthand: "I learned my shorthand from a teacher who was here. I took it privately – and I was lucky, I learned the bilingual shorthand, but I do not use the French at all now. The teacher who gave it to me has gone away now, so I was lucky to get it when I did."

2 *Ibid.*, p. 24.

The number of secretarial jobs, however, is limited in even the largest communities:

> Here we start a secretary at about $170 a month, and this is for a girl just out of school. The range goes up to about $325 [mid-1960s] . The girls in the community who are not secretaries become store clerks, work in offices, or are nurses. For this reason we do not employ married women because there are so few jobs for women in the area. Actually if there is a widow or something like that we have no hesitation at all; but once we feel that her husband can support her she leaves, or, if she wishes she can get a job downtown; but the few jobs that are available for women in the office are left for single girls.

Despite the high turnover, there are not enough secretarial jobs for the girls.

> I have 34 stenographers, but no male secretaries. The Union negotiation contract for females gives a very low pay. This was of course, based on the old days when people would go to business school and females were available. Males don't seem to go into this occupation; if they do they go to a business school but don't take any shorthand because this is women's work, and the reason, of course, is the low salary. We have a fantastic turnover every year in secretarial help and it would be very good to have permanent help. Now there is some talk in the union about having equal pay for equal work. If this was actually put into action it would mean that the secretarial salaries would go up, and under these circumstances I would be in favour of having a male secretarial staff. This would give us a permanence. At the same time we could have an elite group of male secretaries and enough money for them to make a career of it. At the moment half of our secretarial staff is married; when they become pregnant they quite often get leave of absence and return later. We are now building up a secretarial pool, and we have young people coming out of business school and if they have a high salary they have responsible work. Our most skilled secretaries do get around $400 a month, which is very high, but there are very few of these.

Other courses are given in the hope of imparting skills, such as hairdressing, but the final solution to all the girls' problems is often seen as marriage:

> We find that these young girls who haven't got the brains, or who were drop-outs, or who haven't taken enough education are real problems; they hunt for the first man they can find, to get married as quickly as possible. And the first man who comes along does, and this of course starts a vicious circle again, because usually he is not the right kind of person. I just had a case the other day, a seventeen-year-old girl. She was a very cute young thing and didn't have much education, and it was quite evident for a year or so that she really was looking for a man so she could get married, and she ended up marrying an alcoholic. I was talking to one of our top athletes, a very clever boy who had repeated grade eleven, and had failed primarily because he just wouldn't do the necessary work. He's going to marry now. Men tend to find a girl as soon as possible and girls look on marriage as a way out of leaving the town or finding unsatisfactory employment.

Marriage, however, is not always easy in a small and isolated community of single industry (or anywhere else). If a young person is to marry within his or her own religion and ethnic group, and still remain within the age differences traditionally maintained in our society, there are very few partners to choose from. Although "going steady" during the high school years is common, the movement of youth outside the town reduces the potential partners. By the time the rules of endogamy are adhered to, there may be only two or three potential marriage candidates. If there are adjacent communities which can be reached by car, this restriction is not as severe. Many girls, however, are forced to leave the community to find a marriage partner as much as to obtain a job or follow a career line.

OCCUPATIONS OUTSIDE THE COMMUNITY

The third alternative for both males and females is to move outside the immediate area, but remain within the region. This alternative offers a much wider occupational choice. However, the applicant generally lacks the education, expert knowledge, and the primary group relationships which could support him in a strongly competitive situation. It is doubtful if the majority can do as well in earnings or community prestige in the region as they could in their home community.

Finally, the fourth alternative is to move outside the region to an urban area in Canada, the United States, or elsewhere. This type of move involves a tremendous number of unknowns. Certainly, a considerable but casual knowledge of the local industry and its skills is not very useful in a new situation. Education is a more valuable qualification.[3]

Within the community of single industry, the individual's job horizon is restricted; the urban working-class youths are more likely to be acquainted with a wide range of occupational possibilities than those who are raised in a less heterogeneous (occupationally), smaller community.[4] In addition, the occupational impressions offered by daily life are proportional to the actual occupational distribution. The greater the number of miners, the more frequently will young people hear about that occupation and the more often will they be led to choose it.[5]

Directly and indirectly the family has a great deal to do with the occupational configuration of the children. Education for instance is a major determinant of career patterns, but children from low-status families do not have as much chance to stay in school as those from high-status families.[6] The youth from a working-class family receives little education and vocational advice; while attending school, job plans are vague; when young people leave school they are inclined to take the first available job. Lack of education, lack of planning, and failure to explore fully the available job opportunities, all characterize the working-class family; these traits are handed down from generation to generation.[7] Occupational and social status tend

3 See Lawrence Thomas, *The Occupational Structure and Education* (New York, 1956), p. 39. See also Institute of Local Government, Queen's University, *Single-Enterprise Communities in Canada* (Ottawa, 1953), pp. 226-9; Center for Settlement Studies, University of Manitoba, *Aspects of Interdisciplinary Research in Resource Frontier Communities* (Winnipeg, 1970), pp. 35-62, and Center for Settlement Studies, University of Manitoba, *Proceedings – Symposium on Resource Frontier Communities, December 16, 1968* (Winnipeg, 1968).

4 Leo F. Schnore and David W. Varley, "Some Concomitants of Metropolitan Size," *American Sociological Review*, 20 (1955), 408-14.

5 P. F. Lazarsfeld, *Jugend und Beruf*, vol. 8 of *Quellen und Studien zur Jugendkunde* (Jena, 1931), p. 13.

6 S. M. Lipset and R. Bendix, *Social Mobility in Industrial Society* (Berkeley, 1959), chap. 7.

7 S. M. Lipset and F. T. Malm, "First Jobs and Career Patterns," *American Journal of Economics and Sociology*, 14 (1955), pp. 197-261.

to be self-perpetuating; a youth from a family in the unskilled job category sees less, reads less, hears less, has experienced less variety in his environment, and is simply aware of fewer opportunities than the socially privileged young person.[8] But, prepared or not, many of these young people are forced to leave home.

SOURCES OF CONTACT FOR RECRUITMENT OF YOUTH INTO URBAN INDUSTRY

In a study of the transition from school to work by young people in two urban communities it was found that the ways in which youth found a job were varied. They included: (i) the efforts of teachers and other school functionaries; (ii) the personal contacts of families and friends; (iii) individual efforts on the part of the student; (iv) a continuation of part-time work undertaken while at school; (v) the National Employment Service. Research findings showed that guidance services of the schools made little imprint on the students, and few students had any awareness of the National Employment Service (Manpower) (until they lost their first job, when they went to register as unemployed).[9]

Since this study, another approach to the question was tried by the writer. Instead of asking youth where they went for a job, and how they went about it, urban industrial employment officers were asked how they recruited their personnel, and how initial contact was made with young potential employees. The employer signified the point or points of contact used to recruit skilled trades, administrative and stenographic employees, and unskilled workers. The results are found in Table 2.

The figures reflect rather eloquently the patterns under discussion. When recruiting unskilled labour, companies very seldom go to the school, or ask high school teachers for recommendations. Instead, the unskilled worker (who has dropped out of school) applies to the company or has personal and family contacts with it (perhaps he is the son of a loyal employee). Part-time or summer workers and the National Employment Service (Manpower) provide the rest of the initial contacts.

8 Lazarsfeld, *Jugend und Beruf.*

9 O. Hall and B. McFarlane, *Transition from School to Work,* Department of Labour, Report no. 10 (Ottawa, 1962), pp. 57-9.

TABLE 2
Point of contact used by urban companies
in the recruitment of new young employees ($N = 119$)

Source of contact	Skilled trades (per cent)	Administration and stenographic (per cent)	Unskilled (per cent)
High school and teachers	15	26	2
Personal and family contacts	24	28	27
Candidate's own initiative (personnel office)	46	44	46
Part-time (summer) workers	13	7	19
National Employment Service (Manpower)	31	29	31
Active recruitment by firm in school	18	22	3
Private selection agencies and advertising*	0	2	0

*Added by respondent.
NOTE Many companies use several points of contact. The total of each column exceeds 100 per cent.

The picture for white collar workers, both administrative, clerical and stenographic, however, is quite different. Many high schools are equipped to train students adequately in at least some of the basic skills necessary for this category. The high school is the third largest source of contact with these potential employees. A large number of contacts derive from applications to the personnel office of the company. As many are brought to the attention of the company through personal or family contacts as through the National Employment Service (Manpower).

Recruitment patterns of youth into the skilled trades lie somewhere between the white collar and unskilled.

Reading the table horizontally, there are several important features. First, there is a high level of personal initiative on the part of youth. Only about a quarter of the urban contacts are made through personal and family relationships with the company (nepotism again!). Another rather surprising thing is the consistency of some sources regardless of the level and type of skills involved; initial contact through family nepotism remains constant whether the new recruit is white collar, unskilled, or skilled. In much the same way, young people on the three levels of skills approach the personnel office of the company in large numbers. There is a similar across-the-board relationship for contacts through the National Employment Service (Manpower). The Hall-McFarlane study noted that most youth did not utilize the services of the National Employment Service to obtain their first job.[10] The findings here do not necessarily contradict theirs; the earlier study was addressed to the initial job-searching pattern of youth – this table is concerned with the initial point of contact on the part of the recruiting company, when there is no reason that it is or should be the recruit's first job.

The major difference indicated in the recruitment pattern is the use of the school as a recruiting centre for the three skills. The company depends upon the school to categorize those who apply on their own initiative according to educational achievement.

Once the student has left his home community, he or she is not able to utilize high school and teacher contacts, personal relationships, personal knowledge, or influence and knowledge of immediate family. According to the Hall and McFarlane data,[11] girls have lost two-fifths of their contacts with the work world once they have moved away from home. It has been found that, in the city as in the community of single industry, the majority learn of jobs from friends, among fellows in clubs and associations, and in casual gossip. Ginsberg points out that the most likely place to hear of job opportunities is among friends and acquaintances. "There are two groups of people likely to get work – those already in employment who heard about new openings while on their jobs; those with relatives and friends who had an 'in.'"[12] Another study concludes that acquaintances and relatives working in the plant were the most frequent single sources of information on available jobs, followed in importance by random application at plants.[13]

In still another study it was found that successful methods of getting jobs were through application at the local plant, and through the help of friends and relatives. Of the 861 who obtained jobs, 391 applied at the plant, 311 had the help of friends and relatives, 73 got jobs through their previous company, and a handful received employ-

10 *Ibid.*
11 *Ibid.*
12 E. Ginsberg, *et al., The Unemployed* (New York, 1943).
13 G. R. Reynolds, *The Structure of Labour Markets* (New York, 1949), pp. 136-7.

ment through newspaper advertisements, employment offices, and through political influence.[14] Other studies have established that when jobs are scarce, the average unemployed worker turns to friends for suggestions of where to look for work.[15]

Youth in a new or strange community is at a disadvantage. Indeed, an individual's response may first be understood in terms of his primary groups, and secondly in terms of the larger organization in which these groups are implanted.[16] For the vast majority of youth who emigrate from single-industry communities, then, the two most obvious sources of employment - through friends and local industries - are ruled out.

FORCED MIGRATION OF MALES AND FEMALES

Although some youth cannot wait to leave the community, the majority and almost all the parents are anxious that they should remain. In Milltown, a respondent said:

> We have developed a training programme for the young men in the community if they wish to take it. We give them a training along the apprenticeship type after they have finished school. Then they are ready to leave [the community] and they have a journeyman's training and want to leave; and then I have the old man in here, and then the old lady, pleading to have him taken on in the company to keep him at home - but, of course, this is impossible. I just laugh, and tell them that they are grown men - twenty-two or three - and that it will be good for them to get out in the world - that they can't stay at home tied to their mother's apron strings for the rest of their lives. But they think something will happen to them, that they will meet bad company and so on. But, of course, they have to go.

Carlton discusses technical change as one of the reasons for the few jobs available in a pulp and paper town:

14 Couper Clague and E. W. Bakke, *After the Shutdown* (New Haven, 1934).

15 For a summary see Lipset and Bendix, *Social Mobility in Industrial Society.*

16 L. Festinger, S. F. Schacter, and K. Back, *Social Pressures in Informal Groups* (New York, 1950).

> ... the demands of the mill itself are typically changing, and may be altered even more radically in the future. The new complexity of electrical, chemical, electronic and mechanical installations in the increasingly automated pulp and paper mill, for example, make heavier demands upon specialized skills in both plant and office, while eliminating tasks which had earlier absorbed much raw labour. In the bush, as in the mill yard, unskilled, and semi-skilled labour are still required, but these typically draw more heavily on rural, semi-agricultural, seasonal, transient, and student resources. While there is, perhaps, a fairly high rate of turnover here – less in the mill proper – the number of additional places created from year to year is presently quite small. Discounting turnover, several of the mills estimated their annual increment of new places at no more than one to two dozen.[17]

Although the exception rather than the rule, most respondents in one community, parents and children alike, agreed that they did not wish youth to enter mining, the sole industry. Several suggested that this dislike of mining forced many of them to continue longer in school:

> Students dread the mine; I think their fathers have taught them to be afraid of it; I don't think really there are many boys in this school who want to work there. As a matter of fact, I think that they attend the school because they want to avoid going into the mine. I know many who have expressed this point of view. Many of our grade twelvers also leave the town; the girls can get into nursing in that grade and some boys get into departmental stores and so on.

All respondents in all communities agreed that youth very quickly educated themselves out of the jobs offered in the community, and so out of the community itself.

> As far as the children are concerned, the high school graduate really must leave; they usually go to university or to technical school. The industry cannot absorb an unlimited number of children. This is going to be a real problem in the area and I don't think that they should anyway; I think that it is poor to have father-son relationships in industry.

17 Richard A. Carlton, "Differential Education in a Bilingual Community," unpublished PhD thesis (University of Toronto, 1967), p. 331.

This suggests that the higher educated leave, permitting those with lower education to remain in the community:

> The best we ever hope for really is grade 9 or 10 education. After all if you have somebody with grade 12 they are not going to work in a factory – they are going to want a white collar job. The more education you give, the more these people are going to move away from the factory into something else.

Or, in a mining community:

> The graduates of high school are not absorbed by the community. I have always said that one of our major exports is brains. Those who go on to college have a marked interest in mining and in geology. A good number go into engineering.

And another respondent noted "The people who come out of our technical schools – we can't place them in town; there is no machine shop. The closest one is 200 miles away."

Some concern is expressed about the exodus of young people from the single-industry community, on two counts: first, their lack of sophistication, and, second, their lack of appropriate training:

> The community is very concerned about the loss of youth to other communities to find jobs [because] most of them go ill-equipped to enter new industry; so there is a real drive afoot now for the high schools to reorganize completely their technical training programme – expand it, rebuild it, and redevelop it along the lines of the Robarts plan.

With this constant selective migration, however, others are worried about the youth who remain in town: "It is these people who drop out and who don't get absorbed in the work force; they have not enough education to move, and they sort of stay around the town. They shrink – they shrink in outlook, they shrink physically, and they settle for less."

Females, who have occupational and marriage problems in the community of single industry, have a passport to almost unlimited jobs in any larger community in the nation by the simple expedient of a six-weeks' typing course. The males, lacking this easily achieved transferable skill, need far more time to explore the alien world of work in which they find themselves.

Hall and McFarlane make this point, and what they say has relevance for migration:

> ... the girl who fails to adapt to the requirements of a [high school] commercial course can drop out and register for a brief period in a business school from which she can step into a real job. The business school cushions her fall from the academic world. There are no comparable institutions which can help the boy step from his half-completed schooling into the enjoyment of a well-established job.[18]

EMIGRATION ROUTES

In interview after interview, in community after community, respondents gave similar accounts of the destination of youth outside the community. The successes are recounted with great pride as these excerpts suggest:

> As far as youth is concerned, the boys go into university or go into the armed services. The girls become nurses, teachers, or go into clerical work. The number of drop-outs is considerable in high school here but probably not nearly so great as elsewhere.
>
> Two years ago we had 48 who graduated from grade 13 – of this 48, twelve went into teaching, five into nursing, and twenty-eight to university; twenty-three of the twenty-eight were in areas of mathematics, engineering, and science.
>
> Of our last grade thirteen class, seven went to university. There were eleven students in the class; one went to nursing school, two girls to teachers' college, and I'm not sure about the other one. Prior to this over 50 per cent had gone to university, but I think that percentage is growing. I don't know what happens afterwards but I think the professionals come back here.
>
> Grade 12 is the end of general vocational, technical, and commercial work. In our school we have about half of the population taking the straight academic course and half taking the general vocational, technical, and commercial. In general, males stay longer in school, but girls over-achieve. Education is a tool to get out or to achieve something. A lot get out and go into elementary school teaching. Of girls who have Grade 12, we have had twenty-four

18 Hall and McFarlane, *Transition from School to Work,* p. 65.

nurses and twelve taking commercial. Our commercial girls are scattered all over the place; three down to a neighbouring town, two to Ottawa, and so on.

The barriers, hurdles, routes, and alternatives, tend to become patterned and known, so traditional routes emerge.[19] These routes, however, are not identical for all those young people who wish to or are forced to move.

1. Education

One of the easiest ways to emigration is to continue along the educational lines that link the community to the outside world. Thus, the small town high school graduate is able, by virtue of his education, and the fact that high school is part of a larger continuing educational process, to move to an institution of higher education. In a sense, this is a transitional stage, but the route is well marked, well known, and it presents the emigrating student with an "occupation" for a number of years, as well as a ready made social community at the university. This route is open to the few, and the few who have particular accomplishments of an academic type.

While at university the student may explore career and vocational possibilities. In addition to those who have made up their minds early in high school about a career, such as medicine, others use the route to discover a potential niche. Many who graduate with a BA are not sure of their final career lines.

Although university provides the student with a potential respectable career, a social world of rooming houses, residences, friends, activities, and the free and easy companionship of a ready-made peer group, it is accomplished at high cost to his family. Regional universities and colleges[20] notwithstanding, the expense of a university ed-

19 See Robert C. Hanson and Ozzie G. Simmons, "The Role Path; A Concept and Procedure for Studying Migration to Urban Communities," paper presented to the American Sociological Association (1966).

20 Propinquity is important in relating students to their university. The University of Montreal has a disproportionate number of students from metropolitan regions. The University of Sherbrooke has a large proportion of its students from communities under 30,000. Laval has an over-representation from prosperous and from poor rural municipalities, whereas the rural municipalities of medium wealth are over-represented at the University of Sherbrooke. In large measure, this distribution is neither haphazard nor casual, but a product of ecological forces. Jacques Brazeau, Jacques Dofny, Gérald Fortin, Robert Sévigny, "Les

ucation to those families who cannot maintain their offspring at home is high; it seems much more taxing for the family to supply several thousand dollars each year for the upkeep of the student away from home than to absorb room and board into the ongoing daily expenses as the urban family can with its commuting student. This, then, is one route out of the community of single industry into the larger world. By following it young people can remain outside, or return to the community as professional people.

A popular route to work outside the dominant industry has been elementary school teaching. In the past, this required a reasonable high school record and a year of training at a teachers' college, leading to a respectable career in the larger world; a youth could return to the home community to teach if he wanted. The career line is reasonably clear and distinct (there are known precedents in the community), and the youth, once accepted by the training college, leaves the community to enter another ready-made social world. This is a well-used route, and as a result, "small centres of population contributed more student-teachers than would be expected on the basis of chance alone."[21]

Entry into the armed forces provides a similar clearly demarcated career line, with room, board, clothes, money, and camaraderie.

Another similar route, and of particular significance to females, is nurses' training. Again, the route and the necessary procedures are well known; traditionally the hospital provides the girls with occupational training, room and board, a supervised social world, friends, and pocket money. The occupation is respectable, is defined as standing the girl in good stead, whether she becomes a wife and mother or "just in case." Families are willing to part with daughters when they give them into the care of hospitals. The extensive use of this route is seen statistically: cities of 200,000 or more contribute only 24 per cent of the nursing students, communities of 4000 or less 35 per cent, and communities from 4000 to 200,000, 41 per cent of the nurses in training.[22]

Resultats d'une enquête auprès des étudiants dans les universités de langue français du Québec" (Montreal, 1962) (mimeo).

21 William Gerald Fleming, *Background and Personality Factors Associated with Educational and Occupational Plans and Careers of Ontario Grade 13 Students* (Toronto, 1957), p. 23.

22 R. A. H. Robson, *Sociological Factors Affecting Recruitment into the Nursing Profession* (Ottawa, 1967), p. 97. This trend is apparent in the findings of the Atkinson Foundation Study: Fleming, *Ontario Grade 13 Students,* Table I, col. 2.

Other types of post-high school training lack the clear-cut career lines and the pre-formed social world. Courses sponsored by technical schools, and private and commercial schools specializing in such fields as computer programming or applied electronics provide a less clear-cut career line, and admission does not include an automatic room, board, and social world. This sort of move requires more of the student because he has to reorganize a larger part of his life for himself.

The well-marked routes, however, are for the fortunate who persist in school. They also point up the importance of the school system in the community of single industry. This post-partum advanced training is built upon the school system of the community. Whether the student is successful or unsuccessful in his chosen course, he has an opportunity to make friends in a new environment, and to learn to deal with most of the important urban secondary relationships.

2. The Loner

The voluntary or reluctant emigrant who has no scholastic record to support him, however, has a much more difficult time. In the first place, he must find new employment opportunities formally, through the newspaper and employment office, or informally, through gossip, friends, or chance acquaintances. Once a job has been located, he has to compete against other contenders. In a new environment, he does not know the content of the job and he has little idea of the wide range of appropriate roles and occupations open to him. In a strange, and to him impersonal, city, he does not know where to live, where to eat, how to meet friends, or even how to make his way around the city. This is not to suggest that the youth is unsophisticated, but merely that he is not as practised at techniques appropriate to this environment as his urban competitors.

Interview material indicates that many have a scanty knowledge of how to find a job. This basic difficulty has been expressed in a number of ways:

> I'm trying to get a job and I don't know where to start out.
> Well, I hitch-hiked all around. I filled out, I don't know how many, applications for jobs.
> There was an advertisement in the paper this week – said $2.50 an hour – that is, on an established route – and it didn't say what kind

of work it was, but there was no age limit on the job, and I applied and wrote for it in Montreal, but I haven't heard nothing from it. I can't think of any place to go – where to go for work. Every place I've been yet, they either say they will call you, or send for you, or let you know if they need you.

A great number of the respondents discuss their difficulty in coping with secondary, impersonal relationships in job hunting. The filling in of application forms, and never hearing, the failure of the prospective employer to take into account the characteristics and case history of the respondent, all provoke bewilderment in all, and hostility in many:

They told us applications mean nothing.
I tried answering ads and none of these panned out.
I was up in Community H, and mostly everywhere you applied for work, they told you they hired through Employment [Manpower].
A lot of places they told us they'd call us back if they needed us – we never heard from them.
I've been all over the country looking for a job – I filled out three or four applications.
Well I tried. I put my name in a lot of places – the woods. They said they'd let me know.

It is very difficult to know what phrases such as "I've been all over the country looking," or "I wrote away to places," or "I looked in Community E" mean. The vagueness of respondents about what they did when they "looked around" (even under persistent questioning) leads to the conclusion that once removed from the web of personal relationships of their own community, respondents have little idea of the procedures through which employment may be found.

One thing is clear: time and time again, mention is made of personal contacts. No matter how casual or fleeting these associations may be, they are, to the respondent, important, personal, and consequently reliable:

I went looking for a little while in Community E, but there was nothing up around there. Saturday, I went to a dance and was talking to a fellow, and I can get a couple of jobs out there if I want to.
Most people who get jobs say that someone called them on the phone or that they just heard about it.

Some of these personal contacts are based upon fleeting meetings while hitch-hiking. Yet these relationships seem to be of great importance, much greater than filling out forms or formalized job-finding activities. The following, rather complex tale will serve as an illustration:

> A fellow came here and said he wanted to lease a car to pick up six more fellows and go to Ottawa [to look for jobs]. We started up there and his car broke down, and so we had to hitch-hike home through the States, up to the border. We were six miles the other side of Montreal and we couldn't get a drive either way, so we took a bus, and came to the terminal [in Montreal]. One young fellow got talking with a man that said there was work up there and they got a hotel room for the night, and when he got up in the morning, the man that was going to find us work was gone. We waited, but we never seen him after. We had to come back home.

This is part of the activity which constitutes "lookin' around for work, but there was none." It also illustrates the faith in the personal word of an individual. This might be interpreted as gullibility, but rather, it demonstrates the habitual primary relationship traditional in single-industry communities. This personal interaction has a warmth and reliability and is expected behaviour within the home community. It is obvious, however, that these primary relationships, while appropriate in the home town, cannot be extended to include casual acquaintances. It seems that many of the youth, living as they do within a small community where most of their interaction is on a personal basis, have difficulty in distinguishing between primary and secondary relationships. The lack of skill in secondary relationships seems to lie behind the failure to distinguish between a neighbour and someone casually met by chance. Their inexperience in secondary relationships makes formal job application difficult and unsatisfactory.

This same lack of experience in secondary relationships (abilities taken for granted by the majority of professional and white collar personnel) is often a determining factor in deciding against moving away. The inability to handle new situations, divorced from primary group support, is vividly expressed in the following comment:

> If I went – say I went to Community E or somewhere else, I don't know how I would act – you know what I mean? If I didn't like it,

> there'd be nowhere to turn. Here I have my mother, you know – you know what I mean? You can always go and talk to her. But if I was in a strange place and say – nowhere to turn, or anything – it would be different – and so I don't know how it would be.

Stated positively, the same point is made:

> It's an easy life in this town, there are no pressures ... there are a lot of little things we feel about living here, which we do not say. The small things you know. I know that as long as I have $2.00 and someone is in need, I will loan it to him. I can always borrow this amount back from someone else. When you are sick, people visit you and help your family. These are the small unspoken things we feel.[23]

Some young people, confused by the difference between primary and secondary relationships, and finding that their only assets are their own young bodies, become marginal male or female prostitutes; others spend their time moving across the country in search of work, subsisting on hand-outs from friends made along the route and on brief spells of part-time unskilled work. Still others move to construction sites as unskilled labourers, or to new towns of single industry which are going through the first stage of development.

> I find people friendly here, and could never be contented away ... I like to visit away, but people are too unfriendly. Once lived in that city of yours [Montreal]. Had an apartment and the people across the hall wouldn't even speak to us. We soon got tired of putting up with snobs up there. Too much traffic, too much excitement, too much pressure.[24]

3. Relatives

But whether well-educated or unskilled, the migrant is fortunate if he has relatives in the urban area. There is growing evidence that kinship networks form major escape routes for emigrants from small communities. Kin provide a home away from home during the transitional period, and they give suggestions and tips on where work can be found, although few actually go so far as to sponsor the newcomer.

23 Magill, "Migration and Occupational Mobility," p. 26.
24 *Ibid.*, p. 29.

Helgi Osterreich, for instance, reports that "the majority of informants [in suburban Montreal] stress obligations to keep in touch, to be friendly and loyal, and to provide help when needed [to relatives] and to support aged relatives."[25] She finds that 93.4 per cent of her sample feel that they have an obligation to help in time of need, and that such assistance had been given and received by a large proportion. For instance, residence had been received by 64 per cent and given by 67 per cent. But advice on business and money matters had been received by 22 per cent and given by 33 per cent. Help in getting a job had been received by 20 per cent and given by 11 per cent; financial help and long term residence had been received by 11 per cent and 6.7 per cent and given by 22 per cent and 24 per cent respectively.[26]

Butler notes that both groups in his study feel they have an obligation to give financial aid to kin (migrants, 78.5 per cent and settlers 62.9 per cent). A high proportion of both migrants and settlers feel they have an obligation to find jobs for kin.[27] Butler also quotes an informant as saying, "I have got government jobs for the family. You should look for jobs and tell the best way to get them, but not go out and try to use your influence. You shouldn't jeopardize your own position." Butler adds, "Migrants [in construction work] say they always watch for job opportunities because construction sites often have large turnovers of men, and when jobs are available they are not only reserved for kinsmen who may have 'first choice,' but for anybody in their home community."[28] Another respondent said:

> I always thought I would like to go down to X. My brother lives down there, and he told me that if I didn't get anything steady here, to go down there, and he would see that I had a place to stay until I found something. He would certainly help me – try to get me something too. I feel it would be better than going to Ontario, not knowing anybody and having to get out and start

25 Helgi Osterreich, "Geographical Mobility and the Extended Family," unpublished MA thesis (McGill University, 1964), p. 51. See also her article, "Geographical Mobility and Kinship: A Canadian Example," *International Journal of Comparative Sociology*, 6 (1965), pp. 131-44.

26 Osterreich, "Geographical Mobility and the Extended Family," Table 31, p. 81.

27 Peter Butler, "Migrants and Settlers: The Influence of Geographical Mobility on the Retention of Extended Kinship Ties," unpublished MA thesis (University of New Brunswick, 1967), p. 58.

28 *Ibid.*, p. 58.

> from scratch, and he claims he can get me something down there to hold me over anyway, at least until something better comes along. I applied for one job through the paper; just what it was I couldn't tell you.

This same dependence upon family and friends has been noted in the USA.[29] There is a growing number of studies of the process of Canadian migration. This literature covers both the receiving and the contributing end of the process, as well as the major participants in the drama.

4. Friends

Dennis Magill's study of Coalville offers material which is pertinent to the subject at hand. In describing the migration of youth from a declining single-industry coal mining town he states:

> One miner whose two children had both migrated from Coalville explained this movement as follows: "My first son moved from Coalville over three years ago. He had a cousin who lived in

29 See Charles Tilly and C. Harold Brown in their study of immigrants to Wilmington, Delaware. They discuss the auspices of migration, "the social structures which establish relationships between the migrant and the receiving community before he moves." Charles Tilly and C. Harold Brown, "On Uprooting, Kinship and the Auspices of Migration," *International Journal of Comparative Sociology*, 8 (Sept. 1967).

> ... kin groups specialize in certain kinds of aid. They rarely have jobs in their gift. They vary greatly in how much information and how much skill in dealing with major urban institutions they can lend to a newcomer. Their enduring specialty lies in the internal operation of the household rather than its external relations. So we might expect to find kin groups most regularly offering domestic forms of aid at migration – lodging, personal care, food, emotional support, short-term cash. We might also expect to find this specialization in domesticity greatest among those groups relying least on their kinsmen during migration, on the supposition that they develop specialized means for meeting each of their significant problems at migration (p. 144).

Although only a small percentage of their Wilmington sample could be considered as youth at the time of migration, the authors note that 46 per cent of the sample of 190 utilized the auspices of kin, friends, or a combination. In addition, 27 per cent used mixed auspices – presumably some of these used friends and other connections. The percentage that utilized friends and/or kin was considerably higher for non-urban migrants; in this instance, the percentage rose to 53 per cent who used kin, friends, or some combination of these (Table 2, p. 150).

> Ontario, and he went to stay with him until he found work. It wasn't too hard for him to find work ... He worked in a big factory where he didn't need any training ... Later his brother joined him and stayed with him until he found work. A lot of his friends have left here and stayed with him until they found work."[30]

The above explanation was a recurrent theme among mining families when they were asked how their children found work outside Coalville. In the town there were no formalized channels of communication which supplied knowledge about the occupational diversity beyond the community. Instead a complex system of informal communication transmitted knowledge of the outside occupational world through casual day-to-day conversations or letters from friends and relatives already living elsewhere.

> ... One 19 year old migrant, when asked how he heard about work available in [a large Ontario city], explained "A number of my friends have moved here to the city. When I quit school (at grade 8) it wasn't too easy to get work around home. So I figured I'd come up here and look around. I stayed with a buddy of mine when I arrived. He worked in a big shoe factory, and I went down there and asked for work. They took me on ... No, I didn't know anything about the job before, but I knew it was easy to get work though. A lot of fellows come home every summer and you hear about all the jobs open."

Another migrant Coalviller, who worked as a taxi driver, explained how he heard about the work available in the following terms: "I moved up and lived with my brother and his wife. He has lived in the city for five years, and got me a job in the factory where he worked. I stayed at this job until I got my chauffeur's license." Two young migrant Coalvillers noted: "I was finished school [Grade 9], and a bunch of fellows came home for a few weeks from the city. They told me about work there and I went back with them. I still live with them and we all work in the same factory ... It wasn't hard to find work. I went over with one of my friends and spoke to the hiring office: a week later they were after taking me on." Finally, "Our next door neighbour's son worked in the city. They wrote him and I hitch-hiked up and stayed with him and his wife. I met a friend I

30 Magill, "Migration and Occupational Mobility," p. 56.

used to go to school with and we moved up to the city and got work here."[31]

Such statements as "A lot of fellows come home every summer and you hear about all the jobs open," and "They told me about work there and I went back with them," suggest that entry into the occupational structure is greatly assisted by the network of interpersonal relations both within and outside Coalville. Frequently, young Coalvillers from mining families who leave the town do so before they have definite employment; however, they have heard of work available in large centres from relatives, friends, and acquaintances. Further, when they migrate they can count on support from the network of personal relations pre-established in these industrial centres. As one perceptive young migrant explained:

> In the city there is a "Cape Breton Community." A hell of a lot of people leave and come here. There is little else for them to do. When you first move you can visit all sorts of friends and stay with them. They help in getting work and a lot of people will put a fellow up until he gets settled away ... If it wasn't for this help it would be hellish hard to leave. But I know a lot of fellows who don't mind moving because they know so many people away.[32]

RATES OF GEOGRAPHICAL MOBILITY

The discussion of migration routes leads to questions of broader significance. What is the emigration rate from these communities of single industry? Where do emigrants go? Who emigrates? Do they improve their position in the stratification system, do they remain at the same level of occupation as their father, or move to a lower one? It would be very reassuring if we had answers to these questions, but we don't. There is some fragmentary and somewhat questionable evidence that suggests possible trends. Despite the inadequacies, it might be useful to review what evidence there is.

In the Railtown study, the locations of all high school entrants (817) over a twenty-three year period were analysed; 785 could be traced, and 57 per cent of them had left the community of single industry.

31 *Ibid.*, pp. 57-8.
32 *Ibid.*, p. 58.

In his study of a single-industry pulp and paper town, Carlton asked high school students for their educational goals and the *projected* locale of their work. The question was: "Do you plan to work in Northern Ontario or do you expect to move out (e.g. to the south)?" The replies from 1125 students indicated that 52 per cent planned to work in northern Ontario and 46 per cent in southern Ontario; the remaining 2 per cent were undecided. (The same question asked of 224 grade 8 students elicited a 53 per cent response for southern Ontario.)[33] This means that *at least* 46 per cent saw their future outside the community of single industry. To compare the pulp and paper town with Railtown, we find that 62 per cent of the railway town high school entrants *actually* remained in the region (43 per cent in the town itself and 10 per cent in the region), compared with the *projected* locale of 53 per cent in northern Ontario. The Carlton study reports that 46 per cent *plan* to settle outside the area, compared to 43 per cent of the youth of the railway community who *actually* did settle outside of the community and region.

Andrews, in his study of a railway town in the Maritimes, reports that 62 per cent of the *high school graduates* emigrated during the period of 1932-66.[34]

Magill's study of Coalville indicates that the rate of migration of the children over 16, at present in the labour force, was 71 per cent of eighty-seven respondents.[35] The majority of these migrants went to Ontario (66 per cent). Seven per cent remained in the Atlantic provinces, 11 per cent moved to other parts of Canada, and a further 16 per cent went to the USA. In an ARDA study, Connor and Magill note:

> Given the limited occupational opportunities in the project area, there is a very low probability that most students will be able to find employment ... In response to the question – "Considering the kind of job and way of life I eventually wish to have" – fully 75 per cent of the students expect to leave their present home community. Almost equal numbers of male and female students expect to leave their community.

33 Carlton, "Differential Education in a Bilingual Community," Table XI, p. 201.

34 Alick Andrews, "Social Crisis and Labour Mobility, A Study of Economic and Social Change in a New Brunswick Railway Community," unpublished MA thesis (University of New Brunswick, 1967), p. 95.

35 Magill, "Migration and Occupational Mobility." In the preceding generation migration was 39 per cent.

> However, although three-quarters of the students expect to leave their home community, a smaller proportion are either satisfied to leave (28 per cent) or eager to leave (19 per cent) after completing their education. One-fourth (26 per cent) of the students are undecided about their desire to migrate or to stay. Nevertheless, given the high number of students who actually expect to leave, this desire to stay or leave will have little influence on actual behaviour. From the project area there will be a continued and constant flow of "forced migrants" after students complete their education. By and large, these migrants expect to remain within Nova Scotia (37 per cent) or are uncertain of their geographical destination (34 per cent).[36]

In the present context, it is necessary to treat this last set of figures with some caution because the study considers rural development in Nova Scotia. The study area includes only one community of single industry (population 883). There is no assurance that migration from rural areas and from communities of single industry are similar.

A fifth body of data was obtained from a random sample of adult respondents in Minetown, a community of single industry with a total adult population of 3439. Information was obtained on the respondent, his parents, his brothers and sisters, and his children. In all, 64 per cent of the respondents' brothers and sisters lived outside Minetown. In the succeeding generation, 60 per cent of the respondents' adult children have migrated.

The evidence collected in two railway towns, two mining communities, one pulp and paper town, and a rural area containing a groundwood pulp mill, suggests that something like 60 per cent of the youth of the single-industry community migrate. Further, the interviews cited earlier and the fragmentary quantitative evidence suggest that once the early stages of the community are over, the migrations are persistent. If this is so, other communities have received a tremendous number of residents whose background and attitudes are associated with patterns of life characteristic of communities of single industry. Some of the implications of this will be considered in the next chapter.

36 Desmond M. Connor and Dennis W. Magill, *The Role of Education in Rural Development*, ARDA Research Report, no. RE-1, Department of Forestry (Ottawa, 1965), pp. 63-4.

Some caution about these estimates is in order. Four of the studies were made in the Atlantic provinces, which have been experiencing a net decline in population and a very large emigration for a number of years. Only one of the communities can be considered as not in decline. But this objection is countered by the assertion, made over and over again by respondents from all communities of single industry, that there are no jobs for the youth of the community. The number of jobs in any community of single industry is finite, and no matter what the hopes and plans of the youth may be, the great majority cannot be accommodated in the local industry. This, of course, is verified by corporations in any location, for with increased mechanization, fewer men are needed, and although few men are fired, even fewer are hired. This is counteracted to some extent by the increase in occupations concerned with personal services, but this does not take up much slack in the community of single industry.

THE RECEIVING COMMUNITIES

Although the interviews and the evidence indicate that there is a high and consistent level of outward migration of youth, the patterning of the host communities seems more complex. On one hand, the Minetown study shows that the overwhelming majority of the migrants live in communities of less than 30,000 population. The Coalville study finds quite a different situation with the majority of migrants crossing half the nation to resettle in Ontario. Railtown youth remain in Ontario, with about half of them gravitating to urban areas. The ARDA study of students indicates uncertainty about final location, at that stage of their education.

The variety of patterns is such that no one theory seems sufficient to explain the phenomena. There are a number of plausible explanations, and it could well be that they are all useful. Stouffer, for instance, claimed that the number of persons going a given distance is directly proportional to the number of opportunities at that distance and inversely proportional to the number of intervening opportunities.[37] Magill accounts for the attraction of the industrial areas of the New England States and Ontario to the migrants from Coalville by

37 Samuel A. Stouffer, "Intervening Opportunities: A Theory Relating Mobility and Distance," *American Sociological Review*, 5 (1940), pp. 845-67.

the lack of intervening opportunities.[38] (In part the bilingual nature of Quebec contributes to this.)

Clearly, there are a number of variables at work in this whole process. Some like Jan Hubert stress class and family influences, "[mobility] is made easier by the relative independence of children from their parents at an early stage,"[39] or, Crawford, who talks about attachment and support from family.[40] Beshers and Nishuira, on the other hand, account for many differences in terms of internal states of the individual, depending on whether the migrant is "purposive-rational," future-oriented (lists alternatives and their consequences), or is a "short-run hedonistic" person who works at immediate jobs to satisfy immediate wants and desires.[41] This contrasts with the "economic push-pull" theory of Burford.[42] Turner[43] is interested in motives and personal characteristics, while others concentrate on kinship informal networks.[44]

38 Magill, "Migration and Occupational Mobility," p. 54.

39 Jane Hubert, "Kinship and Geographical Mobility in a Sample from a London Middle-Class Area," *International Journal of Comparative Sociology,* 6 (1965), pp. 61-80.

40 Charles O. Crawford, "Family Attachment and Support for Migration of Young People," *Rural Sociology,* XXXI (Sept. 1966), p. 300.

41 J. M. Beshers and E. N. Nishuira, "A Theory of Internal Migration Differentials," *Social Forces,* XXXIX, no. 3 (1961), pp. 214-5.

42 R. L. Burford, "Index of Distance as Related to Internal Migration," *Southern Economic Journal,* XXXIX (Oct. 1962), pp. 77-81.

43 Ralph H. Turner, "Migration to a Medium Size American City: Attitudes, Motives, and Personal Characteristics Revealed by Open-Ended Interview Methodology," *Journal of Social Psychology,* 80 (1949), pp. 229-49.

44 Leonard Blumberg and Robert Bell, "Urban Migration and Kinship Ties," *Social Problems,* 6 (1959), pp. 328-33; Lewis Killian, "The Adjustment of Southern White Migrants to Northern Urban Norms," *Social Forces,* 32 (1953), pp. 66-9; Eugene Litwak, "Geographic Mobility and Extended Family Cohesion," *American Sociological Review,* 25 (1960), pp. 385-94; Osterreich, "Geographical Mobility and Kinship: A Canadian Example"; Ralph Piddington, "The Kinship Network among French Canadians," *International Journal of Comparative Sociology,* 6 (1965), pp. 145-65; Marcel Rioux, *Kinship Recognition and Urbanization in French Canada,* Bulletin of the National Museum of Canada, no. 173 (Ottawa, 1959); Philippe Garigue, *La Vie familiale des canadiens français* (Montreal, 1962); Raymond Breton, "Institutional Completeness of Ethnic Communities and the Personal Relations of Immigrants," *American Journal of Sociology,* 70 (1964), 193-205. Other relevant works are: S. W. Miles, "An Urban Type: Extended Boundary Towns," *Southwestern Journal of Anthropology,* 14 (1958), pp. 339-51; Allan Pred, *The External Relations of Cities during "Industrial Revolution"* (Chicago, 1962); Albert J.

The Minetown study suggests that some migrants are preoccupied with small communities. It is difficult to know whether these people seek the close interpersonal relationships characteristic of this type of community. They may lack their own web of primary relationships within an urban area, either through kin or through friendship and club systems. On the other hand, this could be interpreted as migration being carried out by a step-by-step process; the migrant moves from the small community to the intermediate community to the metropolitan community. Other evidence suggests that the excess population of communities of single industry contributes to the manpower requirements of newly-established communities of single industry.

Part of the difficulty of interpretation arises because many existing migration studies are concerned with the members of the work force who become unemployed. In the concern for the worker, who for one reason or another becomes redundant in a particular work situation, various studies have concentrated upon those who are capable or willing to move, and their relative success in making this move. The difficulties encountered by these experienced (and somewhat rigid) members of the work force are irrelevant to youth who have not entered the work force and are still unencumbered by family.

Reiss, Jr., "Rural-Urban and Status Differences in Interpersonal Contacts," *American Journal of Sociology*, 65 (1959), pp. 182-95; J. C. Russell, "The Metropolitan City Region of the Middle Ages," *Journal of Regional Science*, 2 (1960), pp. 55-70; H. S. Shryock, Jr., *Population Mobility within the United States* (Chicago, 1964); Thomas O. Wilkinson, "Urban Structure and Industrialization," *American Sociological Review*, 25 (1960), pp. 356-63; G. Beijer, *Rural Migrants in Urban Setting* (The Hague, 1963); Janet Abu-Lughad, "Migrant Adjustment to City Life: The Egyptian Case," *American Journal of Sociology*, 67, pp. 22-32; Phillip Fellin and Eugene Litwak, "Neighbourhood Cohesion under Conditions of Mobility," *American Sociological Review*, 28, pp. 364-76; Ronald Freedman, "Cityward Migration, Urban Ecology, and Social Theory," in Ernest W. Burgess and Donald J. Bogue, eds., *Contributions to Urban Sociology* (Chicago, 1964); Arnold M. Rose and Leon Warshay, "The Adjustment of Migrants to Cities," *Social Forces*, 36, pp. 72-6; Lyle W. Shannon and Magdaline Shannon, "The Assimilation of Migrants to Cities: Anthropological and Sociological Contributions," in Leo F. Schnore and Henry Fagin, eds., *Urban Research and Policy Planning* (Beverly Hills, 1967); Charles Tilly, *Migration to an American City* (University of Delaware, Agricultural Experimental Station and Division of Urban Affairs, 1965); Basil G. Zimmer, "Participation of Migrants in Urban Structures," *American Sociological Review*, 20, pp. 218-24.

In addition, many studies have considered migration as a general problem, and thus have sampled a mixed bag which contains both veteran members of the work force and those who have not yet entered it.[45]

The provisional answer seems to be that young people participate in many forms of migration. The variations appear to arise from the route taken, the amount of education and skills, and the priority of values. Specifically, some move straight to the metropolitan area for additional training, or through links of informal sponsorship, or simply because they are "looking for work." Superimposed upon this, of course, are considerations, extraneous to the main thrust of the argument but of great importance to the individuals involved, of language, culture and way of life, such as are found in the community that Carlton studied. Some migrants, then, migrated directly from the community of single industry to the metropolis, with or without the prerequisites of such a move; others travel stage by stage; still others make an intermediate step, they may move again or leave it to succeeding generations to make the next steps. Still others populate the new emerging communities of single industry.

There is no question but that the economic and industrial heartland of southern Ontario attracts youth from communities of single industry from northern Ontario, and lures many from the communities in the Atlantic region and the western Provinces. Draft regulations in the United States have closed the border to many young males who, in the past, moved south in their search.

The cultural and language complexity of Quebec province both inhibits migration out of the province and places barriers to movement into the area. Other less noticeable sub-cultures within English-speaking Canada act as a countervailing force to the attraction of sheer industrial concentration. The sub-cultural values held in the Atlantic provinces might well account for some of the migration trends in the Minetown population. Certainly the French-speaking population of northern Ontario feel more at home in this area than in the English-speaking south.

Then, as historical accident, it is quite possible that the residents of some communities have developed a wide-spread informal com-

45 Tilly's study, for example, is concerned with a heterogeneous group of migrants. Tilly and Brown, "Of Uprooting, Kinship, and the Auspices of Migration," pp. 139-64.

munication network in one or other of the cities. Respondents in Coalville, testify to this, and recent unpublished studies on Maritime pubs, and Newfoundland clubs (with informal membership based upon "home towns") that have grown up in Toronto confirm this. Then, there are always the "loners" who leave without qualification or contact, never to return. Certainly all young people are not of a single type either in qualification or in ultimate goal. This, of course, is all closely related to the migration routes. Some further light may be shed upon this by considering those who migrate.

WHO LEAVE?

Maritimers for a long time have claimed that their main exports are fish and brains, and in their interviews several respondents noted that the community's greatest export was brains. This suggests that there is a general assumption that there is a selective migration. The assumption is that, through time, the community of single industry is left with those with the least intelligence and enterprise, and those from the least privileged minority groups. Certainly a member of a superordinate group, with brains, enterprise, and education is well equipped to move out successfully on one of the migration routes; but there are alternatives for other young people with different qualifications. It must never be forgotten that many intelligent enterprising youths remain in the community by choice, because they like it. We also know that at certain periods, there is little choice about leaving, regardless of the adequacy of preparation for the move.

The data available relative to this question are even more limited because in the study of the pulp and paper town and in the ARDA study, the youth had not yet left the community. No ethnic variables can be explored in Coalville, Andrews' railroad community, or Minetown, because these communities are ethnically homogeneous. The little information available comes from the Railtown study.

Only 18 per cent of the students who achieved senior matriculation remained in Railtown, compared with 34 per cent of those who left school after completing grade 12, and 63 per cent of those whose highest completed grade was grade 9. Further, 122 of the 126 students who left school before entering high school remained in Railtown. There is a remarkable connection between grade completed and location of occupation. "The amount of migration in a particular stream is less among those with a few years of education than among other education groups."[46] However, this marked relationship between education and migration is not an exclusive one. Those with maximum and minimum educational qualifications both remain in Railtown and migrate to urban areas.

Earlier, many respondents suggested that females had considerably greater difficulty than males in finding employment in the majority of communities of single industry. Further, the range of potential marriage partners was restricted. This suggests that we could expect a larger exodus of females. This expectation is confirmed in the Railtown findings. Fifty-two per cent of the male high school entrants remained in Railtown compared to 41 per cent of the females. These figures are conservative because they are based on the students who entered high school. There were only six females among the 126 who did not enter high school; only 4 of the 126 left the community.

SCHOLASTIC ACHIEVEMENT OF ETHNIC GROUPS

In those communities made up of many ethnic groups, the migration rates are quite different for the various groups. The attitudes toward migration rate of ethnic, cultural, and language groups in the pulp and paper town of Carlton's study suggest that there are distinct differences: 35 per cent of the English-speaking young people as compared with 66 per cent of the French-speaking young people see themselves as remaining in their home-town. On the contrary, 31 per cent of the French-speaking population see themselves as living away from the north, in comparison to 61 per cent of the English-speaking population:

> A larger proportion of the English-speaking students aimed at studies beyond the secondary school level, either in a university or technological school, while more of the French students intended to begin work following completion of their high school course, or were undecided. In answering all of the questions involved, a very much larger proportion of French students were undecided, whereas the English students appeared to have more definite long-range plans for education and work. Similar, but

46 Beshers and Nishuira, "A Theory of Internal Migration Differentials," p. 217.

> smaller differences were noticeable in respect of work goals; however, the numbers of French students aiming at occupations of "professional" standing were heavily weighted with rural French students oriented to teaching and nursing. Most obvious of all is the sharp difference in the inclination to employment in Northern Ontario, in which the French students reflect the strong commitment to the north expressed by their teachers and by the French-speaking community at large.
>
> While the projections of students at this level may well have little relation to their long-range achievements, there can be no doubt that such plans will influence the critical choices of secondary school and course, now pushed back to the eighth grade. Decisions made at this time may close, or increase in complexity and difficulty, routes of access to higher education and to the career lines which flow out of these areas of specialized training.[47]

These extreme differences are reflected in the *actual* scholastic accomplishments and migrations from Railtown. Twenty-two per cent of the British group completed grade 13, compared to 5 per cent of the French, 5 per cent of the Indians and 14 per cent of the "other"[48] ethnic groups. Fewer British left school after completing grade 9 than did any of the other groups, and more completed their senior matriculation. Only 10 per cent of the Indians continued their education beyond the first two high school grades compared to 56 per cent of the British. The median grade completed at time of school leaving is as follows: British 11.6, French 10.2, Other 10.0, Indian 9.7. These medians, which indicate the middle values of the grades accomplished with less regard for the extreme values show considerable differences among ethnic educational accomplishments.

The Railtown material shows that there were marked differences in geographic mobility among the ethnic groups. In the British group 38 per cent remained in Railtown in contrast to 53 per cent of the

47 Carlton, "Differential Education in a Bilingual Community," pp. 201-2.

48 The "other" category may seem to have a high standard of education. Actually "other" is a residual category and includes all backgrounds other than British, French, and Indian. This includes eastern and southern Europeans as well as individuals of Dutch, Finnish, German, etc. background. In actual practice, the majority of the eastern and southern Europeans leave school after grades 9 or 10. The northern Europeans, particularly those with a German background, remain at school until grades 12 or 13.

French, 81 per cent of the Indians, and 50 per cent of the "other" ethnic groups.

There were also major differences in the number of Railtown students from each ethnic group who entered the professions. Professional status was achieved by 28 per cent of the British, 15 per cent of the French, 5 per cent of the Indians, and 23 per cent of students from the "other" ethnic groups.

The final question concerns the position held by the youth after emigrating. Lipset and Bendix state that growing up in a small community is a decided disadvantage to upward mobility.[49] There is a limited amount of information on this subject.

In Minetown, 76 per cent of the respondents worked in mining and other unskilled occupations in comparison to 66 per cent of their fathers. (If all the sons of the fathers are considered, that is, by including the brothers of the respondents, then 79 per cent worked at unskilled occupations.) The high percentage of fathers in the skilled and semi-skilled field is partly accounted for by the rural setting and the type of skills of their era, such as village blacksmith or harness-maker.[50] Fifty-nine per cent of the respondents' male children who have entered the labour market were in the unskilled category. The respondents' sons seem to have gained ground lost by the preceding generation. This general trend must be treated with great caution because the general level of skill and skill requirements has changed radically in the three generations.

The Coalville study breaks the generations into two working categories, manual and non-manual. In the second generation 70 per cent of the sample is manual, and in the third generation 63 per cent is

49 Lipset and Bendix, *Social Mobility in Industrial Society*, p. 213.

50 Intergenerational mobility is a particularly treacherous area for research. Among other problems are the changing status and wage associated with particular occupations over a fifty-year period, the difficulty of matching father and son at the beginning, middle, or end of their career, the problem of classifying occupations (such as lumping professional and proprietor). For a discussion of these and other points, see Lipset and Bendix, *Social Mobility in Industrial Society*.

The Minetown data were not gathered initially for a study of inter-generational mobility, and so no attempt was made to control for these variables. For this reason, the figures discussed here are suggestive only; their inadequacy is clear. Their use is justified only in that there is so little information on the final occupational achievements of migrants from Canadian communities of single industry.

engaged in manual occupations. The author links both migration and upward mobility in the following propositions:

> There is a strong correlation between intergenerational occupational inheritance and migration. The greater the consistency of occupational transmission of mining through three generations, the lower the rate of migration from these families. The greater the families' trend of upward mobility in Coalville's occupational structure through a number of generations, the higher the rate of migration from these families.[51]

In Railtown, some indication of upward mobility can be derived from an appraisal of the number of students who have taken professional training over a twenty-year period.

Of the 817 pupils used in the study, 206, or 25 per cent of the total, entered the professions. An important difference is noted when the males and females are compared. Of the 388 males 57, or 15 per cent, entered professional occupations while of the 429 females, 149, or 35 per cent, entered the professions. This does not suggest, however, that the professional training or occupations are strictly comparable (e.g. engineering versus nursing).

In the railway occupations 53 per cent of the youth who went into professional activities, were from families in the managerial group, 28 per cent from the white collar group, 25 per cent from the running trades, 27 per cent from the trades, and 15 per cent from the labourer group.

There are a number of other indications of considerable upward mobility among youth from small communities. We had noted that smaller communities contribute an unexpectedly large proportion of girls for nurses training;[52] they also contribute more teachers' college students than would be expected on the basis of chance.[53] Clute notes that in his sample 47.8 per cent of the Ontario physicians and 64.3 per cent of the Nova Scotia physicians came from communities of 10,000 or less.[54]

51 Magill, "Migration and Occupational Mobility," p. 61. The figures cited in the text are an adaptation of Table 16. For a more general discussion of all the migrants from communities of single industry see, K. Scott Wood and Harold Verge, *A Study of the Problems of Certain Cape Breton Communities* (Halifax, 1966).

52 Robson, *Nursing Profession*, p. 97.

53 Fleming, *Ontario Grade 13 Students*, p. 23.

54 K. F. Clute, *The General Practitioner* (Toronto, 1967), p. 38.

This means that some youth are well equipped educationally, and follow particular routes to occupations with higher status than those of their parents. Others leave, lacking a high school education, to take their places at the bottom of the urban heap. In the majority of cases, both are forced to move. But in some communities there is a conspiracy among parents, union, the company, and the community organizations to force the children to get as much education as they can; they then prepare them for particular migration routes, and a fighting chance of moving upward. In other communities where for generations the school has been defined as the enemy, where employment at a man's pay at fourteen has been a tradition, there seems to be little generational mobility. For these forced migration is accomplished through kin and friends, or on a hit-and-miss basis.

We now turn to the final chapter in which we will consider some of the wider implications of the points discussed in the preceding chapters.

16

Some social implications

The one-industry community grows from the initial construction stage, through periods of recruitment, settling in and transition, and finally reaches fairly stable maturity. However, the maturity and stability are only comparative; the stability is precarious because of the forced migration of youth, and the ultimate uncertainty of the single economic base.

Persistent patterns emerge in isolated single-industry towns of under 30,000 regardless of the type of industry – pulp and paper, mining, railway or manufacturing – and regardless of types of work and skills. The impact of the industry upon the lives of the citizens of the community is extraordinarily great whether it takes an active part in the affairs of the community or withholds its support. The one industry, the single major employer, and the only reason for the town's existence results in the industrial hierarchy forming the major dimensions of the social stratification for the community. In addition, the division of labour within the industry tends to fix ethnic occupations. In terms of job selection, local youth have a high level of informal knowledge about the industry and its occupations, so that outside job seekers are basically excluded; on the other hand the outward migration of youth is tied to the employment needs of the company.

The industry involves the population of the community in three types of mobility. The upward mobility, based on seniority, within the local occupational hierarchy affects the majority of citizens. The town is deeply influenced by the horizontal mobility at the top of the hierarchy; the managers and superintendents move in from another branch outside the community. Their short stay and feeling of impermanence influence their activities in the community. The third is the high level of geographical, and not always upward, mobility of youth.

The size of the community and its isolation introduce other intrinsic factors which affect the patterned relationships. The first is social observability and social control. Behaviour is highly observable and is therefore restricted, but at the same time, peculiar types of social insulation are built by the citizens as protection from eternal scrutiny.

A second factor is the restricted professional and institutional services. The lack of school specialization – commercial, technical and other courses – affects the occupational selection and training of youths, which in turn influences their careers. In addition many of the communities have one or two, if any, doctors and limited hospital facilities; these facts have wide implications for expectations and patterns of behaviour. Legal, dental and other professional services are similarly restricted.

A third intrinsic factor is that the great majority of these small communities are characterized by primary, personal relationships rather than the impersonal, secondary relationships which account for so much urban interaction. The inhabitants have special benefits and obligations arising out of interpersonal skills and relationships.

A fourth intrinsic feature is the community cycle. Many industries began by hiring men, all of an age. Once staffed, few more are hired because these industries are characteristically stable. Thus there are phases of hiring and non-hiring, periods when there are many young people in the community and periods when there are few, periods of heavy outward migration, lean and heavy years in the schools, and so on.

We have noted the peculiar role that the church plays in the community, part recreation sponsor, part a vehicle for social conflict, and a major basis for differential association. The merchants and suppliers of services to the industrial population hold a peculiar position in the stratification system and serve as another source of ritualistic but controlled conflict. Recreation, with all the problems of resources and personnel, acts as an element of social control. We discussed the mechanisms which prevented conflict from becoming divisive controversy, and found that gossip became a major factor in personalized conflict and control.

THE ONE-INDUSTRY COMMUNITY IN CANADA

The community of single industry is significant to Canadian society for several reasons. In the first place a considerable proportion of the population lives in this type of community, and half lives in communities of 30,000 or less. Second, because of the nature of Canadian geography and the distribution of natural resources, there is little chance that the total number of such communities will decrease. At lease one writer has suggested that the number of single-industry communities will increase.[1] The third reason is that many Canadians

1 Ira M. Robinson, *New Industrial Towns on Canada's Resource Frontier*, University of Chicago, Department of Geography, Research Paper no. 73 (Chicago, 1962).

have been brought up in this type of community. Perhaps the majority of the citizens of the larger, more diverse communities of the nation have had their attitudes, expectations, and behavioural patterns moulded within the peculiar social structure of the single-industry community. Finally, this peculiar structure is common to both French and English Canada.

Communities of single industry seem to have a particular flavour. Patterns of life and expectations arise from the single occupational base and the absolute limitations imposed by the size and isolation of the community. If citizens have wants, defined as legitimate, but yet unattainable because of limitations inherent in the system, they often handle these conflicts by "putting up with things" or maintaining the fatalistic assumption that circumstances are beyond their control. We will return to some possible implications of this theme shortly.

THE UNIVERSALITY OF COMMUNITIES OF SINGLE INDUSTRY

The attitudes and behavioural patterns, and the reciprocal expectations characteristic of the community of single industry can be seen from one point of view as being uniquely Canadian. For instance, the isolation and the simplified social structure of these communities are unlikely to be found in the European countries; it is difficult to imagine such characteristics in Holland, Belgium or Great Britain, although, as we have seen, Lockwood describes the social networks of "the one-industry town"[2] of Great Britain, and Belgium, like Britain, has its one-industry coal towns. Other established European communities may have resembled the Canadian communities at some past stage of their development. Doubtless there are many such communities in the USSR. Although many social and geographical characteristics may be common to Soviet and Canadian communities, there are major differences, if for no other reason than that the establishment of the community, the recruitment of personnel, and the obligations owed to the industry and its personnel all take place within a different political and social structure.

2 David Lockwood, "Sources of Variation in Working Class Images of Society," in Joseph A. Kahl, ed., *Comparative Perspectives on Stratification: Mexico, Great Britain, Japan* (Boston, 1968), pp. 100-10.

Communities similar to those that we have described are found in the United States of America. In this country, so similar to Canada in many geographical and social respects, there are many isolated communities built around the work of mining, pulp and paper, and transportation. In fact some social characteristics of the single-industry community are found wherever natural resources are being exploited. Mining communities in South America, Africa, Australia, India, and all other parts of the world have some basic similarities. The differences emerge from the different attitudes and expectations that people bring to these communities from cultures quite divergent from the western technological North American way of life.

We have restricted our discussion to the behaviour patterns found in communities with a single industrial base, limited in size and usually in isolation. By choosing the one-industry community the processes could be examined with some clarity because we did not have to account for a more complex social structure. We have maintained that the patterns persist in this type of community regardless of the industrial processes involved. Even so, analysis has been complicated by the various stages that characterize the growth and development of the community and the large number of idiosyncratic factors that are bound to arise in social life in particular communities. Two questions then arise: is this a particular type of community? Are the behavioural patterns emerging within this type of community unique?

If we modify the self-imposed restrictions we will be able to see if and to what extent the patterns described are characteristic of communities quite different from those under study. First then let us examine the variable of isolation.

ISOLATION

The one-industry community exists to house the employees who exploit the area's natural resources; the location of the community, within a few miles, is predetermined by the location of the resource, the electric power necessary for the process, or the technical requirements imposed by the transportation system that moves the products. For this reason the communities are, almost without exception, found in the sparsely settled parts of the country. Indeed, if we trace them by province we find many communities of single industry in the rugged interior of Newfoundland, none in the farm-based communities of Prince Edward Island, a few in the more rugged parts of Nova Scotia, and far more in New Brunswick. There are a few south of the Saint Lawrence River and only one or two in Southern Ontario – that area lying south of North Bay and Sudbury. The majority of these communities lie in northern Ontario and northern Quebec – the area characterized by the production of pulp and paper, gold, copper, nickel, and where the transcontinental railways pass through the pre-Cambrian shield wilderness. Moving west, the communities of single industry hug the northern boundaries of the prairie provinces; the few to the south are located above the oil deposits and coal seams. A high proportion of the population centres of the Yukon and the Northwest Territories are communities of single industry and the remainder are found in the rugged terrain far from the fertile valleys of British Columbia.[3]

The peculiar location and isolation of these communities almost guarantees that they remain communities of single industry. The economic and technical factors that were instrumental in locating and developing communities of single industry are the same factors which rule out additional industry, diversification of the economic base, and expansion of population. In areas where the communities are close to a larger population and market they become diversified, expand, and so are no longer communities of single industry. One notable exception is the mining community where several competing companies work the same ore body; another is the community with an abundance of cheap electrical power fortuitously located where two basic resources such as minerals and forests can be exploited.

Communities of single enterprise are and remain isolated. Physical and geographical isolation, however, is a relative quality. At one end of the continuum there is the isolation of the community whose only contact with the outside is through infrequent air service; at the other end, is the community surrounded by 50 miles of scrub forests with the closest community 60 miles away by road. People living in a Northern Ontario railway community on the main line of one of the transcontinental railways with dozens of passenger and freight trains daily pausing for servicing and change of crew, may feel, and in some senses are, isolated, and the same thing applies to individuals

3 Many of these communities lie within the so-called mid-Canada corridor. See Richard Rohmer, *The Green North* (Toronto, 1970).

living in the community three hours' drive by first-class highway from a major city.

It is clear that these people are not talking about social isolation as it is usually defined in the social sciences. They are not talking about "failure of the individual through inability preference or whatever to establish or maintain communications with those about him."[4] This isolation is not related to the interpersonal relationships *within* the community, but rather to the relationship between citizens of the community and others in outside communities. The preoccupation with this quality of life persists despite mass communication. McLuhan's global village is not meaningful to them in terms of interpersonal relationships or potential relationships with others. The isolation of the single-industry community seems to refer to the potential relationships of the individuals with other groups and communities outside their own. The phenomenon is probably quite close to the vicinal isolation, the physical separation which isolates and limits accessibility, as discussed by Becker; "nature presents man with his geographical location; culture provides his vincinal position."[5]

That these definitions of isolation are subtle is supported by the preliminary findings reported by Matthiasson. Residents of an isolated community of single industry ranked services and facilities that should be available in a typical resource community; the first four were: entertainment and recreation, income in relation to cost of living, housing and accommodation, and good access to cities in the south. The services in their own community which needed improvement were, in order of frequency of choice, access to cities in the south, communications, medical facilities, and entertainment and recreation. Yet, when given a check list of terms descriptive of northern living, "isolated" was ranked fourth, after "friendly," "expensive," and "challenging" ("gossipy" was fifth). The responses could be interpreted in a number of ways, and the author carefully points out that the findings are still preliminary and incomplete.[6]

4 R. T. Lapiere, *A Theory of Social Control* (New York, 1954), p. 330.

5 Howard Becker, "Current Sacred-Secular Theory and Its Development," in H. Becker and A. Boskoff, eds., *Modern Sociological Theory in Continuity and Change* (New York, 1957), pp. 164-5.

6 J. S. Matthiasson, *Resident Perception of Quality of Life in Resource Frontier Communities,* Center for Settlement Studies, University of Manitoba (Winnipeg, 1970). Also see Center for Settlement Studies, University of Manitoba, *Proceedings – Symposium on Resource Frontier Communities, December 16, 1968* (Winnipeg, 1968).

In extreme isolation there seem to be geographical and measurable restrictions on the interrelationships possible with people of other communities. On the other hand, although there are few restrictions of this type imposed on an urban dweller, he seldom takes the opportunity of making contact with a neighbouring city or village. This suggests that isolation is a feeling, which, while based upon physical fact, has little relation to any absolute standard of geographical location.

The feeling of isolation discussed by respondents in communities of single industry is probably more closely related to their attitudes and opinions on the limitation of alternatives than it is to geography. In this sense, people feel isolated in Vancouver, Toronto, San Francisco, Boston, Halifax, New York, or London. This raises the question, isolated from what? The answer seems to be that the individual feels removed from the possibility of taking part in some desired activity. The feelings of isolation expressed by some respondents, although perhaps extreme in communities of single industry, are also found in diversified urban areas. On the other hand, there are people in both urban areas and communities of single industry who do not yearn for what is not there. This suggests that isolation, rather than being unique to the community of single industry is shared to some degree by many people in many types of communities, both urban and rural.

SINGLE INDUSTRY

We now turn our attention to a second variable, that of single industry. If we leave the population and the degree of isolation constant what happens if we add a second industry to our community? If the second industry has the same resource base, such as two mining companies working on one ore body, there are a series of implications. To begin with, there are two sets of management personnel moving in and out of the community. Inevitably one of the two industries is defined as a better industry to work for and stratification is affected by the greater prestige attached to the Smith Company than the Jones Company. At the same time, however, because there are two work structures and two bases for stratification, there is a more complex set of formal and informal patterns of association. Further, the level of observability is reduced considerably; despite the fact that the size of the community has remained constant there are many activities in the Smith Company which would not necessarily come to the attention of all who work in the Jones Company.

The interaction between people and the role of the two corporations in the community depends largely on the early history of responsibility undertaken by the corporation in the development of the community – the degree of support for local organizations, the support and subsidization of recreation facilities and so on. Corporate competitiveness is introduced by the second industry. The two corporations are vulnerable to polite blackmail by the citizens, their associations, and organizations; almost inevitably the corporations are forced to vie for the goodwill of employees and their community associations. This at least opens the possibility for citizens to feel that their social and political action could affect their lot in life. The addition of a second industry then, provides a potential flexibility in social life.

All other variables held constant, the addition of a second industry does not affect the institutional and professional services available in the community. It does not increase the number of doctors and dentists or teachers or alternative streams in the school system; it does not affect the nature of the relationships with professional people; it does not affect the range of occupational choices open to the youth; it does not affect forced migration or the range of available marriage partners.

If, instead of two industries sharing the same resource base, an industry with a different base is introduced, more widespread ramifications are expected. If, for instance, a pulp and paper mill and a mine share the same community, the social differences are highly intensified. The two resource bases accentuate the differences in reputation of the two firms; the differences in the type of work have important ramifications for the prestige structure within the community. Because the two firms are unlike, different types of expectations are attached to their activities as well as an intensification of their competition. There is a wider variety of local jobs but the migration level from the community remains much the same. Further, the institutional and professional aspects of community life remain much the same regardless of the second industry.

FISHING, FARMING AND COMMERCIAL COMMUNITIES

Social patterns and attitudes in a small industrial community are, however, quite different from those in a community built upon fishing and farming (and perhaps trapping), or in a centre based upon commercial and distribution services. The fishermen or farmers share occupations characterized by an indeterminacy and insecurity often classified as "acts of God." The return for work is ruled by changes in the weather, the season, and other variables not controlled by man. Men often cope with these unknowns by being fatalistic; if this is not a good year, next year may be, but in any event, there is nothing to be done about it. Although all are subject to these uncontrollable events, their social consequences are differently experienced because there are variations in the amount of capital that each man brings to his occupation – land acreage, fishing boats, stock in the store, and so on. His success depends upon the amount of work he does, the hours worked, and the scheduling of these hours, as well as the intuitive or "art" quality of his work – the right time to plant or harvest; where at this tide, in this season, with this moon, the fish are found; what loss leader brings customers to the store. The stratification of fishing, farming and commercial communities, then, depends upon a range of complex variables that are not incorporated in any industrial hierarchy. No individual earns a fixed income; his income is not guaranteed by skills, educational background, learning or age.

At the same time, the individual's position in the stratification structure is obscure because the symbols are far more varied and subtle than would appear from his pay cheque. The individual in a single-industrial hierarchy can spend his money in various ways, but everyone knows the amount he is paid; this knowledge, along with his occupation category, symbolizes his position in a stratification hierarchy. In a fishing, farming, or commercial community the returns are not clearly and definitely known in a monetary sense and the symbols of social status are indeterminate – in order to evaluate the status of a farmer, no one is sure whether to look at the barn, the house, the herd, the number of vacations, the number of paid employees, the clothes, the machinery, the type of car, or the amount of money borrowed, The symbols of position, then, can be highly specialized or very diverse; in this situation curiosity about the innuendo or the real story behind a particular set of symbols becomes tremendously important; it is under these conditions that a high level of speculation and gossip is devoted to the evaluation of the position of the individual.

In contrast with the industrial town, this type of community is made up of many independent but interrelated capitalists. Each man starts with some capital investment, and together with his talents, judgment, and labour, he carries out his work operating under a general level of luck. Although he can blame fate and impersonal forces, he has no industry to blame. He has no industry to use; he knows that recreational facilities, the school, his church and other institutional facilities are a product of his own participation and that he cannot call upon any local industry to assist him to build and maintain them. Similarly his position in the hierarchy and his relation to his fellows is not dependent upon a corporate structure. His relationship with store owners differs because the farmer, fisherman, and store-keeper are all entrepreneurs. In contrast, the institutional complement of professional services is much the same as in the community of single industry; the professional services rendered by doctors, dentists, teachers, and clergy are subject to many of the variables discussed previously. The level of role observability is much lower than in the community of single industry. This is partly because each man has his "own domain" as insulation and partly because status attributes are not achieved within the single structure. Observability is low and the level of curiosity and gossip is high. This way of life comes closest to the Jeffersonian ideal referred to in Chapter 1.

THE COMMUNITY OF DOMINANT INDUSTRY

Occasionally people refer to Oshawa, Hamilton, Sault Ste Marie, or even Ottawa as a one-industry town. This, of course, is a misnomer; they are not one-industry towns but rather communities with a dominant industry. Superficially, the community with a dominant industry has many characteristics of the one-industry town because the giant industry is seen as having an untoward effect upon the whole community. Executive decisions about how much, if anything, is to be contributed to a certain cause, changes in technology, when to lay off employees, raising employment qualifications – decisions in any area – have wide-spread implications for all citizens. The dominant industry, then, is seen as being responsible for the community and it is given a large share of the blame when things go wrong, and perhaps some credit when the community thrives.

It is clear, however, that the social stratification in a community of dominant industry is far more complex than that of a small community of single industry. Whether the dominant industry is surrounded by dependent and contributing industries or whether the other industries have independent bases, each industry tends to have different working conditions, pay scales, rates of promotion and so on. This, then, complicates the over-all view of the general stratification of the individuals and families in the communities as illustrated by attempting to compare the ranking of the presidents of three companies – the large automobile manufacturing company, the firm that supplies it with safety glass, and the firm that manufactures bathing suits in the same community.

COMMUNITY SIZE

We have considered the implications of holding all factors constant and varying first isolation and then the number and type of industries. Now, we vary a third factor, size. And as was noted earlier a very large community of single industry is a negation of terms; a large community involves major changes in allocated community responsibilities and concomitant credit and blame.

The level of observability of the individual and his family is reduced considerably, firstly by the diversification of industry and secondly by the size of the community, so that it is now no longer possible to keep track of all of the citizens of the community.

Once the community has a large population, the role of industry is not so crucial in the non-work facets of community life; the institutions of the community are more varied and larger in number, the recreational services are more diversified with many added participation groups; the range of and competition among the stores is increased; alternative educational streams are found; the quality and number of teachers is increased; the range of medical institutions, doctors, dentists and specialists in the medical and paramedical fields is enlarged. Medical aid is always available and the relationships between the patient and doctor are far less complex than in a small community; with any luck the patient may have a physician long enough that he is able to maintain a continuing medical history.

But although an increase in the size of the community seems to be crucial in changing the whole nature of the relationships between individuals, the assumptions held, the patterns of behaviour, and the distribution of responsibilities, this may be more apparent than real. If we consider, for instance, the metropolitan area, characterized by many industries, many stores, services, and a most complex institutional structure, we find that the round of life of most families is not very different from that of a one-industry community. Many families in the suburbs, in fact, go through the various stages of the development of their community, or their piece of community, as evidenced by the work of White and Clark.[7] Although the family shares a geographical base with a few hundred thousand other families, and potentially has at its service a thousand doctors and a thousand dentists and thousands of teachers and thousands of stores, schools, churches, and recreational outlets, life is restricted to a small segment of this potentiality. Many social relationships are confined to the immediate area. Despite the size of the community, friends and relatives form the bases of the most meaningful relationships.[8]

PERSONAL RELATIONSHIPS

These repetitive contacts with friends and relatives have been confirmed in a number of studies, including Peter Pineo's study of Hamilton:

> ... the people in the Hamilton neighbourhood were involved in primary relationships; and their frequency of contact with relatives outside their own households was roughly equivalent to that found in studies in the United States or England. Sixty-eight per cent reported at least weekly contact with some relative outside their own home.
>
> These people were also in frequent contact with friends and neighbours. Their involvement with friends seemed as intense as their involvement with kin. While 68 per cent reported at least weekly contact with "their best friend in the neighbourhood," in fact, more (37 per cent) reported daily contact with the best friend than reported daily contact with some relative (21 per cent).[9]

7 William H. White, Jr., *The Organization Man* (New York, 1956); S. D. Clark, *The Suburban Community* (Toronto, 1966).

8 White, *The Organization Man,* pp. 30-61.

9 Peter C. Pineo, "Social Consequences of Urbanization," in N. H. Lithwick and Gilles Paquet, eds., *Urban Studies: A Canadian Perspective* (Toronto, 1968), p. 971. Similar trends were found among French Canadians in Montreal by Garigue: Philippe Garigue, "French Canadian Kinship and Urban Life," *American Anthropologist,* 58, no. 6 (Dec. 1956), pp. 1090-101. See also Scott Greer,

Pineo goes on to say:

> Age and number of years spent in the neighbourhood are closely related phenomena in the neighbourhood studied. A gradual accumulation of friends through neighbouring may have produced the larger friend networks among the older residents. When we asked the respondents how they made friends the largest proportion (40 per cent) said that initial contact had been made through neighbouring – they had simply run into them on the street, in the shops, through the children.[10]

It would seem then, that one of the features of interpersonal relationships in the urban area that distinguishes it from the small town is neither the kinship relationships nor the primary relationships, but the lack of in-between civilities. The number of accumulating biographies and obligatory ritual exchanges is not as great. But, this is merely a matter of degree, for before long, the housewife finds out that the sister of the supermarket cashier is ill, and the cashier will

"Urbanism Reconsidered: A Comparative Study of Local Areas in a Metropolis," *American Sociological Review*, 21 (Feb. 1956), pp. 19-25; Helgi Osterrich, "Geographical Mobility and the Extended Family in Montreal," unpublished MA thesis (McGill University, 1964).

10 Pineo, "Social Consequences of Urbanization," p. 202. The following are found among the long list of studies touching on primary relationships within the city: Marc Fried, "Transitional Functions of Working Class Communities: Implications for Forced Relocation," in Mildred B. Kantor, ed., *Mobility and Mental Health* (Springfield, Ill., 1965); Herbert Gans, *The Urban Villagers* (New York, 1963); Philippe Garigue, *La Vie familiale des canadiens-français* (Montreal, 1962); Scott Greer, *The Emerging City* (New York, 1962); Madeline Kerr, *The People of Ship Street* (London, 1958); Peter Marris, "The Social Implications of Urban Re-development," *Journal of American Institute of Planners*, 28 (1962), 180-6; Herald Wilenskius and Charles Lebeaux, *Industrial Society and Social Welfare* (New York, 1958); Michael Young and Peter Willmott, *Family and Kinship in East London* (London, 1957); William F. Whyte, *Street Corner Society* (Chicago, 1943); Morris Axelrod, "Urban Structure and Social Participation," *American Sociological Review*, 21 (1956), 14-8; Wendell Bell and Marion Boat, "Urban Neighbourhoods and Informal Social Relationships," *American Journal of Sociology*, 62 (1957), 391-8; Allen Coult and Robert Habenstein, "The Study of Extended Kinship in Urban Society," *Sociological Quarterly* (1962), pp. 141-5; Oscar Lewis, "Further Observations on the Folk Urban Continuum and Urbanization with special reference to Mexico City," in Phillip M. Hauser and Leo F. Schnore, eds., *The Study of Urbanization* (New York, 1965); Paul J. Reiss, "The Extended Kinship System in the American Urban Middle Class," unpublished PhD thesis (Harvard University, 1960).

enquire about the housewife's little girl who is not accompanying her. The breadwinner knows that his secretary is having "man trouble," or that his fellow-welder's wife has cancer. One by one, repetitious meetings elicit greetings, until, over the years, in the most impersonal of areas, the individual accumulates a number of greeting and speaking acquaintances.

Within this area of kinship, neighbours, and friends there is a high level of role observability; but the urban family is able to carry on activities outside of this web of relationships and so achieve a certain level of privacy. The breadwinner of the family characteristically moves several miles to his work and it is unlikely that neighbouring families have breadwinners working in the same industry. Thus men's successes and failures at work are not common knowledge within the neighbourhood. But as White and others have pointed out, because neighbours are never sure of the social status of the individuals in the neighbourhood, court or street, and as they are never sure which symbols should be accepted as indicative of what degree of success, the level of probing and curiosity is probably more extreme than it is in the community of single industry where the position of the individual at work, at home and in the community is well known to all.

COMMUNITY SERVICES

Although the suburban housewife or the downtown family cannot be considered to be isolated from neighbouring communities, they seldom visit these communities. Within the urban community emergency medical and dental assistance is always available but, as we well know, the urban family tends to place its health requirements in the hands of one practitioner in much the same way that the citizen of the single-industry community does. Although in theory, a wide range of medical generalists and specialists is available to the family, the choice of a doctor is made on irrational and non-specialist laymen's grounds, usually the recommendation of a friend or neighbour. The children go to the neighbouring school and the process by which they get their education is much the same as it is in small communities. Usually the teacher is not under the intense scrutiny of the parents because it is possible for him or her to live in another part of the city. If the child has difficulty in a particular school or with a particular teacher it is extraordinarily difficult to move him to a different school because of suburban and urban school jurisdictions. Similarly the family uses a local church, a small range of convenient shops and a very restricted range of recreational facilities. Although families are always able to go to the museum and to the art gallery, and the parents could go dancing any night they felt like it or attend a different movie every evening, the point is that they don't.

In other words, urban life is carried on basically within neighbourhoods and even when the occupational requirements take the husband outside the neighbourhood, it is within a very restricted area. There are many barriers – real and imaginary, involving money, time, and convenience – that restrict the social economic and work life of the urban family. One English-speaking family, who lived in the eastern part of Montreal, at the time of interview had not been downtown to the main stores or to the central core of the city for five years – it had not been necessary. Many suburban housewives get to the downtown area of their city less often than those who live in the isolated communities of single industry.

In urban centres there are many potential marriage partners, but marriage can be consummated only when propinquity brings the two together. Although migration is not enforced by a job shortage, youth leaves the family home to set up its own establishments, often many miles physically and many more miles socially from parents.

On the other hand the wide range of competing institutions, organizations and structures within the urban areas creates a diffuse level of responsibility for difficulties – labour blames management, management blames government, and the government blames the city. The municipality blames the provincial government, and smog, traffic problems, and school difficulties are all the responsibilities of people who are unnamed and unknown.

The city abounds with facilities and opportunities that are never utilized and for many, at least superficially, the life round of the suburban family is amazingly similar to that of the family in the single-industry community. The basic difference is that the urban resident has alternatives that are seldom used; the availability, whether used or not, affects social definitions which have a great importance to the individual and his attitudes. It is one thing to choose not to select certain alternatives and it is another not to be able to choose. Within our society it is not so important whether one goes dancing or bowling or whether one spends a disproportionate amount of money on food, a house, an automobile or whether one belongs to certain organizations, whether one goes to the ballet every night or goes to a concert twice a week, as it is to have a choice of not doing it. The absent services seem to make the heart grow fonder.

THE COMMUNITY OF SINGLE INDUSTRY AND CANADA

When people share a community, its problems and its limitations, consciously or unconsciously they work out ways of dealing with difficulties and conflicts. Ideas, norms, traditional practices, social expectations, and knowledge are transmitted, created, and shared over the years in the community and at work – these are the cultural facts. Behaviour is also related to the structural facts, such as the patterns of interaction among individuals and collectivities in the community and the division of labour and organization of work.[11] People share a way of life, and responses to problems are accepted because they have met with success. Those who are born and brought up in such a community unthinkingly take over many of these social habits and definitions.

People who share a community tend to share an outlook toward it and the world outside. These attitudes become important because, as W. I. Thomas stated, "if men define situations as real they are real in their consequences."[12] We have noted the preoccupation with isolation on the part of many respondents, but another commonly expressed attitude is that "small towns are a great place to live." These respondents list the advantages – "great hunting and fishing," and "wonderful outdoors life, right on your doorstep"; it is very rewarding to "know everyone in town" – city life is too impersonal, too many people. The extent to which these types of attitudes are transmitted to the young is impressive; when a questionnaire, on the advantages and disadvantages of remaining in their community of single industry (Railtown), was administered to high school students, 90 per cent talked of healthy outdoor life and friendliness.

11 This distinction between cultural and structural facts is analytical only in that it differentiates two distinct ways of looking at the same phenomenon. See A. L. Kroeber and T. Parsons, "The Concepts of Culture and of Social System," *American Sociological Review*, XXIII (Oct. 1958), 582-3.

12 W. I. Thomas and F. Znaniecki, *The Polish Peasant*, 2nd ed. (New York, 1958), p. 81. See also the discussion in R. K. Merton, *Social Theory and Social Structure*, enl. ed. (Glencoe, 1968).

Other attitudes and behaviour deal with persistent problems or intrinsic limitations and restrictions. Interviews disclosed at least two ways of handling these limitations. Despite the complaints, and sometimes the unhappiness expressed by respondents, many talked with a sense of inevitability. Whether the respondent was living in a community of single industry by choice or by default, temporarily or permanently, the comments suggested that there was nothing that could be done about the difficulties because they were inherent in the nature of the community. Further, these problems were minor compared with the fear that technological and economic change might bring about the disappearance of their whole way of life. Indignation is rarely associated with fatalism; people learn to live within limitations.

A second method of coping with limitations was the lowering of the level of expectations, particularly noticeable when interviews from the four stages of community development are compared. At the recruitment stage, respondents are indignant about their housing, medical, and shopping services. In the stage of maturity, young people who have been born and brought up in the community view it with affection for it is the only world they know; their parents have adjusted expectations and behaviour to adapt to an inevitable situation. The rebels who were unable to live within the strictures have long since left.

When people have to share a community with neighbours, acquaintances, and work-mates, they find it useful not to antagonize their associates. When they do not have absolute faith in their doctor, they remember that he is the only person who stands between them and illness. When conflict is considered futile and damaging, the working out of problems and difficulty is constrained, cautious, and conservative. Resignation to events is common.

A great number of people in both French and English Canada live within the strictures of communities of single industry. One-half of the population of the country lives in communities of under 30,000, in which size imposes restrictions only a little less severe. When the migration from these communities is taken into account, there is an additional large proportion of urban dwellers whose basic outlooks, expectations, and behaviour were formed within these small communities.

It is little wonder, then, that when describing Canada, Kaspar Naegele wrote, "Individually by contrast with the individual American the Canadian seems older, more self-contained, more cautious, less expressive."[13] John Porter comments that Canadian literary plots "do not deal with the clash of social forces, social progress, social equality or the achieving of other social mobility. Rather, they tend to be, as R. L. McDougall has pointed out, concerned with personal values, personal relationships and private worlds – worlds of gloom and despair at that."[14]

S. M. Lipset concludes that Canadians are "conservative, authoritarian, oriented to tradition, hierarchy and elitism in the sense of showing deference to those in high status."[15] Whyte and Vallee talk of "a kind of pragmatic reasonableness which discourages open dispute."[16] George Ferguson, comparing general trends in Canada and the USA talks of "the slightly slower tempo of life, the less volatile reaction to events, the more sober, more conservative attitudes of men, the higher degree of sabbatarianism, the greater gift for compromise and the middle way."[17] "If Canada is an 'unknown country' this is, in an important measure, a matter of choice. It is a consequence of a widespread wish to avoid ridicule, emotional display, public quarrels, obvious discrimination, and injustice, and to cultivate instead a certain shrewd and indirect managing of social reciprocities."[18]

This wide range of evaluative phrases has been used to describe Canadians. Taken in sum, then, Canadians are seen to be self-contained, cautious, less expressive than others, diffident, constrained, melancholy, and resigned to misery, in the belief that man is encompassed by forces beyond his control which strike out completely to destroy him. So they seek escape from their feelings of futility and denial in isolation and withdrawal, personal relationships and private worlds. They are conservative and authoritarian, oriented to tradition, hierarchy, and elitism, resigned to undemocratic and authoritarian prac-

13 Kaspar D. Naegele, "Further Reflections," in Bernard R. Blishen, *et al.*, eds., *Canadian Society*, rev. ed. (Toronto, 1964).

14 John Porter, "Canadian Character in the Twentieth Century," *The Annals of the American Academy of Political and Social Science*, 370 (March 1967), p. 53.

15 *Ibid.*, p. 55.

16 F. C. Vallee and D. R. Whyte, "Canadian Society: Trends and Perspectives," in Blishen, *et al.*, eds., *Canadian Society*, p. 849.

17 George V. Ferguson, "The English-Canadian Outlook," in Mason Wade, ed., *Canadian Dualism* (Toronto, 1960), p. 5.

18 Naegele, "Further Reflections," p. 512.

tices. They prefer pragmatic reasonableness to open dispute, and so the conservative syndrome is fostered. Decision-making of elites is accepted and no wrong is seen in the fact that many of the latter virtually or actually inherit their positions. They place emphasis on the maintenance of order and predictability and the persistence of an ascriptive status. To them it seems right and proper for a given ethnic group to appropriate particular roles and designate other ethnic groups to less preferred ones. Canadians are envisaged as having a less volatile reaction to events, and more sober and conservative attitudes of mind together with a high degree of sabbatarianism. They are modest, with a sense of realism, and a gift for compromise and the middle way.[19]

One would be hard put to find a more accurate evaluation of the residents of single-industry communities in Canada.

19 Many consider that the level of abstraction of "national character" is so great that the concept is meaningless; the abstraction obscures regional, linguistic, ethnic, institutional, and individual differences. Some feel that national character is a stereotype which "denotes beliefs about classes of individuals or objects which are 'preconceived' ... a belief which is not held as an hypothesis buttressed by evidence but is rather mistaken in whole or in part for an established fact." (Marie Jahoda, "Stereotype," in Julius Gould and William L. Kolb, eds., *A Dictionary of the Social Sciences* (New York, 1964), p. 694). Stereotypes, of whatever kind, are important because they influence social action. Those who support the sociology of national character claim that it is legitimate: "Like an impressionist painting, national character appears when a body of countrymen are viewed from an appropriate distance. If one observes the population from a great distance its members may be identifiable only as Western or Latin-American or Oriental. If one approaches individuals closely, they appeal as social types ... If one approaches closer still, all the blazing richness of the unique individual comes into focus blurring all else. However, assume an 'intermediate' distance from a group of countrymen and common features they display as nationals appear once more." (Don Martindale, "The Sociology of National Character," *Annals of the American Academy of Political and Social Sciences*, 370 (March 1967), p. 31.) Recently, in the course of research, the writer asked one-hundred-and-forty-four senior high school students in Manitoba to complete the following sentence: "Canadians as a group are known for ...." Sixty-four per cent gave a flattering response, twenty-five per cent gave a neutral one, and 10 per cent an unflattering one; seventy-six per cent of ninety-six senior high school students from Ontario and Quebec gave positive responses, including such words as "peace loving," "democratic," "friendly," "responsible." This suggests that at least some of us like ourselves even if social analysts have described Canadians differently, as seen above. Clearly, these are different perspectives which may be useful depending on the frame of reference and purpose.

Notes on data and sources

The notes throughout the text indicate that a wide range of materials have been used in this study. The major sources may be enumerated.

1. Three detailed community studies. The social characteristics of the communities are:

Characteristic	*Railtown*	*Minetown*	*Milltown*
Population	Under 5000	5000-10,000	10,000-30,000
Ethnic characteristics	Multi-ethnic	Unicultural	Bicultural
Location	Ontario	Maritimes	Quebec
Type of company	Service	Extraction	Industrial
Company housing	Minor	None	Major
Geographical isolation	Isolated	Not isolated	Somewhat isolated

In each study intensive interviews were carried out, with a random sample of the population in the case of Minetown, and with representative samples in the cases of Railtown and Milltown. In each case the researcher lived in the community during the research period and was able to take part in the informal round of community life – on the tennis courts, at church suppers, and so on (but not in the local pub because there wasn't one).

2. Questionnaires returned by management and trade union personnel of the single industry in fifteen communities in ten provinces.

3. Three hundred intensive interviews with key informants in twenty-eight communities of single industry in six provinces.

4. Questionnaires returned by policy-makers in both management and trade unions in fifty-two communities of single industry in all provinces except Prince Edward Island.

5. Interviews and questionnaires from 120 young people from small communities in three provinces.

6. Published studies.

7. Unpublished studies and data, including undergraduate and graduate theses.

8. Magazine and newspaper articles.

9. Census, directory, and statistical material.

Different respondents were interviewed for sources 1, 3, and 5; different questionnaires were issued for sources 2, 4, and 5.

Although this book was not planned to be a source book or a gazetteer, a few comments about the last four sources – the library resources – might be appropriate. Certainly, there is no dearth of material on Canadian communities; there are thousands of articles written by journalists, historians, geographers, architects, educators, economists, engineers, and trade-paper writers. The most useful sources for my purposes in this study have been cited in each chapter

The list of communities of single industry was assembled through a variety of procedures. The easiest, but not the most practical, was to visit the community. A second procedure was the long, complicated process of consulting a plethora of business and industrial directories, lists, indexes, federal and provincial publications, census data, pamphlets, articles, and the like, to assess the available information. It was usually easy enough to establish the fact that a particular industry was in a particular community; it was more difficult to establish if it was the sole industry, and even more detective work was needed to find out if the community was a trading centre for an agricultural hinterland. It was often impossible to locate many track-side hamlets listed in railway time-tables, in official atlases, or in the census material. Cross-checking was difficult because some authorities organized data according to community boundaries while others used township boundaries.

The literature on Canadian communities of single industry is uneven in the sense that a few communities have had hundreds of articles written about them (usually because they were "newsworthy" – a new model town near a new and exciting resource development, or a "problem community" which had lost its doctor or its industry) while others have never been written about. A wide range of well known periodicals such as *Maclean's, Financial Post, Chatelaine, Canadian Geographer, Canadian Geographical Journal, Canadian Architect, Canadian Welfare, Canadian Mining Journal,* have published articles on Canadian communities of single industry. Some articles are of general interest, others reflect the specialized interest of the periodical in which they were published. The *Canadian Periodical Index* is of great assistance in locating this wide-spread literature. *Canadiana* (National Library of Canada) lists catalogues, pamphlets, microfilms, film, and filmstrips, publications of the government of Canada and publications of the provincial governments of Canada. There are many regional bibliographies and indexes such as the *Atlantic Provinces Checklist* (now unfortunately discontinued), and *Bibliography of the Quebec Labrador Peninsula* compiled by Allan Cooke and Fabian Caron (Centre d'Etudes Nordiques, Université Laval, Québec), 2 vols. (Boston, 1968).

Fortunately, two bibliographies on communities were published in 1970. Leonard Marsh's *Communities in Canada* (Toronto, 1970) was designed as a source-book on Canadian communities of all types. In addition to the sources on The Frontiers (section 1) and Small Towns (section 3), section 6 of his book contains valuable material including a reference bibliography and a list of 160 resource-based communities in Canada. Most of these communities were included in the list compiled for this research. Missing are the railway communities and the smaller sawmill towns. The other major bibliography was published by the Center for Settlement Studies, University of Manitoba: Series 3, *Bibliography: Resource Frontier Communities,* 2 vols. (Winnipeg, 1970). The Institute of Local Government, Queen's University, *Single Enterprise Communities in Canada* (Ottawa, 1953) has a list of 155 communities of single industry and a bibliography of several hundred books.

Subject index

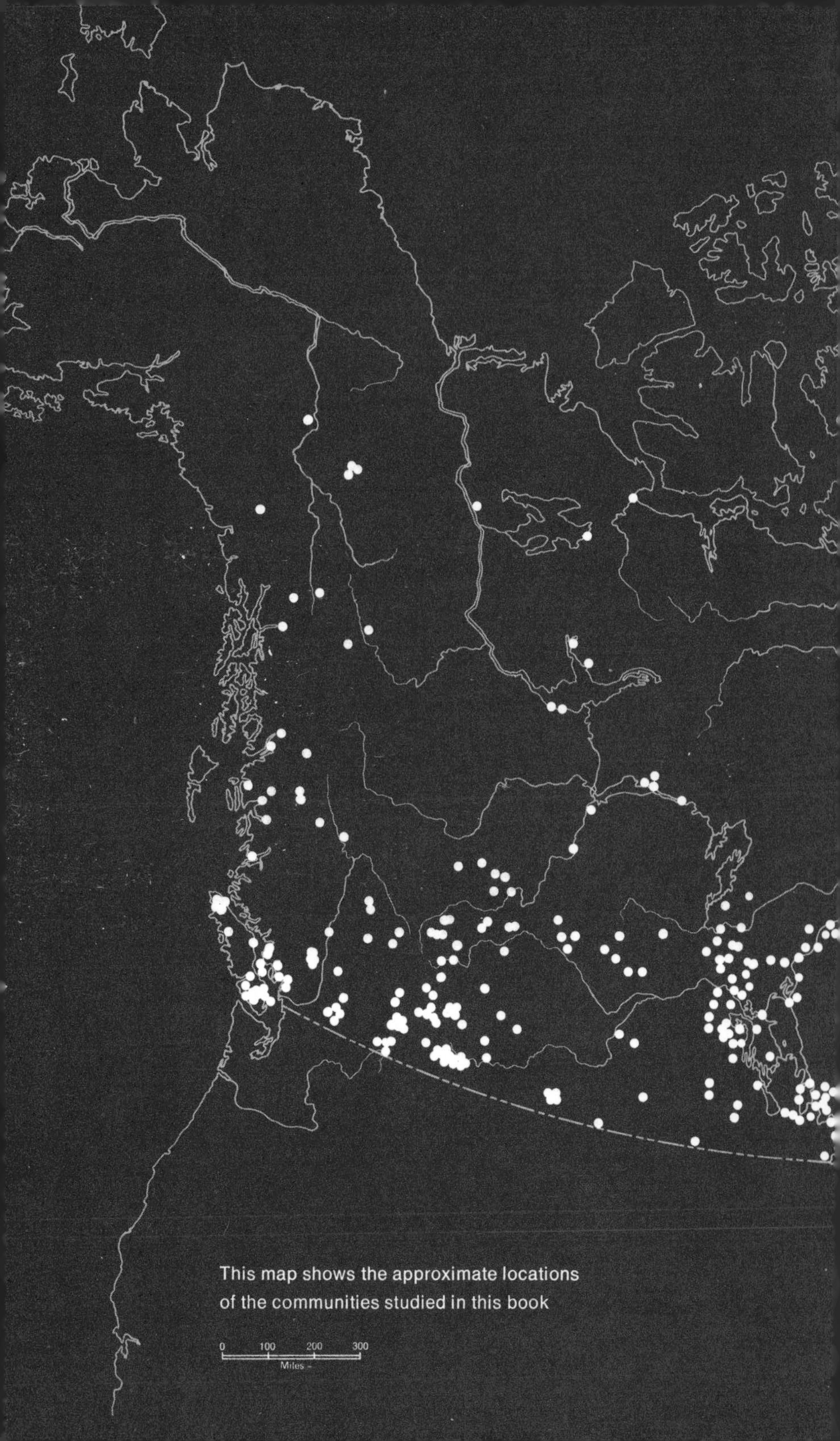

This map shows the approximate locations of the communities studied in this book